Dec/2008.

Whistleblowers and the Bomb

For Robin , Nancy.
If you are reading this
book. you will get to read
my future. real story.

Wishing you to continue
to do for Peace
and democray here.
and for world Free
from N.W.S.
All the best

Vanunu Mordechai

Whistleblowers and the Bomb

Vanunu, Israel and Nuclear Secrecy

New Edition

YOEL COHEN

Pluto Press

LONDON • ANN ARBOR, MI

in association with

THE EUROPEAN JEWISH
PUBLICATION SOCIETY

First published 1992 by Sinclair-Stevenson (London).
Published 1995 in German by Palmyra Verlag (Hiedelberg).
Published 2003 by Holmes & Meier Publishers Inc.
as *The Whistleblower of Dimona: Israel, Vanunu, and the Bomb.*
Published 2005 in Hebrew by Babel Publishers (Tel Aviv).

New edition first published 2005 by Pluto Press
345 Archway Road, London N6 5AA

www.plutobooks.com

in association with

The European Jewish Publication Society, P.O. Box 19948, London N3 3ZJ

www.ejps.org.uk

British Library Cataloguing in Publication Data
A catalogue record for this book is available from the British Library

The European Jewish Publication Society gives grants to support the publication of books relevant to Jewish literature, history, religion, philosophy, politics and culture.

ISBN 0 7453 2400 2 paperback

10 9 8 7 6 5 4 3 2 1

Designed and produced for Pluto Press by
Chase Publishing Services Ltd, Fortescue, Sidmouth, EX10 9QG, England
Typeset from disk by Newgen Imaging Systems (P) Ltd, India
Printed and bound in the European Union by
Antony Rowe Ltd, Chippenham and Eastbourne, England

Contents

Introduction: 5 October 1986

This is a book about nuclear secrecy in a democracy in conflict with her regional neighbours. On 5 October 1986 the *Sunday Times* of London published an exposé detailing Israel's nuclear arms programme. The entire top of the front page of the paper – under the headline 'Revealed: Israel's Nuclear Arsenal' – carried the revelations of a former technician at the nuclear reactor, Mordechai Vanunu. Based on Vanunu's descriptions of the amount of plutonium produced at the reactor, the paper calculated that Israel had at least 100 nuclear warheads and perhaps 200 – ten times most earlier estimates of Israel's nuclear capability. A longer article across two inside pages detailed the structure and history of the reactor plant and provided intimate details of the work processes. Moreover, the paper revealed that Israel was also producing more advanced nuclear bombs, including thermonuclear and neutron. At the foot of one of the two pages, under the caption 'How the experts were convinced', the article noted that ten scientists approached by the paper could not fault Vanunu's testimony.

Mordechai Vanunu spoke to the paper because given the moral questions concerning mass destructive weaponry, Israelis, and the world at large, he argued, had the right to know about the country's nuclear programme. Israeli officials have imposed absolute secrecy over the country's nuclear programme in order that Arab governments should not be under popular pressure to develop their own nuclear counterweight to the Israeli deterrent. Furthermore, Israeli official confirmation that it possesses the Bomb would cause a crisis in Israeli–US relations, with the US cancelling its foreign aid to the Jewish State. The *Sunday Times*'s exposé and Israeli officialdom's reaction to it is a litmus test of whether the perceived need for official secrecy can be reconciled with the public's right to know. Vanunu was abducted back to Israel by the Mossad and tried behind closed doors. He was sentenced to 18 years for espionage and treason.

The single thread running throughout the affair was Israeli officialdom's battle to maintain its posture of nuclear ambiguity notwithstanding the sensational exposé and Vanunu's battle to make it. Whether it is the Israeli government's declaratory response that it will not be the first to introduce nuclear weapons into the region, or the Mossad's abduction of Vanunu, or the closed-doors trial, or official responses to appeals by human rights activists on his behalf, the single motivating factor is secrecy surrounding the Israeli nuclear programme. Ambiguity is the single theme running throughout the Vanunu affair.

The military censor in Israel forbids citizens, including this author, from stating whether or not Israel possesses the Bomb. Nowhere in this book are unqualified references to Israel's 'reported' Bomb made. They are qualified in such ways as by quoting foreign sources or a footnote. On the instructions of the military censor the original edition included the appended statement that 'the book is based on foreign sources, which in no way implies the veracity or non-veracity of the information in the book'. That 'according to foreign sources' Israel possesses the Bomb is no more than a claim. Amorphous terms like nuclear 'capability', nuclear 'potential', nuclear 'policy' could lead, or mislead, one to conclude that all that is meant is Israeli nuclear technical know-how, Israeli scientific personnel, or Israeli possession of resources such that if and when the government took a decision to assemble and construct a Bomb warhead, it could do so. 'Nuclear policy' could refer to nuclear energy policy. Mordechai Vanunu never saw a completed warhead. Israeli possession of the Bomb remains uncertain.

It is highly doubtful whether any foreign government or intelligence agency believes today that Israel does not possess the Bomb. As early as 1960 Arab governmental estimates were that Israel was on the road to developing the Bomb. In the insistence on terminological obfuscations like 'potential', and 'capability' the military censor – whose mandate is to prevent the disclosure of military secrets to the enemy – is an anachronism. There is a point where a secret is so widely believed that it no longer remains a secret, even if a government, due to its own diplomatic and domestic considerations, does not disclose it. For most people the Vanunu affair revisited the dilemma of how an open society protects its secrets. In one sense the affair confirmed that the open society may survive and prosper as much as a closed society while enjoying the benefits of openness. The vast majority of officials who have access to sensitive information do not reveal it, thanks to efficient security procedures. Open societies like Israel have a grey area in which former officials are able to participate in the democratic process even when they use the information, experience and insight gained officially to form their judgements. For example, two of the board members of the Israeli Atomic Energy Commission (IAEC) who resigned in the 1960s subsequently led a group opposing Israel's nuclearisation. And although Vanunu was warned by the authorities not to join the Communist Party while working at Dimona, nothing stopped him doing so when he left.

The interface between Vanunu's moral conscience and that of Israel could not have been resolved in a more unsatisfactory manner than in the tragedy of his 18 years in solitary confinement. True, it is unlikely that in any other democracy in conflict, the clash between disclosure of highly classified information on a subject for which there is a consensus at home, including a consensus that it should remain secret, would have been resolved in a different way. In a non-democratic country it would be 'resolved' more quickly and brutally. But the lack of resolution of this interface is a weak point in the democratic model of government. Democratic societies require means by which those concerned about government inefficiency or other matters of public interest can report them and not have to resort to unauthorised leaks to the media. In the 1980s Israel adopted the 'Whistleblower' rule, under which an official witnessing corruption may without fear of dismissal bring it to public notice or report it to the State Comptroller's Office, a body which inspects the efficiency and working of government. However, this rule does not extend beyond corruption, and certainly not to allegations such as Vanunu's concerning inadequate legislative control of nuclear policy. At no stage in the judicial proceedings against Vanunu did any judge acknowledge that no system existed to enable the Israeli public to receive official information and have an informed discussion on the nuclear issue. Questions which require answers include: how much does the nuclear programme cost; who are the people behind it; who appointed them; how many people are involved in decisionmaking to deploy nuclear weapons; who determines the targets to be attacked; what happens if a prime minister goes insane and wants to press the button; and is the decisionmaking framework sufficient to avoid a disaster?

The founding fathers of Israeli democracy 'based' the availability of 'sensitive' national security information upon those trickles of information which, by hook or by crook, authorised or not authorised, reached the public domain. A democracy where citizens are informed of sensitive national security issues only through that information being published abroad is a weak one. A democracy should be a self-contained system with a formal mechanism for monitoring sensitive national security information which has to be classified, and declassifying the remainder. While the continuing Arab–Israeli conflict and the non-conventional arms race in the region necessitate preserving the military doctrine of surprise, and with it secrecy, the encroaching Middle East peace process and Israel's stated preparedness to discuss regional arms control require a pool of basic data so that Israeli citizens are able to fulfil their participatory functions in determining nuclear policy. The short-term diplomatic consequences of a policy of ambiguity need to be balanced with the long-term requirement for adequate data upon which the public can reach intelligent and informed decisions. Had such a balance existed, Mordechai Vanunu's name would be unknown today.

Jerusalem, July 2005

* * *

The author desires to acknowledge the assistance received from Dr Colin Shindler and the European Jewish Publication Society in bringing the book to press.

Chronology

1954	Establishment of the Israel Atomic Energy Commission (IAEC)
13 October	Mordechai borne to Shlomo and Mazalle Vanunu in Marrakesh, Morocco
1956	Signing of secret agreement between France and Israel for the supply of a nuclear reactor at Dimona
1958–64	French engineers and scientists construct the nuclear reactor and an underground plutonium-processing facility[i]
1963	Vanunu family emigrates to Israel
1969	US President Nixon and Prime Minister Golda Meir reach US–Israeli understanding on Dimona
1973	Nuclear alert at beginning of October Arab–Israeli war
1977	
7 August	Mordechai Vanunu starts work as a night controller at Dimona
1985	
November	Vanunu ceases working at Dimona
1986	
January	Vanunu leaves Israel for the Far East
May	Vanunu arrives in Sydney, Australia
August	Oscar Guerrero contacts the *Sunday Times* Reporter Peter Hounam meets Vanunu in Sydney
early September	Vanunu is flown to London and debriefed by nuclear scientist Dr Frank Barnaby
28 September	*Sunday Mirror* publishes 'The Strange Case of Israel and the Nuclear Conman'
30 September	Vanunu disappears in London
early October	Vanunu is taken by ship from Italy to Israel
5 October	The *Sunday Times* publishes Vanunu's story
9 November	Israeli government confirms Vanunu back in Israel

1987
August   Vanunu trial opens

1987–88   Norwegian–Israeli diplomatic crisis over
                                heavy-water supplies

1988
March   Vanunu sentenced to 18 years' imprisonment

1989
May   Vanunu appeals to Israeli Supreme Court

1990s   Series of legal suits against Atomic Energy
                                Commission by ex-workers or their dependants
                                who had become sick as a result of poor safety
                                standards at Dimona

1990
May   Supreme Court rejects Vanunu's appeal

1991–98   Decline in Vanunu's mental condition as a
                                result of solitary confinement

1991
January–February   Israel hit by 39 missiles in Gulf War

1992
August   Radioactive leak from Dimona reactor

1998
March   Vanunu is withdrawn from solitary confinement

1999
November   Selected protocols of the closed-doors trial are
                                released

2000
February   Knesset plenum holds debate on nuclear arms policy
                                Israel Television broadcasts satellite pictures of
                                reactor

2003
April   Gulf War

2004
21 April   Vanunu is released from prison
July   Supreme Court upholds limitations on freedom of
                                movement and speech imposed upon Vanunu

2005
March   New charges brought against Vanunu for infringing
                                the limitations of speech imposed upon him

1
The Cost of Consensus

In April 1986 the Soviet Union faced the most serious crisis in the history of its nuclear industry when the reactor at Chernobyl leaked. Thousands suffered from radioactive fallout, but thanks to the heavy-handed censorship of the government-controlled media few outside the affected area became aware of the disaster. The disaster illustrated the failure of the Soviet-style media system. For Mordechai Vanunu, who had worked for seven years as a technician at the super-secret Israeli nuclear reactor, Chernobyl was a confirmation of the dangers of excessive secrecy in the nuclear industry. Since commencing university studies in Philosophy while still working as a nuclear technician at Israel's nuclear plant at Dimona, Vanunu had become increasingly troubled by ethical dilemmas concerning nuclear weaponry. The Chernobyl disaster – which occurred when Vanunu was in Australia – was an influencing factor in his decision to go public with his account, published in the media that October.

Lack of responsiveness by Israeli officialdom to local effects from the Chernobyl leak only emphasised the danger of the excessive secrecy surrounding Dimona. If Chernobyl today, why not Dimona tomorrow? An official inquiry into the level of radioactive fallout in Israel from Chernobyl found that 'Israel was totally unprepared and unorganised to deal with a nuclear accident in a distant country. Measures taken to deal with the fallout were ill-organised and unplanned.' The report had been banned by the censor lest it arouse public discussion about the consequences of nuclear energy development. According to Mattityahu Peled, then a Knesset member, 'the Israeli public has a right to know, as do publics in all other democracies where radioactive waste is stored, how distant this is from populated areas, or in what level at sea it is buried, and what are the levels of danger of radiation reaching places of settlement.'[1] Examination of Israeli agricultural produce by government inspectors after Chernobyl was done only selectively despite high levels of radiation being discovered, the produce even being turned back by the West German authorities. The Israeli customer was not notified, nor was it made public that during one week after Chernobyl, children, who are at five times greater risk from radioactivity compared with adults, were exposed to one-tenth the radioactivity they generally absorb during an entire year.

The differences between the centralised media system which characterised the then Soviet Union and that of the Israeli democracy were many. But for Vanunu the dangers of nuclear secrecy were overwhelming. Throughout the years the media in Israel has been under intensive military censorship regarding Israeli nuclear-related information and commentary. In the 1960s even indirect mention of Israel's possessing a nuclear capability was blue-pencilled by the censor, because it made Israel's nuclear option too visible. In 1961 the defence ministry asked Israeli newspaper editors not to publish the articles on the subject by journalist and Knesset member Eliezer Livneh of the Mapai political party 'for reasons of national security'.[2] When in 1968 the Parisian news weekly, *L'Express*, published an article on Israel's nuclear programme – after Prime Minister Ben-Gurion admitted in the Knesset that the Dimona 'textile plant' was a nuclear facility – Uri Avneri, the editor of the crusading *Haolam Hazeh* weekly, wanted to reprint the article. Avneri translated the article word for word but the censor refused him permission to reprint it. A petition to the Supreme Court was rejected. When early in 1967, prior to the Six Days War, Zeev Schiff, *Haaretz*'s military correspondent, wrote a series of articles which included Arab perceptions of Israel's nuclear potential, it was banned by Israel's military censor, Colonel Walter Bar-On, on the grounds that it was based on what the Arabs were saying and not on what the Israelis were saying. *Haaretz* has been subject down the years to requests from Israeli officials not to publish matters relating to the nuclear issue; on one occasion when the censor's guidelines did not allow for a particular item to be banned, a senior Israeli official approached the paper's editorial board arguing that its publication would encourage an 'undesirable' public discussion in Israel. The paper turned down the request. The first programme in 'Mabat Sheni' ('Second Look'), Israel Television's flagship current affairs programme, entitled 'Israel's Nuclear Option', was banned by the Israel Broadcasting Authority's director-general because 'the subject was delicate, and would arouse public discussion, much beyond what had been discussed up to that time. The function of television is to report information and not cause public discussion,' the director-general, who is a government appointee, said.[3] Writing about nuclear and non-conventional warfare was rare, and journalists were discouraged from doing so. 'There is no doubt that this was an error, and I include myself among those responsible for it,' said Schiff. 'The result has been that the majority of writings about nuclear weapons in Israel and the Middle East has come from foreign sources, not a few of which were full of basic errors and, what is worse, also written with the intention of harming Israel.'[4] Ironically, the editors have never discussed among themselves the question of the lack of reporting on nuclear issues.

Censorship is no less excessive in the case of the foreign media. According to Charles Richards, the then Jerusalem correspondent of the *Independent* of London, 'with the exception of the Israeli nuclear story, and one or two other matters, censorship doesn't affect my work as a foreign correspondent.'[5] When in the early 1960s David Rubinger, *Time*'s photographer in Israel, snapped the Dimona reactor from beyond the perimeter fence, he had a 'night-long argument on the phone with the censor. I won in the end because I convinced him that the American U-2 spy plane could shoot more than I could ever photograph from the ground. To this day it's the only picture of Dimona that has ever made it through censorship.'[6] 'We can do a little more than the Israeli media on the nuclear story but in practice we are limited because we have no sources,' said Gideon Berli, a former Foreign Press Association chairman.[7]

While a detailed discussion of Dimona remains in the realm of the utterly forbidden unless foreign sources are quoted, by the 1980s there had been an opening up of the subject. With the considerable undermining of the image of ambiguity, there occurred an easing of the censor's limitation of discussion of the broader issues involved. It parallels greater public and media scepticism of the military in general which followed the 1973 and 1982 wars. Prior to the 1973 war, correspondents acceded to the censor's requests not to publish intelligence warnings about Egyptian and Syrian military manoeuvres lest they arouse public concern. Had these warnings been published, the national emergency callup might have begun earlier, resulting in many fewer casualties.

Knesset members seeking information about the country's nuclear capability were no better off than the population as a whole. Hard information was not forthcoming. The first formal notification of the nuclear programme came in 1960. Prime Minister Ben-Gurion confirmed to the Knesset that Israel was building a nuclear reactor. This came after a US U-2 spy plane photographed the reactor. But Ben-Gurion reassured the Knesset that the reactor was only for peaceful purposes. This was also the reply given by government ministers in the Knesset in 1984 when two nuclear reactors were purchased from France. Concerning other key developments – including US inspections of Dimona in the 1960s, the question of signing the Nuclear Proliferation Treaty (NPT) in 1965, and the Israeli bombing of Osiraq in 1981 – official spokesmen replied that Israel would not be the first to introduce nuclear weaponry into the region. Mordechai Vanunu would later decry the fact that development of the Israeli Bomb was undertaken in a manner which clashed with basic democratic values. Decisions about the Bomb were apparently not taken by the government as a whole but by a handful of ministers. Even though both the Knesset's defence and foreign affairs committee, which has legislative responsibility for nuclear policy, and the Knesset's defence budget committee meet behind closed doors to prevent sensitive information from leaking out, they were not always informed of developments in the Dimona project, including the key decision to construct a plutonium-processing wing. And when Prime Minister Levi Eshkol refused to provide government funding for the Dimona project, Shimon Peres, deputy defence minister, took the matter into his own hands and raised the funding from Jewish donors abroad.

When in 1958 seven board members of the Israel Atomic Energy Commission (IAEC) resigned, their prime complaint was procedural. 'Things were done in the name of the IAEC, which in fact did not exist, without Israeli scientists who were close to the profession participating in the planning – if such planning existed,' claimed Shlomo Aronson, an Israeli authority on his country's nuclear policy.[8] The excessive secrecy was necessary both to ensure France's continued cooperation, which was conditional upon secrecy being respected, and to avoid debate by scientists who questioned the heavy economic burden involved in building the project. But the longer the project took to complete the more difficult it became to maintain the secrecy so hermetically.

At the very moment in the early 1950s when a coterie of Israeli policymakers were clandestinely planning the Dimona project, and instigating construction of its first stages, there was a wide public movement in Israeli public opinion against the Bomb. In 1950, some 310,000 Israelis – or 40 per cent of the population – signed the Stockholm Petition against the spread of nuclear weaponry, resolving that any country using nuclear weaponry as a first strike had carried out war crimes against humanity. In 1951, some 400,000 Israelis signed a similar resolution – a year before the IAEC was established. A Nuclear Physics department was established at the internationally renowned Weizmann Institute of Science in Rehovot and its young scientists sent abroad to learn the subject – their visits financed by the ministry of defence. In 1954 an agreement was signed with France for cooperation in heavy-water and uranium production. Even though the Israeli nuclear weapons programme deterred Arab states and would contribute to the Arab–Israeli peace process, nothing can erase the historical truth that the reactor was built both without full government approval, and against the background of wide public opposition to the Bomb.

That by the 1980s the Israeli public had altered its stance and favoured the development, and even deployment, of the Bomb cannot justify the decision process of the 1950s. (Illustrative of the undemocratic nature of early nuclear policymaking was the defence establishment's ban on a delegation of the Israeli committee for Peace attending a peace conference in Stockholm.) Vanunu felt a moral obligation to inform humanity concerning the Dimona project, about which, he said, little was known. 'There was nobody else in all the world or in Dimona who could come out of Dimona with photos and knowledge and be ready to speak. It had become my responsibility, my own mission,' he said after he was released from prison in 2004.[9] In October 1986 the *Sunday Times* of London would run Vanunu's story across three pages, confirming once and for and all earlier beliefs about Israel's nuclear capacity.

A distinction requires to be drawn between the absence of public debate and the absence of public discussion. 'There were always discussions, always people organising. There were small numbers of people (from the non-strategic sector) who were interested in debating but they were small and the subject didn't generate debate among the wider public,' according to Tamar Hermann of Tel Aviv University's Steinmetz Peace Centre.[10] It is incorrect to say that there had been no debate about the Bomb within informed circles or that there had been no organised opinion. A number of groups had surfaced over the previous 25 years which campaigned on an anti-nuclear platform. These included a group led by Hillel Schenker of *New Outlook*, Mapam's intellectual review; and the committee for Nuclear Disarmament in the Arab-Israeli region in the 1960s, whose leaders included Hebrew University dons, among them Professor Yeshayahu Leibowitz, the scientist and philosopher, the philosopher Professor Gershon Scholem, Talmud Professor Ephraim Urbach, and the sociologist professor Shmuel Eisenstadt. In 1983 the Israeli League for Nuclear Disarmament demanded international inspection of nuclear sites by the UN. Israeli Doctors for Nuclear Peace campaigned concerning the medical effects of nuclear war. In Ichud, Professor Judah Magnes demanded that Israel adopt a neutral stance on the nuclear question in the struggle between the Eastern and Western blocs. There were many articles in Ichud's journal on the danger of Israel becoming the first nuclear power in the region, and on the dangers to the environment.

As early as 1964, a serious study of Israeli nuclear strategy, *Nuclear War and Nuclear Peace*, by a former head of Israeli military intelligence, Professor Yehoshafat Harkabi, appeared in Hebrew and went immediately into a second printing. In 1966 it was published in English. Yigal Allon, the Labour minister, articulated his critique of nuclear deterrence in *A Curtain of Sand*. Academics like Professors Shlomo Aronson, Shai Feldman, Yair Evron, Dr Reuven Pedahzur and journalists like Avraham Schweitzer of *Haaretz*, Haggai Eshed of the now extinct *Davar*, and Ephraim Kishon have discussed the issue. *Netiv*, the right-wing intellectual review, is also a forum of debate among nationalist thinkers.

But discussion has often involved circumlocution. Thus, at the foot of an article by Alan Dowty in the Israeli academic journal *State, Government and International Relations*, which articulated the unambiguous case for nuclear ambiguity, was appended the disclaimer that the article was based entirely on published sources, that the author had had no access to classified information, and that he was not linked to the Israeli government and had not received official or background guidance in preparing the article.

In the 1970s a sea change had occurred in Israeli public attitudes. A 1976 *Haaretz* poll found that 77 per cent of Israelis favoured possession of the Bomb. Of these 69 per cent supported possession unconditionally as opposed to 8 per cent who supported it 'because there are no other choices.'[11] Notwithstanding this, in the 1986 poll by Tel Aviv University's Jaffee Centre for Strategic Studies, in which 78 per cent of those questioned supported the policy of ambiguity, 46 per cent did not agree 'to switch to nuclear weapons in order to deter the Arabs', and 28 per cent 'certainly did not agree', while 22 per cent 'agreed' and 5 per cent 'certainly agreed'.[12]

The contrast between the 1950s and the 1970s may partly be explained as resulting from a growing belief among Israelis that Israel possesses a nuclear bomb capability. It may also be explained by concern among many Israelis about Arab non-conventional arms developments. A 1987 Jaffee Centre public opinion poll found that of the Israelis questioned, 78 per cent favoured secrecy regarding Israel's nuclear capability. When, in the aftermath of the Vanunu affair, Hannah Zemer, editor of *Davar*, raised the nuclear issue in the paper, she, as well as other Israeli editors who did so, were inundated with letters from readers, including reservist army officers, claiming the newspapers had divulged Israel's secrets to the enemy, even though the material had been cleared by the military censor.

Ever since independence there remains in Israel a widespread public deference to authority on the broad range of questions relating to national security. The 'sacredness of security', or *kedushat habitachon*, permeates a society which throughout its 50-plus years' existence has had to face threats to its very existence. Referring to the Davidic psalm, 'The Guardian of Israel Will neither Slumber nor Sleep', a public opinion poll in 1986 asked Israelis whom they saw as the 'Guardian of Israel'. Some 57 per cent replied the Israeli army, 17 per cent the State of Israel, 10 per cent the people of Israel, 2 per cent the United States, and 2 per cent said everyone must guard themselves.[13] 'In the Israeli mentality there is a recognition that there are secret things going on on nuclear matters. The government knows best and doesn't fool around. Also, there are more immediate problems which come before the nuclear issue,' said Menachem Shalev, formerly political commentator of *Maariv*.[14] The fact that a large segment of Israel's population of immigrants comes from eastern Europe and from Arab countries, neither of whom have had experience of democratic participation, has only compounded this attitude. There is also a conscious recognition by many Israelis that freedom of access to information, particularly regarding defence matters, is not an absolute value, as it is in some other Western countries, but is a relative one which has to take its place with other values around the absolute one of national survival. 'The public accepts the ambiguity: if we are not sure we have the Bomb we don't have to think about it,' Professor Dan Horowitz of the Hebrew University argued.[15] According to Mordechai Gur, a former Labour party minister, and himself a former chief of staff, 'The public knows quite well that as a result of the continuous threat by the Arab countries we have to survive and take measures in order to survive. No Israeli wants to know all the details. If you ask most Israelis they don't have the feeling they are being kept in secrecy.'[16]

A truly democratic government that follows a policy of ambiguity in nuclear development or in any other sphere of official policy has to reconcile itself to the principle of governmental accountability. The Israeli case is a litmus test of the tensions involved. According to David Kimche, former director-general of the Israeli foreign ministry, 'Every democracy has a policy of ambiguity about certain subjects. No democracy reveals everything because no democracy wants to be self-defeating. Israel cannot be compared to western Europe. A democracy has first and foremost to preserve its democratic existence as an entity and that's what we are doing. It is a mistake to say that everything in a democracy has to be open.'[17] But does it have to be an either/or situation? Should public discussion of even the broader issues around the nuclear option be officially discouraged?

Acquiescence in censorship by the Israeli media need not be contrary to the theory of a free press. A democracy may impose its own limitations on freedom of expression, such as artistic freedom, as well as on matters concerning national security so long as these are determined by the people rather than the government. It is this which raises moral questions about the validity of Vanunu's action in leaking Israel's nuclear secrets. But the case for justifying the secrecy surrounding the Dimona project is weakened by a conspiracy of Ben-Gurion and a coterie of advisers who carried out the development both without first obtaining wider governmental and parliamentary approval and against the background of the then wide public hostility to the Bomb.

2
The Bomb that Doesn't Exist

It was to create doubt – and eventually resignation and despair – about the Arab dream of 'exterminating Israel from the world's map', as former Israeli foreign minister Abba Eban put it, which moved David Ben-Gurion, the country's first prime minister, to launch a nuclear research programme. Its partly disguised nuclear capability has over the years served to impress on Arab neighbours Israel's determination to survive by whatever means necessary. The nuclear deterrent proved itself in the Arab–Israeli conflict. Days before the breakout of the 1967 war, the Israeli Government, headed by prime minister Levi Eshkol, ordered the assembly of two nuclear bombs after Israeli anti-aircraft fire failed to bring down an Egyptian MIG which flew over the Dimona reactor.[1] In the 1973 Yom Kippur War, 13 nuclear bombs were hastily assembled by the Israelis during a critical 78-hour period.[2] At 10 pm on 8 October, the northern commander, Major-General Itzhak Hoffi, informed his superior, 'I am not sure that we can hold out much longer.' After midnight, defence minister Moshe Dayan solemnly warned prime minister Golda Meir: 'This is the end of the Third Temple,' a symbolic comparison between the state of Israel and the first two Jewish temples destroyed by the Babylonians in 586 BC and by the Romans in AD 70. Mrs Meir gave Dayan permission to activate the nuclear weapons. But before any triggers were set the battle on both fronts turned in Israel's favour, and the 13 bombs were sent to desert arsenals.[3] At the beginning of the 1982 Lebanon War, defence minister Ariel Sharon reportedly proposed that Israel launch a nuclear strike against Syria because, he said, Syria was about to attack the Golan Heights. But prime minister Menachem Begin flatly rejected the proposal.[4] In the Gulf War prime minister Itzhak Shamir ordered mobile missile launchers armed with nuclear weapons to be moved into the open in order to deter Baghdad from using chemical warheads on the Scud missiles launched against Israel.

In becoming the world's sixth nuclear power after the US, Russia, Britain, France and China,[5] Israel's nuclear development reads like a defence technology success story. Early on, a research and planning branch was established in the fledgling state's defence ministry, whose functions included the extraction of uranium from phosphate.[6] A pilot plant also enabled the production of heavy water, which is used in the separation of plutonium from uranium. In 1952 an atomic energy commission was established. In 1954 an agreement was signed with France for cooperation in heavy-water and uranium production; another with the United States involved the building of a nuclear research centre for civilian purposes at Nahal Soreq. The official 'lineage' stops there.

In September 1956 France and Israel signed a secret agreement whereby France would supply Israel with a sizeable plutonium-producing reactor to be built at Dimona.[7] Both France and Israel imposed maximum secrecy, the project being built on a 'need to know' basis. For example, in order to maintain secrecy, French customs officials were told that the largest of the reactor components, such as the reactor tank, were part of a desalination plant bound for Latin America. After buying heavy water from Norway on the condition that it not be transferred to a third country, the French airforce secretly flew as much as four tons of the substance to Israel.[8] Some sections of the project were even kept simply as oral understandings.

The reactor complex is divided into nine blocks or *machon* (Hebrew for 'facility' or 'institute'). Machon 1 comprises the large silver-domed reactor, nearly 20 metres in diameter. Uranium fuel rods remain in the reactor for a few months before being discharged for reprocessing. Machon 2 comprises the chemical-processing plant where plutonium is removed from spent reactor rods. Before reprocessing begins, the rods are soaked in water-filled tanks for several weeks. Machon 3 processes natural uranium for the reactor. Machon 4 is a facility for treating radioactive waste. In Machon 5 uranium from Machon 3 is made into rods coated in aluminium to be sent to the reactor. Machon 6 supplies services to other machons including power and electrical generators. Machon 8 is a large laboratory for research into means to enrich plutonium. Machon 9 is a laser isotope-separation facility which can be used to enrich uranium. In Machon 9 depleted uranium is made into tips of shells for Israeli use. (Machon 7 is unknown.)[9]

Israeli officialdom believes its undeclared capability fills a vacuum created by developments in non-conventional weaponry in Arab countries. In the early 1960s and early 1980s the Soviet Union supplied Iraq with two nuclear reactors but the low megawattage of both nullified their military significance. However, France constructed a reactor with a higher megawattage in Osiraq in 1980. The Israeli airforce bombed the reactor in 1981 prior to its completion. Despite the setback, Iraq kept up its nuclear arms goals. Other Arab countries, including Egypt and Syria, placed the nuclear option low on their priorities. Libya failed in its own attempts to go nuclear. Under the Shah, Iran established a nuclear research centre where an undeclared nuclear effort was begun. The only other Muslim country to make any advancement was Pakistan, in a bid to counter India's nuclear capability.

Difficulties – of both economics and know-how – in producing nuclear weaponry encouraged some Arab states to opt for the poor man's bomb: chemical weaponry and biological weaponry. Countries possessing chemical weaponry included Egypt, Libya, Iran and Syria. Egypt and Iraq deployed chemical weaponry, the former in Yemen in 1967, the latter in its war in the mid 1980s with Iran. Little information is known regarding Arab biological weaponry, but Iraq and Syria reportedly manufactured biological capabilities to spread cholera, typhoid, anthrax and other diseases.

Despite these developments, Israel did not go public with its nuclear programme. 'Israel has no nuclear weapons, will not resort to using nuclear weapons and will not be the first to introduce such weapons into the region,' prime minister Itzhak Shamir told American reporters in 1983. The time-honoured phrase, 'Israel will not be the first to introduce nuclear weapons into the region' has been the Jewish State's sole declared position on the nuclear option. On the day after the *Sunday Times*'s report it was repeated yet again by prime minister Shimon Peres.

Israel has never admitted to possessing nuclear weapons. She has, however, intimated more than once that she is quite capable of producing them, and has played up her scientific and nuclear energy achievements.[10] This seemingly contradictory posturing has been described as the 'bomb in the basement' policy, with the result that Arab states suspect or are convinced that Israel has stockpiled nuclear weapons and would be prepared to use them if faced with annihilation.

Although the phrase 'Israel will not be the first ...' could be considered by foreign observers a bare-faced lie, like a Bible tract it may be talmudically interpreted in many ways to cover precise information regarding nuclear capability. 'The first to introduce' allows Israel to be the second. The term 'nuclear weapons' is consummate hair splitting. Does it mean only assembled nuclear warheads (the 'bomb in the basement' school) or does it extend to unassembled components or even nuclear arms infrastructure (the nuclear options school)? Are 'weapons' only offensive or are they also those intended for the 'peaceful' purpose of deterring an enemy? A nuclear weapon is defined by the Nuclear Proliferation Treaty (NPT), and by others, as one which has been tested. To this day the claim that Israel has tested a nuclear device remains speculative. 'The region' need not refer simply to Arab countries which, with the exception of Iraq and Iran, have been many years away from producing nuclear weapons. It could include US bases and ships. The US stockpiled nuclear warheads at a base in Turkey already as early as 1955. The region may be defined as extending from Morocco to Afghanistan and as including India and Pakistan. That Israel will not be the first to introduce nuclear weapons into the region remains as true today as it was 40 years ago.

While Israel is a member of the Vienna-based International Atomic Energy Authority (IAEA), only the nuclear reactor at Nahal Soreq, which Israel declares is used for peaceful purposes, is open for inspection to the IAEA. Like most other nuclear states, Israel has not signed the NPT, which requires signatories to open all nuclear facilities to inspection. The logic behind the Israeli policy that nuclear capability should remain a matter of supposition can best be understood by considering the consequences of Israel going public. In the event of Israel's disclosing a nuclear capability, it would rally the Arab world, and further complicate an uneasy Egypt–Israeli relationship. Israeli officials argued that it would also create internal pressure on Arab governments to balance Israel's capability. Given the Arab states' technological and economic limitations, they would certainly lean on their supplier states, which would be under a certain pressure to provide parity.

Going public could also seriously complicate the US aid package to Israel. According to the 1976 Symington Clause of the Foreign Assistance Act, a US administration must cut off economic and military grants or credit to any country which imports uranium-enrichment technology or materials without accepting the safeguards of the IAEA on its nuclear facilities. In 1975 Congress held up the planned sale to Israel of Pershing surface-to-surface missiles which could be fitted with nuclear warheads. Most congressional attempts to control nuclear proliferation have failed. One case where it succeeded was that of Taiwan, which in 1987 began constructing a small-scale plutonium-extraction unit. In March 1988, under US pressure, Taiwan agreed to halt work and dismantle the Canadian-supplied research reactor. The US has applied a double standard in implementing congressional controls on foreign aid among the new nuclear nations. Thus, while India has exploded a nuclear device but has not been affected by the Symington Law, Pakistan has at times suffered interruptions in US aid.

The posture of ambiguity emerged in part as a result of a compromise between those Israeli ministers and officials like Moshe Dayan who backed going public with a nuclear option and those, including Labour leaders like Levi Eshkol, Yigal Allon, Israel Galili, and more latterly nationalist Likud leaders like Ariel Sharon and Benjamin Netanyahu who are sceptical about the practical value of the nuclear deterrent, and who believe that Israel's defence should be based on conventional means. It remains unclear exactly when the line that 'Israel will not be the first to introduce nuclear weapons into the region' was first conceived. Some say David Ben-Gurion pulled it out of his sleeve when he met President de Gaulle in Paris in June 1960. The two conversed relaxedly about the future of Algeria, the global political situation and the doctrines of the great philosophers. Suddenly de Gaulle shifted gear, fixed Ben-Gurion with a hawk-like stare and roared: 'Tell me honestly, Mr Ben-Gurion, why do you need a nuclear reactor?'[11] Taken aback, Ben-Gurion assured the French president that Israel would not manufacture an atomic weapon at the reactor and that it would not be the first to introduce nuclear weapons into the Middle East. Even though Ben-Gurion and Shimon Peres – who favoured building the Bomb but without Israel formally confirming it – won out in this debate, the views of their critics came to bear in that the nuclear capability has not been incorporated into the Israeli defence deterrent. It should be kept as a weapon of last resort – never to be contemplated. In short, Dimona should not be relied on.

Total ambiguity about the Israeli nuclear option had a very short lifespan. Impairment of the image occurred at two levels: the political declaratory level and the technical level. In 1956, when Israel and France signed the secret agreement for the construction of the nuclear reactor at Dimona, all the members of the Israeli Atomic Energy Commission (IAEC), except its chairman, resigned because they thought that Israel's nuclear priorities should be economic rather than be defence-orientated.[12] And when the Eisenhower administration asked about the construction of the reactor at Dimona and the establishment of a strict security zone around it, prime minister Ben-Gurion assured Washington that it was a textile plant. This was later amended to a water-pumping station.[13] The first serious challenge to the country's nuclear ambiguity occurred when, in December 1960, an American U-2 spyplane photographed the reactor. The CIA revealed to an emergency session of the Nuclear Energy Congressional committee that what the Eisenhower administration had been led to believe was a textile plant was a large and tightly guarded nuclear facility. 'Israel was on its way to becoming the fifth nuclear power,' a CIA staffer told the committee. It led to a crisis in US–Israeli relations. Washington was upset that it had been lied to and that the CIA had failed to detect it for over three years; CIA head Allan Dulles was sacked partly for this, although the error was so embarrassing that his dismissal by President Kennedy was delayed.[14] The US asked Israel whether it was planning to go into nuclear weapons production. Israeli officials had not arrived at an information policy regarding the secrecy. Israel had little obligation to give the US an explanation, US foreign aid being down to $1 million per year. Ben-Gurion told Kennedy that the Dimona project was intended for peaceful purposes, namely, nuclear energy. The US was particularly concerned at the effect which any Israeli move into the nuclear sphere could have on US relations with Egypt and the rest of the Arab world. Moreover, US pressure on Israel in the matter could earn Washington kudos in Arab capitals. Ben-Gurion had to acknowledge to the Knesset that a thermal reactor was being constructed in the Negev with French assistance, but said that it would be devoted to peaceful ends. Yet surprisingly, deputy defence minister Shimon Peres was still claiming in 1963 that Dimona was a water-desalination plant 'intended to turn the Negev into a garden'. To verify that the reactor was being used for civilian purposes only, the Kennedy and Johnson administrations insisted on inspecting Dimona, making weapons sales conditional on these inspections. According to Kennedy advisor Meyer Feldman, Kennedy agreed to missile sales to Israel only after he was assured that Israel was not developing nuclear weapons. The US insisted on sending its own inspectors to visit Dimona. This has to be seen also against the background of both Kennedy's resolve to rid the world of the nuclear danger, and of the 1962

Cuban missile crisis. American nuclear scientists visited the reactor in 1961 and 1963, while it was being built, and reported that no chemical-separation plant had been constructed. So did inspectors between 1964 and 1967. After the former inspection, the inspectors reported that 'we are concerned that Israel has succeeded in hiding development of the nuclear weapons given that Israel hid from us for two years the very existence of the nuclear reactor, and that questions concerning the acquisition of uranium were met with: "This is outside the terms of the visit," or that "this should be raised within the regular diplomatic channels." ' However, in the following year, the US National Intelligence Agency reported that its inspectors concluded that there was no proof that Israel had developed parts for nuclear weaponry. 'The power of the reactor is too low to produce plutonium. Moreover, there is no proof that uranium amounts have been hidden.' Notwithstanding this, the inspectors were unable to account for 80–100 tons of uranium from Argentina. Future inspections, he added, should seek to verify why the reactor did not work at its full capacity. Years later this mystery appeared to solve itself when Vanunu disclosed that a mock control room was intentionally built to show low levels of power.[15] These inspectors added that adequate inspection was not possible because of the hurried and limited nature of the visits allowed. The team which visited the facility in 1969 submitted a written complaint that it 'could not guarantee that there was no weapons-related work at Dimona in view of the limitations imposed by the Israelis on its inspection procedures'. Vanunu later told the *Sunday Times* about a false wall built on the ground floor of Machon 2 to disguise the service lifts to the subterranean floors beneath which plutonium was separated and bomb parts manufactured. According to Abba Eban, a former foreign minister, identical-looking structures were built at Dimona 'costing us lots of money, walls which led to nothing, entrances that reached nowhere, and windows that did not open'. US inspectors failed to find any evidence for the production of nuclear weaponry. Without their knowledge the Israeli nuclear bomb was developed and produced in underground facilities in the depths of the ground.[16] Even by the eve of the 1967 war, US officials remained uncertain whether or not the Israelis possessed the Bomb. Concerned as to whether the Israelis had acquired a plutonium-processing plant, the US ambassador in Tel Aviv, Walworth Barbour, was instructed by Washington in 1967 to raise the matter with his Israeli contacts.

In September 1969 prime minister Golda Meir and president Richard Nixon reached what would become a historic understanding between Israel and the US on the Dimona project. Mrs Meir promised the US president that Israel would not publicly declare that it had nuclear weapons nor would it conduct nuclear tests. Nixon, recognising that Israel could not be asked to give up the nuclear deterrent at the same time as giving up territory it had captured in 1967, agreed in return not to pressure Israel to sign the NPT. The unwritten understanding – regarded as one of Golda Meir's greatest diplomatic achievements – has become a cornerstone in relations between the two countries. The drafting was completed in a meeting between Nixon's advisor Henry Kissinger, Itzhak Rabin, then Israel's ambassador in the US, and Meir's advisor Simha Dinitz. Kissinger, for whom military power was an underlying premise of international politics, believed that a nation that had lost 6 million of its people could not be left without the 'ultimate weapon'. After the election of Jimmy Carter – who viewed nuclear disarmament as a messianic obligation – Israel was worried because Carter was not aware of the understanding made between his predecessor and the Jewish State. Dinitz appealed to Kissinger to inform the new president about the Meir–Nixon understanding. The former secretary of state went to the White House and the understanding was saved – surviving all changes in US administrations and governments in Washington and Jerusalem since.

The disclosure by the US in 1960 had reverberations in the Arab world, with Egyptian president Nasser taking a lead role in formulating an Arab response. In a speech at Port Said in December 1960, Nasser spoke of the need for a preventive war in order to thwart the realisation of an Israeli nuclear option. In addition to the possibility of military action, Arab politicians and commentators proposed intensive diplomatic pressure on France to end its nuclear cooperation with Israel, and raised the idea of developing an Arab nuclear deterrent.

Nuclear ambiguity was further undermined after a number of unauthorised statements by senior Israeli officials. While serving as president of Israel (a mostly symbolic office), Ephraim Katzir, himself a scientist of some international renown for his work in physical chemistry and biology on polyelectrolytes and an important figure in the IAEC, told a group of American and European scientific journalists in December 1974 that 'Israel has a nuclear potential.' A reporter followed it up with a question about the capability and time limit for realising the nuclear potential, to which Katzir, who clearly knew far more about the Israeli nuclear programme than he could let on, retorted: 'Do you think I'd state a date here in these circumstances?' Another asked whether Israel's nuclear potential was not a worrisome phenomenon. Katzir replied: 'Why should this matter worry us? Let the world do the worrying.' His remarks set off a chain reaction around 'the world, and Israel's foreign ministry quickly got the president's office to put out a clarifier that Katzir was referring to the general potential in Israel of scientists and general scientific-technological experience that objectively could be implemented if so desired'.[17]

Two years later, Moshe Dayan, who had resigned as defence minister in the aftermath of the 1973 Yom Kippur War, told French TV:

> For Israel, the future should include the option and possibility of possessing nuclear weapons without any external control. I think we have the possibility of manufacturing the bomb now. I believe that if the Arabs introduce an atomic bomb

into the Middle East sometime in the future, we ought to have a bomb before they do, yet naturally not in order to use it first.

Dayan was one of Israel's political elite who favoured Israel going public with its nuclear capability, arguing that a military deterrent comprised solely of conventional weaponry had a crippling effect on the national economy. A political row broke out with Moshe Arens claiming that Dayan's remark could severely harm Israel. A few months later, Dayan said during a visit to Canada, 'Israel possesses the scientific and technological capability to produce an atomic bomb, should the Arabs threaten to use such a bomb, but Israel will never be the first to launch nuclear warfare in the Middle East.'[18]

It is not difficult for this sophistry to take on the air of double-talk. Dayan, then foreign minister, told a visiting delegation from the US House of Representatives Armed Services committee in February 1978, when asked about the existence of an Israeli nuclear capability, 'We won't be the first to use nuclear weapons, but we wouldn't like to be the third element to do so.' Itzhak Rabin, who has stuck closer to the official formula, was once asked, after reiterating that Israel would not be the first to introduce nuclear weapons, 'How fast will Israel succeed in becoming the second state to do this?' 'Well, it's difficult to answer that,' he replied, 'I hope the other side won't be tempted to introduce nuclear weapons. I believe we can't afford to be the second, yet we'll have to be neither the first nor, at the same time, the second. And this depends on when one of the sides decided to do it.'[19]

Ambiguity was also impaired by international speculation on whether Israel had carried out any nuclear tests. In September 1979 the US Vela satellite recorded a double flash of light originating from the South Atlantic-Indian Ocean area. The CIA informed the National Security Council that a two- or three-kiloton bomb had been exploded in 'a joint South African–Israeli test'. (Vela is a nuclear-detection satellite which had already recorded 41 similar flashes, all of which were subsequently confirmed as nuclear explosions.) The South African military attaché in Washington made the first-ever request for a computer search on detection of nuclear explosions and orbits of the Vela satellite. Both the CIA and the Defense Intelligence Agency (DIA) concluded that the September 1979 flash had come from a joint South African–Israeli test of a nuclear device. But a scientific panel set up by president Carter suggested that the flash probably resulted from the impact of a small meteorite on a satellite. However, after the fall of the apartheid regime, South Africa's deputy foreign minister, Aziz Fahd, confirmed that it had been a nuclear test. Though he failed to mention any Israeli connection, Israeli experts are sceptical as to whether an Israeli bomb was not the one used in the test, and point to the close Israeli role in South Africa's nuclear development.[20] Many officials in the US defence establishment were aghast and wondered why the White House was 'equivocating'; they accused the Carter administration of hiding behind the 'zoo' theory – avoiding dealing with the political headaches that would accompany acknowledgement of the test.

Israel reportedly carried out an underground nuclear test in the Negev as early as 1963.[21] According to Meir ('Munya') Mardor, who founded Israel's arms industry, Israel successfully tested a 'very powerful weapon enough to deter Israel's enemies' in November 1966.[22] Moreover, it has been suggested that Israeli nuclear scientists are competent enough to design nuclear weapons using implosion techniques that do not need full-scale tests.[23] Testing of the Jericho missile's warhead and its nuclear explosion potential is said to have been carried out by computer simulation, obviating the need to detonate the weapon.[24] One nuclear physicist has argued that ordinary nuclear weapons can be designed and constructed without a full-scale test because a boosted-fission weapon, with some deuterium and tritium gases fed into the centre of a plutonium sphere, has the same basic design as a non-boosted weapon. With the difference being technical rather than scientific the explosive yield can be predicted quite precisely. However, in the case of thermonuclear weapons, with their more complex design, it is thought unlikely that a test could be avoided even if the test is limited to testing the fission trigger and a small section of the fusion stage.[25]

'Ambiguity' should not be confused with nuclear secrecy. The value of the nuclear ambiguity posture lies as much in the enemy suspecting that a country possesses the nuclear weapon as in secrecy. A nuclear capability so secret that its potential enemies do not suspect its existence loses its value as a deterrent. It is the finely tuned balance between the enemy, on the one hand, being uncertain and, on the other, suspecting the nuclear capability which led one researcher to describe the posture as 'deliberate nuclear ambiguity'.[26] Some see the nuclear alert at the beginning of the 1973 Middle East War, in which the Israeli army deployed land-to-land missile batteries for the Jericho missile after Egypt had deployed two divisions of Scud missiles more as a warning by Egypt. According to Professor Yuval Neeman, a former senior army intelligence officer, Israeli army chief of staff David Elazar ordered that the missile batteries not be camouflaged in order that Soviet satellites would pick up the intelligence and pass it to Egypt. Similarly, after Saddam Hussein threatened to scotch half of Israel during the 1991 Gulf War Israeli officials deliberately leaked to journalists that Israel would 'reply 100 times greater', a barely disguised reference to the country's nuclear capability. Shimon Peres would later remark during Vanunu's trial behind closed doors that every utterance about Israel's nuclear capability is closely weighed for substance and timing. While a few of the disclosures to the foreign media over the years may be viewed as intentional these should not be exaggerated; the dents in the image of ambiguity discussed in this chapter were unintentional or came from foreign governmental sources.

The option of Israel going public with any nuclear capability has long been debated within the informed elite of Israelis and by other strategic thinkers. Adherents of going public point to a variety of arguments in favour. A logical mutual-deterrence system would replace random decisionmaking. An undisguised deterrent would not only be clear and precise but credible. A mutual-deterrence system requires a second-strike force to hit back after the enemy force has destroyed some of a country's nuclear forces: the *Sunday Times* suggests that Israel possesses such a second-strike capability.

A major argument of some who favour incorporating a nuclear capability into Israel's formal military deterrent is one of economics. It would relieve conventional weaponry of the brunt of deterring the enemy, enabling qualitative improvements in conventional weaponry to be carried out and reducing the crippling defence budget. The $64,000 question is twofold. First, what effect would this have on the foreign aid budget from the United States? Is the bilateral relationship so important and crucial to the United States that the US administration would agree to the same volume of defence and economic aid when Israel had acknowledged a nuclear capability? Would – and could – the US administration push legislation through Congress which would put the onus on Arab states by requiring their chemical weaponry capability to be placed under international supervision before US aid assistance could be interrupted? In the face of congressional pressure to cut off US aid to Pakistan after Pakistani officials hinted that their country possessed the Bomb, the Reagan administration enacted legislation in December 1987 which would have required India to place its nuclear facilities under international supervision before any suspension of economic assistance to Pakistan.

The second and even more difficult question concerns Arab reaction to an Israeli decision to go public about something they have long believed exists. The photographing by the American U-2 spyplane of the construction of the nuclear reactor at Dimona did not appear to have triggered a major Arab arms race. Given economic and technological limitations to achieving a nuclear potential, it did not become a major issue on Arab domestic agendas. Israel's going public with a nuclear capability when both Arab world attention and superpower attention were otherwise occupied could be as important as any other factor in influencing short-term regional and international reaction.

Supporters of the existing ambiguity policy point, first, to the seemingly crazy actions of some Arab states where decisionmaking is often centralised in the hands of one (not always rational) person. First, a mutual deterrent system assumes rationality on the part of the two sides concerned. Second, an Israeli bomb could pressure Arab states to pursue nuclear parity, increasing the Middle East arms race. Third, a deterrent involving nuclear forces would reduce the flexibility which conventional forces enjoy: nuclear weaponry cannot deal with the problem of terrorists and terrorism. It can serve only as a weapon of last resort. Fourth, going public would add to the diplomatic difficulties in Israel's overt and covert actions against Arab attempts to develop a non-conventional capability, such as the 1981 airstrike on the Iraqi nuclear reactor. And fifth, ambiguity has been shown to work. The Arabs have been deterred, as evidenced in the 1973 war when, after crossing the Suez Canal, Egyptian forces took the Sinai but did not continue into the Israeli headland. Furthermore, it is the incalculability of the irreversible step of going public which leads ambiguity's backers, like Alan Dowty of Notre Dame University, to conclude that 'the current situation is comprehensible, familiar and – in a sense – secure!'

3
Mordechai Vanunu's Gauntlet

Mordechai was born in Morocco on 13 October 1954 to Shlomo and Mazal Vanunu. They lived comfortably in Marrakesh, Morocco in the 1950s. They were Jews raised in poverty who struggled to improve their lot. Shlomo ran their grocery store and Mazal moonlighted as a dress maker. This earned them enough for a house with running water and drainage, a backyard for the children, and an Arab servant. It was life in an Arab country, speaking Arabic and dressing in long Arab gowns and desert sandals, but Shlomo, whose father-in-law Rabbi Ben-Abu was a widely respected scholar, wanted his children to receive a solid Jewish as well as a general education. Mordechai was educated at the Alliance, a French-language, secular Jewish school. It was a life which, if not idyllic, was peaceful and better than that enjoyed by many other Jews in the Arab world.

Life for Moroccan Jews, however, was changing. Unbeknown to the Moroccan authorities, officials of the Jewish Agency, which handles Jewish immigration to Israel, had been in the country since the 1950s encouraging families to emigrate to the young state. Small and large groups of emigrants were secretly organised. The Vanunus were among the last to decide to leave Marrakesh, delayed by their reluctance to leave behind the grandfather, who had become ill. But after he died in 1963 they decided to leave. Shlomo sold the grocery store and the one-storey house. On the day the Vanunu family were ready to leave, Mazal dressed the six children in French-style clothing and straw hats. After reaching Casablanca by train, the family travelled by ship to Marseilles. Shlomo took the opportunity there to buy a refrigerator, washing machine, radio, tape recorder, and even carpets, to take with them to their new home.

When the family arrived in Israel the Vanunus' dreams of the good life in the land of their forefathers were quickly dashed. They were given a large hut with collapsible beds and mattresses. There was no dividing wall. To this day the children remember being told to put the refrigerator and carpet in the middle of the hut. It took the family a number of months, perhaps half a year, to resign themselves to their way of life in Israel. They felt as though they had traded the Garden of Eden for the wilderness. 'We knew nothing about Israel,' Vanunu said. 'We just knew what was written in the Bible, and we expected a very nice place with mountains and water, green and trees.'[1] Shlomo contacted relatives living in Migdal Haemek, and an uncle suggested they go there to a small vacant apartment owned by the state-subsidised housing company, Amidar. They did, but were evicted from it and sent back to Beersheba.

The Vanunus were soon moved to a small house in Beersheba's Daled neighbourhood, where they were to stay for the next eight years. Daled was a conservative area, with many religious people who were politically to the right. But it was also the city's drug centre. It was not easy to bring up a family in an area where so many had at one time or another been charged with criminal offences. Entertainment consisted of a film every couple of months which would be shown on one of the outer walls of a building. Even though Beersheba was an industrial centre, producing ceramics, pesticides and textiles, the only work Shlomo found was in share cropping and heavy labour – quite a letdown from running a grocery store. He cried about the way he was treated in his homeland. He eventually became ill and was hospitalised. Twenty-five years later he had a stall selling religious artefacts in the city market.

His parents had much to despair about and most of it fell on their children, Mordechai would write one day. The children, though, did make their way, and Mordechai himself received a university education and earned a respectable salary at the nuclear research centre.

The family lifestyle became more religious. The radio was no longer left on during the Sabbath as it had been in the more relaxed atmosphere prevalent in Morocco. In accordance with the practice of the very orthodox, Mazal covered her hair all the time instead of only when going to synagogue. Shlomo was looked upon as a rabbi at the small *shul*, or synagogue, where he prayed daily. Mordechai was placed by his father in the junior Bet Yaakov school, an independent network of schools which provided a more intensive Jewish religious education than the state-administered school system. But Mordechai failed to become absorbed in the system.

His father transferred him to the Wolfson *yeshiva*, which was a new boarding school providing a more modern education with many of the secular studies and preparation for matriculation, but also intensive religious studies. 'But Wolfson was not the best possible choice,' Meir, his brother, added. 'It was a compromise. My father wasn't interested in secular studies and general education. His dream was a more religious education.'[2] Initially, Mordechai's photographic memory proved ideal for memorising passages from the Torah and the Talmud, but after some time he became withdrawn, associating with the less religious boys, becoming one of the so-called Gang of Three in the class. The turning point was when be was caught listening to the radio on the Sabbath. A staff meeting was specially convened. 'We were faced with an acute dilemma,' one of the teachers remarked, 'On the one hand, to throw out the boy would ensure that he understood the seriousness of the matter. If we didn't do anything our esteem in the eyes of the religious boys would go down tremendously. On the other hand, it would mean that he was lost for good. There were among us some who did not believe in throwing a boy out.'[3]

By the time Mordechai left Wolfson after matriculation there was, according to Meir,

> a continuous conflict at home, a conflict which was to reach to the very foundations of the family framework. There were noisy arguments. Since arriving in Israel the family had grown further and would reach 11 children. Father and mother lost their traditional authority.[4]

It was a far cry from Mordechai's younger days, when his good nature endeared him to his father, making him his favourite, and when he was a role model for the younger brothers and sisters who treated him with a certain deference.

Mordechai hoped to get into the airforce for his three-year national service and become a pilot, but he failed the exams. Instead, he joined the Engineering Corps, rising to be a squad commander. According to his army certificate, he trained new recruits to the corps. At the end of national service they suggested that he sign on for an officer's course under which he would also engage in engineering studies.

Vanunu first contemplated the nuclear research centre as a place of employment after he heard about it from an ex-school friend who worked there. His friend described it as a good place, good salary but he didn't say what they did and didn't do:

> The NRC was a nuclear reactor but I didn't know anything about it. I had learnt nuclear physics, the previous year at Tel Aviv University [where Vanunu had registered in 1975 but which he left after failing two key exams] so I knew what was 'nuclear', what is 'the atom', but 'Nuclear Research Centre' – nothing. I went to the office in Beersheba, they looked at my background and said 'Fine' and gave me the forms.[5]

Accepted in 1976 as a candidate for trainee technician at the reactor, Vanunu, aged 22, was sent back to school for a crash course in physics, chemistry, maths and English. He passed the exams in the reactor's school together with 39 of the 45 candidates. (A number were not accepted, apparently for security reasons; one was a left winger, another's father worked at the Habimah Theatre.)

He had been asked about his political affiliations at his first interview after he applied to work at Dimona. At that time Mordechai supported Menachem Begin and his Herut party. Typical of many oriental Jews, he looked to Herut in order to be liberated from the Labour party's hold on Israeli bureaucracy and public life, but his support was no more than that of a passive participant.

He worked hard at the reactor, rarely missed a day, and not infrequently stood in for his colleagues. His monthly salary of some $800, relatively good by Israeli standards, enabled him to buy a flat and a car, as well as to save. Vanunu's lifestyle was simple if frugal. 'I didn't want to buy anything for my flat,' he said later at his trial. 'I didn't have a radio or TV. I took from my parents a used bed, a used fridge and a used oven. The money – I put in the bank.'[6] Since 1978 he has been a vegetarian. He gave up smoking.

After working for two years at the reactor, Vanunu began to feel bored by his routine. He decided to return to university. He started an Engineering degree at Beersheba's Ben-Gurion University while still working at the Dimona reactor, some 40 kilometres (25 miles) away, but then decided that he did not want to invest the five years required to complete such a degree. He moved to Economics, but did not settle down there either, and finally began a joint degree in Philosophy and Geography. It is not surprising that he finally plumped for Philosophy; he had been reading Nietzsche at the age of 17. According to Meir Vanunu, one of the courses he attended was Dr Avner Cohen's course on philosophy and nuclear issues. It helped Vanunu to articulate the contradiction between democratic control and excessive nuclear secrecy. He defined his goals as 'acquisition of linguistic abilities, to read more and more books, and to develop orderly thinking and a stable way of life'. He was not a brilliant university student. 'Let us say he didn't shine intellectually,' Dr Evron Polkov, one of his philosophy lecturers, remarked. 'He was an above-average student; at once reliable and hard-working,' according to Dr Lurie, head of the Philosophy department.[7] But he went on to commence a Master's degree in Philosophy and became an assistant to Dr Haim Marantz, a position which consisted mostly of marking undergraduate student papers. He was drawn in particular to existentialism and Sartre because the existentialist school emphasises that a man determines his lot. Lonely man has to make decisions all the time. There is nobody to tell him in which direction to move.

Vanunu's politicisation came suddenly, with a vengeance. The 1982 Lebanon War, and the controversial invasion spearheaded by defence minister Ariel Sharon, was the turning point. He attended demonstrations against the war. When Dr Polkov, whose course on metaphysical realism Vanunu was later to attend, was imprisoned for conscientious objection to serving in Lebanon, Vanunu organised a demonstration for him outside the jail. Opposition to the war widened into a general sympathy for the Arabs on the West Bank, whose very situation Vanunu equated with that of Sephardi Jews. In his own army reserve service he preferred to work in the kitchens, not wanting to have anything to do with the military machine. According to Musa Fawzi, head of the Arab student body at Ben-Gurion University, and a friend of Vanunu, 'Motti believed that mutual respect of the Arab and Jewish peoples would enable them to live together. But as long as there was discrimination against an Arab minority this he believed could not be achieved.'[8]

Through Jewish settlement, Vanunu later wrote,

Israel made the first error. If they would have tried to create a link with the Arabs in the land and not try to make Jewish settlements, push the Arabs out and acquire territory, then one could have found a way to establish a united state.

At an Eastern folklore evening at the university student club in November 1985, attended by over 100 Arab students, most of whom wore the *kefiah* scarf, Vanunu called from the stage, which was bedecked with the PLO flag, in favour of the establishment of a Palestinian state. The only other Jewish student at the evening was a representative from the student union's comptroller's committee attending in an official capacity.

He became his department's representative on the students' union. He later helped to found Campus, a student group which aimed to improve Arab student rights including dorming on campus, as well as the conditions for university scholarships for Arab students. In the legal cases of two Arab students he sought assistance from two leading Israeli civil rights lawyers, Dr Amnon Zichroni and Avigdor Feldman – both of whom were later to figure in Vanunu's legal defence. In one instance Vanunu travelled to an Arab university on the West Bank in order to photocopy the philosophy classics in the Arab language for some fellow Arab students in his department. He managed to get an Arab elected to the student council by ensuring that many Arab students voted in the elections, usually characterised by an apathetic turnout. Even the Left's control of the student union did not contribute to an improvement of Arab student rights, he told the student newspaper, *Berberane*, in a 1984 interview. Only electing an Arab would enable this to be achieved.

By 1984 Vanunu was moving towards communism. In June he attended a meeting in Paris of students from different countries. 'He threw out the labels of somebody who had recently turned to the Left and was at the stage of being "more like the Pope than the Pope himself",' another Israeli delegate, Shlomo Slotzki, noted. At Ben-Gurion University, together with another Philosophy student, Yoram Peretz, he organised a left-wing circle to discuss issues of the day from a philosophical perspective.[9] He also affiliated it to Rakah, the Israeli Communist party. In 1984 he had himself planned to join Rakah, which has 2,000 members of whom some 250 are Jews, but 'my place of work warned me that they know exactly what goes on in the Communist party's branch in Beersheba', Vanunu wrote to a friend.

Vanunu claimed that he contemplated resigning from Dimona in the summer of 1985 but that he was persuaded to stay on, albeit in another section of the complex. According to him, his grade and salary were raised at the time.[10] Apart from the ideological reason which led him to decide to leave Dimona, he had been frustrated by his work.[11] 'There was no challenge. He had advanced as much as he could,' according to Meir.[12] There was no chance to advance further because the shift heads had been there since the reactor was established. He believed that his lack of advancement was due to his Sephardi background. This is despite the fact that today many Sephardi Israelis occupy key positions in the civilian and military sectors of public administration. There was also a sense of inertia. 'Most of the work is automated. You had to find something to do while on shift. Most workers saw their work as simply a means for a salary,' he remarked.[13]

There were weaknesses in the career-management structure at Dimona. The 1980s saw Dimona hit by a series of labour–management disputes including worker protest meetings, demonstrations, and even the blocking of the entrance to the centre. Frustration and embitterment were particularly prevalent among scientists. According to a 1987 survey of relations between workers and the workplace, conducted by the personnel section at Dimona, there was a feeling that after key projects were completed, alternative ones were not set up, budgets were cut, and research teams dismantled. Scientists were offered very generous terms to take early retirement, and the impression existed that those who did not accept did so because they were unable to find employment in the work market.[14]

In December 1985, 180 workers were laid off from the centre because of economic cuts.[15] US analysts speculated that Israel had trouble running the plutonium plant for a number of years, creating a backlog of spent fuel. Vanunu was hired, they reasoned, as part of a large group of technicians to deal with the backlog and the 180 were laid off once the backlog had been reduced. Vanunu was one of those laid off. By agreeing to voluntary dismissal, he received higher compensation than if he had resigned. He lost much of his savings in the Israeli bank shares crash in October 1983.

Shortly before he accepted voluntary dismissal, he finally submitted his application to join the Communist party. On the application form he put down his job as being a student. Had he written that he worked at the nuclear research centre the party would have been suspicious, Uzi Borstein, the party spokesman, added. Like other new applicants to the party Vanunu was put on probation, which usually lasts six months to a year. It allows 'the new candidate to get to know the party, and the party the candidate', Borstein said. In the short period before he left Israel, Vanunu was critical of the work of the party's Beersheba branch. He questioned the ideological background of some of the branch members. He advocated the need to bring lecturers to explain what communism is, to interest the wider public regarding communist economic and political thinking, and to open new branches of the party in the region.

Throughout 1985 Vanunu was debating with himself what to do next in his life. All the options were open: to take up law; to continue his Philosophy studies at Ben-Gurion; to move to the Hebrew University in Jerusalem, the country's most prestigious university; to work in Tel Aviv; or go to the United States or South America. There was to be a new chapter in his life, he noted in his diary. Different ideas were coming to fruition. In addition to changes at work and university, Vanunu wrote of leaving the region, of leaving even the Jewish faith. A new beginning. A life of choice based on his own experiences. By October he had decided to go to the Far East in order, as he told a friend, 'to find himself'. He had a basic curiosity regarding Buddhism. In fact, his interest in religion was one of the motivations for studying Philosophy. But his visa application to visit India was turned down, and instead he decided to stop off in Thailand. He planned to continue on to Australia, and from there to Boston where Meir, to whom he was intellectually close, lived.

In the previous 15 years, Mordechai Vanunu may have grown intellectually, but emotionally he found considerable difficulty in relating to people. To describe him as 'quiet and introverted', as one student colleague put it, was an understatement. His difficulties in forming human relationships are a feature of his diary. In April 1983 he bemoaned the fact that marriage and children would not be experiences he expected to enjoy. Why, he asked in May 1984, did he circulate in places where there are people, particularly girls, if he was prevented from developing relations with them? In the meantime, he concluded, it was better to spend time with his books and writing. At one student party he suddenly stripped naked. Three graphologists who separately examined Mordechai's handwriting each focused on his difficulty in forming human relationships.

Yet by 1985, three months before he left Israel, Vanunu had had a serious relationship. A mutual friend introduced him to Judy Zimmet, an American volunteer midwife at Beersheba's hospital, ostensibly because she wanted to write a paper on philosophical aspects of abortion. She had been in Israel for nearly a year, spending the first part at an *ulpan* (language-study centre) learning Hebrew at the World Union of Jewish Students at nearby Arad. 'We felt good together,' she said. 'Motti and I liked many things in common. We both liked song, trying new things together, new kinds of food, restaurants and films. Motti was very curious.' According to Meir, she felt more for Mordechai than he for her. When he decided to travel to the Far East he said that he wanted to go alone: his loner side returned. 'Our relations were not clear and changed all the time,' Judy said.[16] However, at one point in Australia he wanted to suggest that she come and join him but she had already left Israel and begun computer studies at Boston University. In making Boston the last destination of his trip, Vanunu presumably planned to see her again.

Saying goodbye to his family was not difficult. His visits to his parents had become rare occurrences and when he did visit it was briefly. On Yom Kippur, the holiest day in the Jewish calendar when even secular Israelis stay home, Vanunu went to the sea with Arab friends to go swimming. Few acts could have distanced him more from his father's cherished religion. 'Because my parents are religious I am not only non-religious but anti-religious. I rebelled against God and said there is no god, nothing. Only then can you examine everything afresh,' he said. Apart from Meir, a Hebrew University Law graduate, whom he felt closest to, and Asher, who became a high-school teacher in Jerusalem, the other brothers were Albert, and two younger ones Moshe and Danny who were respectively finishing and beginning their national service. Two of his sisters, Shulamit and Haviva, had married Chassidic Jews (one of whom today heads a Talmudical academy) and lived in Benei Beraq. Nanette, a trained teacher, had a job outside Beersheba. Mordechai was closest then to Bruria, perhaps because she was less strictly religious than the other sisters. And it was to her that he brought his various possessions for safekeeping before leaving, including his diaries.

On 17 January 1986 he sailed from Haifa for Athens, leaving a country he intended not to see for a long time. From Athens he flew Aeroflot, the cheapest available flight, to Bangkok. It included a 48-hour stopover in Moscow, and an opportunity for the aspiring communist to visit the city. The KGB lost quite an opportunity at the airport in failing to discover the undeveloped rolls of film taken inside Dimona which he had stuffed into his knapsack. From there he went to Thailand and Burma, returning to Thailand, where he stayed for a month in a Buddhist *ashram*. He continued to Nepal, where he spent the Passover feast with a couple of Israeli tourists, then to Singapore, and on to Australia. After trying to get employment at the Israeli consulate in Sydney and the Jewish Agency – surprising, given the alienation from Israel which Vanunu felt – he took up taxi driving.

His stay in Sydney was to begin a 'new chapter' in Vanunu's life. While he foresaw some of it, such as the break with Judaism, he could not have anticipated its ending. Living in one of Sydney's sleazy districts, King's Cross and the parish of St John's, he felt a strong sense of fellowship with the area. Its rector, John McKnight, was a well-known youth worker who had previously directed a drug rehabilitation centre. Under Operation Nicodemus the church opened its doors a couple of evenings a week to attract the area's socially disadvantaged for counselling. When Vanunu entered St John's one evening, he began asking McKnight, the assistant rector Stephen Gray, and the lay catechist David Smith, questions about Christianity, becoming deeply involved in conversation with them. It was not Vanunu's first contact with Christian institutions. He had visited Christian sites of interest in Israel, and through the Anglican Church in Ramallah, and its head Georges Rantasi, had obtained money for a fund for needy students at Ben-Gurion University.

It was not long before Vanunu began attending Sunday services and Bible classes, and then moved into one of the church's flats. 'I think the warmth and fellowship and love of the people of St John's just won him over,' McKnight said. Appropriately enough, Nicodemus, who is mentioned in the gospel of

St John as a 'Pharisee and ruler of the Jews' was also a Jew saddled with problems who sought relief by turning to Jesus. On 17 July 1986 Vanunu was baptised by Reverend Gray and adopted the name John Crossman. Although there had been less than three months between his first entering the portals of King's Cross and his baptism, according to McKnight,

> the path for a convert from Judaism is easier because there is so much common ground. Vanunu believed in the essentials of the Christian faith, he believed that there was a God, and he believed that God was active in the world. He believed that God is a God of fairness and justice.[17]

Perhaps it was not surprising that Vanunu changed his religion. 'I had', he wrote in a letter to Judy Zimmet, 'chosen my religion. Nobody can decide for me. Everybody is obliged to choose his faith and find his answers to life.' 'With my university studies opening my mind, I used to think a lot and try to decide what was my own way, not the way my parents had chosen for me,' Vanunu said. 'I had to make my own decisions. That is part of the philosophy of existentialism that you choose your way, your target for life.' Nor was it so surprising that he adopted Christianity. Universalism is a value which he would have found attractive in any framework. 'As a caring Christian community, we were concerned about the whole range of issues – social justice, racism – and only a small group were looking at peace and justice,' said McKnight.[18] If St John's was strong on community work, it was not on church doctrine. 'To what extent he was committed then to any particular Christian doctrine is, I think, open to debate,' remarked Smith.[19]

It would be wrong to underestimate the impact of Church philosophy upon Vanunu's decision to speak out. That the Christian Church had taken a definite stand on the nuclear arms race made it doubly attractive. The outspoken criticism of nuclear weapons by some Christian churches drew Vanunu's attention. The Danish Lutheran philosopher Søren Kierkergaard was the key. Drawing upon Kierkegaard's essay 'Fear and Trembling' (the only work of Kierkergaard which had then been translated into Hebrew), Vanunu stared into an abyss and saw the parallel between his own case and the Binding of Isaac. Just as Abraham had an obligation to carry out God's command and offered up his son Isaac despite the personal cost to him and to his wife Sarah, so every person, Kierkergaard argued, had an obligation to think matters out for themselves and act accordingly. The Lutheran or Protestant outlook that every Christian has a responsibility to think matters out for themselves was in direct contrast to the Catholic obligation unquestioningly to accept hierarchical authority. The university graduate in Philosophy found this approach most agreeable. Like Abraham, Vanunu had a felt obligation to speak out. As one of the very few who had had access to Dimona he felt a moral obligation to inform the world despite the personal cost to himself and his family which such a deed would entail. 'Don't consider what will happen to me if I help you but what will happen to you if I don't help you,' he wrote to a friend. 'In this life I want to help mankind, to give it all I can,' he wrote to Zimmet. On his prison release in 2004 he would say,

> I was thinking, I don't want to be in prison. I want to enjoy life; but since there is nobody in all of the world, or in Dimona in Israel, who would do such an act, it had become my responsibility, my mission.[20]

His conversion was bound up also with his decision to speak out on the nuclear question. In giving, as he saw it, his life to Jesus as a life of suffering, Vanunu was comforted by Kierkegaard's concept that in jumping into the abyss he would have faith and knowledge that God would hold him up. Vanunu embraced Kierkegaard. 'Faith resolved itself into practice not into further intellectual reflection,' a priest at St John's said. So Vanunu set about his mission, albeit with 'fear and trembling'.

In contrast to some Church leaders, the rabbinate in Israel has not taken a stand on the nuclear arms question. This silence mirrors the ambiguity on the question generally in Israel. Yet, given the reality of war and, today, of non-conventional weaponry in the Middle East, this silence is inappropriate. However, in the United States, the various branches of Judaism, in particular the reform movement, have adopted positions critical of the then superpowers' arms race. Though peace figures prominently as a motif in the Jewish liturgy, Judaism is not pacifist in the contemporary sense. Self-defence is an obligation: 'If a person comes to slay you, kill him first,' the Talmudic book of Sanhedrin argues. But, as in the Christian theory of 'just war', military action resulting in civilian casualties, whether by intention or as a foreseeable consequence, is forbidden. Consequently, Rabbi Professor Judah Bleich of Yeshiva University, New York, argues that 'the nuclear bombing of Hiroshima and Nagasaki, despite the resultant diminution of casualties among the armed forces, cannot be justified on the basis of the law of pursuit.' 'Is one person's blood redder than another's?', the Talmud asks rhetorically. Some rabbinical scholars, however, attempt to draw a distinction between the utilisation of weaponry and its deterrent role.

It seems obvious that Vanunu did not fully investigate Judaism's position on the subject of nuclear arms.[21] Perhaps he never understood the deeper spirit of Judaism. Orthodox Judaism has never been happy focusing simply on broad principles, on moral values which can be interpreted in many ways. Instead it has sought to map out a precise code of life, with considerable emphasis on human action, or *mitzvot*. In Orthodox settings, such as Vanunu's home background, there is a danger that some may lose sight of the deeper meaning of these acts.

St John's was running a number of seminars and workshops under the heading, 'Following Jesus in a Suffering World', dealing with Christian responses to such contemporary issues as poverty, race, apartheid, and nuclear arms. The message of the workshop on nuclear arms, McKnight said, was that

> Christians ought to take an active role in working against nuclear weapons and not leave it to major powers to decide for us. It was cathartic for Vanunu. It was the turning point and what he felt he had to do was as a result of the workshop.

At one of the meetings Vanunu gave a talk on his work in Israel. He produced some of the photographs he had taken inside Dimona, displaying them as if they were holiday snaps. 'He was very casual about it, and he did say this is a secret plant which he worked at. I guess I took that with a grain of salt really at the time,' one parishioner said.

The question facing Vanunu was what strategy to adopt in taking an active role against nuclear weapons. The answer came from a freelance Colombian journalist, Oscar Guerrero, who was being employed under a Commonwealth reemployment scheme to paint the church. Within four days of their meeting, Guerrero told Vanunu that he was a freelance journalist, and produced photographs which appeared to show him with such international personalities as Lech Walesa, the then president of Argentina, Raúl Alfonsín, and Shimon Peres. He said he knew many journalists and would help to sell the story about Israel's nuclear programme. Vanunu had already attempted to contact the media while in Thailand but had it not been for the fortuitous encounter with Guerrero, there might not have been any 'Vanunu affair'.

Initially Vanunu had second thoughts. He told Roland Sollitus, another resident of St John's who had become involved in Guerrero's plan, that he wanted to destroy the film and scrap the whole idea. Sollitus told Vanunu that he could not. Vanunu realised he was right, and immediately had the remaining film developed at a local shop.

'I had to overcome many personal barriers to do what I did,' Vanunu was to write from an Israeli prison in September 1987:

> The chief danger was the sacrifice of my personal life to exposure and slander, and of my future plans all on this altar. But the action was worth it. By this action I pointed the path in which I believe, my own philosophy about what must be done, the way in which a man must be willing to sacrifice and risk his life for the sake of an act that is important and beneficial to all, to humanity.[22]

The man who as a boy had helped in the family, helped others in his first year at Wolfson with their Talmudic studies, helped Arab students, was – simplistically and with some political naivety – going to help those who, unlike him, were not privy to Israel's nuclear secrets. And, despite his break with the family, he wrote to Meir to apologise for the family embarrassment and hardship which would surely follow. As it turned out, Meir had since moved and received the letter after the *Sunday Times* published the story.

Vanunu felt that he was in a special, if not unique, position:

I knew the basic data and material. I live my life by travel, search and examination, competing with all kinds of theories and thoughts. In the aftermath of the Lebanon war and the Shin Bet affair my inner soul doubted the country's leadership and their acts. I decided to do it like somebody who sees himself responsible for all matters deciding what is good for the country. I am not a person who has got much to lose in life, a stoic who is happy with little. I had nobody to turn to for advice, nor would I have sought it had there been one.

Moreover, he saw it as a divinely ordained mission:

All these features were gathered in one man as a bomb or mine that waited for a vehicle to explode it. I waited, I hesitated, I thought until I met the journalist. Then the mine exploded and sent me here [to an Israeli jail]. I didn't want to offer myself for this purpose. My question is why did God, Destiny, place this function in my hands. Or, to put it another way, where would I be otherwise today?

The wide popular Israeli belief that the country does possess a nuclear capability raises basic questions about the justification and purpose of Vanunu's act of disclosure. While Vanunu was correct that nuclear decisionmaking has been without proper legislative control, his act of disclosure served no clear purpose. Vanunu seemed unaware of how widespread public belief was in Israel that the country possessed a nuclear capability. Speaking to the author, Vanunu countered that up to the time of his exposé, there were only beliefs, or evaluations. 'Israelis did not know for certain, particularly' – as he told the *Sunday Times* – 'the large size of the arsenal or that it included neutron and thermonuclear bomb capability.'

Despite his signing the Official Secrets Act and becoming sensitised during his nine years' work at Dimona to the obligation to observe secrecy, Vanunu appears to have had few reservations as to the personal danger involved in revealing Israel's secrets. With an unrealistic world outlook it was difficult for him to distinguish the realities and he decided according to experience and impulse. Moreover, a new behavioural mode of challenging existing norms, including challenging the legitimacy of authority, had replaced Vanunu's old set of values. In May 1983, according to his diary, Vanunu had developed his political outlook and become as extreme as was possible in that area. He also noted that he had made more acquaintances among Arabs.

Vanunu's belief that crucial decisions in Israel's nuclear programme were taken outside the parliamentary process, even without the full consent of the Cabinet, is well-founded. At the time of the building of the nuclear research centre at Dimona, the Knesset's Defence and Foreign Affairs committee had received only a general summary of the project – and that only after it had been published in the newspapers. The decision to build the reactor was kept even from members of the Knesset's defence budget committee, which is usually informed of fiscal matters even if they are top secret. Prime minister David Ben-Gurion did not inform the Knesset about the nuclear reactor until 1960; when the US U-2 spyplane photographed the reactor, he reassured Knesset members that it was intended for peaceful purposes only. There was a great outcry in the Knesset, with indignant charges of concealment levelled at the government. Haim Landau of the Herut party and a member of the defence and foreign affairs committee complained that 'the most important fact regarding the atomic reactor was not made known to us, and that was deliberate subterfuge.' But Ben-Gurion was steadfast: 'security' justified the silence. *Time* claimed that the plutonium-processing plant was constructed on Ben-Gurion's and Moshe Dayan's initiative without even the Cabinet's knowledge or consent. Today, nuclear arms policy is made by the 'forum of four', comprising the prime minister, defence minister, foreign minister, and finance minister. In time of war this is widened to include the police minister as well as the heads of the security services and senior defence ministry officials involved in deterrent policy.

Nuclear policy is the responsibility of the defence and foreign affairs committee, which meets behind closed doors. In practice a small subcommittee of four members from government and opposition formally oversee policy. To ensure secrecy this subcommittee does not report back to the full committee even though the latter meets behind closed doors. 'The subcommittee has visited the reactor more than once,' according to Abba Eban, who chaired the committee at the time of the Vanunu exposé. According to Eban, 'follow-up and supervision of nuclear policy is continuous and thorough. I am not able to state the tens of hours during which I participate in such discussions. It is not a matter of reporting once a year. Parliamentary supervision exists.'[23] Notwithstanding this, he would later say that he was 'surprised' by the Vanunu exposé published in the *Sunday Times.*

Vanunu's concern at the lack of legislative control was shared by no less a personage than Levi Eshkol, who as prime minister in the 1960s forced the resignation of the chairman of the IAEC, transferred the commission from the ministry of defence's auspices to those of the prime minister's office, and filled the board with civilian experts. The apparent loss of political control is a direct result of the ambiguity policy. Both the government and the Knesset's defence and foreign affairs committee need to take steps to reassure those Israelis who disagree with the policy of ambiguity that proper legislative control is maintained in nuclear policy making.

Public debate in other countries may be divided among those such as India, Argentina and Brazil where, like the United States, Britain and France, there is wide public debate, and those such as Pakistan where support for the Bomb is equated with patriotism, where a critic could be labelled anti-Islamic, and where public debate on the nuclear programme is less great. Those in Israel advocating public discussion of the basic nuclear issues include some favouring ambiguity. Professor Yair Evron, for example, has argued that

> in a democratic society, a learned and open debate about the implications of strategies that concern the very existence of that society is essential. The problems connected with nuclear issues are so complex that it is doubtful whether prudent and effective policies and strategies could be planned and executed without open and elaborate discussions. Given the reality of non-conventional arms and the possibility of escalation, Israeli officials have an interest in the existence of a consensus of support for the nuclear option.[24]

Moreover, a minority has the right to express its views on subjects of basic importance to a society's existence such as the nuclear issue, whatever the majority's view.

A second question concerned Vanunu's premise that Israelis wish to debate the subject: in fact some 78 per cent of Israelis support the policy of secrecy. Moreover, the general interest in knowing who is a nuclear power and who is not carries much less weight given the Israeli consensus in favour of ambiguity. According to Vanunu, citizens in a democracy have no right to censor themselves. 'In a democracy people demand to know exactly what is going on. In any case, I still have the right to inform them, and they can decide what they wish to do with the information.'[25] The weakness of the argument that the consensus among Israelis favours secrecy is that it was imposed from above as a fait accompli. Vanunu might well have argued philosophically and with considerable justification that the consensus did not evolve after a debate among the public at large about the merits of secrecy or otherwise. How can a society limit its freedom – whether political, artistic or otherwise without first debating the merits and demerits of such a limit? Many governments, including Israel's, make much of the need for secrecy 'in the face of the enemy'.

A number of questions remain regarding Vanunu's motives. The first and most important concerns the absence from his diaries, where he put down his most intimate feelings, of any expression of the need to discuss the nuclear issue openly or of a plan to reveal information about Israel's nuclear secrets. Only Vanunu knows the reason for this, but he did decide to leave Dimona for political among other reasons, and he took the photographs with the apparent intent to bring the nuclear issue to public knowledge. And he was concerned that 'he was manufacturing things which could endanger humanity,' as he told Judy Zimmet shortly before he left his work.[26] If not reflected in his diaries, the latent potential for speaking out about the nuclear programme was sown in his left-wing years of 1983 to 1985. The catalyst which sparked this was the atmosphere and discussions at King's Cross.

The second question concerns his stated goal of informing Israelis, and not just the world community, about the nuclear danger. What level of concern did he have for his countrymen if he left Judaism for another religion? Only Vanunu knows. His identification with Israel was tenuous if it existed at all. 'He was very disappointed about what goes on there. He was often sarcastic,' Judy Zimmet said.[27] A clue may lie in a letter Vanunu sent to his brother Meir on the eve of leaving Australia for London. In it he wrote,

> ... I am going to London to make an agreement with the *Sunday Times* ... What motivates me are primarily political reasons. Despite [the fact] that I have left Israel and do not wish to be involved, I am returning to being involved. I feel that it is my obligation to go public ... I have thought a lot about this step and this appears imperative ... .

Even though he was cutting his ties, he still felt a moral obligation to inform his countrymen.

Third, there are significant differences between civil disobedience at home and evasion of the state authorities by flight to another jurisdiction. Milton Konvitz, a distinguished professor of law at Cornell University, argued that by submitting to the sanction of the breached law, a defendant shows himself – as well as the community – that he has deliberated; that he has weighed and measured; that he is not acting on mere impulse or whim; that he has faced his conscience squarely; that he has made a decision that is of supreme importance to himself.

Vanunu, however, was aware that he would be unable to publish his information inside Israel. Notwithstanding this, his main reason for going abroad was because he was dissatisfied with Israel and wanted to start a new chapter in his life. While in taking the photographs of the reactor he may have wanted to direct public attention to the nuclear danger, he had no clear strategy for this: a chance encounter with a mercurial journalist resulted in the suggestion of selling his story to the media.

In addition, Guerrero's asking price to the *Sunday Times* of £250,000 for the story raises doubts as to the sincerity of Vanunu's motives. It is true that Vanunu did tell Reverend Gray that he wanted 'the money used for God's work. I've asked myself, if I had something to sell, would I take it? I don't think I could resist the temptation of having half a million dollars to use for the Lord's work.' And when the *Sunday Times* told Vanunu that they would have to put his name to the story, he replied that if they did not they could have the story without payment; he was concerned for it to be told. In the final agreement drafted between the paper and Vanunu, he was to receive some of the proceeds from a book ghosted by the newspaper's Insight team. Mordechai Vanunu aspired to teach philosophy, as he had begun to do at Ben-Gurion University prior to his departure from Israel. While the *Sunday Times* did not pay Vanunu for the original disclosure, arguing that they do not pay informers, they recognised Vanunu's need to build a new future for himself and offered an arrangement by which he would receive part of the second rights from the sale of the exposé to foreign news organisations, earnings from appearances and interviews with the media, and royalties, the percentage to be agreed upon, from the book the paper's reporters were planning to write and for which the publishing house Collins had offered a substantial contract. Vanunu damaged his image by letting the matter be tainted by money for Guerrero's role. Feeling somewhat lost in the big world, Vanunu found somebody who appeared to have the right connections through which to publicise his account.

The question may also be asked whether during any part of the three months in 1986 when Vanunu was speaking to the media about his big story, his exclusive information, he had a sense, if only subconsciously, that he was getting the attention which as a Sephardi Jew he felt deprived of. We see in this fabric the threads of Vanunu's dissatisfaction, rebelliousness, political statement, contemplation, disaffection with his country, lack of strategy, and gullibility. Quite a patchwork quilt. Yet things came out much better than Vanunu could have expected in his wildest dreams. Less than half a year after putting on a slideshow about the Israeli nuclear theme to parishioners at an off-beat church, his story was front-page international news. If there were no diary entries and no clear plan beforehand, he articulated his goals after the event from his prison cell. 'The atom [bomb] is a subject', he wrote in November 1987, 'that all citizens need to know more details regarding what is happening in the country, what the government does, in order that they shall not be surprised [by] a further surprise, especially after Chernobyl.'[28] In a poem, entitled 'I Am Your Spy', written at the time of Chernobyl (and since translated into a host of other languages, from Norwegian and Finnish to Bengali and Hindu), he wrote:

> This is not for me. It's too much for me
> Rise, read, rise and inform this people
> You are able. I the screw, the machine-operator
> the technician. You, yes. You the secret agent
> of this people. You are the eyes of the state.
> Espionage agent: Reveal what you see. Reveal to us
> what those who understand, the learned, hide from us.
> If you are not with us we are in an abyss.
> We will have a holocaust. You, only you, sit
> at the steering wheel and see the abyss
> I have no choice. I am small, citizen, your people
> But I will fulfil my obligation. I heard
> the voice of my conscience. There is nowhere to flee
> The world is small in comparison to
> Big Brother
> Behold, I am your emissary. Behold

I fill my task. Take this
from me. Come and judge
Lighten my burden
Carry it together with me. Continue
my work. Stop the train. Get off
from the train. The next station is Nuclear Holocaust
The next book, the next machine, No. There is no
such thing.[29]

Vanunu gave the impression of somebody who was confused. As Ivan
Fallon, the paper's deputy editor remarked, 'he sat outside my office, a
diffident, frightened, but above all – naïve man, with only a half-formed idea
of what he was doing or why he was doing it.'[30]Vanunu may have articulated
his tactics and even his strategy after the event but his underlying concern-
cum-imprecise-objective was what existed beforehand. History is shaped by
deeds and events rather than by intentions. As long as a person is deemed
mentally stable, be he introvert or extrovert, his actions are deemed logically
motivated. 'One is totally convinced when one talks to Vanunu about his
sincerity with which he holds his views against the use and possession of
nuclear weapons,' Dr Frank Barnaby remarked,

He is obviously a complex character. He's impulsive. Also he felt that he should
have had faster promotion than he was getting because he was being discriminated
against as an Arab Jew. These two factors are overwhelmed by his feelings against
nuclear weapons and nuclear war.[31]

4
Devil's Advocate

To uncover the nuclear programme of a foreign country seems a daunting task for even the most experienced journalists. When, therefore, Mordechai Vanunu disclosed Israel's highly classified secrets to the media he was presenting two challenges: first, to the *Sunday Times* editorial team to prove the existence of something which Israel had steadfastly refused to confirm; second, to the Israeli Government itself to weather the threat from the media to its nuclear ambiguity.

The first that the London *Sunday Times* heard about Mordechai Vanunu was when its Madrid correspondent, Tim Brown, told them that he had this incredible story with some photographs.

'It's right up your street', said Brown; but he told the paper he was suspicious of Oscar Guerrero, whom Vanunu had met in Australia and who acted as his intermediary. 'However, he had some photographs which look very interesting.'[1] These were photos which Guerrero said were of the Israeli Bomb, and a couple of photos of the place where, he said, it was manufactured. The photographs which Vanunu had secretly taken inside and outside the nuclear reactor were to be the lynchpin in the *Sunday Times*'s decision to publish his allegations. Guerrero said that he had been approached by a left-wing group in Israel which told him it could introduce him to a scientist who knew about the Israeli Bomb. He had been taken by a small girl, he said, to the outskirts of Tel Aviv and introduced to the scientist. Had there had been no photographs, it is extremely doubtful whether the news organisation would have been tempted to go to the trouble of checking Vanunu's allegations. Brown was also persuaded that in spite of this there was something in what appeared to be the product of a highly imaginative mind after he heard Guerrero making a long-distance call from an adjacent room to his source, the nuclear scientist, ' Professor Vanunu'.

The *Sunday Times* was not the first news organisation which Guererro and Vanunu had contacted. In late July they had been in touch with Carl Robinson, the Sydney-based South Pacific correspondent of *Newsweek*. Calling themselves only 'David' and 'Alberto Bravo', Vanunu and Guerrero said they could prove that Israel possessed the Bomb. Robinson wanted to check 'David's' story through sources and asked him to provide additional evidence, including photographs. *Newsweek*'s New York headquarters began checking the information Robinson filed. But by mid-August 'David phoned back to say he was too frightened to go ahead with the story,' Robinson said.[2] With Vanunu remaining in Australia, Guerrero decided to take a couple of Vanunu's photographs of Dimona abroad in the hope of raising interest among the international media.

The *Sunday Times* was an ideal newspaper to approach given its investigative tradition of nearly 30 years. Many people attribute its reputation to Harold Evans' editorship of the paper spanning the period from 1967 to 1981. Many of the celebrated investigations were made during Evans' period at the helm. The paper named Kim Philby as the 'third man' in the Burgess-Maclean spy ring. Its revelations about the so-called Thalidomide affair and its campaign against the Distillers Company culminated in ten times the amount of compensation which had originally been offered to victims; when faced with a House of Lords injunction stopping the paper from publishing the story, the *Sunday Times* fought and won the case in the European Court of Human Rights. The paper investigated the DC-10 crash over Paris in 1974, and other notable causes included sanctions busting in what was then Rhodesia and British interrogation techniques used on suspects in Ulster. Also under Evans, the paper defied government attempts to stop publication of extracts from the Crossman diaries.

But to appreciate the newspaper's brand of investigative journalism it is necessary to go back to Evans' predecessor in the editor's chair, Denis Hamilton, and to when 'Insight', the paper's investigative team, was first conceived. When appointed editor in 1961, Hamilton was anxious to redefine the function of a Sunday newspaper from being simply a rehash of the week's news. Impressed by the postwar success of *Time* and *Newsweek*, he wanted to introduce two aspects of news-magazine journalism: the 'back of the book' soft news pieces, on business, health and housing, for example, and the type of long cover-story reportage associated with those two news magazines. In late 1962, *Topic*, an attempt to create a British equivalent of *Time*, folded. The decision was taken to hire the editor of the short-lived magazine and apply the news-background concept to weekly newspaper journalism. In its first appearance the news-background section of the *Sunday Times* had some 13 stories, covering two pages, rather than a single long-running story. Subjects covered on the two pages, which bore the title 'Insight', ranged from religion and insurance to shipping and sociology.

Originally, the idea was to use specialist correspondents, but this did not work out. Instead a unit of investigative reporters was created, which would be joined, as a specific story required, by a particular correspondent. The significance of 'Insight', according to *The Pearl of Days*, the newspaper's official history, was that it showed 'that three or four "Insight" men, used to working together, could do a "crash job" on important news stories better than a large news staff used to working independently'.[3]

One of the first major stories 'Insight' undertook was the Profumo affair in June 1963, involving the relationship between the navy minister and Ms Christine Keeler, who was also involved with a Soviet diplomat. In a story which ran to 6,000 words, 'Insight' examined each of the affair's phases.

The technique was applied to politics when, in October of that year, Harold Macmillan, the Conservative prime minister, resigned, and the party appointed a successor in its non-participatory manner of 'sounding opinion at all levels of the party'. Insight's piece that Sunday – for which political correspondent James Margach had sent the team some 10,000 words – guided the reader through the machinations of the political party.

In 1981 Rupert Murdoch purchased Times Newspapers from the Thomson Organisation. It appeared to mark the end of the era of major 'Insight' investigations. When in 1983 Murdoch appointed 36-year-old Andrew Neil, a journalist with the *Economist*, the Murdoch philosophy that newspapers exist primarily to make money was brought to bear. Among the various expenditures Neil axed were those on the investigations:

> As far as Neil was concerned 'Insight' was very expensive and of marginal value. Neil decided that the reality of 'Insight' was hardly worth it. What he failed to see was how important the image of 'Insight' is. In its great days 'Insight' had become a very important strand in the *Sunday Times*'s total personality package.[4]

In 1985, a separate 'Insight' team was reborn. Stories covered by the team, which varied in size from three to five reporters, included the Birmingham riots, corruption in the Bahamas, and the Rainbow Warrior affair, which resulted in an 'Insight' book. Vanunu could not have timed his arrival better. His was just the story to stop the decline in readership. It fitted the mould of what 'Insight' reporting should be about: 'It should be fairly big, something of major concern,' said Phillip Knightley, a former 'Insight' staffer. 'Not something about petty crooks.'[5]

Robin Morgan, editor of the 'Insight' team, sent a reporter, John Swain, to Madrid to check Guerrero's story. Within 24 hours he replied, as Tim Brown had: 'The man's very devious, but he does have these photographs. Where did he get them from?'[6] Swain flew Guerrero to London. Morgan turned to 'Insight' team member Peter Hounam to follow up the story. With a degree in Physics and Electronics, Hounam was an ideal reporter for a story about nuclear physics. Hounam, aged 43, had joined the *Sunday Times* some 18 months earlier from the London *Standard*.

'The photographs looked interesting,' Hounam remarked. 'I was not able to tell very much from one or two shots of what Guerrero said was the Israeli Bomb. But there were one or two photos with things like glove boxes which seemed to be built on a larger scale than would be the case in a university-type physics laboratory,' he added. Hounam showed the photographs of the inside of the reactor's buildings to a nuclear physicist at London University in order to verify whether the pictures, including one showing control panels, were indeed of the inside of what Guerrero claimed to be a plutonium-enrichment plant or rather, say, the inside of an electricity-generating plant. The meeting was not entirely satisfactory because the nuclear physicist was not an expert in making bombs. 'There are very few people in Britain that I would approach without being concerned that the information would feed back to the authorities,' Hounam said. The physicist, noting that he was not an expert on the Bomb, said that rather than being photos of models they were photos of the Bomb itself. But Hounam knew this could not be. 'If it had been a ball of plutonium sitting there in the middle of the room, it would have been quite ridiculous to leave it in the open air. But there was the possibility that the rest of the components were parts for a bomb.' For Hounam a more convincing argument by the professor was that Guerrero's photos showed less a nuclear laboratory and more a production centre. Hounam went back to the office the next day when it was decided to take a risk, a big risk. 'You sometimes have a hunch to follow something through,' he remarked.[7] Meanwhile, Morgan, together with Steven Milligan, the paper's foreign editor, then compared the pictures of the exterior of the Dimona reactor with the ones which the *Sunday Times* photo library possessed: the form of the cooling towers, the palm trees, the shape of the buildings. The library's photos had been taken during the period of Dimona's construction in the early 1960s. Morgan and Milligan kept in mind that there were other desert reactors, like Iraq's, but nevertheless 'felt 90 per cent certain' that the buildings in the photographs were the same as in the newspaper library photos but at a later stage of construction.

Guerrero, according to Morgan, told the 'Insight' team that he had managed the escape from Israel of the country's top nuclear scientist, whom he called Professor Mordechai Vanunu. He had taken the man by boat and plane through a series of safe houses to a safe house in Australia. 'It was crazy that Israel's top nuclear scientist should be spirited away by this young man; if he had, we'd all know about it – or that Israel possessed or was producing hundreds of neutron bombs.' Morgan and Milligan thrashed out their dilemma with editor Andrew Neil. 'We've got a guy who looks like a conman,' Morgan told Neil. 'He doesn't know what he's talking about. It could be a hoax. We have one problem. We have these photographs. They are obviously taken inside Dimona and the pictures we've got are not easily come by.'[8] Doubt and hesitancy would stay with the paper until the story was published – as well as afterwards.

It wasn't the first time in the *Sunday Times*'s history that the fear of being hoaxed had loomed large. The hoax which was at the forefront of everyone's mind was the Hitler Diaries affair in April–May 1983. Murdoch's News International group bought publication rights of what were claimed to be Hitler's diaries from *Stern* magazine. After the *Sunday Times* trumpeted its acquisition of the historical wonder it was discovered to be a massive forgery.

In investigating Vanunu's claims 'Insight' had to answer three questions. First, was the man in Sydney actually Mordechai Vanunu? And did such a man work at Dimona? Second, were the processes depicted in the photographs and described by Vanunu technically accurate? And third, were these processes being carried out at Dimona?

While no two investigative assignments are completely alike, most may be said to pass through three phases. First comes a clue that a news story lies hidden somewhere. The tipoff may be a leak or just a reporter's, or editor's, hunch. The second phase consists of legwork: checking facts, searching through documents, talking to people. If a story is there, this is when it will be unearthed. The last phase is a confrontation with the principals involved, when they get a chance to explain their side of the story, deny the charges, turn away with a 'no comment', or confess. Given that the *Sunday Times* 'Insight' team could not gain access to Dimona, to the participants, or to witnesses, all that it could do beyond checking the accuracy of Vanunu's personal details was to test the credibility of the information. Most of his personal life story could be checked. But while acquaintances could confirm that he worked at the nuclear research centre there was no way 'Insight' could gain independent confirmation that he was one of the select few who had access to the super-sensitive Machon 2 where Vanunu claimed plutonium was produced. They would also have to take his word as to how he managed to smuggle in a camera and take over 50 photographs inside and outside Machon 2.

Morgan and Neil decided to send Peter Hounam to accompany Guerrero back to Australia to meet the mysterious 'nuclear professor'. He arrived in Sydney at the end of August to meet a frightened Vanunu, who suspected Hounam of being from Israeli intelligence, and only two or three hours later did Vanunu open up. 'Guerrero's description of secreting this famous Israeli nuclear scientist in Australia seemed terribly far-fetched,' said Hounam. 'If I could have I would have turned round,' Hounam kept saying to himself in mid-flight.

Vanunu quickly corrected the impression promoted by Guerrero that he was a professor, and told Hounam that he had worked as a technician at the Dimona centre for eight years. The reporter asked Vanunu to describe his working shift, day by day, minute by minute, telling him what processes he regulated. Vanunu went on to describe the structure of the nuclear research centre, and in particular Machon 2. He claimed Machon 2 comprised two floors above ground level and a further six floors hidden underneath, where plutonium was separated from uranium and baked into plutonium 'buttons'. Hounam and Vanunu then closed the curtains of the hotel room where they were meeting and placed the roll of transparencies on a projector. Hounam saw picture after picture of dials, controls, so-called flow panels and other gadgets which showed what he deduced to be a plutonium production process. The flow dials would later enable experts to say whether they were an accurate representation of a plutonium-production process. The value of some of the photos was impaired by their poor exposure. Vanunu refused Hounam's request to disclose the names of others who worked with him at the Dimona reactor, so that the paper could verify that Vanunu had worked inside the reactor; the only name he agreed to disclose was that of the head of the Dimona plant.

Asked how he was able to get a camera into the reactor, and how he managed to take over 50 photographs, Vanunu explained that he had smuggled the camera and film in separately, hidden with his sandwiches and drink. He said perimeter security was relatively lax and that he was free to roam the plant during the long tedious nights. He regularly evaded the endless games of canasta among his workmates, going to the demonstration room on Level 2 where visiting Israeli VIPs – the prime minister, the defence minister, and the top military brass – were briefed.[9] The room had boxed models of atomic devices and a wall-mounted floor plan of Machon 2.[10] 'The room was very important to photograph because this could prove what they were producing there,' Vanunu said. 'I went to the roof of the building and saw there a tower with a guard, but nobody watched me photograph. In one case, someone watched me walk into some of the places I should not go and I gave him some explanation.'[11] Hounam did not send Vanunu's photographs to London for security reasons but did, surprisingly, send written reports. He spent a total of 14 days with Vanunu in Sydney, and had a gut feeling from the start that Vanunu was genuine. 'I knew we had a big story,' he said. When not extracting information from Vanunu about his work and life, Hounam spent hours in a Sydney public library undergoing a crash course in nuclear physics and atomic-weapons production.[12]

Armed with details of Vanunu's personal history received from Australia a reporter, Max Prangnell, flew to Israel to verify the information. A couple of people at Beersheba's Ben-Gurion University were able to identify Vanunu from a photograph. Neighbours and others confirmed that he had worked at the Dimona reactor. Vanunu was able to produce his letter of dismissal from Dimona as further proof that he had worked there. Also approached by the paper were Eli Teicher and Ami-Dor-On, the two Israelis who years earlier had had their own book on the Dimona project banned by the military censor. Another reporter who went to Israel, Roger Wilsher, tried to get close to the nuclear research centre but was turned back near the periphery fence by Land Rovers. Satellite photographs were used to verify Vanunu's description of the centre. In London the 'Insight' team began the arduous task of checking the technical information which Hounam was sending back from Australia. The team was headed by Robin Morgan, who had joined the paper in 1979 as a general news reporter before a three-year stint as an 'Insight' reporter. He concentrated on defence matters, then became deputy home-news editor. In addition to Hounam, the team comprised Prangnell, Rowena Webster and Roger Wilsher. While Webster and Wilsher had done some investigative reporting only Morgan and Hounam could be said to have had hard investigative-reporting experience. In this sense, the 'Insight' team was weaker than it had been ten or twenty years earlier, when all or most of its members had possessed hard experience. The team was joined for this story by Peter Wilsher, an associate editor (and Roger's father) who had been with the *Sunday Times* for over 25 years, to act as devil's advocate and pass a sceptical eye over all the information being checked. In one sense it was an unusual choice because, apart from a period as the paper's foreign editor, most of his experience was in business news. In another sense it was precisely in the fact that he brought no preconceived views that his value as a sceptic lay.

It was clear from the first day the newspaper heard about Mordechai Vanunu that outside expertise would have to be consulted. 'Insight' took Vanunu's description of his work plus the photographs to a scientist whom Roger Wilsher knew at Britain's Atomic Energy Authority site at Harwell, where plutonium-grade material is extracted, to an official at the ministry of defence, and to officials who worked in similar government agencies in the United States, to verify whether they were dealing with a technician who said he extracted plutonium. At this stage 'Insight' 'just wanted to determine the technical aspects of Vanunu's story', and these officials (who were approached in a non-official capacity) were not told from which country the informer came. One of the experts confirmed that the photographs were entirely consistent with what a plutonium-separation plant would look like.[13] Each official consulted said that the informer had not learnt in a university chemistry laboratory or from a textbook, but had worked for a long time in plutonium production. 'It was like a Detroit car worker coming to us, not saying what the product was, just telling you precisely what he did on the production line,' Robin Morgan said.[14] This warranted bringing Vanunu to London to be debriefed by experts. Given that the newspaper had three years earlier been caught out by Professor Hugh Trevor-Roper's error of judgement on the Hitler Diaries, it was surprising that they were prepared to proceed with the investigation of a story which relied heavily on experts' opinions. But the onus of proof lay in an attempt to destroy Vanunu's story, in essence to prove, as one 'Insight' reporter put it, that 'Vanunu was a liar', and this required expertise.

The *Sunday Times*'s choice of Dr Frank Barnaby as chief advisor in the Vanunu investigation was surprising in two respects. First, while Barnaby had worked for six years in the mid-1950s on the British nuclear programme at Aldermaston, he had not actually been working with nuclear weapons for 20 years. Nor was he recognised in the United States as being in the top league of nuclear scientists. Second, would the conclusions of an activist in Europe's nuclear-freeze movement and outgoing director of SIPRI, the Stockholm International Peace Research Institute, be perceived as objective? Although Barnaby had a political viewpoint, he was very methodical. With regard to his no longer being active in nuclear weapons production, he had kept abreast of the subject through his work at SIPRI. 'Because Vanunu knew virtually nothing about the design of the weapons themselves, though he had photos of the models, in terms of his information the paper really didn't need much knowledge of anything of actual weapon size,' said Barnaby.[15]

As he was about to leave Australia for London with Hounam, Mordechai Vanunu was still having doubts about whether or not to publish Israel's nuclear secrets. He was to have these doubts all the way to publication. Two days before his departure in the second week of September, he went to see John McKnight in the St John's parish where he was staying to thrash out his dilemma. 'I took a non-directional approach,' McKnight said. 'My role as his parish priest was to help him just think through the issues and I believe he'd already come to a decision, but I think he just needed to talk through the issue and consequences.'[16] Stephen Gray, the associate minister, said Vanunu had reached a stage where he realised there were two kingdoms, of God and man. 'He had to choose between what he felt was right under God, and what might have been best for his country.'[17] 'He was a person of integrity and was loyal to his country – perhaps not to its administration but certainly to its people,' McKnight added.[18]

The projector cast the pictures on to the screen. The crucially important pictures for Barnaby were those which appeared to show the lithium-separation process. 'From the work Vanunu had been doing in the last two or three years at the reactor, the scientists had gone on to make thermonuclear bombs and the hydrogen bombs,' Hounam said. Such bombs have enough energy to destroy entire cities. Tritium and lithium are only used in thermonuclear bombs. The models showing neutron warheads 'were clearly feasible. But models are models,' he said. The same was true of the control-room photograph which the newspaper was to print on its front page. 'All reactors and reprocessing plants have control rooms – although the flow charts added credibility.'[19] For two days Barnaby questioned Vanunu about every detail, dot, dial and control in the pictures. The 'Insight' reporters in the smoke-filled room took copious notes. Language was not a major problem. Although the debriefing took a little longer, there was no need for a Hebrew translator given that the information was of a technical nature. According to Barnaby, Vanunu both had detailed information of the techniques used, and had worked on the processes. Vanunu was honest about his limited areas of knowledge and did not comment beyond these. The photographs strengthened Vanunu's credibility. Barnaby was left in no doubt following the debriefing that Israel had a nuclear capability. 'Nobody before Vanunu', Hounam said, 'had walked out of Dimona with a whole lot of photographs of what it was like inside and nobody had ever been able to furnish the rest of the world with information on the quantity of weapons that were being produced and the number, the type of weapons that they were beginning to use.'[20]

The quantity of information which Vanunu provided to 'Insight' and Barnaby was clearly much more than the three-page exposé eventually published. 'Insight' was planning some follow-up reports, as well as a book on such aspects as the development of Israel's nuclear programme, the question of nuclear cooperation with South Africa, and the raid on the Iraqi reactor at Osiraq.

The 'Insight' team took the detailed evidence gathered from the two-day debriefing back to the experts earlier consulted. One expert they consulted concluded that Vanunu was a junior technician working at a plutonium-processing plant, given the detailed knowledge of the processes on which Vanunu worked. Some of the British officials consulted, however, were sceptical that the reactor could have been enlarged six times to 150 megawatts without altering the exterior of the plant.

While the reactions of the experts were being canvassed, Peter Sullivan, a graphic artist on the paper, got down to preparing what would be a blown-up three-dimensional diagram of the eight-tier structure of Machon 2, which would run the length of one of the pages of the story. Sullivan sat with Vanunu for 90 minutes to take down his description of the buildings and roads at the research centre. By coincidence the same week that Sullivan was preparing the graphics, a nuclear power station was opened to the public for one day as part of a drive to improve the British public's image of the nuclear energy industry. The technical equipment was useful to Sullivan for gaining an idea of the inside of Machon 2. Sullivan moved the so-called 'Golda Balcony' – named after former prime minister Golda Meir, and from where successive prime ministers and defence ministers have been briefed when touring the reactor – from one side of the diagram to the other. The disappearance of Vanunu meant that Sullivan was unable to carry out one final check on its accuracy.

By the closing days of September – some two weeks after Vanunu had arrived in London, and a month after Guerrero had first contacted the newspaper – 'Insight' had convinced itself of the validity of Vanunu's claims. Reporters noted a change in Vanunu's mood at this point: 'He realised rather slowly that he was a man possessing a unique body of information. But once he had handed that out he was nothing, just another 30-year-old man in a foreign country, and one who couldn't speak the language very well. He didn't like it when he stopped being the centre of attention. It was really getting to him,' an 'Insight' reporter said.[21]

The last stage in many investigative stories consists of confronting the party under investigation. The object of this encounter depends upon the nature of the story and on how much the reporter has already learned. Sometimes the reporter lacks essential material and hopes to fill in the missing pieces. Ideally, as was the case with the Vanunu investigation, the reporter already has enough information to write the whole account and is only giving the other party a chance to give his or her side.

For a news organisation to approach any foreign government to obtain a reaction is a serious matter. It had added importance in this case because in

June 1977 the *Sunday Times* published a four-page 'Insight' report alleging systematic torture of Arab suspects from the West Bank by Israelis during interrogation. That investigation, which took five months, comprised interviews which 'Insight' reporters held with a number of suspects. The editor, Harold Evans, had made a decision not to approach the Israeli embassy for its reaction prior to publication because he feared that the suspects named would be placed in danger. Nor had the reporters spoken to any Israeli officials, such as the police, the justice ministry, the army or the prison authorities while they were carrying out their inquiries in Israel. Subsequently, some of the allegations were shown to be inaccurate.

Peter Wilsher and Hounam took an eight-page summary of Vanunu's testimony, together with some of the photographs, Vanunu's passport number and worker's certificate to the Israeli embassy. It gave the Israeli government the opportunity to shore up its image of nuclear ambiguity either by destroying the credibility of the man or by refuting the allegations about the nuclear arms-production process. Little did Jerusalem know to what extent the very foundations of its ambiguity policy were being challenged at that moment. All the two journalists from the *Sunday Times* did was telephone the embassy to seek an appointment; all they told press attaché Eviator Manor was that they wanted to check a story 'about Dimona'. Manor thought they were doing a story about the black Jews of Dimona, a number of such Jews from the United States living in the town, whose religious status had become controversial. At one stage in the meeting Manor asked the journalists rhetorically, 'If you publish his name, won't it be dangerous for him?'. Hounam replied curtly, 'Well obviously you would know that better than I.'[22] When Wilsher and Hounam left the meeting, Manor telephoned the ambassador, Yehuda Avner, at his residence. He told Avner about the forthcoming 'Insight' exposé but did not refer on the phone to the photographs or to the fact that the reporters wanted confirmation of the story. Manor said he had to come over to see him, but Avner, who was preparing for a public dinner engagement, said that Manor should repeat the standard Israeli position, namely that Israel would not be the first to introduce nuclear weapons into the region. Manor said that this was something totally different, and that Israel was past that stage. He had to see him. When Avner's eyes fell upon the photographs he sat down. 'This is really something,' he murmured.[23] The ambassador reported to Jerusalem. Alarm bells began to ring. Damage control became the order of the day. There was no way to deny the story. The ambassador was late for his dinner engagement. The Israeli government followed a classic rule in government public relations by making 'no comment'. Vanunu had been very anxious for the *Sunday Times* to seek an official Israeli reaction. He, albeit naively, hoped that there would be an official Israeli admission that the information was true and that this would be tantamount to Israel confirming that it had the Bomb.

Andrew Neil read 'Insight's hard copy and passed it as accurate. An unexpected development then occurred. Guerrero, the man who had introduced the paper to Vanunu, arrived in London to claim payment for his introduction. Dissatisfied, he took the story to the *Sunday Mirror*. Interested to see how the *Mirror* would handle the matter, Neil delayed publishing that Sunday. Given that the Vanunu disclosure would make or break his reputation, Neil also wanted one additional check, by an internationally known scientist who would be prepared to lend his name to the authenticity of 'Insight's' story. They decided to approach Dr Theodore Taylor, who had been head of the Pentagon's atomic weapons-testing programme, in which capacity he had designed and tested nuclear weapons and had built plants which produced atomic weapons. Taylor had been taught by the 'father' of the atomic bomb, Robert Oppenheimer. After seeing the photos and transcripts, Taylor concluded that there could be no doubt that Israel had a nuclear capability. Moreover, Israel's nuclear programme was more advanced than earlier estimates suggested, according to Taylor.[24]

One 'participant' whom 'Insight' managed to get to was Dr Francis Perrin, who, as commissioner of France's nuclear programme from 1950 to 1971, oversaw the construction by France of the Dimona reactor – for ostensibly peaceful purposes. In the interview, which the paper published the week following the publication of Vanunu's exposé, Perrin revealed that France, in addition to building the reactor itself, had provided the technology to manufacture nuclear bombs, built the secret underground plutonium-processing plant housed in Machon 2, and supplied some initial uranium fuel. The interview with Perrin confirmed Vanunu's claim that Israel had the technology, the plant and the resources to make atomic bombs. It corrected a 1976 *Time* magazine report – one of the few to have appeared before the *Sunday Times* story – that the plutonium-processing plant was not built until the late 1960s.[25]

'Insight's' examination of Vanunu's claims had therefore passed through some five stages. First, the initial reports of Hounam's questioning in Australia were shown to experts. Second, associate editor Peter Wilsher joined the team to pass a sceptic's eye over their findings. Third, Vanunu was debriefed by Barnaby. Fourth, the evidence from this debriefing was referred to the other experts consulted. Fifth, the hard copy was shown to Theodore Taylor. The reporters had, of course, themselves acted as 'gatekeepers' in their interviews with Vanunu, and there was the confirmation that he had been employed at Dimona.

Neil was surprised that the Israeli authorities did not make any attempt to get him to drop the story. He had even lunched recently with the Israeli ambassador. Neil asked himself whether the absence of any Israeli pressure was evidence that Vanunu's disclosure was an officially sponsored leak. Jane Moonman, then director of the British–Israeli public affairs committee argued,

> If you let the person on whom you are applying pressure know that it is extremely important to you, unless he happens to be a committed Zionist you run the risk of him saying 'Let's go full steam on the story'.[26]

To be sure, the Israeli officials had played with the idea of discrediting the Vanunu story in the *Sunday Times*. Teicher and Dor-On, after being approached by the *Sunday Times* team to confirm what the paper had learnt from Vanunu, decided to inform the Israeli authorities and, following a meeting with the head of field security in the Israeli army, the two were asked to go to London and tell the paper that Vanunu's information was incorrect. But the two, feeling it was professionally unethical to lie to another journalist, declined the official request.

The possibility of an official Israeli approach was anticipated by the newspaper. Hounam said later that had the Israeli embassy given a more detailed answer, including an off-the-record one arguing that publication would do damage, they would have respected the confidentiality of such an answer and not published it.[27] Rupert Murdoch, the paper's publisher, had known pro-Israeli sympathies. He was an admirer of Israel and friend of Ariel Sharon. Murdoch's predisposition towards Israel was reflected in the pro-Israeli coverage and editorial positions taken by the *New York Post* which he then owned. In a telling remark at the time of the 1982 Falklands conflict, Murdoch, on being honoured as 'Communications Man of the Year' by the American Jewish Congress, told his audience that 'the conflict between Argentina and Britain should be taken as a reminder of what might happen in the Middle East: the issue was democracy versus dictatorship and the case for supporting Britain was the same as that for supporting Israel.' Denis Herbstein, a former *Sunday Times* reporter, described 'the real Murdoch' as somebody

who will come into the *Sunday Times* one Saturday night after a spell abroad, take a quick look at the first edition which has a piece on Israeli ill-treatment of Palestinian refugees. He is heard to say 'this bloody paper is getting anti-semitic,' and the message descends pretty sharply through the ranks. Open debate barely exists.[28]

Neil took no risks. 'I was afraid that Rupert Murdoch, an enthusiastic supporter of Israel, would torpedo the story. So I simply did not update him,' Neil said later.[29] On the other hand, one of Neil's colleagues characterised Murdoch's approach as 'quite simple: if it's a good story and sells papers, print it. Murdoch might even have turned around and said "Why not do ten pages instead of three?".'[30]

It would not have been difficult for a dissenting voice to have come out with the story elsewhere had Murdoch and Neil acceded to an Israeli request not to publish. Former 'Insight' editors Bruce Page, Godfrey Hodgson and Phillip Knightley said that they had never been asked, instructed or given a hint by the editorial management to drop investigation of a story. To have done so would have meant the end of 'Insight'. 'If you are dealing with areas where freedoms are paramount like the media, then you will upset a lot of sensibilities if you

start saying "If you don't do what we want there will be repercussions".'
According to Michael Jones, the paper's political editor, 'Mr Murdoch's well-
known Israeli sympathies were never a consideration whether the story ran or
not,' but clearly Neil had to make doubly sure that the story was correct. 'Neil
is aware that if he makes a mistake on a major story concerning Israel it is more
serious than with a story not concerning Israel,' an editorial executive
remarked.[31]

The remaining obstacle to publication was doubt on the part of Neil and
'Insight' regarding Vanunu's motives in divulging the information. The
embassy's 'no comment' raised the question again of whether the Israelis
wanted the story published. Neil increasingly asked himself during the
investigation: was the paper being used by a foreign government? Barnaby's
estimate of the number of Israeli nuclear warheads was much higher than
previous estimates. Barnaby thought that Israel would be pleased for its
nuclear capability to become known – notably to counter Iraqi and Syrian
chemical weaponry. Yet, given the expected negative reaction in the US
Congress, no Israeli government, Barnaby argued, could formally announce
that it had a nuclear capability.[32] Leonard Spector of the Carnegie Endowment
Fund's nuclear proliferation programme shared this view. He even went so far
as to suggest that Shimon Peres, about to hand over the premiership to the
Likud party's Itzhak Shamir under the coalition agreement, might have wanted
to impress public opinion at home in order to prepare the ground for making
territorial concessions.[33]

Leaks may be the stuff of investigative journalism, but they are fraught with
danger. People may leak for altruistic or ideological reasons, but generally
motives are less pure. Some of the most talkative sources are people who have
been hurt by the developments which make the particular story and have a
vendetta against others involved. That Vanunu had been laid off could be
important. Vanunu had struck up a warm acquaintance with Wendy Robbins.
Noticing her medallion which bore her Hebrew name 'Rebecca', Vanunu asked
her, 'Are you Jewish?'. 'Insight' staffers encouraged Robbins to try to find out
his true motives for his disclosure.

There were other theories as well, some attempting to explain how on earth
Vanunu could have roamed about so freely and taken so many photographs.
A variation on the theory that he was working for the Mossad was that the
Israeli authorities simply allowed him to serve their interests. 'Having Vanunu
say it, and adding credibility to his story by subsequently kidnapping him and
putting him on trial, suits the Israeli government very well,' Barnaby speculated.[34]
'My conversations with Vanunu convince me that he was not a willing tool
of the Mossad. But it is entirely possible that unwittingly he was allowed to
serve a purpose – to tell the world about Israel's nuclear weapon activities.'[35]
Though there had been a genuine security breakdown, in the end was Vanunu
given just enough rope? A different possibility the newspaper had to weigh was

that he was working for an Arab or Eastern bloc intelligence service. The motives for Vanunu's disclosure were to concern Neil until the day of publication. 'Governments lie. Middle East governments lie and Western governments lie. All governments lie, and it is the job of journalists to try and expose these lies. I take the view that news is telling the people what governments and powerful people don't want the people to know,' Neil said.

After journalists turned to the Israeli embassy, prime minister Peres, believing that the papers were about to print their stories that weekend, acted to limit the potential damage from the coming publications. The concern was not so much Israeli public reaction itself or even US reaction but Egyptian and other Arab-world reaction. In a step designed to stop the story being taken up further, Peres used the well-tried Israeli system of 'recruiting' Israeli editors. On Friday 26 September the Israeli Editors' Committee was convened. Going back to pre-independence days, this forum has enabled senior Israeli officials to win the 'cooperation' of newspaper and broadcasting chiefs at 'times of need', whereby editors are briefed on sensitive matters in return for either not publishing or delaying information. The Editors' Committee meeting was called for the very unconventional time of the Sabbath eve. 'We were afraid that Peres was going to tell us that war was going to break out that same evening,' remarked Hannah Zemer, editor of *Davar*.[36] Peres – described as 'petrified' by one of the editors – told the assembled editors that the *Sunday Times* was about to publish the revelations of the runaway technician and asked them to abstain from seeking Israeli reactions to the story for the first 48 hours. It was impossible to stop any discussion in the long term. After the first 48 hours editors would be free to print whatever they wanted after clearance from the censor. No objections were raised. 'It was an appeal to our patriotism, and we complied with it,' one editor said. 'I am a responsible Israeli,' said Ari Rath, editor of the *Jerusalem Post*.[37] It was not a difficult choice for editors for another reason: they did not know what the *Sunday Times* was going to publish.

Peres' step in assembling the Editors' Committee had a decisive influence in the *Sunday Times* decision to run the story. Even though the paper's reporters had turned to the Israeli embassy, no decision had yet been taken to run the story given the concern as to whether it was an Israeli disinformation exercise to protect the country's nuclear capability. The *Sunday Times* learnt about this meeting from an Israeli source; Peter Wilsher knew two of the newspaper editors personally. It convinced Neil that Vanunu was a genuine security leak. Censorship had backfired.

Neil might have published that Sunday had the paper not known that the *Sunday Mirror* was also looking into the story. The *Sunday Mirror* article was awaited with a certain interest by *Sunday Times* staffers to see whether it shed further light on Vanunu and his story. But apart from reporting an official Israeli confirmation that Vanunu had been a technician at the Dimona reactor, the *Sunday Mirror* article did not help.

Questions about Vanunu's motives in speaking to the paper resurfaced. On 30 September Vanunu, restless at the continuing delay at the *Sunday Times*, decided to go away for a few days to Italy. (Much later it was discovered that the Mossad had succeeded in drawing Vanunu to come to Rome, from where he was abducted back to Israel.) When Vanunu disappeared on 30 September – and failed to keep in telephone contact with Hounam – the paper was in a quandary whether to publish or not. A meeting of editors was called on Friday 3 October. In addition to Neil, those attending included deputy editor Ivan Fallon, managing editor (news) Anthony Rennell, news editor Andrew Hogg, foreign editor Stephen Milligan and political columnist Peter Jenkins as well as Morgan, Hounam and some of the reporters who had dealt with Vanunu. Those who opposed publication argued that the paper was at a distinct disadvantage in being unable to produce its key witness. The strength of the story depended on an insider confirming the existence of Dimona. Even if the paper was satisfied with the story's veracity, it had to convince the rest of the world. Robin Morgan argued that Vanunu's disappearance was an additional reason to publish because 'if we didn't publish, and there wasn't any witness, the Mossad would quietly put him away somewhere. We had to publish to protect him – an annex to his existence.'[38] Some at the meeting remained sceptical about Vanunu's motives, believing that it was an Israeli conspiracy to project the existence of its nuclear deterrent. It would be Andrew Neil's 'Hitler's Diaries', they jeered. The meeting closed. Most attending opposed publication. Neil closeted himself with Fallon and Milligan, who were both in favour of publishing.

'Andrew was terribly anxious about it. If we had run the story and it had been wrong, the editor would probably not have survived,' said an executive. In deciding to go ahead, Neil was influenced by the news about the Editors' Committee meeting in Israel: 'It was a powerful confirmation of something which was causing Peres anxiety.' Leaving Neil's room, Fallon flashed a thumbs-up to those outside. As he made his way towards the newsroom, a number of staffers approached him saying, 'We want you to know that we regard this as Neil's "Hitler's Diaries".'

The entire top half of the front page of the *Sunday Times* of 5 October carried Vanunu's story under the headline: 'Revealed: Israel's Nuclear Arsenal'. The report summarised the longer article which took up two pages inside. After setting out the details of the structure of the nuclear research centre, the article described Vanunu's background and employment at Dimona, and then gave a brief history of the plant. It continued with a survey of the regional balance of power and the abortive attempts at inspection by the United States. The article then gave a detailed description of Machon 2, where it said plutonium was separated from uranium, and plutonium buttons for the warheads 'baked'. In its front-page article the paper wrote that 'nuclear scientists consulted by the *Sunday Times* calculate that at least 100 and as many as 200 nuclear weapons have been assembled.'

It calculated the number of warheads which Israel had manufactured over the years by using the quantity of plutonium which could be produced during the time the reactor had existed and the known arrivals in Israel of yellowcake, from which uranium is extracted. But Barnaby's estimate, in fact, was 150 weapons. 'Two hundred would be an absolute upper limit. It assumes the same output from the reprocessing plant for the entire period of operations,' he said.[39]

Apart from this, Barnaby could not fault the way the paper had written its report 'given the nature of newspaper articles. I was pleasantly surprised that they'd put so much in. It was a good précis of Vanunu's knowledge.' Barnaby included a lot of what had been left out of the *Sunday Times*'s exposé in a book he subsequently wrote. Of the paper's journalists he thought that only Hounam 'understood totally what was going on – he's prepared to read text books to learn about the subject.' He didn't think there was much in the exposé of specific interest to the physics community, 'but then that's not their readership'.[40]

At the foot of one of the two pages, under the caption 'How the experts were convinced', were the different examinations which Barnaby and 'Insight' had put Vanunu through. Of all sections of the Vanunu exposé in the 5 October issue, it was this sidebar article which showed most changes from edition to edition. The article ended by noting that ten scientists approached by the paper had said that Vanunu's testimony could not be faulted. A comparison between the first and subsequent editions shows that this sentence was omitted from the first edition. 'We were trying to fit this story on the page and we were short of space, so I cut the paragraph at the end,' Morgan said. 'Neil was on the printing stone when he spotted this missing crucial paragraph. It's a reaffirmation that ten experts we approached saw Vanunu's testimony and could not fault it.' To make room for the sentence, another one was dropped which explained the absence of workers in Vanunu's photographs of Dimona. 'Vanunu has a simple answer: "I wasn't going to take pictures in front of my colleagues".'[41]

Certain explanations by the scientists were altered or excluded from this section of the exposé. In the first edition the paper included the qualification made by Dr Theodore Taylor that Vanunu's descriptions of the Dimona infrastructure, and of materials corresponding to the models of weapons components, seemed accurate on the assumption that the photographs were taken at Dimona. But by the paper's final edition this had been dropped. In its place was Taylor's conclusion, which had already appeared on the paper's front page, that Israel had had nuclear weapons for at least a decade, and that, Taylor added, the Israeli programme was more developed than earlier estimates had suggested. These edition changes reflected the anxiety running through the *Sunday Times* newsroom on the night of 4–5 October not only to get the story right but to be seen to do so.

The account ran to a little over 6,000 words. Some previous *Sunday Times* 'Insight' investigations had run to 10,000 or even 15,000 words, one-sixth of the size of an average book. The paper was planning further articles about other aspects of Israel's nuclear programme and to write a book in collaboration with Vanunu, but his disappearance made it impossible to proceed. The exposé published on 5 October was a summary of the key information gleaned from Vanunu, comprising only about 10 per cent of the total information he had disclosed.

The investigation cost the paper £40–50,000. It involved five to six reporters working on the story for five weeks, with visits to Australia, the United States, and so on. By past standards this was not expensive: the Philby and Thalidomide investigations, for example, involved 15 or 20 reporters working for up to three months, and they were estimated to have incurred expenses in six figures. The *Sunday Times* expected to recover the Vanunu expenses through contracts which it had signed with foreign newspapers and magazines prior to its publication of the story. But Vanunu's disappearance put paid to that also. Moreover, the paper's later contribution to Vanunu's defence put the story in the debit column of News International's balance sheet. But the publicity which the *Sunday Times* earned was unexpectedly much greater than originally envisaged owing to Vanunu's disappearance, abduction and trial in Israel. The exposé also helped to crown Neil's three-year editorship of the *Sunday Times*, and showed his mettle as an editor. 'It was the most important story that the paper ran since Neil took over as editor. It was the one with the biggest international implications,' an 'Insight' staffer said. Neil hoped that it would contribute to stopping the paper's sagging circulation, which had dropped some 200,000 in the two previous years, to its lowest figure for some 20 years.

5
The Spoiler

The precise circumstances which made Oscar Guerrero go off and offer the story to the *Sunday Mirror* are a matter of dispute. A relationship of mutual suspicion existed between Guerrero and the *Sunday Times* from the very beginning after Guerrero claimed that 'Professor' Mordechai Vanunu was Israel's top atomic scientist. Peter Hounam did not have an easy time interviewing Vanunu in Australia because, he said, Guerrero was frustrating to deal with.[1] Guerrero claimed that Hounam had left Sydney with Vanunu in the middle of the night, cutting him out of the deal.

The *Sunday Times* denied that it broke its agreement with Guerrero. According to Hounam, 'there was never a question of cutting him out of the deal. We just simply don't do that sort of thing.' While still in Australia, in an attempt to pacify Guerrero prior to his return trip to London with Vanunu, Hounam agreed a deal under which Guerrero was to receive the first US$25,000 from any earnings by Vanunu, such as syndication rights to his story and a planned book. Yet, according to the Israeli paper *Maariv*, drawing on an interview with Hounam a month after the Vanunu expose, 'in Australia Hounam distanced himself from Guerrero whom he saw as a exploiter, and, at Hounam's insistence, Vanunu met him without Guerrero's knowledge.'[2] According to the Israeli Supreme Court ruling in May 1990 on Vanunu's appeal, '... Hounam distanced Guerrero from contact between the paper and Vanunu, and flew together with Vanunu to London. Guerrero, whose requests for a significant payment from the *Sunday Times* were rejected, telephoned in the meantime to another paper, the *Sunday Mirror*.'[3] When Guerrero arrived in London he contacted the *Sunday Times* and spoke to Robin Morgan; Hounam was busy checking Vanunu's story. Morgan tried to reassure him. 'We said "Wait, be patient. We will come back to you. When we've proved the story, that is the time to talk." ' But Wendy Robbins, who worked as a researcher on the story, says, 'Guerrero kept ringing, and kept wanting to speak to Robin [Morgan]. He then asked to speak to me' (Robbins had met him on his first trip to London from Madrid). 'I said, "You'll have to speak to Robin." He said, "But I never get through to him." ' Then Guerrero said that he wanted to meet her in a park at 8 pm, as he had something 'hot' to tell her, later cancelling, saying it was too dangerous. According to Hounam, however, Guerrero telephoned Morgan, 'insisting that he had decided not to pursue his agreement with us. He told Robin that he thought that by now the story was worth a million dollars and he was taking it elsewhere.' The two versions of events came up in March 1992 in the London High Court when Guerrero sued the *Sunday Times*. The main witness to what happened in the crucial period in Australia, Mordechai Vanunu, was unable to give his version of events in court.

The court rejected Guerrero's legal action, as well as ordering him to pay the newspaper's legal costs. Later, after his prison release, Vanunu gave his version of events. He said that

> Guerrero was concerned that he might not be paid by the *Sunday Times*. After Hounam found that he could no longer trust Guerrero [after Guerrero had described Vanunu to Hounam as 'one of Israel's leading scientists'] Hounam tried to get close to me being the source of the story, and felt that he did not need Guerrero any more.[4]

The Vanunu story was not one which a popular British tabloid paper would normally be interested in. 'Foreign affairs are box office poison. Nobody wants to know about them,' remarked Joe Grizzard, a former *Mirror* executive.[5] According to reporter Mark Souster, 'We were asking ourselves, "What do we do with it?" The fact that Israel has a nuclear bomb makes no odds to our readership.'[6] Reporter Tony Frost's scoops in the *Sunday Mirror*, for example, included pictures of the Duchess of Windsor lying on her deathbed, which he obtained from a member of her staff, and the life story of the man who had been Princess Diana's hairdresser for seven years. 'In tabloid terms this was a much more important story than Vanunu,' Frost remarked.[7] But Mike Molloy, the paper's editor, felt Vanunu had a certain relevance:

> You're dealing with readers who essentially don't want demanding papers – otherwise they'd buy the broadsheet ones. But popular entertainment is only part of the paper. All the balancing elements are important. If you give someone a mass of sugary content, ultimately, after a few years, you begin to suffer.

The Vanunu story had a spy element. There was a James Bond feel to it – there was subterfuge, nuclear bombs, snatched photos. The story could have a format which would be totally understood and valued by *Sunday Mirror* readers, he added.[8]

An important factor in the *Sunday Mirror*'s decision to go for the Vanunu story was the knowledge that the *Sunday Times* was on to it.

Tony Frost was an obvious choice to handle Guerrero's story; he had built a solid reputation as an investigative reporter. In 1976 he began a 15-year career on the *Sunday Mirror*, going from staff reporter to chief reporter to deputy news editor and news editor. Later he was to be appointed deputy editor.

The strategy which the *Sunday Mirror* adopted in approaching the story was similar to that of the *Sunday Times* – to check the information and the person bringing it by trying to disprove its authenticity. If Guerrero were proved genuine, the paper would move on to the story itself. Guerrero described himself as an international journalist who had interviewed world leaders. He showed Frost six photos which appeared to show him standing with politicians like Lech Walesa, Argentinian President Raúl Alfonsín, Shimon Peres and the Palestine Liberation Organisation's Issam Sartawi. But something seemed wrong with some of the pictures; Guerrero appeared to be as prominent as his subjects, in some cases more so. Tempers began to fray. Frost did not believe Guerrero's claims about his journalistic background. Guerrero repeatedly said: 'I've got the proof that Professor Vanunu is right ... that Israel has been making neutron bombs.' Then he said, 'I have the same pictures which Vanunu had passed to the *Sunday Times*. I was his agent. I got the pictures copied.'[9] The photos were in a bag Guerrero had been clutching assiduously. But without a contract Guerrero said that he would not show them the photos. Peter Miller, the assistant editor for news, and Frost were hesitant given the question mark over Guerrero's background. Eventually a contract was drawn up, but it included a clause that he would be paid 14 days after exclusive publication of the story. An additional clause required that the information and the photos be found genuine. Guerrero then opened his bag and produced two pictures of what he said was Dimona. He added that it might be possible to get more – but it would cost money.

'You said that you had the evidence,' Frost countered. 'Yes, yes, but they're not here. They're in ... a luggage lockup.' As Guerrero was handing over the two pictures, Frost saw that there were more photos in the bag. A cup of coffee was ordered for Guerrero. According to Frost, 'as the secretary offered him the cup, Guerrero relaxed his hold on the bag. I grabbed it.'[10] That Guerrero had been unwilling to part with these pictures – in contrast to those of him seemingly appearing in the company of international politicians – added to the genuineness of the Dimona photos. 'Although we doubted and were unsure of his motives, we became more and more convinced about what he was selling,' said one of the journalists.[11] They took the material to John Parker, the paper's deputy editor. 'Given the other dubious pictures showing Guerrero in the company of various politicians, who's going to back these up?', Parker asked rhetorically. They had to be shown to experts.

It was Thursday 18 September. Through a 'mole' on the *Sunday Times*'s staff, the *Sunday Mirror* was able to follow the other paper's progress with the story. According to the reporter, 'I had a friend working in the *Sunday Times* who while not actively involved with the story was able to tell me how far advanced they were in their investigation and when they were intending to publish which obviously determined when we would.'[12] According to Frost, 'we were terrified that the *Sunday Times* might publish that weekend (21 September), but the word on the jungle drum was that they were having huge difficulties and that they would not be publishing that weekend.'[13]

The *Sunday Mirror* showed the photos to some five experts, among them a man who had worked at Aldermaston, a Royal Air Force officer with knowledge of nuclear arms, and a Leeds University scientist. The paper's Paris correspondent consulted a French expert. The photos – black-and-white reproductions from the copies Guerrero had shown them – were of four types: exteriors of what appeared to be a nuclear reactor, scenic views of the nuclear research complex, photos showing spherical figures described as bomb components, and components of the Doomsday device. The experts, on being shown the photos, were not asked 'Is this a nuclear installation?' but 'What do you believe this is?'. If they failed to identify them as connected to nuclear weapons production, then, the experts were told, 'Look, we understand this to be ... : Do you agree?' Some of the experts did not want to put their reputations on the line for the paper. Others were non-committal.

The key proof the *Sunday Mirror* wanted was to meet Vanunu. Throughout the ten days Guerrero was dealing with the *Sunday Mirror* he made a number of attempts to reach Vanunu at the *Sunday Times*, as an inspection of the logs of telephone calls at the hotels where he was staying showed. The *Sunday Times* had put Guerrero up at the Tower Thistles Hotel during his first visit to London from Madrid, so Guerrero, not knowing that Vanunu was at a country lodge where he was being debriefed, thought that he might also be at the Tower Thistles. Richard Brecker was sent to the hotel in the vain hope of locating Vanunu, who was only moved to the hotel from 19 to 23 September, by which time the *Mirror* had decided that he was staying at a guesthouse. Hotels in Bloomsbury, Paddington and Victoria were checked out, hotel staff being shown a photo of Vanunu. Guerrero then claimed that Vanunu was staying in a warehouse in St Katherine's Dock with two *Sunday Times* minders, sleeping in sleeping bags. He said that it would be possible to meet Vanunu but only with the minders being present. Finally on Wednesday 24 September, Guerrero said that he could arrange a meeting with Vanunu at Leicester Square men's toilets at 7.30 pm. Tony Frost positioned himself across the entrance on a corner outside a cinema. Peter Miller was on another corner, and Geoff Garvey on a third. Guerrero was at the main entrance to the toilets. They waited for an hour, but Vanunu failed to show up. It was the last they saw of Guerrero. In addition to the dubious pictures of him, the experts consulted failed to give an unconditional OK, and the final proof – a meeting with Vanunu – failed to get off the ground. Guerrero took a cross-channel ferry to Amsterdam and from there via Bangladesh Airlines went back to Australia. He was apparently afraid lest the story on him which the paper was left with would lead him into the hands of the Israelis.

The following day, Thursday 25 September, *Mirror* reporters on the story, and Frost and Miller, met to draw together the various strands of their investigation. Until then the story had had no specific line. Their draft was pegged to the Guerrero aspect but allowed that the photos might well be of Israel's nuclear programme. Miller and Frost met with John Parker, and were joined by the editor. 'Right boys, are we going with the story or not?', asked Molloy. Miller and Frost went quickly through the various aspects. Question: Had we proved conclusively from our experts that the pictures were of the inside of Dimona? Answer: No. Had we proved conclusively from our experts that Israel was manufacturing neutron bombs? No. Molloy became more and more sceptical as reporters ran through their material. Molloy instructed Frost to take all the material to the Israeli embassy in the hope of shedding more light on the matter. The embassy confirmed that there was no Professor Vanunu but that there was a technician of that name who, according to the embassy's spokesman, had been fired from his work because of unstable behaviour.

On Molloy's instructions, the underlying line of the draft was altered from its 'maybe – maybe not' stance to the story's being a hoax. The article, entitled 'The Strange Case of Israel and the Nuclear Conman', raised the question of whether the story was intended to discredit Israel. A sidebar article quoted two scientists as raising serious doubts about the photos' authenticity. One of these, Dr John Baruch of Leeds University, was reported as saying that the pictures could be of any laboratory – even a food-sterilisation plant or car wash. Baruch had, in fact, told Garvey that it might be a nuclear manufacturing facility but that there was insufficient evidence to state this with certainty. If, however, the story was a hoax, it was a highly sophisticated one. Frost, who sometimes clashed with Molloy on editorial policy, says that he complained to him over the way the article was being projected.

Where did the *Sunday Mirror* err where the *Sunday Times* got it right? Both applied similar rules of investigative journalism to the Vanunu story. Both went through the rigours of checking the information and its source. Both were suspicious of Guerrero. And both differentiated between him and the pictures of Dimona. The *Sunday Times* stood at an overwhelming advantage because they had Mordechai Vanunu. Had the *Sunday Mirror* interviewed Vanunu, this would have given greater credibility to the photographs and to Vanunu's story. It is surprising that while the ten experts consulted by the *Sunday Times* said, according to the paper, that 'Vanunu's testimony cannot be faulted',[14] none of the five consulted by the *Sunday Mirror* said so. 'The question of the experts was the one big mistake I made on the whole thing,' Tony Frost admitted. 'I should have sent the material to our US correspondent to show it to an American expert – that's what the *Sunday Times* did.'[15]

Had Vanunu turned up at the *Sunday Mirror* instead of the *Sunday Times* it seems unlikely that *Mirror* reporters would have carried out the rigorous checks, including an intensive two-day debriefing, which the *Sunday Times* did, or have printed three pages on Vanunu's detailed description of the separation of plutonium and uranium which even by 'Insight' standards was intricate.

Molloy seemed not to distinguish between the dubious Guerrero and the pictures of Dimona, despite the fact that he knew that the *Sunday Times* were seriously investigating the story and that they had the man from Dimona. He appears not to have appreciated the significance of Vanunu being the first person with direct knowledge of Dimona to speak about his work, while the *Sunday Times* did a masterly reconstruction, from Vanunu's description of the flow processes, to arrive at an estimate of how many warheads Israel had produced.

In *The Samson Option*[16] journalist Seymour Hersh claimed that the *Sunday Mirror* article was slanted by owner Robert Maxwell at the request of the Israeli authorities in order to discredit Vanunu, and by implication the story which the *Sunday Times* was working on. The fact that the *Sunday Mirror* got it wrong posed for Hersh the question of whether the paper got it deliberately wrong. The Israeli authorities knew the *Sunday Mirror* were following up the story because Molloy instructed the reporters to take the material to the embassy to seek their reaction. It is quite possible that deputy prime minister Itzhak Shamir, who was a good friend of Robert Maxwell, saw an opportunity to bury the Vanunu security leak by discrediting the whole story. Moreover, Hersh claimed that at Maxwell's request, Nicholas Davies, foreign editor of the *Sunday Mirror*'s stablemate the *Daily Mirror* and his boss's right-hand man, provided information about Vanunu's whereabouts which led to his abduction by the Mossad.

There is no evidence that information acquired by the Mossad about Vanunu's whereabouts in London came from Robert Maxwell or his staff. At no time did the *Sunday Mirror* reporters manage to meet Vanunu, even though they persistently told Guerrero they would need to see the subject. Guerrero himself had cut ties with the *Sunday Times* and Vanunu, and did not know where Vanunu was staying. Guerrero attempted to reach Vanunu through the *Sunday Times* reporter Peter Hounam but Vanunu, Hounam said, did not want to meet Guerrero. Yet the details provided by Hersh's main source, Ari Ben-Menashe, an Iranian-born Jew who had worked in Israeli military intelligence, include factual errors which raise serious questions about the accuracy of Hersh's claims.

The *Sampson Option* deals mostly with US–Israeli nuclear relations. When Seymour Hersh offered it to the British publishers Faber & Faber the latter requested a 'British angle' to the book. Hersh, drawing on information mainly from Ben-Menashe, penned the chapter 'Israel's Nuclear Spy'. When Hersh's book was offered to the *Sunday Times* for serialisation the paper was initially very interested, given that the book dealt within the Vanunu case. Hersh and Ben-Menashe were flown over to England and Peter Hounam, who knew more than anybody on his paper about the Vanunu story, held three meetings with them in the space of 24 hours. He caught Ben-Menashe out in many inaccuracies. He had also lied: how had the *Sunday Mirror* obtained its picture of Vanunu?

Ben-Menashe said it had been especially flown from Israel. In fact, Hounam had taken the picture himself when he was in Australia with Vanunu and Guerrero, and had later given Guerrero a copy of the photo. Hounam told Hersh he had been hoaxed, told Faber & Faber the same, and recommended to his editor, Andrew Neil, that he should not serialise the book.

There appears to be more basis, albeit circumstantial, for the claim that the *Sunday Mirror* article was deliberately altered in order to discredit Vanunu. Robert Maxwell was ambivalent in his attitude to the Jewish community in Britain and to Israel. Born into an impoverished religious Jewish family in Czechoslovakia – his father was a farmhand – he had received a religiously orientated education. But when he settled in Britain he began to move away from his Jewish past. He married a French Protestant. After the war he was elected MP for Buckingham. He recognised that social acceptability in the Britain of the 1950s entailed being more English than the English and not identifying too closely with the Jewish community. In 1986 (the year of the Vanunu affair), in an interview with the *Jewish Chronicle* magazine (which took its editors more than 15 months to obtain), Maxwell observed: '... I ceased to be a practising Jew just before the war when I left home. I still believe in God and Judaism's moral code which teaches the difference between right and wrong ... I don't believe in any church, just God. I certainly do consider myself Jewish. I was born Jewish and I will die Jewish.'[17]

But the 1980s were a period of change. By the end of the decade Maxwell was Israel's single biggest foreign investor. His investments, estimated to be worth £250 million, included a computer imaging enterprise, Scitex; a pharmaceutical company, Teva; a controlling interest in the second-largest afternoon newspaper, *Maariv*; and the Keter publishing firm. When Maxwell got involved in something he did it in spades. He became a friend of Shamir, broadly supporting Likud policies, and opposed to the establishment of a Palestinian state on the West Bank and Gaza. He placed his wide contacts in eastern Europe at the disposal of Israel, which had been seeking to reopen diplomatic ties cut in the aftermath of the 1967 Six Days War. His new-found energies on Israel's behalf also gained expression in the news media. The editorial columns of newspapers in the Mirror group became decidedly pro-Israeli during his proprietorship.

When the *Mirror* journalists contacted the embassy's press attaché, Eviator Manor, for an official Israeli response and showed him the material, Manor proposed to Jerusalem that the portrayal of Guerrero in derogatory terms would place a definite shadow over Vanunu and provide an opportunity to discredit the whole Vanunu story. The official reaction which Manor was instructed to convey was that Vanunu had been fired from his work at Dimona because of 'unstable behaviour'. Victor Ostrovsky, the Mossad renegade, claims that Shamir turned to Maxwell and asked him to knock down the story.[18] In an interview with the *Sunday Mirror* following the publication of Hersh's claims, Molloy said that he had told the publisher beforehand of his decision to take the material to the Israeli embassy. Maxwell, Molloy said, neither reacted nor showed any special interest. Yet in the same interview Molloy said that the decision to take the material to the embassy had never been referred to Maxwell. Molloy denies having actually shown Maxwell the material. He didn't see the pictures, nor did he actually have a conversation with him face to face.

6
A Mossad Kidnapping in
New Printing House Square

When the defence establishment first learnt that a nuclear technician was revealing Dimona's secrets to the world's media, they were faced with a number of questions. Principally, was Vanunu giving information to foreign enemy agents such as Soviets, or to the Israeli Communist Party which he had asked to join, or to Arab acquaintances, including one who shared his apartment? Secondly, what information had he given to the *Sunday Times*, or to any other foreign sources with which he had been in contact? A third question was, what would be the political impact, particularly in Washington, including Congress, of Vanunu speaking about his work?

In deciding to abduct Vanunu home, Israel 'had no choice', ex-Mossad head Isser Harel argued:

> To let this guy run free in the world? Tomorrow he would have landed voluntarily or by force in Arab hands and they would squeeze the juice out of him. For both the Arabs and the Soviet Union, it was a once in a lifetime opportunity to get the secrets of one of Israel's most sensitive installations.[1]

Moreover, the leak not only challenged Israeli security but, given Israel's pivotal role as a Western ally in the Middle East, it had important implications for the Western alliance as a whole.

Although defence minister Itzhak Rabin and deputy prime minister and foreign minister Itzhak Shamir were consulted on the decision to abduct Vanunu, as was attorney general Yosef Harish,[2] the final decision rested with Shimon Peres, who as prime minister had responsibility for the intelligence services.[3] In a paradoxical sense Vanunu might be thankful that Peres was prime minister at the time. Had Shamir been prime minister (under the existing coalition agreement he took over two weeks after Vanunu arrived back in Israel), it may be asked whether the ex-Mossad station chief for Paris, experienced in the cloak-and-dagger work of modern espionage, would have decided on what would become the politically inexpedient course of action of abducting an important informant of an internationally respected newspaper. Instead Shamir was left to carry the can and deal with the diplomatic repercussions of the abduction.

One of the Mossad's first clues that a former employee of Dimona was offering secret information to the media about the nuclear research centre came inadvertently from the *Sunday Times* itself. One of its reporters arrived in Israel on 2 September 1986 to check Vanunu's personal details: that he had worked at Dimona, had studied at Beersheba's Ben-Gurion University, and that he was who he said he was. According to Abraham Rotem, a senior Shin Bet official at the time of the Vanunu abduction, the Israeli security establishment learnt only by accident that Vanunu was in touch with the *Sunday Times*:

> It occurred after a British journalist came to Israel to verify whether Vanunu's photos were genuine. Were it not for the patriotism of a well-known Israeli journalist who learnt about the reporter's attempts to verify Vanunu's photos, the Shin Bet would never have been alerted to Vanunu's contacts, and the first it would have learnt about the matter would have been only after publication in the *Sunday Times*.[4]

At Vanunu's closed-doors trial reporter Peter Hounam commented on the visit to Israel by Max Prangnell, a baker-turned-journalist. Armed with Vanunu's photo and passport information Prangnell's task was to verify that Vanunu was the man he said he was and that he had worked at the reactor. 'I told Vanunu beforehand that we would be extremely careful about how we did it,' Hounam told the court. 'I am not sure that it was done very carefully in the end. It should have been.'[5] But it seems that it was not only the attention of the editor which aroused the Israeli authorities. According to Hounam, 'One woman friend clearly knew Vanunu. Unfortunately, Prangnell could not disguise his identity as a British reporter, exposing the danger he might tip off the security services.'[6] Another possibility is that the first the Israelis learnt about Vanunu was from Oscar Guerrero who, according to Louis Toscano, author of *Triple Cross*, contacted the Israeli consulate in Sydney about Vanunu in the hope of making a deal.[7] Vanunu himself recalls that while waiting in the bar of Sydney's Hilton hotel for a meeting with Peter Hounam, he became aware of two Israelis sitting beside him. They tried to engage him in conversation with comments to which he might find himself politically sympathetic. He immediately suspected them of being Mossad agents and left, frightened and suspicious.[8]

After Oscar Guerrero saw off Vanunu and Peter Hounam from Sydney airport on 11 September, he bragged to somebody who had been staying at King's Cross rectory about the great story, showing some of the photographs which Vanunu had taken of the Dimona reactor. This person happened to be a former communications officer with AS-10, who remained in touch with his ex-employers. After an hour's thought the ex-communications officer telephoned

Special Branch telling them that Vanunu and Hounam were en route to London, where the Israeli planned to hand over complete details of the Dimona project together with photographic evidence. According to the *Sunday Times*, a telex was immediately sent off to MI6. Australian and British intelligence have developed close ties since the 1950s at all levels including exchange of intelligence reports, assistance in training, and some joint covert operations. So close is the relationship that AS-10's London base is at MI6's headquarters at Century House. The scale of exchange of information may be seen from the fact that between 1950 and 1974, British intelligence received some 10,000 reports from their Australian counterparts, while transmitting 44,000 in return. MI6 provided AS-10 with a copy of its Far East personality index. In areas where both AS-10 and MI6 are represented, desk officers keep in touch with one another, making it possible to share and analyse intelligence regarding local developments. In places where only one of the services is represented, it can serve as the point of liaison for the other service. In giving the information about Vanunu to MI6 there can be little reason to doubt that the Australians did not inform their Israeli counterparts.[9] But the Mossad already knew a week earlier. According to Toscano there were two Mossad agents on the plane, seated a couple of rows behind Vanunu and Hounam.[10]

When Vanunu, accompanied by Hounam, arrived at London's Heathrow Airport the following day, entering under an assumed name, two British Special Branch men saw him pass through passport control, and the news of his arrival was passed by MI6 to the Mossad. On 21 September, following a meeting between Peres, Shamir and Rabin, where the Vanunu leak was discussed, Peres – anxious that Vanunu should be brought to Israel to stand trial, reportedly telephoned prime minister Margaret Thatcher to discuss the possible implications of the information Vanunu was giving the media.[11]

During Vanunu's debriefing by Dr Barnaby and the 'Insight' team in September, some thought went into the need to protect him. During the crucial days of the debriefing, Vanunu, Barnaby and the 'Insight' staffers stayed at Heath Lodge, a country guesthouse outside London. They thought Vanunu was well protected. So well had the newspaper disguised Vanunu's identity that a year afterwards the proprietor of Heath Lodge still had no idea who his mysterious guest had been.[12]

At the different places where he stayed, Vanunu refused to sleep on the ground floor, insisting on an upper floor. But he also declined the 'Insight' team's suggestion that one of their reporters sleep in the same room as he did. Vanunu wanted his solitude, although he did agree to a reporter staying in a nearby room. After a couple of days at Heath Lodge, Vanunu wanted to see the lights of London. There, he was moved from hotel to hotel. When not debriefing him they entertained him in a bar, in a restaurant or in Vanunu's room. On one of the weekends the paper arranged a one-day tour outside London to relieve Vanunu's boredom while 'Insight' checked the details of his story.

The newspaper devised a plan to ensure Vanunu's safety which on the face of it looked fairly secure. First, the *Sunday Times* planned to organise an international seminar on Israeli nuclear weaponry as a follow-up to the paper's exposé. The seminar, to be attended by internationally respected strategists, would address the dangers not only for the Middle East but for the world as a whole as a result of the nuclearisation of the region. One reporter envisaged the newspaper's report on the seminar including a diagram showing the prevailing-wind factor from any nuclear explosion. The *Sunday Times* also planned for Vanunu to give evidence before a US congressional commission on nuclear proliferation. But come the end of 1986, Vanunu would need, in Andrew Neil's words, to 'open a new page to his life in a new place'. 'We knew we couldn't guarantee his safety for the rest of his life. The Israelis have a long memory,' 'Insight' editor Robin Morgan remarked. He told Vanunu, 'You will be kidnapped, and taken back and punished. You will want to go home because it's your home. "That's my problem, not yours," he replied. His point was a philosophical one. He wanted the information to be known.'[13]

A number of countries were discussed by Vanunu and the newspaper as places where he might make his new life. In addition to Britain, these included Canada and the United States (both his girlfriend, Judy Zimmet, and his brother, Meir, lived in Boston). Australia was also mentioned, but Vanunu had not been enamoured of the country during his four-month stay there. 'What interests them is to drink beer,' he said disparagingly. Another possibility was New Zealand: Stephen Milligan, the paper's foreign editor, knew David Lange, the prime minister and an ardent anti-nuclear campaigner, and believed he could arrange for Vanunu to get citizenship. 'In practice', said Bruce Page, a former 'Insight' editor, 'you have to find a very specific environment. The newspaper has to be very intimately involved with the government in question. That means he would need to settle in Britain. You need to lay out a lot of positions with the ruling party and the opposition. You could improvise on it afterwards. But you have to have it ready before,' he said.[14] Neil said, 'We told Vanunu that we would try to help him get citizenship when all this was over.'[15] But the paper made no known approaches beforehand, presumably because it thought Vanunu's case for application would be stronger once he had become an international political personality. If Vanunu had foreign citizenship and had given up Israeli citizenship, an idea that he himself was toying with, it might have discouraged the Israelis (assuming they were aware of the change) from planning to abduct him in the knowledge of the diplomatic repercussions which would follow.

The Mossad was not far behind Vanunu and the *Sunday Times*. Overseeing the operation was one of Mossad's deputy heads, basing himself in a European capital. The Israeli authorities had gathered a lot of intelligence about Vanunu. They knew he had been to Moscow and that he had converted to Christianity. The reactor's chief security officer – who had known Vanunu personally – called a meeting.[16] Files on his conduct held in the reactor's personnel and security departments would be useful.

The Mossad's instructions were to get him back without causing a breach in British territoriality – no mean feat – which could cause a diplomatic incident. The Shin Bet approached Mordechai's brother, Albert. On 7 September, two Shin Bet officers went to Albert's carpentry workshop in one of Beersheba's industrial areas, and said they needed his help to get Mordechai back from Europe. 'Mordechai is under the influence of people, and there is the fear that he will be pressured to disclose things he does not want to,' they said. 'There is the possibility that journalists from England will contact you to clarify that he indeed worked at the reactor. The moment journalists get in touch with you call the Shin Bet agents.' It is unclear how the Mossad knew of the *Sunday Times*'s intent to send a reporter to Albert.[17] The possibility of Albert travelling to Europe to dissuade Mordechai from speaking to the journalists was raised by the agents. In addition, Albert was asked to let the Shin Bet have a copy of Mordechai's latest letter to him so that it could undergo graphological examination. This Albert refused to do: 'On the one hand they claimed to want to protect Mordechai, on the other they wanted to examine his handwriting!?'[18]

Albert was the only family member approached by the Shin Bet, but not the only 'acquaintance'. A former student acquaintance of Vanunu's at Ben-Gurion University, Ofer Keren – an MA Economics student who was active in a right-wing political group on the campus called Metzada at the same time that Vanunu was active on the left, was asked to help persuade him to return to Israel.[19] And just two days after Vanunu arrived in England and was walking down Regent Street in London's West End together with the *Sunday Times* researcher Wendy Robbins, he was amazed to see Yoram Bazak, whom he also knew from Ben-Gurion University, walking towards him.[20] Bazak's was one of the names given by Vanunu to Peter Hounam in Australia when he asked for people in Israel who could verify that Vanunu had worked at Dimona. (When a reporter tried to reach Bazak in Israel he was away.) Vanunu's first instinct on seeing Bazak was to duck into a side street to avoid him. Bazak, who was accompanied by a girlfriend, Dorit, said they had arrived in London at the end of a European tour. This offered a clue to the Mossad's tactics. Bazak invited Vanunu to dinner on Wednesday 17 September.[21] At dinner Bazak appeared purposely to attempt to draw Vanunu into talking about the country's defence policy in an attempt to raise 'the subject'. When Vanunu asked Bazak rhetorically what his reaction would be if he were to divulge information to the media about his former workplace, Bazak, visibly shaken, replied that he would find a means to get him back to Israel and into prison.[22] This should have alerted Robbins. Instead, Bazak and Dorit took them back to their room at the Royal Scot Hotel. 'It was one of the first stories I had worked on in my life. I knew nothing about conspiracies. To me the thought that the Israelis had sent somebody to bump into him on Regent Street was inconceivable. I argued with Peter Hounam and Robin Morgan, "It's a coincidence. I'm sure it's a coincidence." '[23] According to Robbins, Bazak's girlfriend telephoned Israel. 'Bazak asked Motti not to go downstairs to drink something, as if he was afraid that he would flee,' she said.[24] The incident destroys an assumption by Morgan and Neil that nobody would try to abduct Vanunu in the presence of *Sunday Times* staff. When, according to Robbins, Bazak asked Vanunu not to leave the hotel room, it ought to have sounded a danger signal. 'It didn't really occur to me that somebody could grab him,' Robbins remarked.[25] The 'Insight' team's published account of this encounter, while mentioning the dinner date, does not mention the 'Insight' researcher and Vanunu going to Bazak's hotel room, nor the phone call to Israel, nor Bazak's request that Vanunu should not leave the room.[26]

Vanunu stayed at a number of addresses in London. At one stage he was so frightened that he was being followed that he stayed with one of the 'Insight' reporters. It was therefore surprising that when Bazak asked where he was staying, Vanunu volunteered the information: the Tower Thistle hotel, by St Katherine's Dock, not far from the *Sunday Times*'s offices at New Printing House Square near Tower Bridge. Hounam admitted later that the choice of putting him up next to the newspaper's offices was inept as it would have been an obvious place for the Mossad to put under surveillance.[27] Later, on 23 September, he was moved to the Mountbatten hotel, room 105, registered under the name of Mr John Forsty.

This was also the day when two *Sunday Times* staffers took a summary of their investigation to the Israeli embassy for its reaction, and a succession of two-man film crews stood opposite the entrance of the newspaper offices, ostensibly photographing the picket lines of workers protesting against the introduction of new print technology. The first crew said they were from a students' union; they were tall and sporting stubble. Later, there was a second crew, wearing suits and with a tripod. According to editor Andrew Neil, bogus TV crews who pretended to photograph a labour dispute at New Printing House Square were linked by radio to motorcyclists on the main road.[28] While having no proof, the newspaper thought that these men, whom British police described as having a Middle Eastern appearance, and were not television crews, might have followed Vanunu when he left Wapping to go to his hotel. On some occasions he was smuggled into the newspaper carpark in the back of a car. Sometimes Vanunu was brought to the office via the back entrance to the building. 'We always took him from the back of the building – but what can you do? After all we are just journalists not intelligence agents,' Neil remarked.[29]

Cheryl ('Cindy') Bentov, née Hanin, born in 1960 in Orlando, Florida, whom the *Sunday Times* alleged abducted Vanunu, seemed on the surface an unlikely person to lure him to Israel.[30] Because Peres ordered that no British laws be broken in the process of abducting Vanunu, the strategy adopted was to lure him out of British territory, and only then to take him back forcibly to Israel.

Cheryl Hanin's first contact with Israel was in the late 1970s when she went to the country on a three-month intensive course in Jewish history and Hebrew. Later, after high school, she returned to Israel, joining a Nahal unit (Pioneering Fighting Youth) for protecting new border settlements. In March 1985 she married Ofer Bentov, a major in Israeli military intelligence, who comes from a military family; his father is a retired army general.[31] Hanin could draw on earlier experience in the pay of the Mossad. According to Jack Schiffman, a close family friend of the Hanins, Cheryl once remarked to her mother that 'there were other things that I did for the Israeli government which were even more pertinent and involved than this.'[32]

A right-wing anti-Israeli American magazine, *Spotlight*, which was the first to reveal Cheryl Bentov's Florida origins and which has good CIA sources, alleged that after moving to Israel she went to work for the CIA as a covert operative. If this is true, her marriage to a major in Israeli military intelligence would mean that the CIA had successfully infiltrated an agent into the military intelligence apparatus. *Spotlight* also reported that Mr Peres, in a secure phone call to the White House, personally asked the US for help to 'plug the leak'. But the Americans appear to have been as surprised as others about Cheryl's American past because the principal and assistant principal of Cheryl's school, Edgewater High, were subsequently contacted by both the CIA and the FBI asking to examine her school records. The US authorities do not appear to have been involved in the abduction. Indeed, the CIA station in London turned to its British counterpart to verify whether the Israeli authorities had approached the Thatcher government to warn that they were about to arrange Vanunu's disappearance.[33]

Arriving in London from Israel on 20 September, Hanin booked into the Eccleston hotel at Victoria. Four days later Mordechai Vanunu happened to be strolling near Leicester Square when a lonely-looking woman who seemed to be looking at him caught his eye.[34] Loneliness, the need for human companionship and an understanding human ear in a large, strange city attracted the seemingly like-minded persons. Although she seemed shy, they started talking over a cup of coffee. Vanunu was totally unsuspecting because he thought he'd made the first move. Her name, she said, was Cindy. She declined to give her full name and address, but she managed to get from Vanunu the name of his hotel.[35] Cindy had tried for three days to attract Vanunu's attention as he walked round seeing the sights of London.

Cindy declined Vanunu's suggestion that she come back to his hotel. The two went to see the film *Snow White and the Seven Dwarfs*. By Friday, 'Insight' reporters chanced on the liaison when Vanunu chose to meet the girl rather than attend one of the debriefing sessions with 'Insight'. They immediately suspected she was a Mossad plant.[36] Prangnell managed to catch a glimpse of her from a taxi while waiting for Vanunu. 'She was about five foot eight, she had blonde dyed hair, she was wearing a brown kind of raincoat, and she looked quite stocky. She had a very full face as well,' he said, and added that she was 'probably Jewish'.[37] The paper warned Vanunu but, already upset at what he thought an unnecessary delay in publication while the paper checked the story, he failed to heed their warnings.

On that Sunday the *Sunday Mirror* came out with its double-page centrefold raising grave doubts about Vanunu's claim, entitled 'The Strange Case of Israel and the Nuclear Conman'. Frustrated, not knowing that the *Sunday Mirror* was not a paper to be taken seriously, Vanunu feared that the *Sunday Times* would now not publish, given the doubts expressed about his allegations and about Guerrero's integrity. Moreover, with his photograph splashed in the paper, he had to get rid of the *Sunday Times*'s protection and disappear. Cindy popped the suggestion of the day. 'You can be recognised all over the country. It's better if you go abroad somewhere,' she said, adding, according to Mordechai's brother, Meir, that she was planning to visit her sister in Rome.[38] Initially, he declined Cindy's offer for him to come too, but changed his opinion after deciding that that if the Mossad wanted to get him they could do so in London. Visiting Rome was one way of dropping out of sight of any surveillance.

The following day Robin Morgan of 'Insight' vainly attempted to persuade Vanunu not to go away, but he said he would be back in three days. So did Peter Hounam. 'You must realise that it's quite possible that Cindy is a plant. Can we arrange to meet her?', Hounam asked. 'Vanunu said that evening (Monday) would not be good. I suggested that we should have dinner with my wife and Cindy the following evening, the Tuesday. Vanunu replied, "Fine yeah, let's do that. Let's all go out together," ' Hounam said.[39] On Thursday 2 October, Vanunu was due to sign a contract with the paper for a book on his work on the Israeli nuclear programme, for which he would be paid an advance of £100,000 plus royalties. Morgan accepted Vanunu's argument that somebody might be tailing *Sunday Times* reporters to locate where Vanunu was, but warned him not to leave British territory, to travel only by bus or train and not to hire a car because he would then have to produce his passport and give his true identity. Morgan also advised Vanunu to stay at small bed-and-breakfast establishments. He did not know that Vanunu had already given his true name to Cindy. Cindy decided to bring things to a head and she purchased a £426 business-class ticket to Rome from the Thomas Cook travel agency in Berkeley Street in London's West End. A flight on British Airways would be least likely to arouse Vanunu's suspicions. Showing the ticket to Vanunu, she explained that she would be leaving the next day, Tuesday, and would be staying at her sister's apartment in Rome.[40] Did he want to go? Romance is used in espionage not only for attraction but also to cause pain; and apparent romantic attachment can be withdrawn, causing extreme reactions of disappointment and loss. The entrapment was complete.

Hounam reached Vanunu at 11.30 at night. 'I'm sorry, I am going out of the city. I am not going very far,' Vanunu told Hounam. 'I won't be able to make dinner tomorrow evening.' Hounam warned him not to use a credit card, although he doubted that he had one. He warned him that it would be a terrible mistake if he set foot abroad because he would be easily picked up. Hounam said:

> Indeed, it would be better if he didn't go anywhere, or if he did I suggested that he didn't tell the rest of the office, but just told me where he was going so that I knew if he disappeared, we could trace him. But he wouldn't do that.

He did promise to telephone three times a day.[41] Vanunu then made a long-distance call to St John's rectory in Sydney. During his stay in London he had been telephoning John McKnight every five or six days, talking about what he was seeing during his stay. As time dragged on, and as Vanunu grew increasingly tense at the delay caused by the paper checking his testimony, these conversations had an important cathartic effect. Before Vanunu left Australia, McKnight had given him letters of introduction to a friend of his, the rector of St Helen's Bishopsgate, and another addressed to any Anglican clergyman, asking for assistance should Vanunu be in danger and need refuge. In his last call to McKnight, at one o'clock on the morning of Tuesday 30 September, McKnight was out and the assistant minister, Stephen Gray, took it. Gray said:

> He seemed alone, worried, disturbed, disillusioned. And he spoke about the damage that Oscar [Guerrero] had done – not in detail, but just that Oscar had done them a great deal of damage and that he didn't feel safe any more, that he was feeling very alone, and that he wanted to be back here at St John's with us. He didn't say that he was going abroad.[42]

At 10.30 the following morning Vanunu left the Mountbatten hotel with two small bags to join Cindy for the flight to Rome. Unable to bring Vanunu directly from England to Israel, the Mossad had two strategies available: to woo him into international waters and take him forcibly from there to Israel, or to woo him to another country and, again forcibly, take him from there to Israel.[43] Given the danger of arousing his suspicions by wooing him to international waters, such as on a yacht, the second strategy was more appropriate.[44]

Vanunu, in a letter smuggled from his prison in 1997, vividly described the kidnapping:

> On 24.9.1986 I met an American girl in Leicester Square in London and later met her several times. On 30.9.1986 she persuaded me to go with her to Rome to visit her sister. We left London on British Airways flight 504 and arrived in Rome. There she was met by an Italian who introduced himself as a friend of her sister's and he took us in his private car to a flat in a suburb outside Rome.

As I entered the flat, I was attacked by two men, who then drugged me by means of injections.

Vanunu wrote that he regained consciousness in a car but that as he tried to cause an accident, he was drugged again.[45] Later, in court, Vanunu described the moments of his abduction:

It's something dreadful when you're snatched, kidnapped, they can eliminate you, take you somewhere else. Everything is possible. I was aware that in a kidnapping accidents can happen such as death. That is, even if they didn't intend to kill me in the first place ... I didn't know what was happening exactly. I was sure that that's it, they're going to shoot me, or kill me. Those first two minutes lasted awfully long, and I started to think about my life, I see pictures from the past. In those moments I saw a possibility of death. That is, it didn't matter to them if I came out of this alive or dead. So I assumed that in future also my life won't be worth much.

On 21 September the *Nora*, an old and very slow boat, was on its back to Haifa port after a pleasant, unstormy, training voyage when it received an order from Israel to sail to a certain point 'X' opposite Port 'X' off the Italian coast and await some 'visitors'. Only the captain, his deputy, and the first officer knew who the 'visitors' were. Disguising its military identity and its highly sophisticated surveillance equipment, the ship sailed under a Panamanian flag.[46] Asked by the crew why the ship had turned 180 degrees back towards the Mediterranean just as it was a short stretch from home, the captain replied curtly, 'It's classified.' Even he did not know all the details. The protestations of crew members that they had family members awaiting their return for the forthcoming Jewish high holidays received the reply 'You think you are on *Loveboat*.' By 28 September the ship reached the location – and waited three days. Crew and the sea cadets had no idea how long they would be waiting at that spot. Endless cardgames were played. Water was running out and the captain introduced water rationing and banned showers. Food rationing was also introduced, and those presents for relatives and friends bought by some of the cadets which were edible were eaten.

Then on 30 September, at 11.30 pm, crew members on duty on the ship's bridge monitored a speedboat approaching. Immediately, the captain ordered everybody on the ship to gather and stay in the ship's lounge which was below sea level, where they would be unable to see the 'visitors' join the ship. The captain's deputy lowered the ramp. Two Mossad agents brought on board a drugged Vanunu. They were joined by Cindy. Vanunu was taken down to the deputy captain's two by two and a half metre cabin, which like the captain's quarters was located on the second deck.[47] Half an hour later, the captain informed the crew and cadets in the lounge that the ship was sailing immediately for Haifa, an announcement which brought a heightened sense of relief. The Mossad agents stayed with Vanunu all the time either in the cabin itself or in the adjoining captain's lounge. Questions from some of the curious crew regarding their identity were ignored. It is unclear why Cindy herself made the voyage rather than taking the shorter and more comfortable flight from Rome to Israel – unless there was a chance that she might be arrested for her role in the abduction.

When the ship arrived on the outskirts of Haifa port on 7 October, the crew and the cadets were again ordered into the lounge as a speedboat took Vanunu and the Israeli secret service agents away. The landing, with Vanunu tied to a stretcher, somewhere on Israel's coastline, was made at 4.30 am under cover of darkness.[48]

When the *Nora* docked, the captain announced that anybody who had photographed the visitors should hand over the photos. He warned them not to disclose anything about the mission. The crew and cadets had heard on the radio about the *Sunday Times*'s exposé published two days earlier and about Vanunu but only made a connection – and realised the part they had played in bringing Vanunu back to Israel – once they returned for home leave and opened the newspapers. On the next trip, the crew could not stop talking about it. One sailor even hung a photo montage of Cindy, published by the *Sunday Times*, above his bed.

The sea journey was also memorable for Vanunu. He was unconscious for part of the journey.[49] 'There were moments when I thought I could die. If I would come out of this dead or alive was not important to them. My life in the future was not worth a great deal,' he said.[50] Vanunu's concern was not undue. In another instance the victim of a Mossad abduction died on a flight. An IDF officer, with the pseudonym of Robert Kind, flew to a European capital in the 1950s to sell military secrets to an Egyptian diplomat. The Mossad's Harel, getting wind of the meeting, sent a Mossad team to abduct him back. An attractive female agent managed to woo him to a liaison with some other agents, one of whom injected him with a tranquilliser which knocked him out. But while en route back to Israel in a private plane, 'Kind' suddenly developed breathing difficulties. He died in mid-flight. The place of his burial is unknown to this day.[51]

The whole apparatus of law and order in Italy had been weakened over the years as a result of the challenges to the authorities from the Red Brigade and from right-wing fascist groups. Rome was a base for an estimated 2,000 foreign spies and their 12,000 informers. With its central location in the Mediterranean and long coastline it was not surprising that Italy had become a centre of the internecine Arab–Israeli conflict. The Vanunu abduction occurred at a time of considerable criticism of the Italian authorities for releasing Abu Abbas, who had masterminded the hijacking of the Italian liner *Achille Lauro*, during which an elderly American passenger, Leon Klinghoffer, had been murdered. Vanunu was abducted just when Italy and Israel were negotiating an anti-terrorism agreement involving the exchange of information about terrorist groups. It was perhaps because Italy felt that she had more to gain than Israel from such an agreement that the abduction went ahead.

During the car journey from 'somewhere on Israel's coastline' to prison Vanunu was already being questioned by two Shin Bet officers, Alon, who led the interrogation, and Yehuda, who was the deputy head of the Shin Bet investigations wing. Vanunu was interrogated about whom he had seen, his motives, about whether he had been paid money by the newspaper. According to Alon, he began to speak about his tour from when he left Israel until he arrived in Australia. 'I was very interested in the journey to Thailand and Moscow. I asked him whom he met, with whom he spoke. Then we spoke about Australia – his search for work, for a place to live, the preacher with whom he stayed.'[52] A conversation developed between Yehuda and Vanunu concerning the reasons for his action. Said Yehuda later:

It was the act of a person who was willing to sell out everything, partly for money, partly for status, partly to solve frustrations and partly in order to decide that he was someone. In the vehicle Vanunu said: 'I don't know what I am, I want to start everything over from a vacuum.' I replied that even if he were a Buddhist monk in Nepal, he couldn't have forgotten the Sabbath blessing at his father's table, even if he became a Christian in Australia, he wouldn't be able to erase his past. The first time I met him I thought: 'Here's a person who felt frustrated, who wanted to build himself some status, and if it was possible, also to make 100,000 dollars at my expense. Not bad.'[53]

Vanunu asked at one point whether it was a conversation or an official interrogation. Yehuda told him that he 'was from the Shin Bet and that I was there in the framework of my job, not to conduct friendly conversations'. Vanunu went silent and wanted a lawyer. Alon told him he was empowered to refuse him access to a lawyer for seven days. Vanunu was told that it was in his interest to cooperate 'because the prime minister is personally handling this affair'. 'Later', said Yehuda,

Vanunu wanted to meet with the ambassador of the country from which [he] was brought. I told him: No way! Then he said: 'You have violated the sovereignty of another country and I want to complain about your behaviour.' I told him he would not get that request. He asked me what would happen to him and I explained that a trial should be expected with very serious charges and that it could be expected that he would be convicted and be imprisoned.[54]

When the three arrived at the prison, agent Yehuda sat down to write a report of the conversation en route. The interrogation continued in the days ahead.

With Vanunu's arrival still under a total blackout he was asked to speak in English when in the presence of other people and to assume a different name: he chose John Crossman, the name he had used at his baptism. Later he changed it to David Enosh. It became clear from that the agency did not know how much money Vanunu had received from the British newspaper. Yehuda told Vanunu, 'You were willing to sell out the State of Israel for 100,000 sterling.' 'It was only $100,000,' Vanunu replied. Vanunu said that he wanted to expose the true face of the State of Israel, a crazy state. Said Yehuda later:

> I asked him: 'If you thought that what was going on there was insanity on the part of a few madmen, why didn't you contact the proper authorities?' And Vanunu replied: 'I am not certain that they are not mad as well.'

Vanunu attempted to add the ideological element. 'Gentlemen, you don't know what goes on there. It is important for the world to know.' Also interested in his motives was Yosef ('Joe') Ginnosar, a senior Shin Bet officer in overall charge of the interrogation.[55] He came into the interrogation room, asking why he did it. Vanunu told him. Ginnosar did not ask him further questions and left after a few minutes.

Agent Alon succeeded in developing an atypically close relationship with the man he was interrogating:

> He was an intelligent guy, who understands things, alert, well aware of events. His action combined a leftist tendency, hooking up with Arab students together with a fantastic perception of the Arab–Israeli struggle from the Arab side plus a sense of discrimination. On the one hand, thoughts, ideas, ideals and a life philosophy, and on the other hand, a work place that in his mind produced atomic bombs. On the first day of the interrogation he spoke about having been aware of the danger when he went to talk (about the reactor). He was aware of the outcome, he was aware of the fact that he might be caught, he said that he was afraid of an attack on his life. Vanunu would sink into silence from time to time, clam up and I would circumvent the silences by raising personal matters. The interrogation was very personal. Sometimes I would sit with him in his cell and he would make me a cup of tea. I also brought him books and showed an interest in his field of study, which drew him into a sort of relationship. I did not lie or trick him. I did not internally show a lot of love for him ... I created an artificial interest beyond my real interest. He said that I was a fine person. I said goodbye and he said to me: 'You were just fine.'[56]

Vanunu's lawyer Avigdor Feldman claimed that the interrogation was conducted under pressure from the ordeal Vanunu had just undergone and that his free will vanished completely. 'He was entirely dependent on his abductors, a man without any control over his fate. He was feeling a total helplessness.

Total helplessness.' A climax of the interrogation was when one agent strode into his cell and threw a copy of the *Sunday Times* onto the table in the cell, exclaiming: 'See what you did!' Vanunu slowly realised at that moment that the *Sunday Times* had finally published his story.[57]

When Vanunu disappeared from London with Cindy on 30 September, the paper did not immediately publish the information because they were not certain he was in Israeli hands. If he was not, this would have alerted the Israelis, who would have realised that Vanunu was no longer in the company of the paper's journalists and easier to pick up. In its three-page exposé on 5 October the only reference to his disappearance was hidden away in the sidebar article detailing how the paper had checked the story. It reported that Vanunu had become agitated after the *Sunday Mirror* had published a photo of himself, became concerned for his safety and went to ground.

In a letter to Judy Zimmet in March 1987, Vanunu appeared to hold both the *Sunday Times* and Guerrero responsible for his ending up back in Israel. 'My original programme was to travel from Australia to go to New Zealand, and from there to Hawaii, to Los Angeles and to New York. Guerrero and the *Sunday Times* sent me here, to the Israelis.'[58] According to Ivan Fallon, deputy editor of the *Sunday Times*,

> We should not have lost him, and next time round, if there is a next time, we would take far better care of him. We were very naive. We did not believe that the Israelis would go to the trouble they actually did to kidnap him. Had we done we would have behaved differently. We did go to quite a lot of trouble, but obviously not enough. For that we do feel responsible.[59]

But Neil, smarting from Vanunu's abduction, has over the years tried to put a brave face on his disappearance, and spoken of the considerable measures taken. Asked by the BBC whether he had something on his conscience regarding Vanunu's disappearance, Neil replied,

> It's not a matter of my conscience. He came to us, he knew exactly what he was doing. We spent five weeks checking the story and one of the problems at the end was that because it took so long, he got restless, and wouldn't stay in our care. If he'd stayed within our care and protection he wouldn't be back in Israel now.[60]

The paper had considered using professional security guards – but the idea was rejected. Notwithstanding the *Sunday Times*'s confidence in its ability to protect Vanunu, a newspaper's resources are clearly more limited than the state's. During the period around the publication of Vanunu's exposé, Neil devised a plan for Vanunu to take a tour of Britain. 'I wanted that he should take a bus tour around Britain so that he would be on the move all the time.

But he wouldn't hear of it,' Neil said.[61] He would have been continuously surrounded by a group of 30 tourists, including two of the paper's reporters and a photographer, making it impossible, Neil thought, for anybody to kidnap him. He would have been booked under a fictitious name. It would not necessitate crossing borders, hiring cars (which require passport identification in the case of foreign visitors), registering with hotels, using his driver's licence or credit cards.

The care and protection did not sustain itself in practice. Wendy Robbins said,

There was no central plan or coordination in looking after Vanunu. Apart from Hounam who was genuinely more caring, others had no interest in who he was or what he wanted to do. During the day it was milk, milk, milk. At night: find anyone to take care of him. During the first days Max Prangnell took him to his flat or visited him at his secret location. Hounam took him out. So did Peter Wilsher for dinner. But increasingly the better I got on with Mordechai, the more he wanted to spend time with me. In the evening it was left to whoever was sitting in the office. On at least one occasion Vanunu was left sitting in the office at New Printing House Square, the reporters having left.

According to Hounam there was tension between Vanunu and Prangnell and Roger Wilsher. At times, according to Hounam, he was left alone – in contravention of the instructions given to them.[62]

On the weekend of the *Sunday Mirror* publication, which followed the 'Insight' team taking the story to the Israeli embassy for its reaction, Vanunu, according to the paper, had grown more and more restless and complained about the delay in the story's publication. Feeling vulnerable, lonely and desperate, Vanunu fell for Cindy's suggestion to fly to Rome. He told the paper, Morgan said, that he was going to look after himself, lose himself in a crowd. 'He couldn't take the risk of somebody following *Sunday Times* reporters,' said Morgan. 'He'd just seen his picture in a national newspaper, in a foreign country that he'd visited only once before, he'd known us for four weeks – and he's going to trust his life to us!'[63]

In the days before the *Sunday Mirror* came out with its story – which was after Vanunu had been debriefed – or 'milked' as one staffer put it – and the 'Insight' team was busy checking the story, security for Vanunu appeared to be less stringent than it had been.[64] It was then that Vanunu met Cindy in Leicester Square. 'People couldn't be bothered to entertain him. We had what we wanted, and he was more or less left to do whatever he liked,' said Robbins. Peter Hounam was an exception; his journalistic responsibility expressed itself in his standing by his news source from the initial meeting in Australia to this day.[65] Another researcher said that 'there was a certain naivety among us about the possibility that he could still be kidnapped after he had given us all the information.'[66]

To the credit of the *Sunday Times*, on hearing that the *Sunday Mirror* was planning to publish its account, it sent two journalists to see Vanunu at his hotel, and emphasised the need to take great care of him. Nevertheless, after the report came out, Vanunu was clearly upset. Talking that Sunday evening by telephone to McKnight in Sydney, Vanunu said he was 'upset by it all, and he thought that the *Sunday Mirror* story might have damaged his credibility so that the *Sunday Times* would not publish it at all. He spoke with great fear for his safety,' McKnight said.[67]

On the other hand there is evidence of some sensitivity being displayed. After debriefing him about his work at Dimona, some members of the team debriefed him at some length about his life while others were checking the scientific information partly, according to Morgan, 'because we were trying to keep the guy out of circulation'. But, as an 'Insight' reporter admitted,

> Vanunu was always in control of the story. We never signed an agreement; one was due to be signed prior to publication, two days after Vanunu disappeared. He could say to us, 'I don't like the way you are treating me. I will leave. I'll keep the story and go somewhere else!'

They acceded to his request to move from the country to London. One day, instead of attending a planned meeting with 'Insight', Vanunu insisted on meeting Cindy briefly. Then came his 'decision' to go away for a few days ostensibly to the country, but in reality with Cindy to Rome. He failed to take his own security seriously. According to Robbins,

> ... the pseudonym names which the paper gave him were a joke for him. We would get into a taxi and he would start up with the driver, 'I am John Smith ... .' He often said to me, 'Ah, Wendy, something terrible will happen before I go to my island. They will get me.' But he didn't seem to do anything about it. He couldn't be bothered to get worried about it. Totally fatalistic.[68]

Vanunu should have been made to understand from the beginning, when he first made contact with the paper, that they would only investigate and publish the story if he accepted the terms of protection offered by the paper. A member of the 'Insight' team said:

> The difficulty I didn't anticipate is that you have to insist on full cooperation of the person whom you are protecting because if you don't, if he walks about, then he is prey to anyone who wants to get him. Had we have signed a conventional Fleet Street contract with him, we could have probably had some hold over him and said, 'Look, you are going to have so much money: stay out of London, stay in the guest house we are putting you in.'[69]

Neil was quite within his rights to delay publication until he was certain the story was genuine. 'Insight' had not told Vanunu that they would not publish;

the opposite was true. They attempted to reassure him of the paper's interest but that further checking had to be carried out. Nor was five weeks, when the paper first heard about Vanunu and his information, a particularly long period for checking such a complicated story. The paper had warned Vanunu about Cindy, whom Vanunu had first encountered days prior to the *Sunday Mirror* hoax story, cautioning that she might be an Israeli ploy. 'We suspected something was going on,' Neil said. Nevertheless, had Guerrero been handled by the *Sunday Times* with greater dexterity and professionalism, Vanunu's photograph might not have appeared in the *Sunday Mirror*. Furthermore, Neil's claim that 'if Vanunu had stayed within our care and protection he wouldn't be back in Israel now' appears to be ill-founded. The physical protection which the *Sunday Times* gave Vanunu has been shown to be wanting. Moreover, there is every reason to believe that if the Guerrero episode had not occurred, Israel would have found other means to woo Vanunu from Britain.

It was not surprising that Neil's reaction on learning of Vanunu's disappearance was one of 'extreme anger', according to an 'Insight' reporter. Neil felt he had provided Morgan with all the financial support he required in checking the story. But the real question was whether Neil – and ultimately Murdoch – had provided sufficiently experienced reporters to do the job. Notwithstanding that some of the younger 'Insight' reporters had done some investigative stories, apparently only Hounam and editor Morgan could be said to have truly solid investigative experience. The overall make-up of the team contrasts negatively with the experience which 'Insight' teams in the 1960s and 1970s possessed. For example, when Godfrey Hodgson headed 'Insight' in the late 1960s, 'Phillip Knightley was an extremely experienced reporter who worked on newspapers and had edited a magazine in Sydney. John Barry had won a press award, John Fielding came from the paper's Business News, and Mark Ottaway had considerable reportorial experience,' Hodgson said.[70] The errors made by the 'Insight' team in the Vanunu investigation reflected the lesser experience of journalists on the paper's staff as a whole.

No internal inquiry was apparently carried out within the newspaper regarding the 'Insight' team's handling of Vanunu, his protection during and after his debriefing, or how the reporting and checking of evidence may have forewarned Israel. An inquiry would offer certain lessons for future investigations regarding the handling of characters like Guerrero, security for informers prior to publication, and creation of the best conditions for their survival afterwards.

Questions of judgement also arise because when Mordechai Vanunu first contacted the *Sunday Times* he said that he did not want his name connected with the exposé. Peter Hounam insisted that if the information was going to be published it had to be with Vanunu's name on it because its value was that for the first time somebody who possessed inside knowledge of the Dimona reactor was revealing its innermost secrets. It took Hounam some time to persuade Vanunu that his best security against being the target of a Mossad operation was to attach his name to the paper's exposé. There would have been a story even had Vanunu's wish for anonymity been respected because the 57 photographs which he had taken inside the Dimona complex were themselves of international significance. Of course the story had added value with Vanunu's name. But this should have been weighed against the real danger to Vanunu's survival.

Ever since the Vanunu affair, one of the unsolved mysteries concerns Oscar Guerrero. Was he just the mercurial journalist-type or did he play a more sinister role in the affair? The latter possibility has been supported not only by Louis Toscano, who claims Guerrero contacted Israeli diplomats with the story while still in Australia, but by also by his reportedly having stayed at the same hotel as Cindy in London. A *Sunday Mirror* reporter even claimed to have seen Cindy and Guerrero having breakfast at the hotel together.[71] A possible clue in assuaging these claims came during Vanunu's trial. Alon, asked under cross-examination by the state prosecution lawyer with whom Vanunu had been in contact, mentioned Oscar Guerrero:

> Vanunu spoke about *Sunday Times* journalists and in addition about an exploiter by the name of Guerrero; we still don't know from where he came. Speculation was even raised that he was a Middle East spy or from Eastern Europe because of a certain aeroplane flight he took.[72]

Had Guerrero been linked to the abduction plot it is highly unlikely that the Shin Bet agent would have wanted to initiate discussion of him in court. Further, if Guerrero was indeed working for Israel, why would he have offered the story both to the *Sunday Times* and to the *Sunday Mirror*, which treated Vanunu's claims very differently? Moreover, why would the Israelis have wanted Vanunu to go to London? It would have been less costly diplomatically to arrange an abduction in Australia, a country far less important to Jerusalem than Britain or even Italy.

The Mossad operation was not as successful as it might seem. True, Vanunu was successfully abducted to Israel; questioned to clarify what secret information he had divulged; and stood trial, becoming an example to all who might contemplate disclosing national secrets. But the main Mossad task was to stop Vanunu from disclosing any information about the Dimona project. The failure of the Mossad to stop the publication of Vanunu's information reflects an intelligence agency's limits. That the culprit was brought back is hardly a consolation prize for the failure to keep defence installations like Dimona secure in the first place.

The four-week time span between the Israeli authorities first learning about Vanunu's activities and 30 September, the date of the abduction, and the fact that perceptions of Israeli nuclear deterrent capability were strengthened by the *Sunday Times*'s estimate of 100–200 nuclear warheads, has led some to speculate whether Vanunu was intentionally left on a loose rein and brought back and arrested only after he had given the *Sunday Times* his story. If Peres saw an opportunity to exploit the security blunder and let Vanunu speak, he displayed poor judgement. The fact that a senior Shin Bet director, and the security officer of the reactor, were moved from their posts straight afterwards leaves no doubt that the Vanunu exposé was one of the worst-ever security-related leaks in the Israeli defence establishment. Mr Shamir said as much when addressing the Knesset's defence and foreign affairs committee behind closed doors. It is hardly in the interests of Israeli officialdom to have had such intimate details published of a subject enveloped in ambiguity. The Israelis had no idea precisely what information Vanunu was disclosing. There are easier ways to leak to the international press without providing the details Vanunu did of the inner workings of Dimona.

Despite the operational success of the abduction, it caused fallout in a number of spheres: in London, in Rome and back at home in Israel. After Vanunu's disappearance it was six weeks before the Israeli government surrendered to pressure and confirmed that he was back in Israel and under arrest. Spokesmen engaged in a disinformation effort to explain how Vanunu was taken from Britain to Israel, and ironically they leaked to the foreign media – the very crime of which Vanunu was accused. The media appetite for stories about spies and espionage gives those in power many opportunities to manipulate public channels of information. At first an impression was created that Vanunu had been enticed out of British territory to international waters, where he was arrested, and that no foreign country's sovereignty had been infringed.

The British authorities were keen to dispel any notion that Vanunu had been abducted from British territory. 'Israel', Whitehall sources told the *Jerusalem Post* London reporter,

> would not have been so stupid as to abduct Vanunu from British territory, particularly since Britain has emerged, since the Hindawi trial [of an Arab backed by Syria arrested for attempting to smuggle a bomb on to an El Al plane at London airport] last month, as Israel's staunchest ally in Western Europe.[73]

And a Foreign Office spokesman told the *Sunday Times* that while the government would take an extremely serious view of kidnapping from British soil they could not justify intervention if British law was not broken. The cover-up went a stage further when the *Economist* suggested that Vanunu had unwittingly been manipulated by the Mossad or even that he was a Mossad agent, and that the *Sunday Times* had been the victim of a gigantic public relations exercise to boost Israel's nuclear posture.

For the first three weeks after Vanunu's disappearance, Israeli officials from the prime minister's spokesman downwards claimed not to know anything about his whereabouts, even though he was in Israel and was undergoing interrogation. Under existing Israeli law there is no obligation on the Israeli authorities to confirm that somebody is under arrest. The Emergency Powers (Detention) Law, the essence of which was inherited from the British Mandate, empowers the authorities to detain a person for six months 'for reasons of state security and public security', and as long as the detention order is approved by a district court judge, it can be extended again and again. In cases of security sensitivity like Vanunu's, this process is completed behind closed doors; sometimes only the defendant's lawyer knows the full reasons for the indictment. And the appointment by Vanunu of Dr Amnon Zichroni, a veteran civil rights lawyer, was not made public. Zichroni adhered to the rules of the game. To announce that he was representing Vanunu would be tantamount to a confirmation that Vanunu was back in Israel, which in turn would raise questions regarding how he got there and how he left Britain.

Eight days after Vanunu vanished, and three days after the publication of their exposé, the *Sunday Times* reported his disappearance to the British authorities. The British police visited the room at the Mountbatten hotel where he had last stayed, but failed to uncover any evidence that the law had been broken. Nor was there a record of his departure from any British airport or seaport. Israeli officials hoped that media curiosity would die away. Military censorship in the Vanunu affair could be summed up in two words: damage control. When the *Sunday Mirror* came out with its hoax story about a nuclear conman a week before the *Sunday Times*'s disclosure, the Israeli censor initially banned Israeli media from publishing reports from London despite both the convention that military censorship does not suppress quotes from the foreign media and the meeting of the Editors' Committee a day earlier at which Peres confirmed that foreign sources could be quoted. A few hours later on the Saturday night the censor finally passed the reports quoting the *Sunday Mirror*.

Vanunu's disappearance was a difficult story for Israeli reporters to cover. Information they gleaned came from Vanunu's family and later from his lawyer, as well as from the prison service, the Shin Bet, and the Cabinet. Israeli reporters with contacts in the intelligence establishment tend to use these sparingly. In this case, officers were tight-lipped. A key source was the justice ministry, which would normally have been very reticent. But the Shin Bet affair months earlier, when the attorney general, Professor Itzhak Zamir, resisted government pressure to cover up the deaths of two Arab terrorists arrested in the 1984 Tel Aviv-Ashkelon bus hijacking, and which later resulted in Zamir's dismissal, turned the press and the justice ministry into unlikely bedfellows. Menachem Shalev, then the *Jerusalem Post*'s justice affairs reporter, said,

> The Ministry of Justice had used the press in order to combat what it felt was the politicians' destruction of justice. To the extent that reporters got Justice Ministry officials to speak about Vanunu it was because they felt they owed us something. Yet it was a futile attempt to get anything past censorship which had not already appeared in the foreign media.[74]

'The *Sunday Times* was made into the Bible,' remarked Mark Geffen, then editor of *Al Hamishmar*.[75] Things began to fall apart with the bizarre arrival in Israel of Reverend John McKnight of St John's rectory. He turned to the prime minister's office, which has formal responsibility for the security services, but was given the runaround, with one official suggesting he try another, and with phone calls unreturned. 'McKnight has no standing, and we see no reason to meet him,' an official said. McKnight said, however, that he managed 'to speak to somebody who had seen somebody who had seen Vanunu and was able to confirm that Vanunu was being held in jail' – a reference to a member of the Vanunu family who had been in touch with the lawyer representing Mordechai. In front of some 100 foreign newsmen McKnight, speaking in the elegant surroundings of the American Colony hotel, situated on the green line which once separated Israeli-controlled West Jerusalem from Jordanian East Jerusalem, the Australian parson brought to the world the news that Vanunu was alive and well, albeit in an Israeli prison.

Initially, Israel's military censor told newsmen that they would be unable to report McKnight's news conference but later retracted this. Thomas Friedman, the *New York Times*'s Jerusalem correspondent, suspected that the Israeli authorities subsequently realised that it was an opportunity for them to let it be known that Vanunu, as everybody suspected, was indeed back in Israel without formally acknowledging it. 'The Israeli intelligence services would seem to have an interest in letting both Israelis and foreigners know that anyone who tries to sell Israeli state secrets abroad will be hunted down and brought back to face an Israeli trial,' Friedman opined.[76] But this Machiavellian view is hardly plausible given the desperate attempts of Israeli officials to put a damper on an embarrassing episode in Israel's relations with London. Rather, the authorities realised it was difficult to stop 100 newsmen from reporting a news conference they had attended. It showed the vulnerability of the open society.

But prime minister Shamir said, 'Israel has its own considerations in avoiding a public comment on the case of Mordechai Vanunu. The government will say what it finds fit to say, and it will fulfil its duty to its citizens.' Were it not for two separate developments, 'nothing', claimed *Yediot Aharonot*, the country's largest-selling afternoon newspaper, 'would have been disclosed. Shamir, Peres and Rabin haven't given a fig for Israeli media and national opinion'.[77]

Two developments forced the Israeli government's hand. The first was that the *Sunday Times* turned to lawyer Amnon Zichroni, asking him to petition the High Court of Justice to ascertain Vanunu's whereabouts. Unbeknown to the *Sunday Times*, Vanunu himself had turned to Zichroni to represent him. Since the paper had no legal standing in Israel, the petition formally had to come from Vanunu's family. It wasn't easy to get the family to agree, since they had been warned by the Shin Bet not to discuss the affair. Once they did, Zichroni wrote to the prime minister saying that unless the government formally confirmed Vanunu was back in Israel he would petition the High Court which, if successful, would be tantamount to such a confirmation. The game was up, attorney general Yosef Harish argued.

The second development was an orchestrated campaign of questions in the British Parliament to prime minister Margaret Thatcher and her ministers regarding how Vanunu had left Britain. Conservative MP Denis Walters asked the foreign secretary to 'press the Israeli government for clarification about the involvement of the Israeli intelligence service in the alleged kidnapping of Mr Vanunu in London and his subsequent illegal removal from Britain'. So did other MPs. Comparing Vanunu to the case of the former Nigerian government minister, Umaru Dikko, discovered at a British airport drugged in the hold of an aircraft en route to Lagos, Anthony Beaumont-Dark asked how Mr Vanunu 'could vanish from a London hotel and, like a rabbit out of a hat, had appeared in Israel'.[78] British officials privately pressed Israeli officials for more information about how he had disappeared.

The foreign press corps in Israel – the tenth largest in the world – followed the story aggressively, particularly the contingent of correspondents representing the British media. Shamir blamed the fact that the affair had come to light 'on the media, on all kinds of people, on this terrible curiosity. But', he told Israeli Television, 'let us leave this, we shall overcome it despite this exposure.' Asked about the attacks it provoked on Israel, Shamir replied, 'Israel is not being attacked, and I do not feel attacked.'[79] In an abortive attempt to stop the Thatcher government from acceding to British MPs' demands for clarification from Israel, officials in Jerusalem told specific British correspondents about the Peres telephone call to Mrs Thatcher prior to the abduction in which he told her of the need to bring Vanunu home and that no British laws would be broken in the process. Israeli officials were careful not to say what Mrs Thatcher's reply had been. The message was clear: if more information was divulged the British government would implicate itself in his abduction. One MP, Dale Campbell-Savours, asked Mrs Thatcher in Parliament whether she had had any discussions with Mr Peres or with any other member of the Israeli government regarding Mr Vanunu prior to his departure from Britain. 'No' was the reply: 'prior' could be interpreted as just before, as opposed to nine days, as was the case. Asked by Campbell-Savours, 'whether any member or official of the Israeli government communicated to the prime minister or her office to procure the return of Vanunu from the UK,' the prime minister's reply again was 'No'. He was not 'returned' to Israel from Britain; he was returned from another country.

On 9 November the Israeli government broke its silence and in a formal statement confirmed that Vanunu was in Israel, under arrest, and the subject of judicial proceedings:

The government of Israel announces that Mordechai Vanunu is legally under arrest in Israel, in accordance with a court order following a hearing in which a lawyer of his election was present. All the rumours to the effect that Vanunu was 'kidnapped' on English soil are without foundation. Moreover, there is no basis for the report that Mr Peres contacted Mrs Thatcher in order to tell her something that did not happen.

In addition to attorney general Harish's argument that the appeal to the Supreme Court meant that the government had to make a statement, the prime mover was Peres, who wanted to relieve the pressure on Mrs Thatcher. Just a month earlier Britain had severed diplomatic ties with Syria over that country's involvement in the Hindawi affair.

But prime minister Shamir opposed the statement, arguing that the British, who were not pushing the issue, had said there was no evidence of a crime being committed on British soil. Nor was there evidence that Vanunu had even entered or exited from London Heathrow's immigration controls. To say anything would – and did – stimulate more questions.

The debate about Vanunu's disappearance attracted some 50 MPs, a larger number than might have been expected. Most were seated in the chamber, but a few hung around out of sight of the public – among them the chief whip, John Wakeham, and Mrs Thatcher's parliamentary private secretary, Michael Alison. Denis Walters called for an official government inquiry into Vanunu's disappearance. There were several ways in which Vanunu could have found himself in an Israeli prison but one that could be ruled out was that he arrived there 'of his own free will'. Logically, it followed that he must have been abducted 'almost without doubt, by Israeli agents', he said. Anthony Beaumont-Dark, who initiated the debate, said that an international jurist should be allowed to interview Vanunu, thereby 'allaying our fears'. Opposition foreign affairs spokesman Donald Woods said that 'the British government cannot expect to get away with their current line, particularly in the light of allegations that the prime minister herself was consulted.' In reply, the home office minister, David Waddington, said that an official inquiry was impractical, since Britain had no power to ascertain from Israel, in the absence of any evidence that a crime had been committed, how Vanunu had got there. However, given the concern in Britain, Waddington, going further than his foreign office colleagues, urged Israel to explain how Vanunu had reached Israel. As regards the lack of evidence of Vanunu's entry to and exit from London Heathrow immigration control, the minister explained that with 35 million passing through passport control yearly only limited records were kept.

The seeds of an intelligence crisis between Britain and Israel preceded Vanunu's disappearance. In the summer of 1986, a bag containing eight forged British passports was discovered in a telephone booth in West Germany. Also in the bag was a genuine Israeli passport and envelopes linking the documents with the Israeli embassy. The incredible claim has been made in West Germany that the passports were to be used to kidnap West German nuclear scientists engaged on constructing an Islamic nuclear bomb. The foreign office got a formal apology from the Israeli ambassador to London, Yehuda Avner, but only after the matter had been raised some seven times.[80] In a meeting with foreign secretary Sir Geoffrey Howe in January 1987, Mr Peres gave assurances that it would not happen again.

But the straw that broke the camel's back was the discovery by British police in August 1987 of an Arab terrorist arms arsenal in a Hull flat. In the late 1970s, Ismael Sowan, still in his teens, left his village to the south of Jerusalem to study Engineering at Beirut University. Before he left, the Shin Bet recruited him to inform on the activities at the university of the Palestinian organisation Fatah.[81] Either at the prompting of his Israeli masters or quite by chance, Sowan rented a Beirut flat belonging to Abder Rahman Mustapha, who was in charge of Commando 18, a section of Force 17 which had responsibility for the PLO's special operations abroad. But in 1984 Ismael moved to London to continue his studies – only to find his old landlord Mustapha in charge of security at the PLO office there.

On the orders of Albert, his Mossad handler at the Israeli embassy, Sowan renewed his friendship with Mustapha, regularly visiting him at the PLO's London office.[82] The Israelis suspected that Mustapha was holding an arsenal of PLO arms and ammunition smuggled into Britain in the early 1970s and now much depleted.[83] Mustapha seized the opportunity to ask Sowan to store a few suitcases for him since, he said, he was selling his house. In the six cases were four rapid-fire assault rifles, seven fragmentation grenades, nearly 70lb of plastic explosives, detonators, timing devices and 300 rounds of ammunition.

In April 1987 Mustapha was expelled from Britain on suspicion of involvement in the killing of three Israelis on a yacht at Larnaca in 1986. On 14 July Sowan went to Israel with his bride. Just before that, on 6 July, Mustapha secretly returned to London, and eight days later Al Al-Adhami, an Arab cartoonist known for his anti-Arafat cartoons, was shot and killed on Arafat's orders. Mustapha left London the next day, and police suspected him of the killing. News of it reached Sowan in Israel. With Mustapha being sought by British police, it would be only a matter of time before British detectives closed in on his Hull flat. He had to tell the Israelis about the suitcases. He renewed contact with the Shin Bet, and met 'David' in Israel. Yes, 'David' agreed, the matter of the suitcases was very serious indeed, but Sowan need not worry. Somebody would be in touch with him when he got back to Hull, and the whole matter would be sorted out. Sowan flew back to Britain on 5 August; the days passed but there was no word from the Israelis. Finally, on 12 August there was a knock on the door. Two Hull policemen stood outside. Sowan bowed to the inevitable and invited the detectives in. On 16 June 1988 Sowan was sentenced at London's Old Bailey to eleven years' imprisonment for possessing explosives and firearms. He was released in 1974 after serving two-thirds of his sentence.

The court case showed once again how British streets had become a hunting ground for Israelis and Palestinians squaring off in their internecine war. Moreover, it shed public light for the first time on the Israeli government's involvement. The verdict was promptly followed by the British government's expulsion of a 'diplomat', Arie Regev, Mossad's liaison with MI6 and MI5.[84] The decision was initiated by the foreign office and by MI5, Britain's domestic intelligence agency responsible for counter-espionage. It had been opposed by MI6, which was well aware of the value of the Mossad as a source of information to Britain.[85] The Mossad had broken the basic rule that foreign intelligence services are supposed to keep the host country's intelligence service aware of what they are doing. After all, had the British been informed the cartoonist might still be alive.

When the arms cache was discovered, a horrendous dispute erupted between MI5 and the Mossad.[86] In an unusual step Mrs Thatcher wrote to Mr Shamir after Sowan's arrest, saying that the British would have no alternative but to limit Mossad activities if it did not fall into line.[87] But the Mossad still did not inform MI5 about what they were doing, so the same message was given to Mr Peres by Sir Geoffrey Howe.[88] While diplomats from the Soviet Union, Syria, Libya and Cuba had been expelled from Britain, it was the first expulsion of someone with diplomatic status from a friendly country.

There may well not have been the crisis between the two countries without the Sowan trial. But it is equally clear that it required the earlier cases – most notably the Vanunu disappearance and the parliamentary and media criticism – to provoke the diplomatic repercussions which followed Sowan's sentencing.

The Italian connection in the Vanunu abduction seemed to remain safely concealed. The connection came to light when on arrival at the Jerusalem District Court on 21 December, 1986, where his remand was extended, Vanunu outwitted his guards by flattening one of his palms against the window of the police van. On it was written:

Vanunu M
was HIJACKEN [sic]
IN ROME ITL
Came to Rome
BY BA FLY 504

The police officers accompanying Vanunu initially did not understand the message; when they did – after Jerusalem press photographer Dan Landau snapped the outstretched arm – they forced his hand away from the window of the van. Inside the courthouse Vanunu's hand was washed. However, on his way out from the court, an Israeli reporter fired questions at Vanunu in Hebrew, asking him where he had been kidnapped. Vanunu shouted back 'Rome', before a police guard clamped his hand over his mouth. Vanunu was proving to be the man Israel could not gag. Israeli censorship attempted to close the security leak by banning publication of the message written on Vanunu's palm. Israeli newspapers appeared with pictures of his hand with the message blacked out. But it had been seen by many journalists and photographers as well as bystanders. Damage control failed again: in a report under the byline of its London-based defence reporter, Frank Draper, the London *Standard* revealed the news of how Vanunu reached Israel from Britain. The ban on the media was lifted. But the paper's Jerusalem correspondent, Bernard Josephs, had his accreditation as a foreign correspondent suspended. 'It will not be possible for somebody to take the law into his own hands and decide to publish something even though its publication has been prohibited,' the military censor, brigadier-general Itzhak Shani, said.[89] 'In order to defend the censorship law, local media and other foreign correspondents, I didn't see any other alternative but to take the step,' he added.[90] But Josephs claimed that he 'didn't mention Rome or any other word on Vanunu's palm. I showed police officers investigating the matter a copy of the fax of the report I wrote, and there was no mention of the words that Vanunu wrote.'[91] *Standard* editor John Leese said that Vanunu's message 'came from an entirely different source and our story was compiled in London'.[92]

In the wake of censorship lapses with Vanunu, and earlier matters, an interdepartmental inquiry was launched in November 1986 to find ways of stopping foreign correspondents from evading censorship.

The palm message had all the promise of a diplomatic crisis in Israeli–Italian relations with a replay, or even worse, of the mini-crisis with London which had only just settled. And while in the British case Peres had prepared the ground by speaking to Mrs Thatcher before Vanunu's disappearance, no such contacts appear to have been made with Rome. The abduction from Italy once again confirmed how foreign intelligence services used Rome as a staging ground for their operations.

Partico Liberate, Italy's liberal party, which formed part of the government coalition, raised in Parliament 'the freedom of movement of the Israeli and US intelligence services on Italian soil' as well as the question of possible links between these services and Italian intelligence. 'It is intolerable that Italy should take on a colony status,' a member said.[93] The small Proletarian Democratic party asked how a kidnap could occur at an airport under the intensive surveillance of the police's anti-terror squad. The only explanation, the party said, was 'that the kidnap was the product of cooperation between Italian security and Israel's secret service'.[94] The question of connivance by the Italian intelligence services in Vanunu's abduction focused attention on Italy's ties and dependence. Despite the restructuring of the intelligence services in 1977 there still seemed a need to invest the Italian parliament's committee for the security services with adequate powers to know in advance about intelligence actions which could be illegal or detrimental to national interests. However, according to Fulvio Martini, who headed the Italian external intelligence agency, SID, at the time there was no coordination with the Mossad. Even after the abduction, Martini's contacts had not informed him informally of what had happened. Had they done so, it would have enabled the Italian authorities to ride the tide of domestic criticism after Vanunu wrote on his hand 'Hijacked in Rome'. Under Martini there had been unusually close ties between Italian external intelligence and both the Mossad and Israeli military intelligence (Aman). These went beyond the normal exchange of intelligence between two foreign friendly intelligence services. Martini's close ties were one factor in the Mossad's decision that the European country which would involve least repercussions in carrying out the abduction was Italy.

Israeli officials had to play out the criticism resulting from Vanunu's palm message. Ambassador Mordechai Drory said he had no information about the case. Italian prime minister Bettino Craxi said that he awaited a satisfactory reply from Israel: the Israeli authorities' 'no comment' was significant. Craxi saw no reason why Vanunu should lie, but ambassador Drory claimed that Vanunu was 'desperate' to stir up publicity about his case. He hoped that Italy 'won't pay attention to any desperate attempt by a person detained under serious charges and awaiting judgement to draw attention and world public opinion with these types of statements'. 'Vanunu's claim sounds as if it came from a cinema movie,' foreign ministry spokesman Ehud Gol said, and political director Yossi Beilin said, 'Tomorrow Vanunu might say he came via Tanganyika.' While Israeli officials denied that any Italian law had been broken, they did not explain how Vanunu had got to Israel. When asked what action Italy would take if it was true that he had been kidnapped on Italian soil, Craxi replied, 'Protest would be the minimum.' He paused and then added, 'But it would also be the maximum because we could do no more.'[95]

The tone was set. Italy would go through the motions of protesting infringement of Italian territoriality, and Jerusalem would dutifully reassure her, as it had the British government beforehand, that her territoriality had not been infringed. The palm incident did not extend to the two countries' diplomatic relationship, and the subject was reportedly not raised during a trip to Italy by Mr Peres in early January 1987. Italy's deputy prime minister, Arnaldo Forlani, visiting Israel at the same time, said that the affair would have no impact on Italian–Israeli relations. 'We've asked for clarification and the Israeli government has given us adequate assurances.'[96] The Italians were not entirely satisfied with Israeli explanations, revising their earlier optimistic assessment. There was to be a judicial enquiry by the deputy Rome prosecutor, Dr Domenico Sica, into whether Italian territoriality had been infringed and whether charges should be brought against anybody. The Italian judiciary has been in the vanguard against the lawlessness affecting the country, and it has taken on the task at no small risk: a Genoa prosecutor investigating the Red Brigade was one of the first victims of the group's campaign of assassination in 1976.

Judge Domenico Sica sought answers to two questions: what was Vanunu's reason for coming to Rome, and how did he continue en route to Tel Aviv? The task facing Sica was arduous, if not impossible, from the outset. A man in a foreign country on his way to court held up his hand with the scrawled message that he had been kidnapped on Italian soil. An investigation was being opened of an incident learned of from the media. There were no eyewitnesses in Italy to Vanunu's disappearance. The only facts were the writing on the palm, and the list of passengers on British Airways Flight 504 from London to Rome on 30 September 1986, which included the name of Mordechai Vanunu. As a *notitia criminis* it provided enough information for the Italian judiciary to have to open a formal investigation.

Sica had conducted many investigations into terrorist crimes, including the murder of president Aldo Moro by the Red Brigade. Italian magistrates have broad powers of investigation and arrest. In addition to spending a couple of hours at Rome's Fiumicino airport to see whether Vanunu could have been kidnapped inside the airport itself, Sica turned to the Italian police's anti-terrorist squad and to the domestic intelligence agency, SISDE (Servizio Informazione Sicurezza Democratica). The facts that Vanunu had appeared on the British Airways' passenger list, had purchased a ticket and checked in a piece of luggage at London Heathrow, were quickly verified. But for Sica there remained the nagging doubt of whether Vanunu had actually come to Rome or whether it was all a piece of disinformation by Israel to create an impression that he had been abducted from Italy and to disguise the real manner in which he reached Israel.

In addition to there being no hard evidence of an abduction, there had been no flight continuing to Israel until the following day. By the end of the first week of investigations, Sica's attention turned to the possibility of Vanunu's having been taken to Israel by boat. In 1987 the *Sunday Times* had published allegations naming an Israeli cargo boat, the *Tappuz*, as the one used to bring Vanunu from the Italian port of La Spezia. (The *Sunday Times*'s claim was superseded by an Israeli newspaper claim that the *Nora* had been used.) Italian officials investigated which Israeli ships had arrived at Italian ports around the time Vanunu was supposed to have reached Rome and found that the *Tappuz* had been the only one.[97] Moreover, they discovered the false destination the ship had given, claiming it was bound for Marseilles having sailed from Barcelona, and that it was heading for Israel.[98] When the *Tappuz* called at La Spezia in August 1987 Sica ordered a surveillance operation to be carried out. The van which the Israeli embassy had hired on the day Vanunu reached Rome, and which had the return journey distance to La Spezia on its odometer, was also discovered.[99]

Some of Sica's information came from Mordechai Vanunu's brother, Meir, who twice visited Sica, in the spring and July of 1987, and from *Sunday Times* reporter Peter Hounam, whose paper published details which Meir gave it about Vanunu's abduction. Meir obtained the information by talking in Moroccan dialect to his jailed brother. The 'Insight' team located a couple of the passengers on Vanunu's flight, but none recalled seeing him. The woman who had been sitting in the seat next to Cindy could not remember Vanunu.

Sica completed his inquiry in June 1988, reaching a sensational conclusion: Vanunu was working in liaison with the Mossad to deliberately publicise Israel's nuclear capability. The whole affair had been a disinformation exercise. Sica dismissed as romance Meir Vanunu's account of how his brother had been taken to Israel. The judge's arguments were fivefold:

(1) Despite wide investigation, Sica found no one who could confirm that Vanunu had arrived in Rome.
(2) That Mordechai Vanunu used his real name on the flight was proof to Sica that Cindy wanted to leave evidence behind.
(3) He dismissed Meir Vanunu's claim that his brother had been taken to a third-floor fiat in a densely populated area of Rome where he was drugged and spirited off to Israel. 'This was the most unsuitable and dangerous place from which to carry an unconscious body. It is obvious that a group of specialists would never have committed such an error,' Sica said.
(4) Sica was unimpressed by Vanunu's message on his palm. Since Vanunu had himself admitted that he did not know English well, how could he have written that message?, Sica asked. Vanunu's other writings in English show 'elementary mistakes', he said; somebody else must have written it.
(5) Sica had seen 52 of the photographs which Vanunu had taken, and which the *Sunday Times* had passed on to the judge with copies to the Italian atomic energy authority, ENEA. These dispelled his last doubts. They showed in perfect chronological order the various stages in the making of a nuclear warhead. No people appear in any of the photographs, even those showing instruments which would normally be watched constantly. Sica wondered how Vanunu was able to make this 'tourist's presentation' of such a top-secret operation, given the security measures in effect at Dimona. He concluded that the photographer was acting with the full consent of those in charge.[100]

The judge did not suggest what the operation was for – or who was behind it – but said, 'It would not take much imagination to link it to the Israelis' desire to frighten their neighbours with their nuclear achievements without having to answer to the Americans for their boasts.'[101] Meir Vanunu said: 'If this is a disinformation exercise, release my brother. If the Italian judge is correct, my brother should be sitting on the seashore, and not in an isolated prison cell while all his family suffer.' Once Vanunu had completed his mission he ought to have been on a first-class El Al flight to Israel to receive a hero's welcome at Mossad headquarters.

Each of the arguments presented by Sica may be questioned:

• Sica claimed that despite 'wide inquiries' he failed to find one person who saw Vanunu reach Rome. It is unclear from the term 'wide inquiries' whether Sica contacted the 130-odd passengers plus flight crew. All the passengers could have been traced since the airline had their names and addresses.

• Sica claimed that the usage of Vanunu's real name on his air ticket was proof of his wanting to record the impression that he had gone to Rome. The first lesson any spy learns – including Vanunu, if Sica is correct that he was working for the Israelis – is not to use his or her own name. Was the small credibility to be gained from the use of his real name worth the Italian public, political and diplomatic fallout which could – and indeed, did – result? And why did Cindy travel under her alias, Cindy Hanin, instead of her real name? No, Vanunu used his own because that was the name on his passport and, not being a spy, he had no forged passport. (It is true that in London he used a pseudonym at the hotels where he stayed but he did not have to show his passport.)

• Sica argued that a professional intelligence service would not have taken Vanunu to a densely populated place in Rome lest it arouse suspicion. On the contrary, it may be argued that it is much easier to conceal a person in an anonymous-looking block of flats. Vanunu travelled to, and entered, the flat of his own volition, accompanied by Cindy. Only once inside, Meir Vanunu claims, was he drugged. The unconscious man could have been taken out to a waiting van during the hours of darkness when there was little chance of being noticed.

• If Sica is correct that Vanunu's English was inadequate to write the palm message, and that somebody else did, why did the Israeli censor ban its publication? And why was a criminal investigation begun against the correspondent of the news organisation which broke censorship and published the palm message? If it was written by somebody else, why did it contain three errors: (i) 'hijacken' instead of 'hijacked'; (ii) 'hijacked' instead of a more suitable word, 'kidnapped'; (iii) 'fly' instead of 'flight'. Indeed, these errors are proof that though Vanunu's English was by no means perfect it was enough to get by. Meir Vanunu agrees that his brother did not know English well but like any serious university student he had picked it up in the course of his studies. Vanunu's English competency was adequate for him to be debriefed by Dr Frank Barnaby without the *Sunday Times* requiring an interpreter.

• With regard to Sica's statement that the 52 photographs which Vanunu had taken were all in chronological order and therefore had to have been taken with official sanction, a 'chronological order' is a subjective not an objective sequence. A chronological order may be made out of any number of photographs. In fact, Vanunu had taken 57, not 52; the others had been damaged by sunlight, according to the *Sunday Times*. Would an officially sanctioned PR job include spoilt photos? Sica would perhaps answer that these were included to give the others a degree of genuineness. He also argued that the absence of any people in the photographs was evidence of official collusion and that if Vanunu was acting on his own there would have to have been people there. But of course, Vanunu could not have taken the photographs with people present. The absence of people is perhaps the best proof that it was a genuine security leak. If it was a disinformation effort, the government would have ensured that people could be seen, to add to the credibility of the scenes. And how many people would Sica expect to be working and seen in those parts of the nuclear research centre? Finally, Mr Shamir referred on several occasions to the security fiasco of Vanunu's disclosure and that lessons had been learnt.

The biggest weakness in Sica's conclusion that the Vanunu disclosure was a disinformation effort was the 18-year sentence handed down. Also, what need was there for Cindy's role if it was a disinformation exercise? (The *Sunday Times* saw Cindy in London and subsequently spoke to her in Israel.) And why did the Shin Bet contact Mordechai's brother Albert on 7 September to verify Mordechai's whereabouts, telling him that his brother was about to reveal secret information to the press?

Andrew Hogg of the *Sunday Times* 'Insight' team said that Sica's conclusions showed that Italy was trying to avoid political embarrassment: 'It's unbelievable. It appears as an excuse not to investigate it in depth.'[102] Meir Vanunu did not have a great deal of hope. In October 1987 he said that he was becoming convinced that the Italian authorities had agreed to Israeli requests not to investigate the affair. Given all this, it seems that rather than draw conclusions which produced as many questions as answers, Sica ought to have returned the file to Italy's state prosecutor as lacking adequate evidence for a final conclusion. Sica did have pieces of circumstantial evidence: the false destination of the *Tappuz* cargo boat and the van hired by the Israeli embassy, to name but two. The final impression, whether by design or consequence, is of a cover-up useful both for calming the domestic embarrassment over yet another foreign national disappearing on Italian soil, and for maintaining good Italian–Israeli relations.

Sica's verdict was not the end of the Italian connection with the Vanunu affair. Various interest groups, among them the peace movement, some 800 Italian scientists, the Italian Federation of Democratic Lawyers, as well as individual parliamentary senators and journalists, protested against the verdict.

In 1994 an Israeli newspaper published new allegations about Vanunu's sea journey to Israel. *Kolbo*, the local newspaper of Haifa, Israel's port city where the country's navy is headquartered, discovered the Israeli naval craft disguised as a Panamanian ship which had been used. Its reporter, Mordechai Alon, who himself had spent his military service as a reporter on the navy's newspaper, heard from members of the boat's staff how the boat had picked somebody up, and how Cindy, whose photograph was later published, had travelled with them back to Israel. The boat, which had been on a routine journey, was about to return to Haifa when it was ordered back to the Italian coastland, where it waited for three days. Then, the entire crew were ordered to stay in the officers' mess while a speedboat with two men and a woman brought somebody on a stretcher on board.[103] The disclosures showed that the earlier *Sunday Times* report that the boat used to transport Vanunu was the *Tappuz* was incorrect.

In the months it took Alon to research the story, his phone and that of *Kolbo*'s editor were bugged by the Israeli security authorities, as the latter attempted by all means to ensure that the truth about the sea journey would never see the light of day. Alon was followed, his phone line cut, his neighbours questioned about him. He was threatened with standing military trial if the story ever broke. When the story was submitted to the censor for clearance, it was rejected in its entirety. A revised version with less sensitive information was prepared but it was very heavily cut. The censor indicated to the paper that it was being cancelled not because it contained narrow military information but because it included diplomatically embarrassing information in naming the country, reportedly Italy, from which Vanunu had been abducted. Italian territoriality had been violated. Israel had taken great pains to ensure that no reference made by the media was reported to Italy.[104]

Kolbo then appealed to the High Court against the military censor's decision. With the real possibility that the courts would allow the original article through, the censor caved in before the matter reached the courtroom. After the *Kolbo* disclosure, Vanunu campaigners approached the Italian ministry of justice again to reopen the Sica inquiry. But the ministry replied that this did not amount to new evidence.

Yet another consequence of the Vanunu affair was the revelation of the true identity of Cindy, who lured Vanunu from Britain. In July 1987 'Insight' reporter Peter Hounam walked up the path of 5 Strauma Street in Netanya, and rang the doorbell. Cheryl Bentov answered the door. Hounam introduced himself as a reporter from the *Sunday Times* and said he wanted to discuss a certain matter with her. She kept her cool and took him into the lounge. Hounam was accompanied by another reporter, David Connett, who had seen Cindy twice in London in Vanunu's presence and whose function was to positively identify her. Hounam told her that according to the paper's evidence she was the person who had lured Vanunu from London. According to the reporters, she did not deny it. Her sole reaction was 'Are you going to publish this?'. Then suddenly she got up and almost screaming said: 'I deny this, I deny everything.'[105] One of the reporters photographed her at that moment, but they never published the photo. Then she ran into the bedroom.

Practitioners of espionage are notorious for expending tremendous resources on devising clever ruses and subterfuges. Fake identities throw a cloak of impenetrability over an intelligence service's operations and enable it to undertake operations which political leaders would otherwise not approve, operations for which agents themselves are not accountable. When Cindy met Vanunu for the first time, she described herself as an American trainee beautician. In covert special operations, which may last for months or even years, the Mossad selects a real-life person who remains totally unaware that his or her identity has been usurped.[106] This is designed to withstand limited investigation by police authorities or rival agencies. The person is chosen because their age group and general physical characteristics roughly correspond to those of an Israeli agent.

Cindy Hanin did not exist on 30 September 1986, the day Vanunu was abducted. By 2 November she did exist. On that day Cynthia Morris, from Orlando, Florida, married high-school friend Randy Hanin. The ages were similar: Cheryl was 26, Cynthia, known to her friends as Cindy, was 22. Cynthia was a trainee beautician. Cheryl's choice was to be her undoing: Cheryl Bentov, née Hanin, was Randy Hanin's sister. A trail of clues left by Cindy led to her exposure. Although she gave Vanunu only her cover first name, Cindy, when she purchased her air ticket to Rome she also used the cover surname Hanin.[107] The *Sunday Times* employed the services of a private detective agency which located somebody in Orlando, Florida, with the name Hanin. The agency subsequently found her school, Edgewater High, where they spoke to the principal and deputy principal, and obtained a school picture of her. Hounam then flew to Florida and discovered from her father, Stanley Hanin, that his daughter had moved to Israel in her late teens. The local rabbi, Dov Kentof, added more details about Cheryl and the family. Obtaining her address in Israel from her father, Hounam was led to Kibbutz Bet Alpha. But the couple had moved to Netanya. The *Sunday Times* was going to carry a 6,000-word article in its colour magazine about how they had succeeded in tracking her down, and the subsequent encounter in her flat in Netanya. But after 'Insight' found the crucial piece of information that in London she had booked into the Eccleston hotel in Victoria, giving as her address her father's address, the paper ran it as a straight news story.[108]

Though she was safely back in Israel, the naming of Cheryl Bentov as Vanunu's abductor was a further chapter in an affair which had caused no small embarrassment to Israel's friends. Whilst the fallout in Britain and Italy should have been envisaged by those planning the abduction, the disclosure of Cindy's identity was due to carelessness and could easily have been avoided. 'By assuming the identity of a close, living relative', wrote Hirsh Goodman, then the *Jerusalem Post* military correspondent, 'Cindy (or rather her masters) left herself open to exposure, and Israel's secret service open to ridicule.'[109] The day Hounam stepped into the Bentov bungalow in Netanya was the last the couple stayed there.

But it was not the last Cindy heard from the *Sunday Times*. In the summer of 1997, Uzi Mahnaimi, the paper's Middle East reporter, was asked by the paper's editor, John Witherow, to locate her. In January 1998 he found her in

Florida and had her photographed as she left her house. How did the paper locate Cindy? Mahnaimi first turned to a well-known detective agency, but it failed to trace Cindy. An Israeli intelligence contact in Florida told Mahnaimi that he 'knows where Cindy is' and gave him a general description of her. She lived in Orlando. The contact described how she looked, and in what kindergarten her child was. The location was not so surprising because her father lived in Orlando, as the paper had revealed years earlier. Within two hours Mahnaimi was on a plane to the USA. Meanwhile the paper despatched a team of photographers from New York. The reporter had two objectives: to photograph and to interview her. After Mahnaimi located her house, he hired a car with single directional windows. Without Cindy knowing, the photographer snapped her as she left her home. They had to be extremely careful because had Cindy discovered she was being followed she would have gone to ground immediately. After Cindy was photographed, Mahnaimi telephoned her at her house. 'Tell us your story once and for all and we won't bother you again. Otherwise we will never leave you alone,' he told her. She replied 'I am definitely not prepared to.' She did not, however, deny that she was Cindy. 'I have nothing to say.'[110]

It would be wrong to overemphasise the diplomatic costs of the operation. Peres rightly gauged that Western leaders would 'understand' the need to abduct Vanunu. Yet the abduction cannot be considered an entire success. Public and parliamentary reaction in Britain and Italy, as well as in Australia, was considerable. If there was broad understanding among Western governments in 1986, there were also the Sica judicial inquiry and the expulsions from Britain.[111] These reactions raise questions regarding the political expediency of the decision to bring Vanunu home for trial.

'If a traitor is under the hand of the state you can give him a summons,' said Isser Harel, who as well as being Mossad chief during most of Ben-Gurion's premiership, authored a study on intelligence services and democracy. He went on,

> The latter [a summons] is easier and avoids the dangers to Israel at the political, security and diplomatic levels which an abduction causes. But Israel is a democratic and humanitarian country. To wipe someone out is a much more serious business. Just assume what the Italians or British or anyone else would say to a killing which occurred in their territory![112]

Even if Vanunu's killing would have been expedient, avoiding the political and diplomatic fallout which followed his abduction, a separate question is whether Mossad chief Nahum Admoni and his colleagues would have been prepared to carry it out, being aware that in earlier intelligence blunders – such as the killing of Arab terrorists after the end of the 1984 Arab hijacking of the 300 bus travelling from Tel Aviv to Ashkelon – Israeli politicians declined to carry the can.

Another factor in Peres' decision appears to have been the need not to set a dangerous precedent. Peres said, 'even though Vanunu's information about the nuclear weapons is untrue, Israel should still prosecute him because he does not have the right to discuss such matters. He violated state secrets.'[113] 'A man cannot spit on his country about one of the most critical issues and get away with it,' a security source remarked.[114] Not to do anything would mean that other dissident Israelis who had access to highly sensitive information could disclose it abroad without fear of being held to account.

But was this largely a cosmetic claim to cover an action which contravened international law? After all, given diplomatic and public reaction abroad, would the abduction have been ordered had it not involved a highly sensitive disclosure where the authorities were concerned what else Vanunu had divulged and to whom, beyond that which appeared in the *Sunday Times*? And, given the patriotism and sense of duty which still pervades Israel over sensitive matters, was there a need to set an example? As *Maariv*, putting a brave face on the security leak, remarked: 'It is remarkable, despite hundreds or even thousands having access in Dimona, that Vanunu was the only one.'[115]

Vanunu was not the first person to be brought from abroad for trial in Israel. The most famous case was that of Adolf Eichmann, abducted more than 25 years earlier. For Ben-Gurion – whose protégé Peres was – it was a case of bringing to trial an enemy of the Jewish people. But there were striking differences between Eichmann and Vanunu. Vanunu had not murdered anybody, whereas Eichmann was not just an enemy of the Jews but an international outcast. Vanunu may have been an outcast for the majority of Israelis, but he was no international outcast. Moreover, he claimed moral goals for his action.

Israel had other options. One was not to take any action. There was a certain value in letting a former nuclear technician advertise the country's nuclear capacity to foreign opinion. The photographs themselves were a scoop, but the message being carried by somebody who was breaking the law was that much more effective. Although Israeli officials were concerned as to whether Vanunu had revealed to foreign agents or to the newspaper more information than would subsequently be published, Vanunu could have been expected to give the most important information to the newspaper, which could have been expected to publish it. His revelations would have been put down as another uncorroborated report in a long series over the years. Instead, the abduction and trial served to confirm what Vanunu claimed.

Another option, theoretically, was extradition. It was ironic that illegal means were used to bring to trial somebody who had broken the law. Israel's extradition agreements with both Australia and Britain – the two countries where Vanunu was known to be divulging the information – are limited to a specific list of offences, among them murder, manslaughter, piracy and hijacking, and do not include the unauthorised disclosure of official information. The only remotely related categories covered by extradition are fraud and bribery (Vanunu was to receive part of the proceeds from the syndicated sale of his story and from a book planned by the paper). It was surprising that Israel's extradition laws had not been revised to the more modern 'no-list system' rather than a specific table of offences. According to Dianne Stafford of the international branch of Australia's attorney general's department, 'Australia's modern extradition practice has been to negotiate extradition treaties that apply to serious offences generally (carrying imprisonment of at least one or two years) without regard to the offence's denomination.'[116] According to P.J. Monk of the British foreign office's nationality and treaty department, 'the crime would have to be an offence in both countries (i.e., the dual criminality system)'.[117] Given that both Australia and Britain have an Official Secrets Act, Vanunu's crime would have been covered. Had Israel had a no-list extradition treaty with Britain it is possible that Vanunu's action would have been seen by the Thatcher government as a political offence.

Another option which would have avoided abduction or disappearance, would have been computer espionage. Electronic, photographic and radar intelligence have been tools of Israeli intelligence since the 1950s. An example was in the late 1980s, when a West German Computer Science student managed for two years to gain secret access, through global communications networks, to military information in more than 30 computers in the United States. Undetected, he obtained data relating to nuclear weapons, intelligence satellites, the Strategic Defence Initiative, the space shuttle, and the North American Air Defence Command. The West German, moreover, was able not only to read material stored in the computers, but could print it out as well as alter the original information.

The *Sunday Times* had transferred onto their computer details of the two-day briefing which Vanunu had given Dr Frank Barnaby as well as of subsequent sessions between Vanunu and the 'Insight' reporters. 'While the computer used in the Vanunu investigation was not on-line to anywhere, and a number of files were used specifically for this investigation which only certain people had access to, the computer itself was accessible to anybody in the building,' a member of the 'Insight' team said.[118] Israel could have ascertained what information Vanunu had given other than what had appeared in the published report by gaining unauthorised access to one of the cables at the *Sunday Times* Wapping site. It would have to be assumed that whatever Vanunu might have revealed to Arab sympathisers or even enemy agents was in the detailed testimony he gave the paper, and it could certainly be assumed that a news organisation's computer system would not be particularly secure against intelligence surveillance in contrast to, say, the computer system of a defence establishment.

After having eavesdropped on Vanunu's debriefing, Israeli agents could have disrupted the *Sunday Times* computers and the report being prepared for publication by the paper, by infecting them with viruses or other disruptive programs. Yet, the strategy chosen was to bring the man home.

The Israel defence establishment enjoys a dominant influence in external intelligence matters, with the Israeli foreign ministry left in a subordinate role in policy making. Defence's kingpin role reflects the external threats faced by Israel. According to David Kimche, the former director-general of the Israeli foreign ministry and a former number two in the Mossad,

> a problem we have had on many subjects is that the defence establishment has not always understood the political connotations of some of their activities. It's very difficult because it's inbuilt: the people in the defence establishment don't always understand the importance of the political side. It's a very sad and sorry thing but this is the fact.[119]

The overwhelming majority of Israelis backed the decision to bring Vanunu home. Typical was *Maariv*'s reaction:

> We are not moved by the fact that someone took the trouble to bring Vanunu to Israel. We say 'Well done' and we don't give a hoot whether he was brought legally or by subterfuge, by sea or by air, alive or dead. And if he has not been brought here, we will encourage every initiative in this direction.[120]

The liberal daily *Haaretz* chimed in, 'No foreign state can prevent Jerusalem from bringing a traitor and spy to Israel.' The paper expressed understanding for 'the need to minimise the dissemination of information on sensitive matters' such as nuclear research, and said that the only area of the whole affair which should arouse concern, and for which the public required an explanation, was the security leak.[121] The only dissident press voice was *Al Hamishmar*, the organ of the left-wing Mapam: 'How far does Israel's jurisdiction extend? Is it permissible or not to bring persons to Israel through the use of coercion – which is perhaps appropriate for spy movies and irresponsible regimes, but not for lawful states?', it asked. 'Israeli public opinion must discuss all these issues without exposing – be it a millimetre – what is or will be considered a bona fide military or security secret.'[122]

Shamir, who had subsequently taken over as prime minister, replied to questions about the affair: 'Israel will say what it finds correct to say and will fulfil its obligation to its citizens.'[123] The reply was reminiscent of his comment in the affair involving Jonathan Pollard, an American in US naval intelligence who spied for the Israelis: 'What happened is usually known to those in the know, and whoever does not know should continue not knowing.'[124] However patriotic the former Mossad officer was, he displayed limited regard for public and parliamentary accountability in the rough and tumble of Israeli politics. Although his attitude may have been more fitting for Israel 20 years earlier, the seventy-year-old politician was not out of tune with the rightward direction which Israel's increasingly Sephardi or Oriental population has taken: the attitude is that national security matters should be left to the defence establishment which 'knows best'.

Reaction or no reaction at home, the fallout abroad serves to pinpoint attention on the way the original decision to abduct Vanunu was made. It was taken in the inner cabinet comprising prime minister Peres, defence minister Rabin and foreign minister Shamir without the involvement even of key advisers. Nor was the full Cabinet consulted either before the abduction or afterwards.[125] On 16 November, seven weeks after Vanunu left Britain, the full Cabinet was briefed by Shamir. As questions were increasingly raised in Britain and elsewhere about Vanunu's disappearance from London, Israeli ministers informally expressed dissatisfaction with the handling of the affair. 'We appear as a non-law-abiding country but one which kidnaps its citizens,' a minister said. By taking decisionmaking out of the formal procedure, the then prime minister Peres made a decision[126] to abduct an informant of an internationally respected newspaper without weighing the full consequences. And by later initiating Israel's confirmation that Vanunu was back in Israel, Peres committed a primary transgression of the rules of covert espionage: public confirmation of an operation.

It is one thing for those who engage in covert action to have no automatic right to be free from being subjected to the very kinds of behaviour they themselves engage in, but it is another for civil servants to be forcibly brought from one territory to another in contravention of international law and conduct. It offends the basic concept of national sovereignty. Moreover, Vanunu was no longer even a government-employed official; he was a civilian who had had access to secrets of the most important kind, and he had broken the Official Secrets Act which binds officials who have access to secret information to observe silence unto the day of their death. If Vanunu could be kidnapped, cannot also anybody who breaks the law and reveals information about, say, their basic training during national service? It was the enormity of Vanunu's crime which decided the Israeli government to act illegally in bringing him back to stand trial, rather than any intrinsic difference between these two cases. And if a Vanunu may be abducted, can, say, a Soviet Jewish scientist who emigrates to Israel, or an East European émigré in the West, to determine how much information they may have revealed to their hosts about their former country? And may Iran, Libya or Iraq take steps against dissidents among their nationals in foreign countries?

The Vanunu abduction, concerning a leak about a very sensitive defence installation, satisfies many people's criteria for covert action, but it must he asked whether less covert means could have been used – particularly given that his disclosures posed no immediate danger to the country's survival.

7
The Security Fiasco

Vanunu's revelations about Israel's atomic secrets were the result of one of the biggest security lapses in the story of the Jewish State. The lapse was doubly disturbing because Vanunu was no spy and had not hidden his pro-Arab sympathies. Security personnel at the reactor learnt of the fact that Vanunu had revised his views about nuclear weapons, having undergone a crisis of conscience, some two years after this occurred. 'If an overt security risk like Vanunu could get away with it, imagine what someone more subtle could have achieved,' a security source remarked. 'The Vanunu leak was a serious breakdown in security procedures. The matter has been examined and solutions proposed,' prime minister Itzhak Shamir told a closed-doors meeting of the Knesset's defence & foreign affairs committee.[1] One Knesset member asked whether anybody knew 'how many Vanunus there are' who might have passed state secrets to foreign sources.

The nuclear research centre has an intricate system of security measures. These include an electrified fence, sand within the perimeter fence which is raked periodically to betray intruders' footprints, and missile batteries which have orders to shoot down any aircraft that strays into the airspace above – as one Israeli pilot found to his cost in 1967.[2] According to the *Sunday Times*, the fleet of buses that brings the staff to work passes one cursory security check some five kilometres before reaching the reactor, and a more rigorous one a kilometre before the entrance.

In 1977, Vanunu began work at Machon 2 – that part of the reactor where plutonium is separated from uranium, providing nuclear bombs with the required fission. In addition to the general pass given to all those working at Dimona, he had Pass no. 320 which gave him entry to Machon 2. On his first trip to Dimona after acceptance, in February 1977, the first thing Vanunu and other trainees had to do was to sign the Official Secrets Act, the penalty for infringement being 15 years' imprisonment. And it does seem that he did not reveal even to his closest associates the exact nature of his work, despite his pride in beginning work in the highly sensitive installation. 'He spoke only in general terms. We knew that he worked in the nuclear research centre,' his brother Meir said. 'Never did he let out a word about his work. We just knew that he worked there,' his mother said.[3] His girl friend Judy Zimmet, said, 'I knew it had something to do with atomic projects. I had figured that out, but he only spoke of chemicals and controls.'[4]

He went through every department of Machon 2, which afforded him an overview of the various stages in what, Vanunu later claimed, was a programme for constructing nuclear warheads. While security instructions formally allowed for workers to be given access only to their own areas of responsibility on a need-to-know basis, in practice Vanunu 'learnt about all sorts of units in order to replace or fill in for other people. Work managers were also happy when a worker knew more units than his own in order to fill in,' he said.[5] In 1978, for example, he moved to another section of Machon 2 and later to unit 95 of Machon 2, the lithium 6 plant. For a short time in August 1979 he worked in Machon 4 where radioactive waste is treated.[6]

Yet the system collapsed. That Vanunu was able to leave the country with the information and the films when he was under suspicion as a security risk indicates that the Vanunu affair may not have been a once-only security lapse. That a section head of the Metallurgy department, where weapons were rumoured to be manufactured, left the keys on top of a locker, enabling Vanunu to walk in, indicated gross negligence.[7] It was here that Vanunu photographed spherical models of bombs. It involved a whole series of hiccoughs, unjustified complacency and exaggerated trust. As Zeev Schiff of *Haaretz* put it, 'the right hand of the security didn't know what the left hand was doing. All the parts of the engine rotated on their axles, but not one was properly connected to the other.'[8]

Responsibility for internal security at all defence institutions falls on Malmab, which supervises security at the ministry of defence. In practice this includes securing all defence installations. Formally, Malmab is fully answerable to the Shin Bet (Israel's domestic intelligence agency, similar to the FBI), whose security wing is responsible for the protection of VIPs, including the prime minister, and for the protection of Israeli diplomatic posts abroad. Today the line of administrative accountability is more in the name than in the reality, with Malmab developing into an operation of its own.

When the nuclear reactor was constructed in the 1950s, the then deputy defence minister Shimon Peres assigned to the chief security officer of the defence ministry, Binyamin Blumberg, responsibility for securing the reactor.[9] The activities of his office, designated the Office of Special Assignments, expanded beyond securing the reactor to include the acquisition of materials related to scientific matters. Malmab's own power of influence inside the reactor was limited by the Israel Atomic Energy Commission (IAEC), the body in overall charge of Dimona. Bureaucratically zealous in resisting interference by outside bodies, IAEC insists that its own personnel handle security inside the reactor. Thus, the reactor's chief security officer was an IAEC official, not one from Malmab. The head of Malmab at the time of the Vanunu fiasco, Haim Carmon – who replaced Blumberg in 1979 – had earlier expressed reservations about the competence of the chief security officer, known only as 'C', but was unable to remove 'C' from his post since 'C' was not a Malmab employee. However, in an attempt to beef up Dimona security, Carmon attempted to sidestep 'C' by appointing his own deputy at Malmab, Yehiel Horev, as a kind of external supervisor of 'C'.

The security arrangements at Dimona ought to have thwarted Vanunu's plans. 'C' knew about Vanunu's political activities at the Ben-Gurion University campus. 'C' reported the matter to the personnel director of the plant, and to the director-general of the reactor, Avraham Saroussi. A copy of his report was also sent to Carmon. Vanunu was placed under observation – which entailed that his work bosses could not take action against him without the approval of the security officers. Indeed, from 1984 onwards Vanunu was summoned on three occasions for a pep talk concerning the need for security. 'There was information that he was associating with all sorts of groups including minorities [a term used in Israeli jargon to refer to Israeli Arabs] which certainly worried us,' 'C', the chief security officer, said later. At the first talk Vanunu admitted that he was 'meeting with a group that dealt with discrimination. We talked about the need to maintain secrecy at Dimona. We warned him.' A second talk with Vanunu took place after 'C' obtained a copy of the university students' newspaper in which Vanunu was interviewed and quoted as saying 'Of course, the only way is to go underground!' Naturally, to 'C' as a security officer 'this not only switched on a red light. So I read it to Mr Vanunu. He said that the passage about the need to 'move underground' was not a quote of his own words, but that the interviewer herself wrote this as an expression of her own ideas. I got the impression that this was really not what he said.'[10]

In May 1985 Vanunu was summoned to a third meeting with security officials, this time at Israeli defence headquarters at Hakirya, Tel Aviv. There he was reportedly asked to sign a declaration admitting that he was friendly with Arabs including those close to the Palestine Liberation Organisation and that he had passed them state secrets. He refused to sign it, arguing that while he had many Arab friends, a few of whom might be linked to terrorist organisations, he emphatically denied that he had passed them state secrets. The implications of these ties were explained to Vanunu who, according to the security officials, undertook to discontinue them. While he delayed his application to join the Israeli Communist party he continued meeting his Arab friends. He even added that the reactor's management 'should not worry because I intend to quit pretty soon and then all will be very quiet.' He said he was planning to study for a second university degree. According to 'C', Vanunu had mentioned his future plans on a number of occasions. 'I remember asking him, "Do you have anything specific in mind?" He said he still did not. "I need to find a direction in life." He did not discuss anything definite.'[11] Before he left his job in September 1985 he was summoned to a routine meeting given to all departing staff, reminded of the need for secrecy, and warned that if secrecy was not respected he would be brought to trial.[12] When 'C' heard that Vanunu was leaving, he suggested that Vanunu's movements in and out of the country be monitored. But nothing was implemented.

It is clear from this that the Dimona authorities were aware of the potential security danger which Vanunu posed. They even planned to move Vanunu from the super-sensitive Machon 2 to the less-sensitive Machon 6. But the system failed. Vanunu managed to smuggle a camera in to work, where he snapped 57 photos. Moreover, the security system failed to stop Vanunu, once abroad, from making contact with such unauthorised bodies as the international media.

After the Mossad's kidnapping of Vanunu back to Israel, security personnel in Malmab, in the IAEC, in the Shin Bet, and in the police carried out a number of investigations. Vanunu was interrogated for several days after he arrived back. The first interrogation was carried out by Shin Bet agent Alon. 'My goal was to find out what Vanunu knew, what information experts who questioned him like Barnaby learnt from him – the facts, details, these are the things which the opponent, the enemy, the journalists desire,' said Alon.[13] Vanunu was later given the *Sunday Times*'s article and told to underline everything that was inaccurate in it, or that he had not told the *Sunday Times*. The Israeli authorities hoped thereby to gauge the damage done by Vanunu. Since Alon had no expertise in nuclear-related matters, 'Giora', a nuclear physics engineer at Dimona, was brought in to assess the damage done by verifying what information Vanunu had passed on while abroad. 'I told Vanunu that since the matter is sensitive it is necessary to check out the matter point by point with an expert.'[14] Vanunu was questioned by 'Giora' – the two knew one another from when Vanunu worked at the reactor – both about the information he had passed to the *Sunday Times* reporters and about his visit to Moscow. Said 'Giora':

> We went through the photographs which journalists in London had brought to the Israeli embassy spokesman, and which had been sent back to Mossad headquarters near Tel Aviv, and talked about what he saw in them, and what he had told the *Sunday Times* journalists.[15]

But this was not a very efficient manner of damage assessment because Vanunu's testimony to the *Sunday Times* (including two long days of debriefing by Barnaby, which was taped) was ten times longer than the published article. Security personnel were apparently unaware of this. Since the tapes reached both Barnaby, who used it in preparing his book, *The Invisible Bomb*,[16] and also two US-based academic researchers of nuclear proliferation in the Middle East, the damage assessment was unreliable. 'We were terrified that he had divulged names of people at Dimona. In Thailand he had told somebody about his work, who suggested they could connect him with journalists but Vanunu did not want to go into details,' 'Giora' added.[17] (This was a possible reference to Vanunu befriending the daughter of British journalist Sandy Gall while visiting Thailand.)

Yehiel Horev remarked later, 'When we received *The Sunday Times*'s article we sat and read what was published. We wanted to verify what had already been published before and what was new.'[18] According to Horev, an official from the IAEC carried out a detailed analysis of 'what was new information in the article, and what was already known.'[19] Horev argued that the exposé made the bombing of the Dimona reactor an option for Arab states. But his assessment is questionable because Arab states have suspected since the 1960s that Dimona is the home of Israel's nuclear project.

Scientists and technicians at Dimona were questioned about their ties with Vanunu.[20] Measures were taken by the IAEC against senior officials at the reactor, including its head.[21] By coincidence or otherwise, 'C' had just then moved from his post as chief security officer, a post he had held since 1979, to the reactor comptroller's section. Another head to roll was that of Malmab chief Haim Carmon. To 'alleviate' his dismissal he was promoted to be an assistant director-general of the defence ministry responsible for foreign relations. Horev replaced Carmon as Malmab chief. This was a little surprising given that Horev himself had been the external supervisor of 'C'. The Horev appointment was later justified in that Horev had been on study leave at the time of the Vanunu exposé.

Moreover, Horev, together with a Shin Bet official,[22] carried out an internal inquiry into the fiasco. 'We had an internal committee of inquiry and found that things were not done properly. The system failed and very serious conclusions were drawn. It's clear the system failed,' Horev said.[23] But a former head of the Shin Bet's security wing, Abraham Rotem, criticised these steps. Moving personnel was inadequate: 'This was little more than moving dust.' He called for stronger steps:

> There was a failure of coordination between and within Malmab, the Shin Bet, and the Atomic Energy Commission. Only an official public inquiry would ensure that adequate steps are taken. This requires a fundamental investigation of all of Vanunu's activities and the security controls which he jumped, including to photograph the installation – in order to ensure that nobody else had exploited the loophole.[24]

Measures taken to improve security at Dimona since the security fiasco presumably include not employing people of extreme political views, keeping a check on any changes in ideology on the part of existing employees, and better routine security inside the research centre. Other measures could also be taken. For example, in the aftermath of a series of espionage cases in the US, including the Walker family spy ring for the USSR, the US army established a free-of-charge telephone number enabling people to report on workers with access to sensitive places or information who arouse their suspicions. In its first year it received over 2,000 calls. There is an obvious requirement to check such reports with the utmost care. Yet even these measures do not stop anybody from leaving the country and revealing the information abroad – except by way of their awareness that they may share Vanunu's fate.

Horev requested that Malmab's authority be widened to include appointments of security officers at defence installations such as the Dimona reactor, appointments currently made by the Shin Bet.[25] Horev had sought to expand his powers and turn Malmab into a separate intelligence entity from the Shin Bet. Prime minister Ehud Barak, in an attempt to further improve security at the Dimona reactor, appointed former Shin Bet head Avraham Shalom – against Horev's wishes – to make the reactor proof against leaks of information.

The question remains whether the intelligence services should be left to investigate themselves. The internal committee of inquiry comprised Horev himself and Shin Bet officer Avner Barnea. To allow them to investigate themselves not only enables a cover-up by those responsible, but is a dereliction of legislative control over the security services. Geula Cohen of the right-wing Tehiya party requested that the Knesset debate security procedures at Dimona, and specifically how Vanunu could have been employed there, but she withdraw the request under pressure from the government.

Cohen's attack was levelled more against the Shin Bet than against Vanunu, and therefore appeared as a further episode in the long-running political battle for legitimacy between Israel's right and left. Nevertheless, her remarks – and their rejection by left-wing politicians – had deeper implications: whether officials in an intelligence service or in other sensitive defence posts are able to carry out their tasks, like other civil servants, irrespective of their political views. Support for this came from a surprising quarter, Raful Eitan, then a party colleague of Cohen's. Eitan is also a former chief of staff of the Israeli army. He called Cohen's view a double-edged sword, arguing that 'today's rulers might purge holders of the opposite view, and tomorrow's rulers might purge the security men left in their jobs.' Heads of sensitive organisations have adequate means for checking trustworthiness. 'I know a great many loyal people who today could be described as members of the leftist camp, and who are just as outstanding fighters and loyal Israelis as everyone else, if not more.'[26]

It is ironic that the Labour party's Ben-Gurion, who doubled as defence minister while prime minister, set the precedent that leftists should not be employed in sensitive posts. Another member of the Tehiya party, Professor Yuval Neeman (who played an important role in Israel's nuclear programme), then identified with the Mapam, was initially barred by Ben-Gurion from being appointed deputy head of Israel's military intelligence. Subsequently, Ben-Gurion was persuaded that Neeman was no longer politically active in Mapam. By the same token, those with right-wing views would not be employed in certain internal security posts. Indeed, while Ben-Gurion allowed former members of the pre-state underground groups of the Irgun, led by Menachem Begin, and the Stern gang, one of whose leaders was Itzhak Shamir, to serve in the external intelligence arm, the Mossad, he did not want them in the Shin Bet. Although there have been brief periods since the inception of the state in which left-wing parties have been regarded with suspicion, today, with the exception of the Communist party, even members of far-left parties – for example, Ran Cohen, from the Citizens' Rights Movement – are in highly sensitive posts in the military and defence establishment.

The liberal-orientated *Haaretz* editorialised that in a free society even those who support a Palestinian state should not be discriminated against in the general labour market. But 'in sensitive places people whose political views are likely to be translated into actions should not be employed.'[27] *Haaretz* was discussing Vanunu rather than the Shin Bet. The question comes down to whether a worker can carry out his or her task responsibly without allowing any personal views to influence it; Vanunu was not able to do so. Without a commission of inquiry, it is unclear whether those Shin Bet officers and Dimona officials responsible for security at the reactor failed because a political view may have consciously or subconsciously influenced them not to weed out Vanunu. But the public and parliamentary consensus in favour of the nuclear element and the involvement of the security services ruled out an independent inquiry. Had its effects been more immediate, such as a nuclear accident, it is most unlikely that a public commission of inquiry could have been avoided.

8

The State of Israel v. M. Vanunu

The shroud of ambiguity which the Israeli authorities placed over the diplomatic and intelligence aspects of the Vanunu affair also characterised Vanunu's trial. But while denial and disinformation are part of the diplomat's craft, the independence of the Israeli judiciary and the rule of law changed the rules of the game.[1]

Days before Vanunu's case was due to come up before the courts in March 1987, Mordechai, on brother Meir's initiative, dismissed his lawyer Amnon Zichroni. Mordechai Vanunu had picked the name of Amnon Zichroni from a list of lawyers who are approved by the defence authorities to see classified material. A veteran lawyer of left-wing causes, during the time Vanunu had been a student at Beersheba's Ben-Gurion University he had turned to Zichroni on behalf of Arab students on the campus. But Meir was concerned that Zichroni was not raising the matter of the abduction, and also wanted the issue of the illegitimacy of nuclear weaponry tested in the courtroom. In the months since his brother's abduction, Meir had increasingly linked the case to the international anti-nuclear movement. Zichroni's style of maintaining ties with the Israeli establishment, including the intelligence community, aroused the concern of the Vanunu brothers. Zichroni was a personal friend of Yossi Ginnossar, a senior Shin Bet officer who, according to Meir Vanunu,[2] had led the team which interrogated his brother. During the mystery over Vanunu's fate immediately after his abduction, Zichroni refused to break the stringent censorship and admit that his client was back in Israel and under arrest.

Zichroni was asked on the BBC radio programme 'The World at One' (10 November 1986) by presenter Brian Widlake, 'Where is Mr Vanunu being held?'

Zichroni: I cannot comment.
Presenter: But have you discussed that with him?
Zichroni: I cannot comment on it ...
Presenter: Does Israel have the equivalent of the British Official Secrets Act?
Zichroni: We have a special Act which deals with such cases.
Presenter: Would I be right in thinking that Mr Vanunu is subject to that Act?

Zichroni: I cannot comment on it.

Presenter: Mr Zichroni, you're being excessively cautious, can you tell me why?

Zichroni: I cannot even comment on your last question!

Presenter: On why you're being cautious?

Zichroni: Yes.

Presenter: Is this because you are under some pressure from the Israeli authorities?

Zichroni: I am not under pressure, but I cannot comment on it.

It was little comfort to the Vanunu family that Zichroni had been instrumental in getting the authorities to lift the veil of secrecy and confirm that Vanunu was alive and in custody by threatening to go to the High Court to obtain this permission.

Zichroni's replacement, Avigdor Feldman, had a solid reputation as a human rights lawyer. He had defended Arabs appealing deportation orders, Druze residents of the Golan Heights, and had got the administration order imposed on Palestinian activist Faisal el-Husseini reduced by half. Former legal advisor to the Israeli Civil Rights Association, Feldman had over the years been concerned about the poor legal services available to Arabs and the lack of overall success in Arab appeals to the Israeli Supreme Court. He was one of the Israeli monitors of the New York-based group Human Rights Watch. The holder of an MA in international law, he had been a visiting scholar at Harvard University, and as a young lawyer a member of Zichroni's legal practice for 14 years. For the poet intellectual-turned-lawyer, the Vanunu case presented a number of significant and stimulating issues which could have long-term implications: the rights of the individual against the state and the limits on how far an individual may act, how a democratic society grapples with the nuclear issue and whether Israel could set her own rules.

Before Feldman took over, he talked at some length with Vanunu to determine what he meant by wanting Feldman to 'politicise the case'. While such issues as the morality of nuclear weaponry and legislative control over the nuclear research programme could be presented in the courtroom within the framework of the legal arguments, Feldman was not going to delegitimise the court system. The line of legal defence which he proposed was that Vanunu had acted from ideological motives, and had not damaged state security in revealing the nuclear secrets. He would claim that the opposite was true: Vanunu had wanted to 'assist' the public and inform them of the nuclear programme so that they could reach a viewpoint on the subject. Nor had he sold any secrets to an enemy; he had leaked them to a newspaper.

According to Feldman, the law is a product of political institutions. The function of the law is to find a legal peg on which to give political expression to the client. Vanunu expected that his legal defence would search in the penal system for something which justified and defended Vanunu's motive.

The prosecution case against Mordechai Vanunu appeared clear-cut. According to the charge sheet Vanunu, on commencing a training course at the nuclear research centre at Dimona, had signed a declaration which committed him to observe secrecy about his work, and was told of the importance of this. But, particularly from the beginning of 1985, he had collected, prepared, copied and held in his possession classified information. He visited top-secret areas of the nuclear research centre and photographed 'top-secret objects' and installations, and hid the information at home. This information allegedly included the physical and organisational structure of the centre, classified 'developments' there, classified operating procedures and production processes, and 'code names of terminology of various secret developments'.

In Australia, continued the indictment, Vanunu gave a man named Oscar Guerrero, 'who presented himself as a journalist', secret information as well as photographs he had taken at Dimona:

When he passed the information to Guerrero, and subsequently to the *Sunday Times*, the accused intended to impair the security of the state. The accused delivered the information in the knowledge that it would be published by the newspaper, and that it would in this way be likely to reach the enemy. By his acts, the accused intended to assist the enemy in its war against Israel.

The most obvious section of the criminal law regarding state security and official secrets under which to charge Vanunu was 'aggravated espionage'. According to Section 113 of the Penal Code:

(b) A person who delivers any secret information without being authorised to do so and with intent to impair the security of the State is liable to imprisonment for life

(c) A person who obtains, collects, prepares, records or holds possession of any secret information without being authorised to do so is liable to imprisonment for a term of seven years; if he [or she] thereby intends to impair the security of the State, he [or she] is liable to imprisonment for 15 years.

The charge that Vanunu had impaired the security of the state suggested that the information he gave the *Sunday Times* was accurate. But, anxious that the charge sheet should not undermine the posture of nuclear ambiguity, officials were quick to point out that under the law it is irrelevant whether the information was accurate or not. 'Secret' information could include signs reading 'Keep Out' surrounding the nuclear research centre.[3]

The Vanunu file was in the hands of Uzi Hasson, a veteran of the state prosecutor's office. A Hebrew University law graduate, Hasson had spent most of his career in the Jerusalem division of the state prosecutor, apart from a spell in the main national office of the state prosecutor where he headed the fiscal department. In1987 he returned to the Jerusalem division as its chief prosecutor.

He could call on considerable experience in criminal appeals to the Israeli Supreme Court. In drawing up the Vanunu case Hasson was assisted by Dorit Beinish, the deputy state prosecutor.

The two were considered the best team to handle this sensitive case; they had worked together on a number of earlier cases. These included the controversial so-called 'Jewish Underground' trial when some Jewish residents of the West Bank had been given sentences of up to life imprisonment for the murder of Arab residents.

As the Beinish-Hasson team put the final touches to the Vanunu indictment for espionage, a charge of treason was added. Its addition reflected differences between the Shin Bet and the justice ministry, and within the ministry. According to Section 99 of the Penal Code:

(a) A person who, with intent to assist an enemy in war against Israel, commits an act calculated so to assist him, is liable to the death sentence or to imprisonment for life.

(b) For the purposes of this section, 'assistance' includes delivering information with intent that it fall into the hands of the enemy or in the knowledge that it may fall into enemy hands; and it is immaterial whether or not war is being waged at the time the information was given.

Notwithstanding that prosecutions have a tendency to include the maximum number of charges, the treason charge raised some official eyebrows because Vanunu had given the information not to an enemy but to a news organisation. Some thought that it would be difficult to convict Vanunu on this count.[4] Moreover, attorney general Harish wanted to press for the death penalty given the seriousness of the charges[5] but other officials argued for life imprisonment, saying that a death sentence could be imposed only if the offence was committed during a period of armed hostilities, i.e., war. The only death sentence ever carried out in Israel's history was that on Adolf Eichmann, in charge of logistics in the systematic Nazi extermination of the Jews, who was abducted from Argentina in 1960 by Mossad agents. But Harish relied on a legal interpretation that Israel, in the absence of peace with neighbouring states, was in a constant state of armed hostilities. However, the final decision was to demand life imprisonment.

There were, in essence, two court cases. Parallel to his trial on charges of disclosing official secrets, Vanunu was attempting to put the state of Israel on trial for abduction. Shortly after he was brought back to Israel, the security services and Vanunu had engaged in some plea bargaining. Vanunu would be charged only with aggravated espionage and not with treason if he agreed not to raise the subject of his abduction. But once Vanunu had divulged that information on the palm of his hand, the offer was withdrawn. It could have knocked three to five years off the 18-year sentence he was to receive.

According to Feldman, since Vanunu had been brought to Israel illegally the court had no jurisdiction. If the judges accepted Feldman's argument Vanunu would have to be freed. There was a precedent in US law (which is admissible in Israeli courts): the prosecution of a drug smuggler, Francisco Toscanino, who had been sentenced to a long prison term for smuggling a great quantity of heroin. A US federal court of appeal overturned a lower court's decision on the grounds that he had been abducted from South America by US narcotics agents and brought drugged to the United States. Until the federal court decision, US justice had drawn a veil over what happened before a trial, saying that it was irrelevant how a person was brought to court.[6]

There were precedents too in Israeli law for people having been brought to Israel by the use of force. Most notable was the case of Adolf Eichmann. The court had rejected Eichmann's defence that it had no jurisdiction, arguing that the court was not interested in how a person was brought to trial. What was relevant was whether it had legal power – which it had over anybody in Israeli territory. One difference between the Eichmann and Vanunu abductions was that while Argentina had waived its rights in the case of Eichmann, Italy was not known to have done so regarding Vanunu.[7] However, only states, in contrast to individuals, had standing in international law and could claim its infringement, and there was no extradition agreement between Israel and Italy. Unless someone had been extradited under an existing treaty, the court would not investigate the circumstances in which a person was detained and brought to Israel.[8] Yet there have been developments in international humanitarian law. According to the International Covenant on Civil and Political Rights (Article 9), 'no person should be subject to arbitrary arrest or detention,' which includes the abduction of a person by agents of one state to another state. Thus, argued Feldman, Israel, which had incorporated the Universal Declaration of Human Rights into its legal system, was obligated to return Vanunu to Italy.[9]

The court rejected Feldman's argument[10] – its precise reasons were not made known – in line with the principle that a court could try anybody under its jurisdiction and was not concerned how that person had reached its jurisdiction. Vanunu hoped that his abduction would be raised in the Italian courts or at the European Court at Strasbourg, but Feldman was sceptical given the verdict of the Italian prosecutor, Judge Domenico Sica, that Vanunu was 'an Israeli agent'. Feldman preferred the possibility of pursuing the Israeli government because its official agents had used force to bring Vanunu to Israel.

At the outset of the trial the minister of defence had used his powers to issue an order barring the court from discussing either Vanunu's work at Dimona or his abduction, on the grounds that this was likely to impair the security of the state. Under the Penal Code (Section 128) a court can order that the accused or his counsel not be present at a particular legal proceeding or not inspect some particular evidence. Said an official: 'It was a funny situation. Vanunu knew – or thought he knew – what was true or not. There was an assumption that the prosecution lawyer knew what was true or not. The only persons that could not know were the three judges.'[11] In Spring 1987 Avigdor Feldman appealed to the Israeli Supreme Court to lift the ministerial order, saying that it would he impossible for the defence to be conducted under these conditions. Feldman planned to challenge the admissibility of the confessions the Shin Bet had obtained from Vanunu during his interrogation by getting his client to testify about his feelings and reactions during his journey front Italy and his initial imprisonment.

Judge Gavriel Bach received explanations from Feldman as to why Feldman needed the information. He also heard from the Shin Bet and security staff at the Dimona reactor. Bach took the rare step in Israeli legal history of limiting the defence minister's order, and decided to let Vanunu describe how he had been brought to Israel, how he was held, for how long, and what his feelings were. It was the first time, according to Bach, that a defendant was being prohibited from giving testimony at his own trial, and Bach ruled that to justify limiting Vanunu's evidence the court had to be convinced that the state's security would indeed be impaired. Quoting another liberal maverick of the Israeli judiciary, Judge Aharon Barak, Bach said that a judge had to weigh the relative importance of each piece of evidence, between complete unimportance and vital relevance. When this had been done, a comparison had to be made with the importance, from the point of view of state security, of not disclosing the evidence. If its importance for the accused outweighed considerations of security, its disclosure could be authorised in the interests of a fair trial. Bach ruled that Vanunu could relate to the way he had been arrested abroad, how he had been brought to Israel and imprisoned and his feelings and fears during the entire period. That the trial was behind closed doors reduced the danger of evidence being disclosed.[12] The decision, and its publication, sent a minor shockwave through the senior ranks of the intelligence community. However, said Bach, Vanunu could not name the country where he had been arrested (even though he had already named it in the palm incident) or the place where he had been held, the identity of his abductors or even the type of transport in which he had been returned to Israel. These, argued Bach, were irrelevant to the trial and would only make it cumbersome.

Born and educated in Berlin, Bach, prior to his appointment to the Israeli Supreme Court, had worked in the state prosecutor's office for some 30 years. In 1969 he had been appointed state prosecutor, and in 1982 made a judge in the Supreme Court. Among Bach's rulings, which were noted for their liberality, were his ruling which cancelled the distinction between the sexes regarding pensions; a ruling against the Israeli Broadcasting Authority action in the early 1980s forbidding the broadcasting of interviews with Arabs who said that the Palestine Liberation Organisation, headed by Yasser Arafat, represented the Palestinian people; and his ruling in the so-called Nachmani case in favour of Ruth Nahmani's right to have a test-tube baby from an embryo of her divorced husband.

As the trial was about to open, Feldman subpoenaed the court charging that the traumatic manner in which Vanunu had been returned to Israel nullified the accuracy of the confessions taken from him by the Shin Bet immediately on his arrival back. Vanunu had reportedly been brought back in the dark cabin of a ship, and then imprisoned in a closed, airless cell. The Shin Bet had given Vanunu the impression that he would be imprisoned for years without anybody knowing it.[13] The confession which Vanunu claimed he had been forced to sign included the statement that he had received money from the *Sunday Times* for the story, and this profit motive gave the prosecution reason for charging that Vanunu intended to commit treason.[14] Vanunu waited for his opportunity to describe in graphic detail his treatment at the hands of the Shin Bet, but he kept within the boundaries of the revised order of the minister of defence and did not refer to the transport used to get him to Israel, nor to the country from which he had been abducted.[15] If Feldman could get the court to accept that the confessions had been obtained under great psychological pressure, the prosecution's charges would be invalid. But Israeli courts allow evidence obtained by illegal means, provided the means do not affect its reliability. In the United States, by contrast, to deter law enforcement agencies from employing illegal tactics, the 'fruits of the poisoned tree theory' prohibits a court from using such evidence even if there is no reason to doubt its reliability.

Inevitably, the cloak of secrecy which had enveloped Vanunu's arrival back in Israel spread to his trial. The judicial system allows for a 'closed-doors' trial for security reasons, and a number of security-related trials, including espionage, have been so conducted. The only information to reach the public is a brief notification at the end of the trial that a person has been found guilty and the name of the offence.

On 30 August 1987 a police transit van, its windows blacked out, backed up to the rear entrance of the court building at the Jerusalem District Court complex in the downtown Russian compound. There, a specially erected sacking canopy shielded Vanunu as he was led into the building. Police sirens wailed to drown out any comments Vanunu might try to shout out to waiting journalists and television camera crews in a way similar to when he had held up his palm months earlier with his message, 'HIJACKEN IN ROME.' Vanunu also had to wear a helmet. This would be repeated each day Vanunu arrived at the courtroom. Inside the courthouse itself, where normally journalists and the public are free to wander around, security guards with Uzi machine guns kept them away from the specially partitioned courtroom on the ground floor. Cheap plywood panels, unpainted and unvarnished, had been inserted between the windows and window-bars in the first-floor courtroom – producing complaints from the judges about the intolerably stuffy atmosphere there.

'The state has a paranoia on security,' Avigdor Feldman remarked.[16] On the eve of the trial Feldman appealed to the court for it to be open. Given Vanunu's wish to raise the question of the morality of nuclear weaponry, and his argument that the public had a right to nuclear information, the openness of the trial was particularly important. The popular image Vanunu had acquired as a traitor and a spy had to be dispelled and his true motives understood.

But the court rejected Feldman's appeal, insisting that proceedings be held behind closed doors. Hopes were dashed that only that part of the trial which dealt specifically with Dimona and the abduction would be closed. Indeed, Feldman had argued that even the information about Vanunu's work at Dimona was no longer secret now that it had been published in detail in the *Sunday Times*. The same was true of the abduction story, which had also been followed by the newspaper. But the prosecution countered that there was additional information which witnesses – for instance, from Dimona and the security services – might raise in testimony, and Vanunu might have additional information which he had not yet divulged.

Not only would that section of the trial dealing with Vanunu's work at Dimona and his abduction be closed, as would the testimony of the prosecution witnesses, but so would the testimony of defence witnesses, including experts from abroad whose evidence was mainly philosophical and based on information already known. The prosecution did not oppose the principle of the testimony of defence witnesses being open to the public but, if it were, they and the security services would demand that Vanunu be removed from the courtroom. Vanunu agreed to this so that nuclear debate in the court could be public, but the judges decided that it was more important for Vanunu to be present at his trial than that it should be open to the public. Also rejected was the possibility of defence testimony being fed to journalists in an adjoining room because there might be an outburst from Vanunu. There were two other possibilities: one was for Vanunu to sit in a special soundproof booth (as had been used in trials in Germany of members of the Baader-Meinhof group) with directional glass to enable him to see the courtroom but not for anybody in the courtroom to see Vanunu, lest there be a repetition of the palm incident. The other possibility was for each day's proceedings to be published after vetting by military censors, which was agreed.

Defence and prosecution lawyers met at the end of each day to agree on what could be released, but in practice the system was ineffective. For example, after the prosecution allowed the testimony of one foreign expert, Professor George Quester, in its entirety, much of it was blue-pencilled by the military censor.[17] And when Feldman wanted to release some of Mordechai Vanunu's description of his background – his childhood, studies, army service and political views – the judges objected, saying that its publication might imply that the judges were sympathetic to his testimony. The only sentence permitted from testimony lasting two days was 'I did this from ideological motives.'[18] By taking a maximalist rather than minimalist view of security concerns, the judges in effect encroached upon the democratic principle of open trials.

The credibility of the trial and its verdict were not enhanced by the judges' decision that the trial should be held behind closed doors. Implicit in the judges' designation of the information as secret, and in the decision that the trial would be behind closed doors, was an indication of what their verdict would be. The presiding judge, Eliahu Noam, was known as an arch-conservative, inclined to fully rely on the thinking of the defence establishment. But according to one witness, Dr Frank Barnaby, the scientist who had debriefed Vanunu on behalf of the *Sunday Times*, 'the judges made no effort to cut short the testimony. They allowed, as far as I could see, the defence as much time as was needed to make the case and they listened with interest. Genuine interest, I think.'[19]

30 AUGUST 1987

' "Ultra secret", "the most supreme defence considerations" – these are the most superlative words possible in Hebrew to describe Vanunu's action,' said Uzi Hasson, opening the prosecution in The State of Israel v. M. Vanunu. Through protocols of the conversations between Vanunu and security agents who arrested him, Hasson learnt from interviews given by Feldman in the Hebrew press on the eve of the trial that the defence planned to argue that Vanunu had no intent to endanger national security, but to inform the public. Hasson told the court:

[T]he facts of his action are the determinants, not the question of criminal intent. But if you want to discuss intents then we are talking about somebody desiring public attention, desiring money. The defence plans to turn the trial on its head by placing the state on trial instead of Vanunu, and to claim that Israel has produced nuclear weapons and broken international conventions, but I hope to persuade the court that the prosecution remains the prosecutor and the guilty the guilty.[20]

In constructing his case that Vanunu had acted 'with intent to help the enemy', Hasson was at a handicap since there was not a scrap of evidence of contact – or intent to contact – the enemy. Hasson's strategy was to distance the court as far as possible from Vanunu's claimed ideological motives because not to do this would have risked undermining the charge of intent to help the enemy. Another byproduct of the ideological gap being raised would be acknowledgement of Israeli possession of the Bomb. Instead, Hasson related the 'intent to help the enemy' to a desire by Vanunu to take revenge on the Israeli social system which had discriminated against the Moroccan-born Sephardi.

'In personality terms', Hasson told the court,

Vanunu was an introverted person, egocentric, a loner, of a composite and complex mental makeup, who concluded that he hadn't found his place in Israeli society and in this country. His life search in general, and in particular in Israeli society, led him more and more to the Left, coming near in outlook to the Arabs.

According to Hasson,

[T]he more Vanunu's inclinations grew in these directions, the more hostile he became towards the nuclear research centre. This feeling grew in the 1982 Lebanon War and after it, and hardened when he was scheduled for dismissal. The cancellation of the dismissal notice did not change his feelings; indeed, insulted, he decided to hand in his notice. He resigned because, according to him, his superiors wanted to be rid of him. The interruption of work, and the insults beforehand (which originated in the conversations and warnings from security personnel following the discovery of his left-wing tendencies) strengthened his decision – reached at the beginning of 1986 – to cut himself off from Israel and begin a new life abroad, and aroused a desire to take revenge against all those who had caused him that pain.[21]

This may also have been the reason, Hasson said, for changing his religion. He continued,

Vanunu is an intelligent person, who in spite of his social background made majestic efforts to advance and to achieve a more respectable position than his parents and family had. Regrettably, he could not do so; nor did he raise a family. His routine work, without hope and perhaps even opportunity of advancement in it, brought him to the conclusion that he had not achieved anything in his life.

'And from this', Hasson argued, 'came his desire for self-publicity, to do something significant which would take him out of anonymity and prove his uniqueness. The possibility of monetary, or other, benefit (required for starting a new life) was among the reasons' for his action, even though Hasson admitted, there was no direct proof that Vanunu managed to receive any significant payment from the *Sunday Times*. Partly in the hope of thereby thwarting Feldman's subpoena that the confessions had been wrongly obtained and should therefore not be accepted, Hasson called as witnesses the four persons to whom Vanunu had given confessions in order to show that the confessions were not made under duress. The senior police officer concerned was deputy commissioner Shimon Savir, who headed the criminal investigation department of the Israeli police. The first of three Shin Bet agents was Yehuda X, deputy head of the Shin Bet investigations division. Prior to joining the Shin Bet he had filled a series of senior police positions, including commanding one of the country's regions and heading the force's Bureau of Special Tasks. Yehuda's involvement in the Vanunu case went back to when Vanunu was still abroad.[22] The second agent, Alon X, had been involved in the kidnapping. A Shin Bet veteran, he had headed one of the agency's departments for nine years. The third agent, '195', had held Vanunu and transported him to prison.

The first witness, deputy commissioner Savir, who had served the arrest warrant on Vanunu after he had been kidnapped back to Israel, described his conversation with Vanunu, which had been held in the presence of agent Alon X. Savir related how when Alon X said that Vanunu had told Savir that Vanunu had given the newspaper the photos for money, Vanunu[23] interrupted, saying 'No payment had been made.' Yet there was also discussion of a book contract.

Prosecutor Hasson turned to Savir: 'As a veteran police investigator how would you describe Vanunu's mental state, compared to that of other prisoners?'

> *Savir:* I've had hundreds of similar cases, defence and criminal. In some instances when a person is caught carrying out a crime, when you sit with them there is a certain amount of tension.
>
> *Hasson:* How would you describe his alertness and sense of orientation?
>
> *Savir:* He understood every word. Not only did I read what I wrote but he read it himself and only afterwards did he sign. He also requested a lawyer.[24]

Feldman countered that the court should seek the opinion of a psychiatrist regarding Vanunu's mental state. Two psychiatrists – for the defence and prosecution – later testified for a total of three hours. The defence psychiatrist claimed Vanunu had signed the confession under duress, whereas the prosecution's psychiatrist said there was no connection between Vanunu's mental state and his signature.

The first Shin Bet witness to testify was agent Yehuda X, who had accompanied Vanunu 'as he was brought ashore on a military stretcher somewhere along the coast of the Mediterranean Sea. I was also present at the jail when the confessions were written down', Yehuda told the prosecution. 'It was not somebody who was in a state of terror that he was about to die. There was no indication in his behaviour that he was terrified.'[25]

Encouraged by the prosecution to testify concerning what Vanunu had told him, Yehuda X painted a negative picture of the accused. 'Vanunu said he wanted to expose the real mask of Israel,' he said. Yehuda said that he had asked Vanunu 'why if he thought what was being done at Dimona was crazy he did not turn to official Israeli channels.' According to Yehuda X, Vanunu said 'I am not certain that the authorities themselves are not crazy. Also, if I told somebody I am not sure that they would not jump on me.'[26] Yehuda X added that en route from 'somewhere on the Israeli coast' to the jail, Vanunu described 'the agreement between him and the *Sunday Times* – which in the end was not signed – for 100,000 sterling or 100,000 dollars'.[27]

The question of the kidnapping led Feldman to related aspects of the affair. The authorities had known for sometime that Vanunu was in touch with the media. And yet they had not stopped him. Perhaps, Feldman suggested, the Israeli authorities had an interest in the information about Vanunu's work at the reactor being published.

Feldman said, 'I want to persuade the court that the state's behaviour both regarding the *Sunday Times* publication and in bringing him home did not point to great concern that publication would damage security. I will prove this.' Feldman continued:

> The Israeli embassy in London knew about the matter in time to stop publication. The Israeli authorities knew about Vanunu about a month beforehand. The time it took for the state to react does not suggest a state facing an imminent danger. We claim that even if there was no intention at the outset for Israel to publicise information about its nuclear programme, the government had an interest in Vanunu disclosing that Israel possessed 200 nuclear warheads.[28]

The testimony of the next Shin Bet agent, Alon X, who had been in overall charge of the operation to bring Vanunu to arrest, offered the prosecution a further opportunity to show that the confessions were legally obtained. Vanunu understood that the information he gave Alon was given in the context of a 'formal investigation and that he had a right not to say anything'. Furthermore, 'Vanunu was very calm, and alert, and took an interest in everything happening ... He took care in how he worded his answers.' Asked by Hasson whether Vanunu spoke from fear of death, Alon replied that he did not see any 'fear. Nor did Vanunu say he was afraid.'[29]

Indeed, Alon X had developed an unusually close relationship with Vanunu for an interrogator: Vanunu told Alon that 'he was 100 per cent.' However, it became clear from Alon X's testimony that Vanunu had not been allowed to meet a lawyer initially; his first meeting with Amnon Zichroni, Feldman's predecessor as Vanunu's defence counsel, was on 20 October, two weeks after Vanunu was arrested.

Alon X also testified concerning the various pieces of evidence which the prosecution had shown the court, including the *Sunday Times* article, photographs which Vanunu had taken inside the reactor and later given to the newspaper, as well as Vanunu's special pass to Machon 2 at the reactor. It was important to Hasson to reassure the court that the information disclosed in the *Sunday Times* article had come from Vanunu. Showing the photographs Vanunu had taken inside the reactor was also a further means for Hasson to bring out the terrible damage to national security which Vanunu was accused of causing. At one point, when Hasson produced in court a copy of the *Sunday Times* article, reprinted on a separate sheet of paper, defence lawyer Feldman interjected and demanded that a witness be brought to confirm that what appeared in the reprint had first appeared in the newspaper.

Feldman's cross-examination of Alon X provided Feldman with fertile ground to weaken the prosecution case. His tack was the veracity of the confessions obtained. The fact that Alon X prepared the confession only at the end of each day – because 'the dynamics of the relationship between the one being interrogated and the interrogator would be interrupted if I had to also take copious notes' – raised for Feldman the question of the accuracy of the indictment. That Alon X was unable to produce the notes from which he had prepared the final confession only strengthened Feldman's doubts.[30]

Feldman said that 'Alon [X], as the principal investigator, did not gather all the information contained in the confession – which later formed the basis of the indictment sheet – only from Vanunu himself but also from other sources.' Moreover, the very behaviour of the state authorities proved that they weren't in practice so concerned about Vanunu's information being published. While the government did not have a master plan when Vanunu was still working in Dimona, to the effect that one day he would leave and publish the story of the Bomb and thus meet the state authorities' aim of projecting Israel's nuclear posture, the manner in which the state authorities acted – or did not act – after they heard about Vanunu's contacts indicated a certain ambivalence on the part of the government towards the forthcoming publicity.[31] 'At the end of the day', Feldman said, turning towards the judges,

> the court will have to determine: (1) Was the security of the state damaged? (2) Did Vanunu intend to damage state security? And (3) What were the natural consequences of Vanunu's action? We will show that there was no necessary, causal connection between damage to state security and publication. Had the damage been so immediate, the state authorities would have acted in a completely different manner.[32]

This was presumed to be a reference to the Mossad's reputation for undercover operations of one type or another. Feldman went on:

> There is a thesis of which I want to persuade the court, that the state in fact speaks with two voices. Here in the courtroom we suspect that publication was very damaging, but in practice the state, knowing that something is about to be published, says to itself that it's not so bad, it won't help the enemy so much. In short, there is a policy that from time to time things are thrown to the press. I want to persuade the court that Vanunu did not help an enemy in time of war.[33]
>
> [...]
>
> *Feldman*: I won't ask anything further about the file. I will ask if he [Alon X] knew what was in the file. Later, I might ask about one or two quotes from it, such as his quotes that Vanunu went with Arabs, that the nuclear research centre said, 'We need to fire him.' Will he [Alon X] confirm that he learnt of this from [Vanunu's] personal file, not from the defendant himself?[34]
>
> [...]
>
> *Feldman*: Your main source for Vanunu's personal details was the personal file.
> *Alon X*: Yes.[35]

Feldman moved back towards his main goal of proving that Vanunu's motivation was ideological and that he had no intent to damage state security.

While the law was interested in the results and not the motives of an action, Feldman argued that Section 99 of the Penal Code alluded to a special intent. The law read: 'A person with intent to assist an enemy ...'. A person who did not have this special intent could not be charged, Feldman postulated. This would also enable Vanunu and his defence lawyer to raise such questions as the right to know and the obligation to speak out. It was the very opposite of what the prosecution wanted: to acknowledge that Vanunu's motives were ideological would imply the existence of the Bomb. Feldman's first step would be to weaken the prosecution's claim that Vanunu's motive was money (which itself was no more assisting the enemy than was disclosing the secrets to meet the public's right to know).

> *Feldman to Alon X:* You told Vanunu that you believed that he did not do it for money?
>
> *Alon X:* I told him this.
>
> *Feldman:* And you believed it?
>
> *Alon X:* I told him that as part of building up credibility and a relationship.
>
> *Feldman:* The question is, do you believe it?
>
> *Alon X:* The matter is complex. I have no doubt that also involved were philosophical factors and proximity to the Left, Arab–Jewish relations, and what Vanunu coined 'the crazy government'. Also involved was the financial factor, to what extent I cannot tell. If you will allow me, I will explain the basis for the claim about money. It was after Guerrero promised him a lot of money that he developed the pictures.[36]
>
> *Feldman:* This is just your interpretation.
>
> *Alon X:* This is not an interpretation. These are facts. I heard it from his own lips.
>
> *Feldman:* This is your interpretation of the facts.
>
> *Alon X:* You asked me. So I explained why I thought so.[37]
>
> *Feldman:* Do you believe that the ideological motive was there originally, or was the ideological element added on only retrospectively?
>
> *Alon X:* I think there was a philosophical dimension to his action. I wouldn't give a weighting to the ideological as opposed to financial factors.
>
> *Feldman:* The nuclear subject did not come up at all?
>
> *Alon X:* On the one hand, ideology, ideas, thoughts, philosophy of life. On the other hand, his work, which according to him involved building nuclear weapons. His view of 'crazy people' in the government, with many nuclear bombs – obligating the world to know.[38]
>
> *Feldman:* That the world should know.
>
> *Alon X:* That the world should know.[39]
>
> *Judge Brenner:* If we assume that he did it just for money, I don't see the legal distinction – but perhaps one exists. The law on assisting an enemy has nothing to say on whether the intention was to receive money or whether it was part of another plan ... . The problem is that it is necessary to prove that here there was

an intent to assist an enemy in war, and now all this is a matter of motives. Honourable counsel [Feldman] is raising a lot of questions about motives.[40]

The judge's intervention gave Feldman his cue to return again to the question of the very essence of intention. The law's stating 'intent to assist an enemy' rather than merely 'assistance to an enemy' implied, Feldman reasoned, a special type of intent – which was clearly absent here. But Brenner retorted that 'there was no difference in whether the motives were money, ideological, personal'.[41]

So ended the first day of The State of Israel v. M. Vanunu.

31 AUGUST 1987

With the testimony concerning the kidnap by the Shin Bet agents complete and the court shown how the confessions had been taken, the next stage in the prosecution's case was to prove the damage to state security which Vanunu's story had caused. Hasson called as a witness 'Giora', a nuclear chemical engineer who had worked at the Dimona reactor since its early days in 1959 and who in his own words 'knew everything that occurred in Dimona'.[42] As recounted earlier, 'Giora' had been brought in by the Shin Bet to interrogate Vanunu about the technical aspects of the latter's action – something which was well beyond the competence of the Shin Bet agents. In the words of 'Giora', 'my goal was to know what exactly Vanunu had passed on, in what detail, and to whom he had passed it – something which frightened us.'

Wanting to prove that reactor employees like Vanunu would have known of the need to respect silence about their work, Hasson first questioned 'Giora' about security arrangements at the reactor. 'Can a camera be brought in?', asked Hasson. 'Certainly not', replied 'Giora'. 'There is a sign warning that it is forbidden to bring in a camera and certain other things.' The testimony of 'Giora' showed that security measures included entry controls at the site.[43]

'Giora' quickly established his expertise. He had seen the *Sunday Times* article, the photographs which Vanunu had taken inside the reactors and passed to the newspaper, and Vanunu's own notes of the court processes. Hasson took 'Giora' through his paces, getting him to explain to the court what appeared in the photos, and to confirm that what appeared in the photos were sections and objects inside Dimona. 'If somebody that specialises in nuclear matters looks at the photos and receives an explanation is he able to understand something?', Hasson asked. 'Certainly', 'Giora' replied.[44]

Taking his case one step further, Hasson sought to show the damage which Vanunu's disclosure had caused to the nuclear ambiguity posture, and to Israel's foreign relations in general. 'From time to time', Hasson began 'speculation appears in the press and books about Israel's nuclear potential. As a Dimona man what is wrong with what is published?' 'Giora' replied that 'it can result in heavy pressure on Dimona and on the State of Israel. Even details which are not correct can cause damage.' Hasson continued: 'What is wrong if Israel confirms or denies its nuclear potential?'

> *Judge Brenner:* I am surprised at your question – This is a question for a nuclear engineer?!
>
> *Hasson:* This is a question to a chemical engineer who is part of the defence establishment.
>
> *Brenner:* This is a political matter.

Hasson rephrased his question in other terms: 'The State of Israel has a stance of neither confirming nor denying that she possesses a nuclear capability. As somebody from the defence establishment, what's bad about confirming or denying?'[45] In not calling technocrats from the defence and foreign ministries to testify, Hasson failed to show to maximum effect the damage allegedly caused to Israeli foreign and diplomatic relations by the Vanunu exposé.[46]

The next witness, the super-secretive head of security at the ministry of defence (identified by the media as Yehiel Horev, but identified in court protocols only as 'the witness'), was, like 'Giora', called by the prosecution to prove the damage caused to state security but was only marginally more qualified to assess that damage. In the hope of persuading the court of the reliability of his testimony concerning the damage, Hasson first got 'the witness' to describe his wide areas of responsibility for securing the reactor and to give information about its work. Then Hasson asked 'the witness' about the photographs which had been submitted separately by the *Sunday Times* and the *Sunday Mirror* to the Israeli embassy in London for its reaction – thereby proving that the photographs shown in court were the actual ones received by the two newspapers from Vanunu.[47]

The reluctance of 'the witness' to speak – drawing on his experience as the protector of the defence community's secrets – helped the defence because had he been more forthcoming it would have helped to prove the damage to state security more decisively.

Beginning his cross-examination of 'the witness', Feldman returned to his strategy of trying to show that Vanunu had been allowed to leak information in order to project the nuclear posture. 'What were the physical security arrangements? Dimona was not as secret as some try to make out,' Feldman charged. 'An internal committee of inquiry was established which found that the security system collapsed. Conclusions were drawn,' 'the witness' countered. 'If you are trying to hint at an intentional leak, it was rather the collapse of the security system.'

If it was a real security leak, Feldman's next tack was to reduce the actual amount of damage allegedly done to state security.

Feldman: You spoke about the bombs at the reactor ... I think it was well-known information that the heart of the reactor is not where the defendant, Mordechai Vanunu, worked.

Hasson: The minister of defence's order does not allow discussion of the physical structure of the reactor.

Feldman: I will rephrase my question. Is there a way to shut down the entire functioning of the reactor, other than via the place mentioned in the *Sunday Times* story [the plutonium-processing facility at Machon 2 where Vanunu worked]?[48]

'The witness': There is no simple answer. It depends on whether you have pre-warning in time, and on the situation inside the reactor.

Feldman: Can you confirm that in Dimona that there is – as open sources confirm – a nuclear reactor, something the whole world knows, without referring to whether they are producing something?

'The witness': I said so.[49]

In attempting to disprove the charge that Vanunu had damaged state security, Feldman moved his questioning to the subject of Israel's bilateral relations. Feldman began by raising the subject of Norway and its demands for return of the heavy water it had supplied for the Dimona reactor.

Feldman: Norway! – do you know about this from press reports, or directly?

'The witness': Directly.

Feldman: What does Norway claim? Why does it want the heavy water returned?[50]

'The witness' attempting not to disclose the ambiguity posture – notwithstanding that the testimony was being given behind closed doors – shrouded his answers in the same ambiguity which has characterised Israeli nuclear policy:

'The witness': I will answer you by referring to what has appeared in the press.

Feldman: Tell me what you know, not what has appeared in the press. I too can read the press.[51]

For Feldman it was unacceptable to prove that state security had been damaged by simply referring to press reports, which anyway were not always accurate.

'The witness': According to publications [Norway] feels that it was a partner in the creation of Israel's nuclear potential because it supplied heavy water, believing it was only for peaceful purposes.

Feldman: Do you know this from seeing a letter from the Norwegian government, or was it brought to your attention?

Hasson: This is irrelevant.

Feldman: Irrelevant! You want to say that damage was done to state security. Then this is not relevant? He said that damage was done to state security. I want to know how he knows.[52]

Norway was not the only country to which the damage caused by Vanunu's exposé to state security could allegedly be traced:

Feldman: Do you have access to intelligence material about what is really happening in Arab countries? What was the influence of the Vanunu exposé there? How did they relate to it? What did they think about it? Did it cause them pangs of trembling, as a result of which they decided to do something?

'The witness': This is in the framework of general evaluations. I have no hard intelligence data which says that as a result of Vanunu there were more practical steps.

Feldman: As a result of the publication of Vanunu's exposé was there more pressure on Israel to join the Nuclear Proliferation Treaty.

'The witness': One senses more pressure to join. Is there a direct connection with the Vanunu exposé? ... Our evaluation is that there is some connection. The Vanunu affair accelerated matters in a general sense. The greatest pressure came from another direction – from the USA.[53]

Feldman: Had 'the witness' read the *Sunday Times*'s exposé? Had he broken it down as between what was new in the exposé, and what had been previously published? There was a clear need to identify precisely what new classified information had been exposed by publication.

'The witness': I read the article when it came out. We did a breakdown of the article according to headings, and sorted out what information had already been published elsewhere and what had not.

Feldman: Do you have the breakdown? I want the witness to bring it.

Presiding Judge Noam to 'the witness': Do you have written material like this?

'The witness': Much time has passed and I don't remember all the activity. I remember how we sat down and read it. I don't remember if somebody recorded and made comparisons, but we made an evaluation of the dangers. An examination of what was new and what had been previously published was made within the Atomic Energy Commission. I will look for the document and bring it.

Hasson: The minister of defence's order requires that only I see it.

'The witness': Only you, the prosecutor.[54]

Feldman's next tack was to turn ambiguity on its head: 'Since Israel claims not to have nuclear weapons, you cannot charge somebody with revealing what the state does not possess because by implication it does not exist.'[55]

Judge Tal corrected Feldman: ' "The witness" did not say we have no Bomb. He said that the position is that Israel will not be the first to introduce nuclear weapons into the Middle East.'

Feldman corrected himself: 'On the assumption we won't be the first to introduce nuclear weapons into the region, since no state in the Middle East has nuclear weapons it follows that Israel also does not have nuclear weapons ... This will be one of the central defence arguments.'

Feldman was exhaustive in tackling the concept of state security from all possible directions. Are not most states, Feldman asked, in favour of international reporting of those states possessing nuclear weaponry? Presiding Judge Noam interjected: 'This is not relevant.' Yet Feldman continued: 'Most states regard unsupervised nuclear weapons as illegal. Vanunu's action was not illegal: he had an obligation to speak out.' But this was too much for the presiding judge. 'Finished [with this point],' Noam interrupted.[56]

1 SEPTEMBER

The classified document which identified which items of information in the *Sunday Times* article were new in the public domain and which were not, and the question of whether the defence lawyer would have access to it, opened a Pandora's Box of how a person could be charged with crimes specific knowledge of which was withheld from his own defence counsel. How could somebody be charged if the information or part of it was already known? Hasson appeared to want to overcome the dilemma posed by the minister of defence's gagging order by instead bringing to court the author of the document, not 'the witness' himself. 'If Feldman wants to question him about the document he can do so, but I won't show him the actual document,' Hasson said.

Feldman: Make a selection from the article of what is permitted and what is not.
Hasson: It's impossible to make a selection.
Presiding Judge Noam: If it's classified information then there is nothing to be done.

Feldman interjected that Judge Bach had lifted part of the minister of defence's gagging order; and information not previously known could be permitted to the defence if it came within those categories allowed for under Judge Bach's ruling. 'I don't understand why you cannot remove from the classified folder such information published for the first time by the *Sunday Times* as was freed by the Bach ruling, and on the basis of this I will question the witness.'[57]

Hasson's antics were too much for Judge Brenner. Brenner was exasperated by the strict interpretation which Hasson was making concerning what the court could see. 'In what way does it help?', Brenner asked, going on to remark:

We are still left hanging in the air even with the information which [counsel for the defence] is allowed to see. We don't know the defendant revealed information of a most general nature. Relative weighting of information we certainly cannot know about. Precise data concerning the information we cannot know about. Yardsticks for comparison we won't have.[58]

It was not atypical of Brenner's neutral approach. Appointed to the bench at the age of 46, Brenner was not regarded as one who automatically accepted the establishment's view, and in a stream of judgements over the years had gone against the state prosecutors. Coming from a poor background in the mixed city of Haifa, he had counted Arabs among his friends while a youth. He paid for his law studies at the Hebrew University by working part-time as a librarian in the Law faculty library. Notwithstanding his open mind, for example, towards Palestinian-related judgements, in defence-related matters he remained inclined towards the security establishment's perspective.

> *Feldman:* I want to see the information itself, so that I can question the witness.
> *Presiding Judge Noam:* But Hasson cannot show it to you.
> *Feldman:* ... such information as I am able to see.
> *Judge Tal:* If there are minimal paragraphs which the defence can see, perhaps they could be copied onto a separate sheet.

At that point the court decided to leave the two lawyers themselves to work out a mutually acceptable manner in which Feldman could see selections from the report.

The next witness was the official who had been head of security inside the reactor, identified only as 'C', and who was moved from his post immediately following the *Sunday Times*'s disclosure. He was called as a witness by the prosecution in order to tell the court that Vanunu had been periodically warned about his obligation of secrecy, and had signed a declaration to this effect. Hasson was able to show the court that the reactor authorities had taken reasonable precautions and that Vanunu knew that he was breaking the law by divulging the information.

In his cross-examination of 'C', Feldman sought to disprove the picture created by Hasson that Vanunu divulged the information out of bitterness towards the system. 'Do you agree that Vanunu did not show signs of bitterness that his work was being terminated?'[59] (Vanunu had been made redundant with other workers in an economic cutback, which offered the reactor authorities a way to free themselves of Vanunu after he declined to be moved from Machon 2 to a less sensitive part of the reactor.) But 'C' was only partly helpful. He told the court that 'at a certain point Vanunu told security staff at the reactor that there was also a feeling of bitterness, among other things.'[60]

> *Feldman:* Yes, but your feeling is that he left of his own volition, that he wanted to leave.
> *'C':* It was agreed; he undertook to leave, so he left. On his last day we had a meeting at which he said that we could carry the responsibility for the fact that he had decided to leave.[61]

Feldman was little more successful when he sought to place the blame on the reactor authorities for Vanunu being given access to classified information that he did not need – and which he subsequently divulged to the newspaper. Perhaps the reactor authorities bore partial responsibility for the disclosure in not limiting access to sensitive sections of the reactor complex only to those workers who had access.

> *Feldman:* Do you know whether Vanunu knew only about the particular branch of work he was engaged on?
>
> *'C':* I don't examine the heart of a worker. It's difficult to come here and say that a worker only knows about his own area. We don't widen access except on a need-to-know basis. But I don't rule his head or his heart.[62]

The comments of 'C' ignored the way in which Vanunu was able to move freely about the reactor site and snap 57 photographs which would prove to be a deciding factor in the *Sunday Times* going ahead and investigating Vanunu's story.

So ended the testimony of the witnesses for the prosecution. The testimonies of the head of security at the defence ministry, of 'C', and before them that of 'Giora', were so sensitive that not a word about the three witnesses or their testimony reached the outside world. A total blanket of secrecy was imposed. It contrasted with the earlier section of the prosecution testimony when the sole fact that Shin Bet agents had given testimony had become known. Journalists speculated about the blanket silence. Was the court angry with the few crumbs which had come out about the Shin Bet testimony? 'No', was the reply. 'If so, what happened, Mr Feldman?', shouted one reporter. Uncharacteristically, Feldman kept his lips sealed. 'I am forbidden to say anything.' 'How many witnesses testified?', a reporter threw back. 'I can't say,' said Feldman. 'Did Vanunu testify?', another shouted. 'I can only say that the discussions were held behind closed doors from A to Z. This includes the closed doors.'[63] Prosecution lawyer Hasson was even less forthcoming; he simply hurried away in the direction of his nearby office at the state prosecutor's Jerusalem division.

9
Press Disclosure = Espionage + Treason

'The judges should dismiss the case,' lawyer Avigdor Feldman told the court as he opened the defence. Vanunu had neither damaged state security nor had he had any intent to do so. Therefore, Feldman said, there was no case to answer. Moreover, according to the statute book the responsibility for proving intent fell on the prosecution, not the defence. The prosecution had failed to bring any proof of Vanunu's intent. Vanunu's intent was the reverse of what the prosecution claimed – it was to enable the public to know.

But the prosecuting lawyer, Uzi Hasson, countered that it was impossible to enter a person's heart to determine his intention: intent came from the act in itself.[1] The very fact that Vanunu disclosed highly secret information placed the onus of proving Vanunu's intent on the defence. Judge Shalom Brenner challenged him: 'If you say that Vanunu intended to pass secret information to an enemy, then why did he not go to the enemy? Why did he require an intermediary, the *Sunday Times*?' Hasson replied somewhat lamely, 'It is not possible to know the unequivocal reason for this.'[2]

2 DECEMBER

The defence called as witnesses individuals who had worked on the *Sunday Times* story: journalist Peter Hounam, and scientist Dr Frank Barnaby; individuals familiar with Israeli policy who could assess the questions of the damage done by the exposé to state security, and of parliamentary supervision of nuclear policy: Israeli politicians Shimon Peres and Abba Eban; and US academic Professor George Quester.

But the defence's first witness was Mordechai Vanunu. He had long awaited an opportunity to explain – albeit behind closed doors – his motives for speaking out. It was an opportunity for his lawyer to place a question mark over the validity of Vanunu's confession by claiming it was taken by his interrogators under duress. 'You are kidnapped,' Vanunu began. 'They can get rid of you. They are able to take you to another place. Anything is possible. In a kidnapping something can go wrong and end in death. In other words, even if they did not intend to kill you ... or even if it's unclear whether they started shooting at you,

you're in a situation where in the first and second minutes, you don't know what is happening ... [you think,] if I come out of this alive it is not important to them; so I prepared myself for the fact that my life was not worth much to them.'[3]

Afterwards, Vanunu's testimony turned towards his biography. He described to the court different stages of his life – from early childhood in Morocco, to the difficult years for his parents as immigrants, to his national service in the army, to his university studies, to his being accepted for work at Dimona. He moved on to his philosophical outlook: he was drawn to Sartre and existentialism. 'God is dead,' Vanunu said 'and it is for man to make decisions, to find for himself a purpose and goals in life. What you do is what you think is the right thing.' This would give a clue to his act of revealing the country's nuclear secrets. He went on to describe how he was drawn to human rights causes. While in the student union at university he saw at first hand discrimination against Arab students in getting work, scholarships, and access to student dormitory accommodation on campus. 'I claim that equality in rights should be enjoyed by everybody – it is not necessary to discriminate because they are Arabs,' he told the court. 'I began to meet them and speak with them.'[4]

Wishing to prove that Vanunu did not consider the danger to state security, nor was even concerned about it, Hasson asked Vanunu: 'Did it ever occur to you [to ask] who knows and who doesn't know?'

> *Vanunu:* No ... The Israeli government is producing [its nuclear capability] and not saying anything ... tricking [people] ... I did not know who knows and who doesn't.[5] Everything that I did was to confirm what was already known.[6]
>
> *Judge Brenner:* Did you take into account that publication could endanger the security of the state?
>
> *Vanunu:* I thought about it and I was sure that it would not endanger state security.
>
> *Hasson:* I want to understand. You say, 'I am a good citizen.' If so, don't you think you have to think twice before you do something that perhaps will damage the state?[7]
>
> *Vanunu:* Yes.
>
> *Judge Brenner:* I want to focus on the question. Did the possibility that your action was likely to cause damage to state security cross your mind?
>
> *Vanunu:* Certainly. I am not able to ignore things which come up.
>
> *Judge Brenner:* Did it come up in any way?
>
> *Vanunu:* In any way ... perhaps in a small way. My action could damage the policy of the government.[8]

Though he described his innermost feelings, Vanunu was careful not to mention even once the circumstances of the kidnapping or the country from which he had disappeared.[9] The day was almost a disappointment. 'I know you are expecting to hear about the drama of Vanunu's testimony', Feldman remarked to waiting reporters afterwards, 'but there wasn't any'.[10]

6 DECEMBER

Vanunu's testimony was followed by that of Dr Frank Barnaby, the nuclear scientist who had debriefed Vanunu for the *Sunday Times*. During three hours of testimony Barnaby described how he had met Vanunu. While Barnaby said there was nothing new in the revelations,[11] he told the court that part of the value of the *Sunday Times*'s exposé lay in the fact that the information came from somebody on the 'inside'. The photos which Vanunu had taken inside the reactor had persuaded him.[12] In effect, Barnaby weakened Feldman's case that there was nothing new in the revelations to warrant Vanunu's being charged under Section 113 of the Penal Code with passing on 'secret' information. The weakness in Feldman's argument was that there was no real knowledge about Israel's nuclear capability – there were assumptions and evaluations. Vanunu's actions, Barnaby added, had helped the cause of non-proliferation.[13, 14]

7 DECEMBER

The next witness called by the defence was Peter Hounam. As the member of the *Sunday Times* reporting team who had developed the closest contact with Vanunu, his testimony would throw light on Vanunu's ideological motives – ostensibly to save the region from the danger of nuclear weaponry – showing that he had no intent to damage state security. Hounam would help Feldman to build a picture of Vanunu's true goals in divulging the nuclear secrets. Feldman began by asking Hounam: 'You tried to find out why Vanunu was doing it, or why he was giving you this information?'[15]

> *Hounam:* The one thing that kept coming up over and over again in conversations in the office was his motives. I was asked my opinion on this. And I had to go back to Vanunu again on this because there was a view that it was all too good to true to be presented with all these photographs and this information about the inside of Dimona. Why was this guy doing it? There was a puzzle that a guy who had come from a fairly simple and humble background, who had worked as a junior technician, should suddenly get into his head that he should tell the world what was going on in Dimona. It did seem that he was going through a lot of thinking about his attitude to philosophy and things like this. Vanunu said it was quite wrong that Israel should have been continuing with secret production of atomic weapons quite beyond the needs of Israel for defensive purposes. What was of even more concern to him was the fact that scientists and the production people had gone on to make thermonuclear weapons including the neutron bomb and the hydrogen bomb.[16] He had a very strong feeling that the world

should know that this was going on. So I said to him, well, you are an Israeli, why do you think that? He then pointed out something I didn't know, that the programme was not only not known outside Israel but also that there was only a very small group of people within the Israeli government that ever knew what was going on inside Dimona. And he was genuinely worried that it was going to lead to some sort of nuclear war in the Middle East.[17]

Wishing to strengthen the ideological underpinning of Vanunu's action, Feldman turned to the question of whether Vanunu was owed money. The taint, emphasised in Israeli media reports at the time of the exposé itself, speculating about six-figure sums received by Vanunu, created an impression that he had damaged state security for financial benefit. Given his relationship with Vanunu, for Feldman, Hounam was well-placed to confirm that Vanunu had not received a penny from the newspaper.[18]

Hounam: It has been the policy of the paper under Andrew Neil's period as editor not to pay for information. Vanunu was telling us everything we wanted to know, and not placing any conditions on this. It was more than good enough. It was the ideal situation. As Oscar Guerrero [who had introduced the Sunday Times to Vanunu] had been to us as a journalist he would be quite rightly owed some sort of fee for what he had done. Guerrero was trying to get the Sunday Times to pay a huge sum of money for the story. In one meeting in a pub, while in Australia, Vanunu said to me, 'Look, forget about Guerrero, it's my decision to give this information. What about publishing all this information and the photographs for nothing?'[19]

Feldman's next strategy was to show that Vanunu had had to give the paper's reporters a large amount of classified information, not in order to damage state security but in order for the paper to prepare its story: 'Can you tell us at what stage the bulk of the information was disclosed to you?'[20]

Hounam: During the first two or three days I met Vanunu in Australia I had all the information I needed. First of all, obviously, I needed to be able to sort of paint a human-interest type of picture – an interesting picture of what it was like in Dimona. So I needed little physical details, like the layout of the complex. In particular I needed details of the building where the plutonium was made, Machon 2. So I wanted to get a fairly detailed picture of what it was like in this underground building. I therefore started to build up a diagram, which I asked him to sort of fill in details of. I needed to know in fairly minute detail the flow rates of chemicals and the type of chemicals that were being used in the production process, so that they could be checked technically – not so interesting from the point of the view of publication in the newspaper, except in one vital point, and that is that the quantities did indicate how much plutonium was being made and therefore how many weapons were being made. The same applied to lithium and tritium manufacture. I needed to know something about the security of the place, because people would want to know about that, to know how he had managed to get these photographs.[21]

Feldman then sought to show that Vanunu did not have any intent to damage state security.

Feldman: Did you think that publishing something which had nothing to do with the issue of nuclear weapons, only with the reactor, would damage the security of Israel?[22]

Hounam: Vanunu's view was that he felt if it was brought out in the open that it would be more likely that pressure would be put on Israel to cooperate with some sort of Middle East nuclear free zone and things like that.[23]

In order to knock down the impression which Feldman had tried to create, that there was nothing new in the information given out by Vanunu and which had been published elsewhere beforehand, Hasson, in cross-examining Hounam, sought to strengthen his case that new information had been given out. Hasson asked: 'You saw something new, and you saw proof?'[24]

Hounam initially supplied the prosecution with the goods:

Hounam: From the beginning I thought there was something new. Nobody had ever before walked out of Dimona with an account of what it was like inside. Nobody before had walked out of Dimona with a whole lot of photographs of what it was like inside, and nobody had ever been able to furnish the rest of the world with information on the quantity of weapons that were being produced and the number, the type of weapons that they were beginning to develop.[25]

Knowingly or unknowingly Hasson could play on the 'news value perspective' through which Hounam as a reporter saw matters, in order to prove that it was new security information, previously unpublished, which had been disclosed.

Hasson: You saw some interest in publishing something new.

Hounam: Yes, as long as you qualify that by saying what I saw as new, because what I saw as new would have been different from what a security man would think [of] as new.[26]

Hasson: Did Vanunu tell you anything concerning Dimona that you did not publish, or that was not published in the article on 5 October 1986?[27]

Hounam: There were a lot of technical details – that would have been of use to help anyone making the Bomb, that [were] just too boring to put in the story.[28]

Hasson moved from the question of whether Vanunu's information was new to dealing with the allegation that the information damaged Israel's bilateral political relations. 'Did he tell you anything', Hasson asked, 'about the political connections of Israel with other foreign countries concerning Dimona?'[29]

> *Hounam:* I asked him because I was extremely interested in whether there was a link between the Israeli operation at Dimona and South Africa. The only thing he told me, and I am not sure that we published it because I didn't think it was relevant [was] that he overheard people saying that they had been in South Africa. But he said he did not know whether they had been there on holiday or for some official purpose.[30]
>
> *Hasson:* That's South Africa. Did he speak about another foreign country?
>
> *Hounam:* No.[31]

Anxious to build up the picture that Vanunu well understood the seriousness of his action in speaking to the press, Hasson asked Hounam whether Vanunu ever discussed the question of his own safety, that he might be kidnapped by some Arab secret service, by the KGB or something like that.[32]

> *Hounam:* It may have come up, but he was more concerned with being kidnapped by [the] Mossad.[33]
>
> *Hasson:* But it came up.[34]
>
> *Hounam:* If it came up, it did not [make] an impression on me so that I would remember now, 15 months later. I was concerned about his safety, and vis-a-vis Israel finding out about it.[35]

As further proof that Vanunu was aware of the possibility of the damage to state security from the exposé, Hasson asked Hounam: 'Did you discuss what the result would be after the article was published?'[36]

> *Hounam:* If there was overwhelming proof that Israel was producing the Bomb, then pressure would come from Western countries, particularly America, on Israel to dispose of the Bomb – and that would facilitate the declaration of a nuclear free zone in the Middle East.[37]
>
> *Hasson:* What did you tell him? Did you tell him you were right? Did you tell him that he was not right? Or, didn't you comment at all?[38]

Hasson was disappointed because he did not get the answer he wanted. Hounam replied from the perspective of a newsman, not from that of a security officer: 'I think I would have allowed him to go along with the idea because it was in my interest to try and persuade him to tell the story.'[39]

Hasson: The question of whether Vanunu understood the damage caused could also be examined by asking whether the *Sunday Times* evaluated the damage the exposé would cause. You said that inside the *Sunday Times* there was hesitation, a moral hesitation to publish or not to publish because it would endanger Israel.[40]

Hounam: If the Israeli embassy had come back and sort of shared with us certain knowledge and agreed that the information was correct but had explained to us ... why it would be very damaging to Israel if it was published, we would then have been faced with a decision over whether or not to publish the article.[41]

[...]

Hounam: We are not sort of moralistic about it. It depends what you mean by the danger to the national security of Israel. It could mean two things, you see. You could be thinking of whether or not you were worried about the security of Dimona. It gives anybody a target for more information. And we obviously thought of that. And we also thought about the other side of it, which was the general policy effect on Israel's foreign policy.[42]

Hasson wanted to weaken the defence's case that Vanunu acted for the ideological motive of the public's right to know, and to show he acted rather for psychological or monetary reasons. He asked, 'Is it true that you got the impression that he wanted to detach himself from his religion, from his country, from his family, from his friends, from everything that was in the past?'[43]

But Hounam was a reticent witness. 'Although we talked about his attitude towards religion, my opinion was that at that stage he was not a committed Christian,' Hounam replied.[44]

Hasson: This was not the question. The question was whether your impression was that he thought that afterwards he wouldn't be able to come to his homeland again. So the natural impression would be that he wanted to detach himself from his country, from his people, from his past.[45]

Hounam was aghast at the question: 'That wouldn't make an impression like that on me. Because being British, becoming a Christian – sorry, becoming a Jew if you are a Christian – [it] wouldn't immediately come into mind that you were becoming less patriotic or less interested in one's country.'[46]

Hasson: I didn't say anything about patriotism. Don't mix it. But about revealing what is regarded here as a secret, and you, of course, knew that he wouldn't be able to come to Israel again. Right? It gives the impression he wanted to undo his ties with his country.[47]

Hounam: I do want to say that I think he saw it as a sacrifice. That it was something he had to do and that he recognised that he probably would be unable to come back to Israel again, but he genuinely believed that that's what he had to do.[48]

Hasson: And if he wanted to see his family.[49]

Hounam: According to the present policy of the government, of course, that's true. If the policy of the government were to change, no doubt there might be circumstances in which he would be allowed to return.[50]

Hasson: You talked about it?[51]

Hounam: We talked about it. It wasn't a very real proposition, let's put it that way.[52]

For Hasson, having proved that Vanunu understood the implication that he was carrying out a crime, this led again on to the question of financial returns to provide for his future. Like the prosecution's search for a psychological explanation for Vanunu's deed, the 'money factor' was also important – not only as a clue to explain the damage to state security – but also in order to avoid dealing with the ideological issue of Israel and the Bomb.

Hasson: You had concern about how it would be afterwards? It seems to me to be very immoral not to help him financially after you took his story?[53]

Hounam: You may consider it to be wrong but the fact is that that was the policy of the paper.[54]

When the cross-examination was over, Hounam went over to Vanunu – whom he had not seen since he had disappeared in London. 'I said, "Look after yourself and keep fighting" and he said "Thank you very much, Peter." It was a very emotional moment for both of us. Tears came into his eyes,' Hounam said. For Hounam the whole court experience was bizarre. 'Here in front of the Jerusalem District Court was the man (me) who had persuaded this alleged spy to become a traitor. The judges and lawyers were treating me with respect, almost deference, and yet in theory I could be in the dock alongside Vanunu.'[55]

The next witness was Mordechai Vanunu's brother, Albert. He had been approached by the Mossad some four weeks prior to publication of the *Sunday Times*'s exposé while the newspaper was preparing its story with Vanunu's help. For Feldman, the fact that four weeks had gone by until Vanunu was finally abducted suggested that there was not the danger to state security which the prosecution suggested; had he really posed a danger, the Israeli authorities would have acted sooner.

Feldman: I want you to testify about a specific incident in which people from the prime minister's office visited you. When was this?[56]

Albert Vanunu: 7 September 1986.

Feldman: Where was your brother at the time?

Albert Vanunu: In Australia.[57]

12 DECEMBER

In seeking to prove the degree of real damage to state security, Feldman continued his defence by calling top decision makers as witnesses. Feldman wanted to call the cream of Israel's political elite: Itzhak Shamir (who was prime minister at the time of the Vanunu affair), Shimon Peres (foreign minister), Itzhak Rabin (defence minister) and Abba Eban, chairman of the Knesset's defence and foreign affairs committee. Presiding Judge Noam opposed any of the politicians giving testimony; Judges Brenner and Tal agreed, but to two politicians only. They would be able to show what damage, if any, had been caused by the *Sunday Times* article. It would also be an opportunity to raise the question of the level of democratic control over nuclear policy making. This alluded to Feldman's next line of defence. It concerned Vanunu's aims in making his disclosures. His client had no 'intent to assist the enemy' (Section 99 of the Penal Code) or 'to impair the security of the state' (Section 113). His goal was to inform the Israeli public and the world community about the nuclear programme. Feldman quoted Section 94, found at the beginning of the Penal Code chapter on state security and official secrets:

> An act shall not be regarded as an offence under this chapter if it has been, or appears to have been, done in good faith with intent to bring about, by lawful means, a change in the structure of a state or the activities of any of its authorities or in the structure of a foreign state or activities of any of its authorities or in the structure or activities of an agency or organisation of states.

Through Vanunu's breach of the law the public would be informed of something previously hidden from them, and would then express opinions through the democratic process.

'There must be some sort of equilibrium: how can a citizen vote if he doesn't know? Is the Likud government for or against nuclear weapons?', Feldman asked.[58]

The sight of Israel's three top ministers giving testimony would have upgraded the trial from being simply a criminal trial of a person accused of divulging national secrets to one which placed the Israeli democratic process and nuclear arms policy under the scrutiny of the judicial lens.

In calling Eban, Feldman sought to 'expose the non-democratic process through which decisions were made; even key Knesset committees didn't know'.[59] Legislative control of nuclear policy did not exist except in theory, Feldman charged. Even the defence and foreign affairs committee, which itself met behind closed doors, did not discuss nuclear matters; that was left to a miniscule four-man special sub-committee of the main committee. The desire and practice was always that the sub-committee should be multi-party, i.e., having members both of the government and of the opposition, and this is the situation to this day.[60] 'Is it correct', Feldman began, 'that the system for legislative supervision of nuclear policy is different from that of other aspects of defence and foreign policy?'[61]

Eban – who had armed himself for his court appearance with a volume on the law concerning international treaties[62] – began: 'In practice the overall committee (the defence and foreign affairs committee) gives decentralised powers to a sub-committee. It is not the only committee to function like this ... I want to add that follow-up and supervision are continuous, thorough. I am not able to state the tens of hours in a year that I spend participating in such discussions. Parliamentary supervision exists in the most efficient way.'[63]

Judge Brenner: Perhaps your committee knows [about developments inside the Israeli Atomic Energy Commission] just from individual contacts its members have?

Eban: Knesset members know that we have inside the committee a network of forums dealing with all matters concerning military alerts, concerning deterrence, concerning the secret services, and, by parity of reasoning, Knesset members assume that the nuclear theme is also discussed.[64]

Judge Brenner: Have there not been demands in the Knesset to improve parliamentary supervision?

Eban: I don't see any lack of satisfaction in the Knesset or among the public about the amount of attention we pay to this. There is no public or parliamentary pressure for a definitive statement.[65]

Feldman: If so, your committee has full knowledge of what goes on?

Eban: Correct.

Feldman: Has the committee visited the reactor?

Eban: It has visited it – more than once.[66]

Feldman: As somebody who had filled senior positions in successive governments and parliaments, is it not correct that this is not a normal situation for democratic countries?

Hasson interjected. He was worried that the trial might degenerate into discussing the inadequacies of parliamentary supervision, and the question of whether Vanunu's step of informing the citizenry could be justified. 'If the defence's intention is to come up with demands to the Knesset as to why it functions in this or that way, I don't think it is the job of this court. The constitutional rule of the State of Israel is not on trial.'[67]

Presiding Judge Noam to Feldman: Do you want to give your reason [for this line of questioning] before the court decides?

Feldman: We claim that the level of parliamentary supervision is unsatisfactory. The witness was called to testify as to whether there is adequate or inadequate supervision. I don't see why I can't ask this question.[68]

Hasson: The witness was called here to answer the question whether there is, or is not, supervision. And the witness has said what he had to say.

Judge Brenner: The defence's question was on a matter of opinion. The defence is entitled to oblige witnesses to address questions of parliamentary supervision but not to give general opinions about democratic societies.[69]

Judge Tal: The defence thinks that it is important for Israel as a democratic country that nuclear research from the defence perspective should be discussed publicly, at least in the parliamentary framework. Does the witness have any view?[70]

Eban: If every citizen considered himself qualified to inform the public I don't think it would be possible for the defence infrastructure in Israel to exist.[71]

Eban failed to note that existing public and media discussion about nuclear matters is based on speculation and on what has already appeared in that same public/media arena – creating a vicious circle of evaluations. But Eban saw two problems in a public debate taking place: 'We are still surrounded by enemies, and this could produce pressure on policymakers to act in a manner in which they would not otherwise act. It's the pressure of the enemy rather than the journalist which is the central factor.' Eban avoided the question of 'exaggerated secrecy', by which critics characterise Israeli governmental policy. Yet in another sense Eban went to the heart of the dilemma, asking rhetorically: 'Given the nuclear secrecy, was Vanunu justified in acting in the way he did?' Eban replied: no. Later he added as a closing remark: 'There is much research and many seminars on the subject.'[72]

Eban was also asked about the specific incident of the Vanunu exposé. His answer shed light on how the Knesset's defence and foreign affairs committee had functioned during the Vanunu crisis. Feldman asked Eban if he had seen the *Sunday Times* article.

Eban: I read it.[73]

Feldman: Were the pictures in the *Sunday Times* of the inside of Dimona recognisable to you?[74]

Eban: No. When I read the *Sunday Times* it was a surprising revelation.

Eban's answer that he was surprised suggested therefore that there was inadequate parliamentary supervision. But neither Eban nor Feldman took up this point. Instead Eban said: 'I took an interest in what Vanunu had passed on to the *Sunday Times* because it was a matter for the committee to examine whether the laws of secrecy had been broken, and what were the implications of the giving of the information to a foreign source.'[75]

Feldman moved on to the question of the impact of the exposé and the alleged damage to state security:

Feldman: As a result of the *Sunday Times* article did international pressure increase for Israel to sign the Nuclear Proliferation Treaty?[76]

Eban: Throughout the period I served as committee chairman there was pressure. International public opinion increased the calls regarding Israel's non-signature.[77]

Feldman: Can you pinpoint any other serious repercussions from publication of the article?

Eban: I think the exposé turned on a red light in enemy states on the need for them to take steps in the nuclear or other areas. There was more tension, more voices heard in favour of strengthening projects on this subject in enemy countries.

Feldman: Can you give concrete information?[78]

Eban: No. I've decided not to. The court can believe it or not, as it wishes.[79]

Feldman failed to follow this up by discussing whether the exposé had damaged security or not, due to the limits set by the minister of defence. But how could his client be on trial for allegedly damaging state security without hard, specific proofs being offered, and within the security of the closed-doors trial? Judge Tal intervened.

Judge Tal: Did publication of the article influence the supply [to Israel] of materials required for nuclear research?[80]

Eban: There is certainly more supervision by foreign governments [regarding supply of materials]. It's been reported in the press that we are engaged in a dialogue with the Norwegian government [from which Israel received heavy water].[81]

Feldman achieved his goal of the court discussing whether or not there was adequate parliamentary supervision of nuclear arms policy making – with two of the judges themselves (Brenner and Tal) asking informed questions. But, like Horev's testimony earlier, Eban's raised questions about whether – and if so to what extent – Vanunu's exposé damaged national security. That the only country specifically mentioned (according to the protocols released) was Norway – and this more in terms of diplomatic damage – raises profound questions as to exactly what 'damage to state security' Vanunu had caused. Similarly, even the difficulties in obtaining a supercomputer from the US can only be included under the rubric of damage to state security if diplomatic damage from disclosure of the Bomb is defined as damaging 'state security'. Questions about the exposé raised in Congress may be categorised as diplomatic damage rather than security damage.

Yet Feldman was largely satisfied with Eban's testimony. 'Though he said largely what was expected, he enabled me to build the defence I wanted – an extreme one of claiming civil disobedience. Leaving the courtroom after his 90-minute testimony – which Eban was at pains to note he came to give because he was ordered to by the court, he told waiting pressmen, 'I did not meet Vanunu, shake his hand, or look in his direction.'[82]

Feldman sought to expand the argument from one of the public right to know to one of a moral commitment to speak out. At the Nuremberg trials it had been recognised that an individual was not only obliged to refuse to carry out an 'illegal' order but had to do everything in his or her power to see that the order was legal.[83] Since Dimona was not open to international inspection, nor had Israel signed the Nuclear Proliferation Treaty, Feldman posited that Vanunu was under a moral obligation to reveal the information despite having been sworn to secrecy.

The defence had wanted to call Professor Richard Falk, an international lawyer at Princeton University, who had defended conscientious objectors conscripted to serve in Vietnam. But the judges said Feldman should include Falk's views in his summing up at the end of the trial.[84]

4 JANUARY 1988

There is a point at which 'common knowledge' is a contradiction in terms with the notion of secrecy. In basing his defence on the argument that the exposé did not damage national security, and that the information had been published earlier, Feldman called as a witness Professor George Quester, a nuclear proliferation expert at the University of Maryland. By inviting foreign experts to testify, Feldman also sought to overcome the minister of defence's order banning discussion of such questions as whether the exposé had caused damage or whether it was true.

Given that Professor Quester clearly was not privy to classified information about the Israeli nuclear programme, Feldman wanted to open up at least this section of the trial to the public. A number of ingenious ideas were raised to ensure the maintenance of state security, and in particular ensure that Vanunu would not exploit the opportunity of open court to divulge more information. Feldman, in making a formal court appeal to open the Quester testimony to the public, said that security men could sit on either side of Vanunu and place their hands over Vanunu's mouth in the event of any outburst. Another possibility would be for Vanunu to sit in a side room with the court discussion being fed to him. Addressing the court, Vanunu said he had revealed all he had to reveal. He had nothing to add about the kidnapping; however, if the court did not trust him, he was prepared to leave the court.

But Hasson opposed any open court session, given that even a question there could contain secret classified information. Vanunu also had additional information not so far revealed, Hasson claimed.

Judge Tal, tiring of the seemingly endless security precautions insisted upon by the prosecution, intervened:

Judge Tal: Assuming that the defendant still has information which has not been disclosed, until when [will the precautions apply]? Because at some time he will either be released or imprisoned.

Hasson: If he is innocent, then he didn't reveal anything.

Tal: I don't know if its impossible that he will be released for other reasons ... .[85]

Not realising that he was foretelling the solitary confinement which characterised Vanunu's imprisonment, Judge Tal added, 'In prison its impossible to hold a person isolated completely from the entire world. The question is that there is no secret in the world that will not be revealed in the end. It's just a matter of time. Does not the principle of open trials weigh against the fear that the defendant – despite his promise not to scream – will scream something very short, which could be interrupted, because necessarily there will be some point in the future when if he wants, he can disclose it? I ask myself this question aloud.'

But the court rejected Feldman's request. 'Classified information would still come up – intentionally or unintentionally,' said Judge Brenner.[86]

'I am personally convinced', began Professor George Quester, 'that there is no novelty in the *Sunday Times* article. It is easy to demonstrate that the facts mentioned in the *Sunday Times* article were published in many other places in earlier years.' Quester appeared well-qualified. In addition to authoring many articles on nuclear proliferation, he had also been a consultant to the Department of State and the Pentagon. 'I have brought along some examples of literature that illustrates there is no novelty in the *Sunday Times*'s exposé. To bring all the literature would have exceeded the weight allowance I was allowed on the aircraft!'[87]

Feldman: But Vanunu's study was presented by the *Sunday Times* as a scoop. It made headlines. It made the front page. How do you react to this?[88]

Quester: The press tries to sell newspapers as well as to give news, and there is not enough news in the world, so we reinvent it.[89]

Feldman: In the *Sunday Times* article there were pictures taken from inside Dimona. Did the pictures make a change, make a difference?[90]

Quester: Not for anyone who knows the subject matter. Someone who is a total amateur might say that if they have pictures they must prove something. But experts do not need the pictures to prove what is possible and what is not possible. Reactors are similar all over the world.[91]

Feldman: The *Sunday Times* report includes numbers for the production of plutonium and an explanation about the possibility to produce nuclear weapons from these numbers. Do you find anything new about the numbers?

Quester: Anyone can say the stockpile is doubled because we assumed X, Y and Z had learnt to make bombs more efficiently. The *Sunday Times* article is no different from my own estimates, and those of Peter Pry [author of *Israel's Nuclear Arsenal*] and Leonard Spector (author of *The Undeclared Bomb*).[92]

Feldman: In terms of numbers of bombs, what would you say is significant information in terms of numbers of bombs, between zero and 1; between 5 and 10; and so on?

Quester: Any number greater than ten, and that number was passed a long time ago.

Feldman: What you are saying is that 11 or 100 doesn't really make a difference?

Quester: For the purpose of bringing Sadat to Jerusalem, for the purpose of getting the Arabs to realise that you cannot dream, dream, dream about pushing us into the sea, eleven or 111 is the same.[93]

Feldman then raised the question of whether a distinction should be drawn between the material in the *Sunday Times* article, which came from somebody on the 'inside', and previous material which was on the level of speculation and explanation.

Quester: Where one gets the information is always difficult to trace. Whether one believes the information to the 100 per cent level is never certain. And the same is true for the *Sunday Times* article. I would say, and I have said it in print, that about half of those rumours have been instigated by agents of the Israeli government. And I believe that.[94]

This gave Feldman the opportunity to suggest that Israel wanted the information to be published:

Feldman: Do you have an idea for what purpose Israeli agents would spread this kind of information?

Quester: It's a very simple answer. The purpose is to achieve deterrence. The purpose is to convince the Arab states that they cannot hope to defeat Israel. That is a viewpoint that is shared, I think, by virtually all the experts I know in the area of international strategy. That this is sensible for Israel to do, that it serves the national interests of Israel and that it is perfectly consistent with the pattern of rumours being leaked by the Israeli government. Israel serves its own interests well by keeping the Arabs afraid, and the Soviets and other hostile powers afraid, of the possibility without at the same time definitely confirming that possibility. A definite confirmation of that possibility would run the risk of irritating American public opinion and international opinion. Anything, a definite proof that would needlessly tell the Arabs that they have less to be afraid of, and that they can again dream of a good military victory.[95]

Feldman: So actually, what you are saying is that the *Sunday Times* article was instrumental to keeping up this [deterrence] which the Israeli government is interested in?[96]

Quester: The first reaction of many of my colleagues was to say, aha, this is another rumour launched by the Israeli government itself. Subsequent events, including the arrest of Mr Vanunu, have led me not to believe that anymore.[97]

Feldman moved on to the specific question of damage to national security. 'Can you comment on whether the international arena was changed drastically after Vanunu's exposé?'[98]

> *Quester:* I would say it had not changed at all. It is just keeping things the way they were and that without something like the Vanunu disclosure, without any news items, the outside world might begin to forget.[99]
>
> *Feldman:* If Vanunu's revelations made a difference, what moves would governments make?
>
> *Quester:* The US Congress would get very upset. I am very impressed by how little difference it has made on the US.[100]
>
> *Feldman:* How do you explain the passiveness of Congress?
>
> *Quester:* I think it's because the Americans also know the subject. They're saying there is nothing new. We knew that before.[101]
>
> *Feldman:* Have you been following Arab reactions after Vanunu?[102]
>
> *Quester:* The typical reaction of any Arab would be, we have been telling you all of this all along. This is not new.[103]
>
> *Feldman:* Did the article toughen the world attitude towards Israel in terms of joining the non-proliferation regime?[104]
>
> *Quester:* Pressure on Israel to join the NPT is very small because most of the world assumes that Israel will not join.[105]

Vanunu's defence also prepared a chart which listed earlier published reports on Israel's nuclear capability.[106] The reprocessing faculty referred to by Vanunu had already been noted by Fuad Jabber, author of *Israel and Nuclear Weapons*; by Steve Weisman and Herbert Krosney, authors of *The Islamic Bomb*; and by Peter Pringle and James Spigelman in *The Nuclear Barons*. An arms expert had a year earlier estimated on NBC News that Israel had at least 100 nuclear warheads, and possibly over 140. The reactor's enlarged megawattage had been reported in 1982 in a book by French journalist Pierre Pean, *Les Deux Bombes*. But the chart had not found any earlier claim than Vanunu's that Israel had thermonuclear bombs.

Cross-examining Professor Quester, Uzi Hasson sought to overturn the impression left by Feldman and claim that all was not known before Mordechai Vanunu. Up to Vanunu, Hasson would claim, it was all speculation. Vanunu was the watershed in confirmed information as opposed to rumours.

> *Hasson:* Mr Quester, can you agree with me that all that was published (prior to Vanunu) about the Israeli nuclear potential or capability was mere speculation?[107]
>
> *Quester:* I would not use the words 'mere speculation'. There are factual details that have been published over the years about the existence of Dimona, on [nuclear] materials transferred on the high seas, on material missing in

Pennsylvania [references to reports about how Israel obtained raw materials for its nuclear programme].[108]

Hasson: What are the sources of these rumours? No one who is in an official position in the Israeli government.[109]

Quester: Well, when the Israeli governmental representatives purchasing F-4s asked that they be equipped to carry nuclear weapons, they were official representatives of the Israeli government. When President Katzir made a statement he was the President of Israel.[110]

Hasson: What would you say, how would you react if I said to you that the sources concerning the missing materials are Arab and Russian sources?[111]

Quester: I would say that I do not believe that the *New York Times* or *Washington Post* or American academics based their conclusions only on Arab and Russian sources.[112]

Hasson: You said earlier that you will not use the term 'mere speculation'. What term would you use?[113]

Quester: An estimate that any government (Arab or US) would make. High probability, but no certainty of nuclear materials being collected in Israel ready for assembly into weapons.[114]

Hasson: But when you say that there is high probability you are basing this upon information which is from speculative sources.[115]

Quester: We are talking about a word in English, 'speculation'. My impression is that when governments talk about what is happening here in Israel with regard to nuclear weapons, for 25 years they have not been saying this is speculation.[116]

Hasson: And this is your basis: because governments talk about it for 25 years, it cannot be mere speculation.[117]

Quester: I would not use mere speculation talk about what may change Soviet or Egyptian or American policy with regard to Israel. Speculation to me is what a government would say: interesting, but not proof.[118]

Hasson: Talking about proof, there is no proof that Israel has a nuclear potential.

Quester: I agree with that.[119]

Hasson: You agree with that. And if anybody is looking for proof, Vanunu gave them a little bit of proof. Bear in mind two facts: (1) the claim that he worked at Dimona; (2) that he had what Dr Frank Barnaby here called corroborating evidence: the pictures from inside the reactor site.[120]

Quester: I don't agree with that statement.[121]

Hasson: You don't agree with that. OK, the difference is between you and Barnaby. Frank Barnaby said that Vanunu's description of lithium deuteride could have been gained only at first hand. Would you agree with that?

Quester: No. I believe that the UN General Assembly's report on Israeli nuclear weapons mentions rumours on thermonuclear hydrogen bombs in Israel and mentions lithium deuteride.

Hasson: I have here the UN General Assembly report about Israeli nuclear armaments and I can't see any mention. Let's go on. And did you know that Israel is producing 40 kilos of plutonium?[122]

Quester: That I think is speculation, and I still don't know it, because the article is speculation.[123]

Hasson: What I am trying to say is that it was published for the first time in the *Sunday Times*, from Vanunu's mouth.[124] ... Did you ever see a scheme of the reactor in Dimona before it was published in the *Sunday Times*?[125]

Quester: In Peter Pry's book. The book is right here. We can check it.

Hasson: Did you ever see before Vanunu any models of Israel's alleged bombs?

Quester: There are models all over the world.[126]

Hasson: Did you ever see code names or names of special areas in Dimona?[127]

Quester: No. But it is not something that I would have paid attention to that doesn't tell me anything.[128]

Hasson: Did you read in the *Sunday Times* that Israel had built some walls so that the Americans would not know about the six storeys underground [at Machon 2]?[129]

Quester: I have heard the stories before about American visitors and what they saw and they didn't see. I have even talked to some of the Americans [inspectors] who visited Dimona and they told me that they had walked away feeling that had not seen everything they were supposed to see.[130]

Hasson: That was not the question.

Quester: I will answer the question this way. If the Americans read the *Sunday Times*'s account, I think they would not be surprised.[131]

Hasson: Mr Quester, as a reasonable man, if [you] heard about Israel's nuclear potential, after Vanunu's story with the photos, would you say that your belief that Israel has a nuclear potential had been strengthened or weakened?[132]

Quester: This is a question I thought about a great deal. My honest answer is neither one.

Hasson: Neither one. It seems to me that we, you and I, are different ... men.

Quester: The reaction of my colleagues is there is nothing new here. We knew this before.[133] ... If I have seen a road accident in eleven pictures, and someone gives me a twelfth picture, it doesn't change my view of the accident. If there was a different picture I would say I was wrong before. This is not a different picture.[134]

Hasson: If you heard people saying that there are rumours about an accident, and you saw the picture of the accident, what then?

Quester: The pictures in this account, especially the way it was written – and it wasn't written by Mr Vanunu, it was written by the *Sunday Times* – doesn't increase my confidence. I was a 99 per cent before, I am a 99 per cent today.[135]

When considering George Quester's argument that Vanunu's information had been common knowledge, it needs to be noted Professor Theodore Taylor's view, on being shown Vanunu's testimony by the newspaper, was that the Israeli nuclear programme was more advanced than suggested by any previous reports Taylor had seen.

6 JANUARY 1988

The climax of Vanunu's defence was to have been the testimony of Shimon Peres, the foreign minister. Feldman hoped to show from the testimony of one of the undisputed architects of the Israeli nuclear programme that Vanunu had, in practice, raised the issue of the country's deterrent posture – and thereby contributed to national security. But three days before Peres' court appearance, the then prime minister Itzhak Shamir issued a gagging order banning court discussion of five aspects of nuclear policy. As a result, Feldman would be unable to get testimony 'about the most important point'. This gagging order was in addition to the minister of defence's order at the outset of the trial. The details of the Shamir order were not released but they included that 'it would not be possible to bring proofs of a confirmation or whether something was correct or incorrect about certain [unspecified] matters'.[136] Similarly, 'details of the parties in the legislature and executive branches which are involved in decisions concerning the nuclear research centre at Dimona' could not be raised 'with the exception of the fact that the legislature supervises the activities of the centre'.[137] Israeli law allowed Feldman to appeal to the Supreme Court against the new order by prime minister Shamir. Shamir's gagging order was highly helpful to Peres. And the manner in which Peres subsequently dealt with questions in the courtroom was evidence of a 'community of interests' between the witness and prime minister Shamir, who also backed a secrecy stance on nuclear matters. Thus, to Feldman's question as to whether there exists 'an intentional policy of ambiguity on the question of whether Israel possesses the nuclear bomb or has the potential to build the Bomb', Peres was uncooperative:

> *Peres:* Israeli policy as presented to the Knesset is based on two points: (1) that Israel will not be the first to introduce nuclear policy [sic] to the Middle East; and (2) that under certain conditions Israel would be prepared to agree to, or even prepared to initiate, a nuclear-free zone in the Middle East.[138]

Feldman did not sit still, but pursued the matter, digging up some old quotes by Peres himself. 'Is it correct', Feldman continued, 'that Israel has a policy, tactical or strategic, of international ambiguity, as we heard from the witness Mr Quester? Mr Peres, addressing the Knesset on 5 July 1966 regarding the visits of American inspectors to Dimona, said: "I don't know if the State of Israel has to calm Nasser regarding what we are doing or not doing. The Arabs suspect us. I know that the suspicion is a deterrent force. Why do we need to dissipate the fears, why do we need to interpret them?"

My question, Mr Peres, is whether it is correct that Israel makes use of the fear, the possibility, that Israel has the nuclear Bomb, for international political purposes.'[139]

> *Peres:* Israel did not create the suspicion. If it exists it was created by others. Beyond that I am not prepared to go. Not every citizen is able to decide. There are very serious decisions in every country regarding these subjects. And somebody who takes upon himself to go beyond what he has to say takes on himself powers which are contrary to the national interest, and even the law. And because of this I am not prepared to say more.[140]

Feldman was up against a stern, bureaucratic wall of silence: 'Is it clear to the witness, Mr Peres, that the discussion here is behind closed doors and that nothing stated here will go outside? Things of the most secret matters of the state have been said here.'[141]

> *Feldman:* Without any intentional reference to Vanunu's disclosure, does Israel at times benefit from the suspicion, doubt, possibility that she possesses nuclear weapons or has a nuclear arms 'potential'?[142]
>
> *Peres:* My answer is unconditional. If I thought so I would say so but not at this opportunity. I have weighed whatever I have said. Whatever I have said here is to the good of the country. I have nothing else to add.[143]
>
> *Feldman:* But I quoted what you said. In your reply you did not refer to it, namely that the suspicion that Israel has the Bomb is a deterrent. What is your reaction?[144]
>
> *Peres:* When I am not in an official capacity I allow myself to comment in the acceptable parliamentary manner. Formally, if you ask me what is good for the country, I will say things which have already been said. I will remain in that framework.[145]

Feldman adopted a new tack in his attempt to prove that Vanunu did not damage national security:

> *Feldman:* What were the foreign policy contacts which are not classified, following the article in the *Sunday Times*?[146]
>
> *Peres:* What do you call contacts?[147]
>
> *Feldman:* Were there any contacts made by the US or other governments as a result of the publication? Perhaps initially we should stay with the US?[148]
>
> *Peres:* Regarding the subject or the man?
>
> *Feldman:* Regarding the subject as linked to the publicity.
>
> *Peres:* Formal contacts, none.
>
> *Feldman:* I want to read to you – and please confirm or deny it – from an article by Hebrew University International Relations lecturer Yuval Steiglitz from the

journal *Politika*: 'Clarification of the doubt on ... the question of Israel's nuclear deterrent ... will come only when Israel formally declares clear and unequivocal proofs of the development or deployment of nuclear weapons.' I quote further: 'Any development which does not answer one of these conditions, for example Vanunu, evaluations, pseudo-intelligence evaluations, about Israel's nuclear potential are part of the complex disguise which enables the maintenance of the nuclear image.' Do you agree with the assumption?[149]

Peres: I see no need to identify with any article.[150]

Feldman: [You do] not identify [with it].

Peres: Or relate to it.[151]

Clearly exasperated at being asked to testify on behalf of Vanunu, the architect of the Israeli nuclear project interrupted Feldman:

Peres: I am forced to say, I am surprised that you see me as a witness for the defence. I am not a defence witness. It's an error in perceptions, and therefore I want to answer you that I think that the government in every democracy, not to speak of non-democratic ones, decides what to say, how to say it, and when to speak on this subject. Anyway this article has all sorts of implications whether Vanunu had or did not have to [speak]. My view is unequivocal in this. Therefore, I am not prepared to identify, indirectly or in any other way, with this commentary.[152]

Feldman: Since you referred to me directly, the situation is as follows. Your appearance should not be interpreted in any way as confirming or supporting the defendant. The only reason that we thought to call you was that you can bring specific information. What I asked you was as follows: Even today, even after Vanunu and his photos, no country, even the United Nations, is able to say unequivocally that Israel has the Bomb. Can you confirm this?[153]

For Feldman it was yet another attempt to show that Vanunu had disclosed nothing new, and that he had not damaged state security. Peres well understood this:

Peres: The world is very varied, the UN is not like the Arab states, the US is not like European governments. There is no single reaction. If you ask me, the Vanunu article is damaging.[154]

Feldman moved on to the question of democratic or parliamentary supervision of nuclear arms policy:

Feldman: Was the government decision to decide what it is permitted to say on this subject taken in the full body of the Cabinet or in a more limited forum?

Hasson: His question is not allowed under paragraph 4 of the restraining order [a reference to Shamir's gagging order].

Feldman: A journalist from the *Yediot Aharonot* newspaper heard you state at a meeting with journalists that the Vanunu disclosure strengthened Israel's nuclear deterrent. Is this correct?

Peres: I don't know anything about it.

Peres' answer appeared to contradict a comment he had made on November 1986, a month after the *Sunday Times* article appeared, when, addressing a closed meeting of Knesset members of his Labour party, he had said that the article had not weakened Israel.[155]

Feldman: You did not express in an open forum ...

Peres: ... In an open forum, certainly not.

Feldman: At a closed forum there was this expression [of your view].

Peres: I don't think that this is what should be done. My answer is negative.[156]

Another measure of 'damage' allegedly caused by the article's publication was international pressure on Israel to sign the Nuclear Proliferation Treaty (NPT). 'Did the article strengthen pressure on Israel to join the treaty?', Feldman asked. Hasson again came to the witness's assistance: '... Just to remind the witness that he cannot discuss classified secrets.'

Peres: I can refer you to the press. The Soviet news agency referred to the publications. ... There were also publications in the US calling for Israel to sign the NPT, even though these did not specifically relate to the Vanunu matter.

Feldman: Did the Vanunu article not contribute to pressing the Arab governments towards calling for a nuclear-free zone in the Middle East.

Peres: I only know of the reverse, namely that the article may have had an effect on the regional arms race, turning on a red light.

Feldman: I want to know the wattage of the red light, how 'red' it was, and where it was 'red'.

Peres: The information is based on sources and details I am not prepared to disclose.

Peres' inclination not to allow the defence to widen its examination provided Feldman with the moment, for which he and Vanunu had waited, to raise the general subject of military censorship, which contributes to the lack of public information on, and lack of democratic control over, nuclear policy.

Feldman: Is it correct that the military censor has the strictest instructions to censor any items on the subject of Israel developing, or having decided to develop, a nuclear potential?

Hasson: What is the connection of the censor's instructions with our matter? It doesn't influence whether the defendant is guilty or innocent.

Presiding Judge Noam: Why is it relevant?

Feldman: The defence argues that the fact that Israel is developing, or is about to develop, a nuclear potential is among the subjects that a democratic state is not able to keep secret from its electorate. Our claim is that if the defendant revealed these facts, acting innocently, he intended to change governmental policy through ways which are not illegal.[157]

Presiding Judge Noam: OK. We will allow the question.

Feldman: Is it correct that the nuclear subject appears on the list of subjects that have to be submitted to the censor for prior approval? And is it correct that information that even just hints at or broaches the possibility that Israel decided at a particular moment to develop a military nuclear potential is forbidden from publication?

Peres: These details, whether correct or not, are forbidden from being printed. Otherwise they would be published. One among other factors is the embargo on the State of Israel. For example, there are those [countries] which supply us with parts, and with regard to the embargo we have undertaken not to disclose the source of the purchase, and therefore the government is obligated in many cases to classify the source of the purchase.

All matters dealing with the nuclear subject from its beginning to this day are classified at the ministerial level as 'most secret'. Until today we have avoided publication of everything related to nuclear activities in Israel and we have taken strict steps [to see] that these matters should not leak out. The nuclear subject was accorded a 'preferred secret' status – and we dealt with it in this way also regarding security clearance procedures. As the defence minister I gave an instruction that the nuclear subject should be guarded in the most secretive way.[158] We weighed everything, whether to say it or not, and what we said we said, so that whatever we said was stated from the most serious consideration, and from what was good for the country. Beyond that I have nothing to add.[159]

To the best of my knowledge what happens in the nuclear reactor, how the reactor functions, is classified information, and people stand trial for serious offences if they attempt to receive information in an illegal way and make unauthorised use of it. These are crimes of the most serious kind, involving cardinal punishments in countries I know of.[160]

Judge Tal: I want to raise a number of questions. Let us assume that a person wants to raise the question of whether it is desirable for Israel's security to develop a nuclear arms potential. Do you regard a public debate as something which is damaging or should be censored?[161]

Peres: I think it is damaging but I wouldn't censor it because this is a democratic country.

Judge Tal: Assume that a person believes that Israel should not develop nuclear weapons, and he uses information rather than views to make his case – information that was already published, data regarded as accurate by those published sources, or UN sources or researchers, do you think it should be censored?

Peres: If the person received the information as a result of their work where they had taken on an obligation not to publish the information, I would censor it. If the person just gathers quotations to strengthen their case, I would not interfere.[162]

Feldman was disappointed by Peres' testimony. Prior to Peres' court appearance, Feldman had appealed the Supreme Court against Shamir's gagging order. In order not to delay Peres' court testimony until the outcome of Feldman's Supreme Court appeal, it was decided to go ahead, and deal later with any changes resulting from the appeal. Judge Bach, who had also dealt with Feldman's earlier appeal against the defence minister's order, lifted one of the five forbidden themes which, Bach said, it was 'very essential and important to Vanunu should be addressed'.[163] The judges at the Vanunu trial ordered Peres to provide written answers to some 20 questions which could now be addressed concerning nuclear policy. Despite the court order Peres did not reply to all the questions.[164]

Ironically for somebody who emphasised the import of secrecy, Peres brought along to the closed-doors trial his spokesman, Uri Savir. The judges assumed he was a security guard. Only towards the end of Peres' testimony did Feldman alert the judges to the man's true identity.

17 JANUARY 1988

'The Vanunu exposé was an unprecedented exposure of what goes on at the nuclear research centre,' began Hasson in his summing-up. 'If the treason charge under Section 99 of the Penal Code is unproven, this is not the case with the espionage charge of passing secrets to the enemy. Moreover, with regard to the actual crime, there is no difference between the defence and the prosecution.'[165]

The difference, Hasson said, was twofold: (1) Did the defendant intend to carry out the crimes attributed to him? and (2) did he have an obligation, as he claimed, to disclose the information and speak out?

Hasson's initial tack in his summing-up was to avoid the minefield concerning whether or not Vanunu had the intention to help the enemy, but instead to focus on Vanunu's motivations. In contrast to Feldman's intellectual explanation of Vanunu's motives, Hasson presented the court with a socio-psychological analysis of the man. These motives were manifold. First, revenge. Finding himself on a list of personnel cuts must have produced in him an element of revenge. Second, Vanunu's introspective character meant he never made real progress. Repeating more or less verbatim the argument he had presented during the taking of testimony, Hasson went on to say: 'In personality terms Vanunu was an introverted person, egocentric, a loner, of a composite and complex mental makeup, who concluded that he hadn't found his place in Israeli society and in the country. His life search in general, and in particular in Israeli society, led him more and more to the Left, coming near in outlook to the Arabs.' According to Hasson, 'the more Vanunu's inclinations grew in these directions, the more hostile he became to the nuclear research centre. This feeling grew in the 1982 Lebanon War and after it, and hardened when he was scheduled for dismissal. The cancellation of the dismissal notice did not change his feelings: indeed, insulted, he decided to hand in his notice. He resigned because, he said, his superiors wanted to be rid of him. The interruption of work, and the insults beforehand (which originated in the conversations and warning from security personnel after the latter heard about his left-wing tendencies) strengthened his decision – reached at the beginning of 1985 – to cut himself off from Israel and begin a new life abroad, and aroused a desire to take revenge against all those who had caused him that pain.' This may have also been the reason, Hasson said, for changing his religion.

The publicity was a means to achieving something. 'Vanunu is an intelligent person', Hasson continued, still repeating his earlier argument, 'who in spite of his social background made majestic efforts to advance, and to achieve a more respectable position than his parents and family had. Regrettably, he could not do so; nor did he raise a family. His routine work, without hope and perhaps without even the opportunity of job promotion at the centre brought him to the conclusion that he had not achieved anything in his life. And from this', Hasson argued, 'came his desire for self-publicity, to do something significant which would take him out of anonymity and prove his uniqueness.'[166]

The third motive was financial. The possibility of monetary or other benefit (required for starting a new life) was among the reasons for his act, even though, Hasson admitted, there was no significant proof that Vanunu managed to receive any significant payment from the *Sunday Times*.[167] Hasson quoted the letter which Vanunu had sent his brother: 'I am going to London to sign an agreement with the *Sunday Times* to publish what I know about Dimona.' 'And I'm speaking about the words "to sign an agreement" ', said Hasson. To avoid the court concluding that this evidence was taken during the Shin Bet interrogations, which Feldman had sought to criticise as having included undue pressure, Hasson added: 'This is not a word that the Shin Bet interrogators put in his mouth. This was a word Vanunu chose to use when he was still free.'[168] Hasson exploited Vanunu's thriftiness, and care in keeping a written record of his expenses, as a clue to his desire for money. But if Hasson's line was correct, it failed to explain why Vanunu did not push the *Sunday Times* for a formal written agreement much earlier on in his contacts with the paper.

Hasson then stopped, seeking to prioritise the different factors which led Vanunu to act. Hasson placed revenge first. The disclosure gave him the publicity he craved and needed: he would prove to himself that he could do it. But since Hasson sought to paint a picture of a Vanunu desiring to take revenge on the reactor authorities, why not also throw in the money factor, reasoned Hasson. There was a combination of factors, each one leading to, or strengthening, the other.

Hasson moved on to discuss the actual crime or, in legal language, the *actus reus*: 'There is no doubt that the defendant knew that he was doing something illegal from the moment he did it.' Hasson brought various examples from Vanunu's, and Peter Hounam's, testimonies showing that he was aware of the illegality of his step.[169]

To remove any question that the information divulged by Vanunu was not useful to an enemy, Hasson presented the court with an all-encompassing definition of 'sensitive information'. Quoting Judge Zilberg, 'modern war was total, and encompassing all aspects of national life, the economic potential, public morale, level of culture, political parties, education – all these are matters which the enemy wants to know about as a target of war. By itself each one is not important.'[170]

With regard to the claim that Vanunu's information was already known, Hasson argued that even though it was already known, information like Vanunu's serves as a confirmation of earlier information. Hasson sought to disprove the testimony of defence witness George Quester as 'most unreliable'. 'To every one of my questions he said it was correct but added there was nothing new in the information.' Yet even Quester, Hasson reminded the court, said that Vanunu's information had helped the Arabs and 'would be used by the Arabs as a justification for their own nuclear arms development'.[171] Hasson moved on to quoting other witnesses. 'Peres,' Hasson reminded the court, 'said, "we weigh what to say. These details, whether correct or not, are forbidden from being printed. Otherwise they would be published." ' Hasson quoted reactor engineer 'Giora' to the effect that 'there are now problems in buying certain things from the US. Also, the people who work at the reactor were now marked, and would become targets for foreign intelligence agencies when they travel abroad.' Hasson also quoted defence witness Dr Frank Barnaby to the effect that the testimony of Vanunu surprised him.[172]

Hasson turned his attention to the defence argument of an absence of legislative supervision. 'I don't see how in the criminal law framework the defence can bring in the question of legislative supervision. [Vanunu] didn't say, "there is an absence of supervision and I will therefore try to clarify it." He went directly to the last possible measure which it's possible to take. If you think there is no supervision, before you damage the country of your birth, you first turn to official channels. If they say they don't want to speak to you, and a more careful eye cannot be kept on the matter ... you haven't lost anything.

But to come and fire with all the heavy cannon possible and publish everything from A to Z in all its details without an honest attempt to clarify this, in my view, negates any claim of the defence. Vanunu said', Hasson reminded the court, 'I didn't know who knows, who doesn't know. I wanted the citizenry to know.' Argued Hasson, 'If Vanunu felt the supervision was inadequate he could have contacted the defence and foreign affairs committee and explained to them that the situation is inadequate. If one wants to be enfenced by democratic rules, one has to work within the democratic framework, and one of its rules is to observe the law and the security secrets of the country.'[173]

Hasson then turned to the question of the legality of nuclear weaponry in international law which had been raised by Vanunu's defence to justify his speaking out. Hasson said that according to the Nuclear Proliferation Treaty a state signatory is able to cancel its signature at three months' notice, and can develop whatever it wants. Also, the treaty itself initially had a limited lifespan of 25 years, albeit subject to renewal.

Judge Brenner interrupted Hasson:

Judge Brenner: When Vanunu began work at Dimona he accepted [an obligation] on himself not to speak out. Vanunu is saying that this is illegal. Mr Feldman has entered international law under Section 24 (a) (1) of the Penal Code. This law requires a citizen seeing something unfolding to stand up. Therefore, everything that he did was not that he acted against the law but carried out the law.[174]

Hasson: Which 'law'? The law to reveal? The law to go to a newspaper? One needs to hear from the defence which law.[175]

Judge Brenner: He is claiming that he is obligated because of solely humanitarian reasons to stand up and act to implement the law.[176]

Hasson: Under international law, a war of defence is permitted, a war to defend a state's territory is permitted, and somebody comes and tells the whole world, and damages state security, saying I had an obligation to. This is unacceptable. This is anarchy. In his book on international law, Lauterpacht says that nuclear weapons in retaliation are permitted. From this it may be deduced that one may possess them (without which one could not retaliate in event of attack). Even one who says that the deployment of nuclear weapons is forbidden agrees that it is permitted on military targets. There are even those who justify the nuclear attacks on Hiroshima and Nagasaki on the grounds that [they] shortened the war and avoided even more casualties than the attacks themselves.[177]

Judge Tal: I want to understand. If a person in order to come under Section 94 [of the Penal Code] – under which 'an act is not regarded as an offence if it is done in good faith to bring about, by legal means, a change in the structure or the activities of the state' – is required to act through legal means, for what does he need the protection of this paragraph? What crime has he committed? A person commits the most serious crimes involving state security, with the most serious penalties, and he wants to come under paragraph 94 and says he thought that

'I am helping state security.' They say to him 'Yes, but you should have acted through legal means'! In other words he transgressed no law. This is tautology.[178] I don't understand.

Judge Brenner: We are not discussing intent to destroy state security. A person finds a case full of pictures of the nuclear reactor. The person obtained the information without breaking the law or the obligation which he signed in his place of work. He didn't break the law. This is the implication of Section 94.

Hasson: This is certainly what I accept.[179]

Hasson's summing-up turned to what would become a key determinant in the case: the question of criminal intent. The defence had argued that the drafting of the laws of espionage and treason appeared to require a 'special intent' [According to Section 113 (espionage), 'a person who delivers any secret information without being authorised to do so and "with intent to impair" the security of the state' is liable to imprisonment. Similarly, under Section 99, a person 'with intent to assist an enemy in war' is liable to the death sentence or to imprisonment for life.] Feldman pointed to a gap between action and intention. Sometimes, the action was itself evidence of an intention but the very citation of the word 'intent' in Section 99 suggested that a special, stronger intent was required. Simply passing secrets to the enemy was not adequate proof of this required special intent. While Hasson acknowledged that a special intent was implied, his question was: what was it?[180]

According to Hasson, 'Intent is something within the soul of a person. How can the prosecution prove intent? The intent of every action, whether done from a distant motive or near intent, requires to be derived from the results. For example, a person charged with illegal entry with intent to steal. He says he had no intent to steal. This is not a matter of believing or not believing him. Life experience suggests that a person does not break in unless he has an intent to carry out a burglary. Accordingly, "special" intent means you knew, you waived the result, namely the damage of state security ... knowledge of a high level of likelihood that something would occur from a specific act.'[181]

Judge Brenner: What did he want from the result?

Hasson: What did he intend in damaging state security? What did he want in the result? Everything.

Judge Brenner: This is not adequate. This 'special intent' is no different from a 'regular intent'.

Hasson: The intent is the fact that you know – because if it was not the desire you would not have done it.[182]

Judge Brenner: You're making light of it. The problem is how to prove this special intent. Is there a subjective intent that cannot be proven by the consequences of the action? In the so-called Beiski murder the subjective element was added: the judges said that you can't prove it by assuming that a person intended the natural results of the action. The best form of proof is when somebody says, 'I did it because I intended X, Y or Z' – which does not leave you in a situation of a result that cannot be proven.

A second question. We are applying a common denominator to all the illegalities in this section of the Penal Code – whether in damaging territoriality, whether in helping the enemy, or whether in damaging the security of the state. Again, I ask myself, is it not necessary to prove objectively an intent to assist the enemy?[183]

Hasson: If the defendant answers 'Yes' to the question, 'Did you intend to assist the enemy?' this is easy, but who will admit this? Nobody will be saying something like this.[184]

Judge Brenner: Is this the *specific* intent to assist the enemy?

Hasson: This is the *specific* intent to assist the enemy.

Judge Brenner: This is absurd. He took photos, put them with an explanation in a sealed bottle, floated it on the high seas. Then you come and say it is unclear where it will get to on the high seas – to X, or Egypt, or Lebanon or Syria.

Hasson: It is possible that not caring where it gets to is equivalent to intent.

Judge Brenner: This non-caring where it gets to is like the special intent of an illegal action for which the penalty is death?![185]

Hasson: We are not looking at the punishment but at the basis of the transgression.

Judge Brenner: There are different schools of thought regarding the level of proof vis-a-vis the level of punishment.

Hasson then proceeded to give the court a stream of legal precedents in which the Israeli legal system had used the results of an action as the determinant of guilt. 'In one case, the defendant passed secrets to a foreign agent as a result of carelessness, not out of intent to damage state security. The only goal was to ease the way for him to visit his parents in [the agent's] country. The claim was rejected as a justification for the action. Proof that he intended to damage state security was fulfilled by the knowledge that it was a type of information that there was a great chance would cause the supposed results.'[186]

'Let us assume that I believe him. Do we free him – because the defendant says, "I was aware, I weighed it, but decided that it wouldn't damage state security." ' Vanunu knew that the *Sunday Times* article would reach [Israel's] enemies. In a conversation with his family on 25 October 1986, he told his brother, 'Look, why do I need to go to enemy intelligence? I know that everything I published will be analysed by the KGB, MI5, the CIA … I said to our mother, "Peres can no longer tell Reagan that we don't have nuclear weapons. Now everybody knows, even the CIA and KGB. All the world knows." ' Vanunu, asked by Hasson whether he had been worried that the information would reach the Arabs, had replied, 'No, when it was published certainly it would reach the Arabs, but the goal was first to reach the Israelis.'[187]

Vanunu was aware of what Hasson called 'the debate in Israel on the nuclear question'. Hasson had showed him in court two folders of cuttings of newspaper articles and Vanunu had acknowledged it. And 'despite this he published his exposé. Why? Because he says the debate was too involved in the principles and didn't get down to the details.'

Hasson quoted Judge Brenner, questioning Vanunu: 'Did it not pass through your head that it is something which might damage state security?' Vanunu had replied, 'Certainly I thought about it, and thought that it would not damage state security.' 'In any form?', Judge Brenner had retorted. 'Perhaps it will damage governmental policy,' Vanunu had replied.

'And this is what he wanted,' Hasson continued, 'to change government atomic policy.' Hasson quoted Vanunu: ' … the government will be required to change its policy. I don't know how this process will go but I saw the end goal – to change government policy.' 'Now', went on Hasson, 'it is possible that the court will attempt to distinguish between state and government – that what hurts the government does not necessarily damage state security. The court has to determine that the government fixes the policy.'[188]

Hasson's next issue concerned the definition of 'enemy' and 'war'. 'Anybody in this country knows that Arab governments exploit every opportunity to gore the State [of Israel]. "Assisting the enemy" does not have to be in actual battle or in military matters but also in political matters. Therefore I say the defendant knew, took it into account, and wanted to help the enemy.' In widening the definition of damage to state security to embrace also diplomatic effects, Hasson went beyond the norms that damage to state security concerns damage to the military, and fell dangerously near the line separating democracies from non-democracies.[189]

Judge Tal interjected:

Judge Tal: Is the term 'war' in Section 99 only a war with weaponry in order to kill and conquer, or does it, as you say, extend to economic boycott war? The question is, what is the intent of the clause? The second question is, does there need to be an actual situation of war in 'assisting the enemy'?

Hasson: The definition of 'enemy' is not easy. According to Section 91 of the Penal Code, an enemy is one who acts as a fighter, or maintains a situation of war, with Israel. With regard to Egypt this is a problem because it does not define itself as fighting, or being in a situation of war with, Israel. Section 96 of the Penal Code distinguishes between the death penalty for an offence when military conduct takes place and other times when the death penalty is not applied – implying that the latter is included in a more all-embracing definition of 'war' and 'assistance to an enemy'.

Hasson concluded his summing up by dealing with the issue of Vanunu's speaking to a newspaper, not an enemy state:

> *Hasson:* To make such a distinction would be most dangerous because it gives a *heckhsher* [a term for kosher food but used in popular Hebrew inside Israel in a wider sense of 'behaviour regarded as acceptable'] to everybody to publish the most secret information in the press. The law does not say how information is passed; the law talks of the passing of information. Indeed, to go via a newspaper rather than directly via a foreign government means that one doesn't endanger one's own life. By going to a newspaper one gets publicity. Section 111 refers to information passed to a foreign government or [intended] for one, i.e. not necessarily passed directly to one. I thank the court.[190]

22 JANUARY 1988

Defence lawyer Avigdor Feldman began his summing-up by arguing that the prosecution had not provided proof of intent to assist 'an enemy at war with Israel'. The prosecution had equated an enemy at war with Israel with intent to damage state security. There was a need to distinguish between the two terms, Feldman said:

> *Feldman:* Further, I will claim that intention to reveal nuclear secrets is not intention to damage state security. Moreover, the very nature of the testimony brought by the prosecution was inadequate to prove 'assistance to an enemy in war'.

In 'assistance to an enemy' one has to prove that the act can cause damage to state security. Furthermore, Vanunu did not anticipate the damage which would almost certainly result, and if he had not anticipated the damage there was also no proof of intent. Since the development of nuclear weapons – away from the eyes of the public and the world at large – is an international crime, any injury to the secrecy was not damaging state security.

A central thesis of Feldman's summing-up concerned the concept of intention. Feldman pointed to a gap between action and intention. There is no transgression in passing the information, postulated Feldman. 'The punishment is only for intent. The seriousness of the punishment of treason – even amounting to death – suggests the need of culpability. If the prosecution is right that there is no difference between "high expectancy of results" and "intent", what did the law makers have in mind when they drafted Section 99 with its reference to a "special intent"?' Feldman quoted Professor S.Z. Feller's magnum opus, *Fundamentals of Criminal Law*, to the effect that the connection between the one who acts and the action is ethical – the internal motive which helps one to carry out an action.[191]

Judge Tal: I want to understand something. If a person sells state secrets for monetary benefits, the damage to state security does not exist. According to Feller, what will be the sentence?

Feldman: Innocent.[192]

Judge Tal: This is the problem with learned articles by learned professors. He has to say something new. By contrast, the approach of the court conforms to what is past precedent. Let's take a serial killer. He doesn't know his victim, it does not interest him. One cannot attach to him a specific intent to murder ... He knows there is a very high likelihood that this will be the result but from his inner soul, as Professor Feller puts it, he doesn't want it. The reverse is true – he has mercy on him.[193]

In basing much of the defence on 'intention', Feldman gave himself a task that was not easy. Israeli law, like some other legal systems, differentiates between motivation and intent. Motivation concerns the basic goal of an alleged criminal, intent concerns the means used to reach that goal. Over the years Israeli courts have not been interested in the motivation of an individual – although it can be relevant for sentencing – but in the intent or action of an individual as it affects society, or, as in the Vanunu case, the security of the state. Vanunu was not unlike a doctor who, wishing to undertake heart research, takes the heart from a living person for laboratory examination. The person, of course, dies. The doctor did not want to cause the death, but would be charged with murder because it was highly probable that the person would die. The legal definition of acting with intent is of the action of one who foresees the results and in so doing accepts them. Thus, in 1960 Czech-born professor, Kurt Sitte, was convicted by an Israeli court of passing secret information to foreign agents even though he did not wish to harm the security of the state but did so out of concern for the welfare of his relatives. In its ruling the Israeli Supreme Court said that 'in offences against state security a person is responsible for such consequences of his action as are highly probable.' According to the law on treason, 'assistance to an enemy in war' includes intent that information shall fall into the hands of the enemy or in the knowledge that it may fall into the enemy's hands (Section 99 (b) of the Penal Code). Those who drafted the law appeared to be concerned that where the security of the state was at stake, society might not be adequately protected.

The difficulty posed for Vanunu by the wider definition of intent – as embracing the probable effects of an action – was particularly real regarding the charge of espionage, according to which 'a person who delivers any secret information without being authorised to do so and with intent to impair the security of the state is liable to life imprisonment.' Even the unauthorised gathering of information made Vanunu liable to a seven years' imprisonment (Sections 113 (b) and (c)). But the prosecution had a weaker case with the treason charge. It was pushing the matter to accuse Vanunu of having 'intent to assist an enemy at war with Israel'. Vanunu acted in good faith and never intended to 'assist the enemy'. The fact that the clause read 'a person with intent to assist an enemy in war' suggested that a special type of intent was required. Feldman also proposed that assistance to an enemy, including mere knowledge that the information might fall into their hands (stated in Section 99 (b)), first required the special intent which preceded 'assistance' in Section 99 (a).

Feldman then turned to the definition of 'enemy':

> Feldman: In referring to assistance to an enemy Section 99 is surely not referring to a collective term but to a personalised, specific term. Specific content requires something more than the general conflictual state in which Israel finds itself.

This led Feldman to argue that passing the information to a newspaper was not a case of the specific intent underlying either the law of treason or the law of espionage. The law of espionage specifically concerned a state, not a non-state like a newspaper. For example, it implied leaving or entering the sovereignty of a state; intention to bring about military actions against a state; serving in enemy forces.

> Feldman: In every judgement in which knowledge is equated with 'intention', it requires to be clear that the person you pass the information to is an enemy state, or an agent. The traditional understanding of espionage implies that someone specific receives the information – which in popular parlance does not include a newspaper – and it is usually carried out in a hidden act, not one done in public, certainly not at a press conference. The 'intention' here was the reverse of espionage: his 'intention' was for the information to reach as wide a platform as possible. Thus, the conditions for 'intent' do not exist in this instance.[194]
>
> Judge Tal: One can propose the opposite thesis. Somebody who wants to be really efficient can in a single act inform everybody: if he or she publicises something in a newspaper, 200,000 people will read it including the specific person who wanted to get the information.[195]
>
> Feldman: This is precisely my point. One cannot say that somebody who publishes a piece of information in a newspaper did not intend that the information would reach the enemy and damage state security; but in contrast this is not the 'near certainty' when a person goes to an enemy – an act which itself screams that there is an intent to damage state security. Espionage and journalism do not go hand in hand.[196]
>
> Presiding Judge Noam: What about the nature of the contents of the information? Let's say a person goes to the BBC and reveals the most secret programmes of a country. He is not going to a foreign agent, but the nature of the contents of the information is not important?![197]
>
> Feldman: It is certainly important. All I am saying – and this already is leading to my client's acquittal – is that the passing of the information is not enough.[198]

Judge Brenner: It's possible, as Feldman suggests, that giving information to a newspaper is clear. When one puts a note in a bottle in the ocean there are any number of possibilities [as to where the bottle gets to]. But in this case there is an additional element: when a person discloses the most secret details of the State of Israel he needs to know it will also be read by the enemy including Arab states, that it will be useful to the enemy. Perhaps he didn't think, he didn't intend to damage state security, but he knew this [that it would help an enemy state].[199]

Feldman: We are dealing with a criminal case. The prosecution has to prove beyond any doubt that the defendant intended to damage state security. It is precisely the significance of the information, on a subject of great public dispute, that there are different views, that his intent was not to damage state security. This fact gives me greater freedom of movement.[200] Our claim is that there is an alternative 'intent', one which is at least equal to 'intent to damage state security'. It is rather like a country which produces and distributes heroin in the world. A man comes and, thinking that heroin is dangerous, and that there is an international treaty against narcotics, reveals [the information] to the media. Or like somebody in Nazi Germany, a German army officer, who passes the information to foreign correspondents because he himself is unable to. You can't say he is damaging state security.[201]

Presiding Judge Noam: And therefore it is permitted to Mr Vanunu to reveal the most secret programmes of the country?[202]

Feldman: The court will have to decide this. Moreover, there is the legal weight of Section 94. There is a need to distinguish between one with intent to damage the security of the state and one with another intent. And we are discussing intent because the behaviour is the same in both. The alternative intent is not criminal but originates from being terrified that nuclear weapons are secretly held by the state and pose a damage to the security of the entire world.[203]

Presiding Judge Noam: So, from the nature of the content one can learn about the 'intent' of an act.[204]

Feldman: Yes, it is possible to.

Judge Brenner: A person says to himself, 'I know that this act will cause damage,' but that person is not bothered by this because his alternative goal is preferred. Without even resorting to Section 94, what do you say?

Feldman: Acquitted, because this is a different 'intent'. And even if I take the example – bad for the defence – of a doctor who removes the heart of a man in order to do some medical research, the man will certainly die even if this is not his intent. But in our case the prosecution has failed to prove the damage caused – and such proof is necessary in criminal law. Abba Eban has said [in his testimony] that there was no pressure as a result of the Vanunu disclosure. In the witnesses it called, the prosecution did not measure up to the proofs necessary to prove the damage done. They didn't call the experts from the defence establishment to prove the so-called damage. Eban said the disclosure turned on a red light in the Arab world; I asked him to give details but he couldn't. Peres said a similar thing; when I asked him to be specific, he declined. They spoke of damage to the country; nobody – I checked – spoke of damage to state security. By contrast, I called experts of international standing like George Quester, who could easily stand up against defence commanders and Mr Peres. Quester said, 'I do not think that Vanunu damaged the security of Israel; perhaps even the contrary is true.' The need for proof beyond any doubt is vital in criminal law.[205]

Feldman moved his summing-up toward the question of the international danger of nuclear weaponry. 'All know is what the nuclear bomb is, what the implication of atomic war is – apocalypse. The whole world will be destroyed', Feldman quoted from the book *Nuclear Weapons and The Future of Humanity* by Avner Cohen, which equates nuclear weaponry with genocide.[206]

Feldman concluded his summing-up by arguing that if the court concluded that Vanunu had not acted for ideological reasons but for money – even though once Vanunu reached London, and Oscar Guerrero became excluded from the picture the money element did not come up, according to Peter Hounam's testimony – the prosecution still had to prove the damage which Vanunu had caused to state security. And even if the prosecution proved damage, it still had to prove intent.

The three judges wrote their judgement together, but until the week of the verdict (at the end of March 1988) they pondered at length whether Vanunu should be sentenced for aggravated espionage only or for treason as well.[207] They finally reached a unanimous decision that he was guilty of both aggravated espionage and treason. The court rejected every one of the arguments brought by Feldman. The judges decided to accept that the confessions had been obtained by the Shin Bet with [only] a reasonable amount of pressure.[208] Of the defence that the information had been given to a newspaper and not to a foreign agent, the judges said that publication in a newspaper was in effect testimony that Vanunu 'intended to bring all information he had gathered and publish it for the knowledge of every enemy of Israel even without making direct contact with them.'[209] Of the argument that 'assistance to an enemy' had to prove damage in practice, the court said that 'damage' could be measured in the very prohibition of the act, even if the enemy did not see the information. And on the question that 'assistance to the enemy in war' was limited to periods of armed hostilities, the court said that 'in war' included periods between wars because most Arab countries had been in a continuous state of war with the Jewish State. The court also rejected the argument that information about Israel's nuclear capability had been published earlier (but their reasoning was censored).

Feldman had also argued that the charge of aggravated espionage did not apply to Vanunu since he had not had 'intent to impair the security of the state'. Whereas the Penal Code section on treason implicitly stated that 'intent' included merely 'the knowledge that the information may fall into enemy hands', no such definition of 'intent' was given in Section 113 on espionage. The judges ruled that Section 99 defined the essence of 'intention' for Section 113 as well. However, this interpretation was questionable because the part of the Penal Code covering state security and official secrets is itself divided into six articles, among them 'General provisions', 'Espionage' and 'Treason'. If the wider interpretation of intent had been intended by the drafters of the penal law to be applied in other sections dealing with state security, this should have been included under the 'General provisions' at the beginning rather than under a specific section, namely, that dealing with treason. The judges had, in effect, applied a ruling on one specific article from another and separate specific article, that on 'Treason'.

The judges were divided over the question of what motivated Vanunu. In a majority decision, Presiding Judge Eliahu Noam and Judge Brenner accepted Hasson's psychological analysis of Vanunu, which in effect nullified Vanunu's claim that he was ideologically motivated. Judge Zvi Tal, however, said that the overriding factor was ideological – 'a world outlook which concretised during Vanunu's activism at the Ben-Gurion University. Vanunu was on the far Left of the political spectrum.' In trying to determine Vanunu's true motives, the judges looked for earlier evidence of his anti-nuclear position. A letter he had sent to his brother, Meir, before flying from Australia to Britain, was of some importance for Judge Tal. Vanunu had told Meir that 'he had decided to do it primarily from political motivation. Even though I left Israel and don't want to be involved I am returning to the involvement. I feel it is my obligation to publicise the information.' But Judges Noam and Brenner thought the letter was an attempt to justify his action 'because for any intelligent person the action amounted to treachery towards his motherland'. The ideological explanations were there to disguise any suggestion of his being a spy or traitor. To understand Vanunu's motives, the two judges said one had to take into account his desire to join the Israeli Communist party, and his subsequent desire to cut his ties with the country and not return. They also said that Vanunu's diaries showed a constant wish for self-publicity and a financial incentive, but did not support a strong ideological motivation.

Yet Israeli press reports about his diaries suggested that Vanunu's progressive thinking was very much present. The absence of diary entries about the Bomb or his work at Dimona could be to his credit, in that he had been careful not to reveal the classified information even in his own diary. He did not discuss his work even with his family or girlfriend. What might have persuaded the judges otherwise would have been indications of legal activities after he left Dimona such as press articles with anti-nuclear content or his involvement in interest groups. The judges seemed unaware that, while staying at King's Cross in Sydney, Vanunu had been actively involved in a workshop on peace, which also focused on the nuclear arms issue. The Noam-Brenner line, if generalised, would imply that an individual's self-proclaimed political views and actions are tied to deep socio-psychological forces rather than to intellectual and rational considerations. Also implied in Hasson's picture of Vanunu was that he was as extreme on the nuclear issue as he was on other political matters such as the Arabs and the future status of the West Bank. It would indeed not be surprising for an individual who reached a broadly radical outlook on life to be anti-nuclear.

For those who knew Judge Tal, his approach was also not so surprising. Regarded on the bench as a special type of person, he related to all who came before him, men, women, defendants, state prosecutors, with equal regard, listening patiently and sympathetically to their case. When initially appointed to the bench, he had dealt with many criminal cases, and it took him time to distinguish between when he was being told a lie and when the defendant had a genuine explanation for his or her behaviour. When in private practice he not infrequently sought an ideal solution, such as helping to reunite a couple on the verge of divorce, notwithstanding the loss of earnings which would otherwise have accrued. His particular forte was Hebrew law. A religious law scholar, he studied at the Kfar Haroeh religious high school after emigrating from Poland to Palestine in 1935. He not infrequently raised a Hebrew law angle in court, while being careful not to clash with the existing modern Israeli law.

Notwithstanding the fact that two of the judges rejected the ideological motives Vanunu claimed, the court concluded its ruling by noting that the 'worst crimes in the history of humanity have been done from ideological motives. No ideological goal sanctifies the use of means. Moreover, the danger from ideological criminals is perhaps greater than from other types of criminals.' Quoting law professor Itzhak Zamir, the court said that ideological criminals not only transgress the law but place the state infrastructure itself in danger. Since they are often seen in positive terms, they become a focus of demystification for their respective causes, and will take measures and engage in violence 'perhaps to the extent of rebellion and uprising against authority, that is, against democratic society'.

When the judges announced their verdict, Vanunu addressed the court and said that he did not regret publishing the information, but with hindsight he would not have done it. As he read the 60-page verdict he could not hide his disappointment, and intermittently put his head in his hands. Vanunu had expected to be found guilty of espionage only. 'I am not a traitor, I didn't intend to damage the security of the state. I am very disappointed that the court did not accept the message which I tried to give it: that I did what I did for ideological reasons,' Vanunu said to Feldman.[210]

He was sentenced to 18 years' imprisonment, less than the 20 demanded by the prosecution. His having being held in solitary confinement, cooperation in the Shin Bet interrogation, and expression of some regret in his final statements to the court all contributed to the judges' decision to reduce the sentence. Had the issue of the Bomb exercised the Israeli public, it is most questionable whether Vanunu would have been given the harsh sentence he received.

Asher Vanunu's reaction to the verdict and sentence was: 'Mordechai didn't murder, he didn't rape. He had good intentions. Nobody understood him.' But his father Shlomo said: 'My honour had gone. It is a disgrace to the family. But this is my son. Do you know a father that doesn't love his son? What can I do? We were more successful with our daughters: they married men of Jewish learning. And this son destroyed our life, and honour.' Meir Vanunu, who like Asher had hoped the court would not find Mordechai guilty of treason, attacked the court 'for not succeeding in rising above narrow state interests, and pronouncing on the nuclear issue in general'.

The arguments Avigdor Feldman raised in Vanunu's defence in the Jerusalem District Court were heard again at the appeal before the Israeli Supreme Court in May 1989. A tendency for the Supreme Court to discuss broader legal questions – in the Vanunu case these included such basic definitions as those of 'motivation', 'intent', 'assistance to the enemy', 'damage to state security' – gave Feldman hope that it would recognise some of the weaknesses in the penal system on which he pinned his client's defence, and which he had unsuccessfully raised at the earlier trial. The minority opinion of Judge Tal, that Vanunu had been ideologically motivated, gave Vanunu some hope that the Supreme Court would address the deeper-seated issues which underlay The State of Israel v. M. Vanunu.

The appeal was chaired by Meir Shamgar, president of the Supreme Court. A former advocate-general of the Israeli army, Shamgar had a particular interest in defence matters but had shown a general inclination to accept prosecution claims in classified intelligence evidence.[211] As advocate-general he had introduced the application of international law to the military administration of the West Bank and Gaza, and later, as the government's law advisor, made it possible for residents of the West Bank and Gaza to appeal to the Supreme Court.

Feldman restated his argument that the expression found in the law of treason – 'a person with intent to assist an enemy in war' – implied a special type of intention. That treason was mere knowledge that the information might fall into enemy hands presupposed this special intent. Vanunu had never had such an intent to assist the enemy. But Judge Shamgar rejected the need to prove 'certainty' concerning the result of his actions; a 'high probability' was sufficient. A person was assumed to intend the natural and probable consequences of his actions.

Feldman argued that Vanunu's motives had been incorrectly interpreted by the majority of the District Court, Judges Noam and Brenner. Hasson's portrait had been one-sided, and he asked the Supreme Court to accept the minority opinion of Judge Tal that Vanunu had been motivated primarily by ideological factors. But the Supreme Court said that under Israeli law, motive was immaterial regarding criminal responsibility. The law existed to protect the organs of government and was interested only in the intent of a person as expressed by their actions. Shamgar quoted British judge Lord Devlin to the effect that 'rebels and high-minded spies could be heard to argue that defeat in a battle would serve the best interests of the nation because it would be better off under a different regime.' There could be no question of good faith where a person published secret information in the knowledge that there was a 'high probability' that the publication would damage state security, Shamgar said. Feldman then argued that the Vanunu exposé, rather than causing damage to state security, had strengthened the country's nuclear posture. Shamgar replied that Vanunu did not have authority to decide what was in Israel's defence interests; that authority rested with the government.

Feldman restated his argument that, under Section 94 of the Penal Code, Vanunu had acted in good faith to bring about a change by lawful means, through pressure from informed public opinion. Shamgar said that 'the attitude that the ends of motivation justify the means is the antithesis of democratic rule'. There was no contradiction between democracy and secrecy: all free states recognise the right of competent authorities to enforce secrecy for the protection of the state. It appeared that Vanunu had confused democracy with anarchy. Feldman countered that 'secret' was what the authorities saw fit to keep secret. In a narrow sense, nuclear issues were under legislative control because Section 113 (d) recognised a category of information 'that the security of the state requires to be kept secret – information which the government, with the approval of the Knesset's defence and foreign affairs committee, has declared to be secret'. Nuclear information fell under this heading.

Notwithstanding his concern for defence interests, Shamgar had a reputation for defending freedom of expression. In trials involving libel, for example, he had attached more importance to freedom of expression than to an individual's reputation. In rejecting Feldman's appeal, he was in effect saying that nuclear matters should remain secret. Shamgar sees the Supreme Court as a seismograph of public attitudes, and has noted that law requires public legitimacy. Wide public support for Israel's possession of nuclear capability, and agreement that the subject be secret, creates the strong emotional public involvement which Shamgar knows is a key to national security. But, in a wider sense, certain criticism by members of the Knesset's defence and foreign affairs committee itself over the years about their being inadequately briefed by government officials suggests that Shamgar's perception of the legislative control of nuclear matters is inaccurate. His judgement also ignored the rights of minority groups in a democracy to be informed and to discuss this issue of crucial importance. Shamgar lost an important opportunity to focus attention on these lacunae in Israel's democracy.

Shamgar also questioned whether Vanunu really wanted to reach the Israeli public. After all, why publish the information in a British newspaper whose

Israeli audience was miniscule? 'Rather, it was a blow at Israel from abroad in front of all its inhabitants,' Shamgar claimed.[212] The judge failed to deal with the censorship which had existed in Israel on all nuclear matters prior to Vanunu's exposé, and which would have stopped any local publication. Although fringe interest groups had campaigned against nuclear weapons, there had been no debate on the subject among the wider public. And, although Feldman's argument that Vanunu had acted in good faith to bring about lawful change may be questioned, Vanunu, Shamgar argued, could have breached secrecy in a less drastic way. Notwithstanding the lack of formal procedures, he could nevertheless have contacted the state comptroller's office or the Knesset's defence and foreign affairs committee. In going to a leading foreign newspaper Vanunu had breached secrecy on a wanton scale.

The defence derived some satisfaction from the trial. A debate on the nuclear issue was held in the end – even if the press benches were unoccupied and the rest of the world could not follow it. The judges were there, as was history, if only for the record, and international experts had come to testify. Even if the debate-of-sorts was not essentially about whether Israel should have the bomb, and whether its possession is morally justifiable, the questions cropped up within the framework of Vanunu's motivation and whether he had impaired state security. It was the first time an Israeli court had addressed itself to the status of nuclear weaponry in international law and the right of the individual to disclose official secrets to the media.

In contrast to the defence, prosecutor Hasson did not 'tango' – or stoop to the opportunity which the trial offered to present the case for governmental secrecy and the need for administrative procedures to effect policy change. Nevertheless, in his summing-up, Hasson gave expression to a countering of those of Feldman's arguments which he used to justify Vanunu's action.

The judges, though encumbered by limitations in discussing the nuclear subject, reached a considered verdict. Even Feldman later acknowledged that Hasson put up a most respectable case.[213] However, the omission in the Israeli penal system of a law specifically prohibiting unauthorised leaks to the news media left the judiciary with the task of charging with treason and espionage somebody who had leaked classified information to the media for what he proclaimed to be the public good. The case raised important questions about the relationship between the state and the individual, but the judges had to confine themselves to interpreting the existing law. This conveyed an incorrect impression that the court simply 'passed the buck' it had been handed by the government on to the prison authorities, which, in turn, confined Vanunu for an enforced 18-year-long silence.

According to Professor Mordechai Kremnitzer of the Law Faculty of the Hebrew University, 'Vanunu's action could have helped an enemy, but treason was an inappropriate offence with which to charge him. It went too far. One needs to distinguish between information given to the media and the normal type of espionage for two reasons. First, when something has appeared in the media it is possible to take steps to repair the damage, which one is unable to do when the information was conveyed in secret. The injured country has an advantage when it knows what the enemy knows. Second, the treason charge comes close to stopping freedom of expression and the public's right to know. There was a difference between going to a foreign intelligence agency and to the media. There should therefore be a separate offence in the penal system of revealing classified secrets to the public.'[214]

The Vanunu case paralleled a case before the US courts involving a civilian naval intelligence analyst, Samuel Loring Morison, who also worked as a part-time American editor of the London-based *Jane's Fighting Ships*.

In 1984 Morison passed US satellite photos of a new Soviet aircraft carrier he had spotted on a colleague's desk to *Jane's Defence Weekly*. The Reagan administration used the 1917 Espionage Act to charge Morison with espionage. He was the first person ever to be so charged by a US court for leaking classified information to the news media. He invoked the First Amendment, pointing out the danger of a citizen being tried for thus leaking information. But the US circuit Judge Donald Russell rejected this. 'The mere fact that one has stolen a document in order [to] deliver it to the press, whether for money or for other personal gain, will not immunize him from responsibility for his criminal act. To use the First Amendment for such a purpose would be to convert the First Amendment into a warrant for thievery.' In October 1985 Morison was sentenced to two years' imprisonment.

There were similarities and differences in how the Israeli and US courts dealt with the respective cases. If in the Vanunu trial much of the discussion concerned whether to extend his crime from espionage to treason, the Morison trial never considered this: it was a question of whether or not it was a case of espionage. Two of the three judges, who agreed with Judge Russell's verdict, were concerned with the media's and the public's right to know. Judge James Wilkinson said that 'the First Amendment interest in informed popular debate does not simply vanish at the invocation of the words "national security" '. In the Morison defence as well, questions of motivation, and of actual damage to the security of the country, were raised. The US government contended that Morison, by making the photographs public, had alerted Soviet intelligence to the capabilities of US satellite intelligence-gathering techniques. The defence argued that the Soviets were aware of the capability of US satellites, and even had a stolen manual of the KH-11 satellite which had been used to take the photos. They also argued that Morison, a patriot, was warning of the Soviet threat. But Judge Russell said that he had been fired not 'by zeal or public debate but by self-interest to ingratiate himself with *Jane's*'.[215]

In 2001 a former head of research and development in the Israeli army, brigadier-general Yitzhak Yaacov, was arrested for allegedly supplying classified information, including about nuclear matters in which he had been involved, to an Israeli journalist and to an Israeli academic researching the country's nuclear development. His arrest sent a shockwave through the political/defence elite. He may have been arrested partly for just such a purpose: to send a warning that even senior officials and retired veterans are subservient to the secrecy laws. Yaacov had provided the information in order, it was suggested, to ensure his name would enter the history books for his contribution to Israel's defence. In contrast to Vanunu, there was genuine disquiet that a respected retired member of the defence establishment could be arrested for leaking to the media. Nobody made the comparison between the case of Yaacov and that of Vanunu despite the similarity between the two cases, perhaps in order to avoid damaging Yaacov's chances. Yaacov's suspended sentence was very different from the 18-year imprisonment imposed on Vanunu for committing a similar crime. This suggested a 'two-tier' attitude: one for ordinary low-grade technicians, and another for top brass. It also suggested that despite the fact that the judges were not overly preoccupied with the question of Vanunu's 'intent', it played a decisive factor in the difference between the sentences imposed on the two men.

The internal contradictions in squeezing press leaks into the laws of espionage and treason under the existing legal system were addressed in 2001 – belatedly for Vanunu – by the Knesset's law and statute committee, which discussed the need to define more precisely the terms 'espionage' and 'treason'. Among questions raised by the committee were the question of whether somebody who merely unauthorisedly has classified documents in his possession should be subject to the existing laws of espionage and treason; whether the current practice by defence-related agencies in Israel of imposing on all documents a carte-blanche classification of secrecy should be revised in favour of a more selective approach whereby only those documents would be so classified which could damage state security or which come under categories of 'secret subjects' to be approved by the Knesset's defence and foreign affairs committee; and whether the law should not differentiate in the punishment between secrets passed to enemy states, to friendly states, and to the media.

Yehudit Karp, the government's deputy legal adviser, acknowledged the need to revise a law instituted when perceptions of defence issues were different. While the defence agencies – the Mossad, the Shin Bet, and the ministry of defence's security department – are critical of some of the changes proposed, the Shin Bet acknowledges the need to differentiate between secrets passed to enemy states and those to the media. Yet while committee chairman Ophir Pines noted that brigadier-general Yaacov did not engage in treason or espionage in speaking to some journalists, he declined to extend it to Vanunu's case: 'Vanunu also attempted to damage state security,' Pines said.[216]

*   *   *

In 1999, twelve years after the trial was over, the pall of thick secrecy which surrounded the trial disappeared to some extent when the Israeli courts acceded to an appeal presented by *Yediot Aharonot* newspaper for the release of the protocols of the Vanunu trial. The court ruled that a blanket classification was no longer acceptable, and ordered the authorities to examine which sections of the court protocols could be released to the public. Eventually, some 1,170 pages of testimony, about 40 per cent of the total, were declassified.

The protocols released provided highly valuable testimony of senior Israeli officials and policymakers. The information in the protocols was valuable both for the light it threw on Israeli nuclear policy and in providing details of the Vanunu kidnap. In the former category, most telling was the testimony of Dimona engineer 'Giora', who appeared to confirm the speculation about the Israeli Bomb. Asked by prosecution lawyer Uzi Hasson, 'Are the objects in the *Sunday Times*'s photographs objects that exist at the reactor?', he replied, 'Yes'. 'Would an expert understand what the objects mean?', the judge asked. 'Of course', 'Giora' said. But there was little hard information in the released protocols about the nuclear programme itself; much of the material deals with the importance attached to the ambiguity policy and the fact that in highlighting activities at Dimona, Vanunu's action drew international pressure upon Israel. Shimon Peres and Abba Eban in their respective testimonies claimed that the Vanunu exposé had damaged Israeli interests but pinpointed only partly what actual damage had been caused to state security. According to Peres, the Vanunu exposé had damaged Israeli–Norwegian relations. Also, the exposé made more difficult the purchase of a supercomputer capable of being used to simulate nuclear explosions. Also, questions about the nuclear programme were raised by members of the US Congress. There were vague claims that the Vanunu exposé strengthened the Arab arms race. Eban's testimony provided hitherto unknown information about parliamentary supervision by the Knesset's defence and foreign affairs committee and its little-known sub-committee on special matters dealing with the Dimona reactor. Yet equally important was Eban's admission in court that he was 'surprised' by parts of the Vanunu exposé.

The historical value of the protocols lay more in the information and details of the kidnapping. These helped to clear away some of the theories and speculation and build a more authoritative account of the Mordechai Vanunu affair. The testimony of the head of security at Dimona, 'C', shed light on the personnel-vetting procedures at the reactor. It showed that the personnel department had become aware of Vanunu's political activities on the Ben-Gurion University campus while he was still working at the reactor, and that he had been warned on at least three occasions prior to leaving Dimona not to divulge any information about his work. It demolished one theory, that there had been no security fiasco, and that Vanunu had deliberately been allowed to roam and freely to photograph the inside of the reactor complex, in order for the information to be published, thereby heightening the country's nuclear deterrent posture. The protocols also cleared up a certain mystery about the identity and role of Oscar Guerrero in contacting the *Sunday Times* and, later the *Sunday Mirror*. Some British journalists speculated about having seen him together with Mossad agent Cindy. But in the testimony given – behind closed doors – by Shin Bet agents, it was clear that the Israelis had no idea who he was. Also, from the testimony of Albert Vanunu that Mossad agents had approached him on 7 September 1986, it was clear that the Israelis knew at least a month beforehand about Vanunu's contacts. It also revealed that the Israelis considered sending Albert to Europe in the hope of persuading his brother not to reveal his story.

Information slipped into the released protocols unintentionally. Uncensored testimony about how Vanunu was 'brought ashore on a stretcher – and taken into a car on the coast – was accidentally left in[217] – together with the censored page with this description excluded.[218] Under the minister of defence's order, the court was forbidden to refer to the types of transport used by the Mossad to return Vanunu to Israel. The protocols unintentionally cleared up the mystery of whether Vanunu was flown from Europe by El Al, as news reports at the time suggested or, as has been shown to be the case, by sea. But the name of Italy as the country from which it is widely believed Vanunu was abducted does not once appear in the censored version. Another oversight was the publication of the names and career background of two Shin Bet agents Alon X, and Yehuda X, and of 'Giora', the nuclear engineer at the reactor.[219] Yet another error was that the name of the ministry of defence's security departmental head was left in at one point;[220] it was the first time that the previously classified name had been disclosed – but the slip never became known and a Knesset member disclosed the name a year later in the Knesset plenum.

The protocols provided a moving description of Vanunu's emotional feelings at the moment he was kidnapped. Perhaps most important is that the protocols provided a version – albeit censored – of the debate inside the courtroom about the rights and wrongs of nuclear secrecy. The questions and remarks of two of the judges in particular, Judge Shalom Brenner and Judge Zvi Tal, show how serious an attempt was made to weigh the legal arguments from all sides.

Yet the processing and censoring of the protocols was uneven. Entire sections of the testimony of certain witnesses were excluded. Bits of the testimonies of Abba Eban, 'Giora', Shimon Peres, and Mordechai Vanunu which had been excluded from the main sections of their testimonies were later left in in the summings-up of the defence and prosecution lawyers. But most surprising was that the judges' verdict and reasoning were excluded. Even though a summary of the verdict had been released when Vanunu was sentenced in 1988, there was a clear interest for the justice ministry then to release the full 60-page verdict which contained an important message about the need for secrecy and for respecting the democratic process.

On 24 November 1999 excerpts from the court testimony were published by *Yediot Aharonot*. Their publication brought a flood of criticism from Israeli politicians from across the political spectrum. The publication of the protocols, it was charged, would invite diplomatic pressures upon Israel. Witnesses at Vanunu's trial had given testimony behind closed doors, assuming that the 'sensitive' discussion would never see the light of day. Otherwise they would have spoken even less candidly than they did. Officials in the Israeli Atomic Energy Commission and elsewhere in the defence establishment said an error had been made in allowing so much to be published. In contrast to the 1,170-page Vanunu protocols, in another security-sensitive trial – that of Nahum Inbar, an Israeli arms dealer sentenced for selling chemical weapons to Iran – only 82 pages of the protocols were released. Yehiel Horev, the head of the defence ministry's security department, had appointed one of his assistants, Amiram Levine, to handle the matter. Levine had worked in the defence ministry's security department since 1981 as head of the 'special affairs' division. Levine's boss was furious that hundreds of pages of protocols had been released. Levine said he had been under intense pressure from the justice ministry, whose lawyers had persuaded him that the government would be unable to withstand an appeal to the courts. But his boss was not mollified, and Levine was moved elsewhere in the defence ministry, to the post of assistant to the ministry's comptroller.[221]

The big mystery of the protocols was the probing of Vanunu's motives. Feldman complained that the protocols gave Vanunu's voice a punctuated and distorted nature. 'I supported full publication, not partial publication. The publication was very selective, representing the position of the Shin Bet,' Feldman charged.

Yet testimonies by Peter Hounam and by Shin Bet agent Alon X gave expression to Vanunu's ideological motives, and the fact that his goal was not financial. While there may be truth in Feldman's claims, many of the white spots from the censor's blue-pencilling appear to be in contexts referring to sensitive defence-related matters, rather than discussion of views. The published protocols suggest that Vanunu's intellectual process to justify his deed was incomplete at the time – posing the possibility that the thought process achieved its fruition in the years after the trial.[222]

10
Friends from Afar

Vanunu was held in solitary confinement for the first twelve years of his imprisonment. His cell, in an isolated wing of Ashkelon prison, measured three by two metres; it had a bed, shelf and table and a small window above head height. Initially, his light was kept on for 24 hours a day, and there was a close up camera because the authorities feared he might do damage to himself. He spent much of the day reading. His choice of literature was eclectic: Thomas Mann, T.S. Eliot, Franz Kafka, Baruch Spinoza, and William Shakespeare. He was allowed out to an isolated exercise yard for two hours a day, and he did yoga on his cell floor.

The solitary confinement was characterised by very limited contact with the outside world. The only people with whom he could talk were his family, whom he was allowed to see for half an hour every two weeks, or an hour once a month. These visits were subject to being suspended; in 1992, after Vanunu was verbally abusive to a warder who awoke him at 2 am, they were cancelled for a month. All meetings were in the presence of the prison governor or a senior prison warder, and a security agent. He could speak with his lawyer any time he wished, in practice once a month or once in two months. Another contact was a priest who used to celebrate Communion once a month, mostly on Sunday.

After Mordechai's's arrest, Meir, his elder brother, who since childhood had had considerable influence over Mordechai, was his primary contact with the outside world. But after Meir disclosed classified information about the abduction he was unable to return to Israel for years lest he face arrest, and lived in London for much of the time. The main contact with Mordechai fell on the more reserved brother, Asher, a secondary-school teacher of History and Citizenship. Another brother, Danny, attended to every one of his brother's variegated and whimsical demands, even if he, like Asher, had little sympathy with his brother's actions.

Mordechai's contacts with his parents were spasmodic at best. Initially, they cut ties, resuming them later to a small degree. His father, Shlomo, never fully recovered from a stroke. His mother, Mazal, found seeing her son behind bars so depressing that she visited only infrequently. The couple, suffering abuse from their neighbours in Beersheba over their son's deed, moved northwards to Bnei Beraq, living near their two married daughters.

Seeing his relatives and his lawyer was hardly compensation for being unable to form or maintain other relationships. The authorities agreed to his using cassettes, which could be vetted, but Vanunu was not given access to a telephone, a privilege accorded most Israeli prisoners. A small consolation was a radio, generally forbidden in Israeli prisons because prisoners might fight over which stations to tune in to. He listened often to the BBC World Service, and he also had a television set.

Initially, he kept up a wide correspondence despite the rigorous censorship of his outgoing mail. He wrote to the Israeli media and politicians on nuclear matters, and to individuals like Peter Hounam and Frank Barnaby. In the early years of imprisonment, the Reverend John McKnight, who had converted Vanunu to Christianity, wrote about once a month. But by 1990, the fourth year of his imprisonment, Mordechai wrote seldom, even to Meir. In a letter to him in early 1991 Mordechai wrote, 'I have written you many letters – but they don't let me send them to you. I have a lot to tell. They're still using their powers to shut my mouth – but they're unable to shut my brain. When I am free, I will speak ... I have nothing to lose.' According to US campaigner Sam Day, who edited a collection of Vanunu's letters from prison, *Faith Under Siege*, 'the letters show a sharp break in Vanunu's state of mind'.[1] By the 1990s he was getting more mail than any other inmate at Ashkelon prison. At Christmas he would receive some 1,000 cards or letters.

His faith in Christianity was sorely tried by the prison conditions – and broken. During the first five years, he read the Bible daily. Initially, he remained convinced that he had done God's will and that the courts would recognise that he had acted for the good and give him a light sentence. He looked forward to the weekly visits of Brother Gilbert Sinden, of St John's Cathedral, where he performed the Eucharist. The centrality of his new faith was evident in the first years of his imprisonment while he awaited the decision of the courts. In February 1987, six months after his arrest, he wrote to Reverend David Smith at St John's in Sydney, 'I find love in Christianity and Jesus. Everyone has to open his heart to find this love.' In July of that year he wrote to Smith,

My spirit is good and I believe that all my suffering will be ended soon. My faith and the words of St Paul keep me strong, and my prayers give me power to wait for my freedom, and you helped me to know Christ.

This unbounded faith worried Sinden, who wrote to Smith that

Vanunu does seem to think that he will be acquitted at his trial or at worst given a very light sentence. I sense the atmosphere of this land. I feel it is important to build him up to be ready to receive a very harsh sentence.'[2]

When Vanunu did not indeed receive that light sentence he nevertheless remained convinced that God would save him at the Supreme Court hearing. When this did not occur either, it challenged his Christianity:

> My belief and faith has suffered a great weakness. I am not practising any religious things, and I am no longer interested in faith and religion. This life in prison cannot make a man more religious. The hard life sends a message to believe only in material things and to be more earthly. However, I am still a Christian. This is my identity.[3]

In a letter in July 1987 Vanunu even charged that John McKnight and the other churchmen were 'cooperating with the security services cartel'.[4] Indeed, for four years until 1995 Vanunu ceased to maintain contact by post with his brother Meir and with supporters and protesters. He told his adoptive mother, Mary Eoloff, that he 'read the Bible daily for the first five years of imprisonment but now I get my strength from within myself'.

According to Dr Ruhamah Marton of Doctors for Civil Rights, 'To sit in isolation in a cell is one of the most terrible experiences imaginable. A person is left in a vacuum, like rotting wood, doesn't feel anything. Loss of his system of senses is comparable to death.' While for the first years of his imprisonment Vanunu was concerned with his trial and the court appeal, there was now little for him to hope for. At the beginning he had delusions that he was being followed by the security services. By 1991 he had spells of dizziness, and difficulties in concentration. By 1996 the isolation had become so severe in duration that he suspected all around him. He suspected that music programmes and the BBC were intended to manipulate his mind and drive him crazy. He even suspected his lawyer, and subsequently suspended contact with him for a time. His friends were Mossad agents. By 1997 he was reading hidden meanings in the postage stamps and letters sent to him.

In 1995 the then police minister Moshe Shahal set up a committee to investigate the legal basis for holding Vanunu in solitary, following a request from Dedi Zucker, chairman of the Knesset's statute committee, concerning the length of Vanunu's solitary confinement. Prison regulations, while not specifiying how long a prisoner may be held in solitary, suggest days or months. The committee's report acknowledged the serious psychological consequences of prolonged isolation and recommended various steps to alleviate the isolation, including that a prisoner held in solitary should share his cell with at least one more prisoner in solitary. Perhaps most important in the report – which was only recommendatory – was that the power to hold a prisoner in solitary should require the special permission of a court judge instead of, as at present, just that of the prison authorities.

International criticism of Vanunu's imprisonment conditions brought two ministers to Ashkelon to inspect them, David Libai in 1993 and Avigdor Kahalani in 1997. Justice minister Libai, a Tel Aviv University professor of criminology, and an acknowledged dove, was one of the few justice ministers in Israel's history to have made a point of visiting prisoners. When police or 'internal security' minister Kahalani entered his cell in 1997 Vanunu asked him to intervene. Kahalani told him: 'I have no powers. It is all determined by the Shin Bet.'

> *Vanunu:* You are the minister, you can intervene.
>
> *Kahalani:* You disclosed state secrets, and now you want to be together with Arab security prisoners?!
>
> *Vanunu:* I did not reveal state secrets. I saved the country. You won't use nuclear weapons again.
>
> *Kahalani:* I don't know whether or not we have the Bomb. What I do know is that as a soldier I fought on the front to defend you. You damaged my security and that of my children. You need to pay for this.
>
> *Vanunu:* Who gave you the right to kidnap me?
>
> *Kahalani:* We have the rule of law, and you need to pay for what you did.[5]

Asher Vanunu attempted to enlist some left-wing Knesset members to improve Mordechai's prison conditions, but with little success. He turned to the Israeli Association of Civil Rights, which represented Vanunu in 1995. But owing to the latter's suspicions about the assocation, its involvement ended. The solitary confinement was routinely renewed every six months by the prison governor upon instructions from the Shin Bet without recourse to the courts. Feldman appealed to a Jerusalem court in 1991 to have solitary confinement ended, but the prosecution charged that the incident in which Vanunu wrote on his palm the details of how, according to him, he had been kidnapped from Italy was evidence of his determination to continue disclosing information.

During one appeal by Vanunu for an easing of his prison conditions, Judge Zvi Cohen said that these were without doubt difficult, but the key was in Vanunu's hands. Cohen recommend that another prisoner, chosen by the prison governor, join Vanunu in his cell. Although Feldman suggested that Vanunu at least try it for an experimental period, Vanunu – suspecting the cellmate would inform on him – turned down the offer, claiming that the authorities did not have the right to decide who the cellmate should be. The authorities proposed that he be placed with another Jewish security prisoner, but Vanunu wanted to be with other Palestinian security prisoners (there are 700 Palestinian prisoners and 40 Jewish prisoners at the high-security prison). Feldman claimed that Vanunu, rather than being held in solitary confinement, should be brought to trial in the event of his disclosing more information. Underlying the policy of solitary confinement was a clash between what Vanunu saw as his right and responsibility to disclose information and what the authorities saw as their right to protect secrets. Some perceived the solitary confinement as an attempt by the security authorities to seal Vanunu's lips by driving him crazy.

There were also bizarre court appeals. Vanunu appealed to know whether 'Cindy' had been murdered: 'Is it possible that this woman has been killed by those who planned the kidnapping?' He also appealed against Shimon Peres' election as prime minister on the grounds that he had given the order to kidnap Vanunu.

The solitary confinement engendered sympathy among anti-nuclear and human rights groups around the world. For these groups, Mordechai Vanunu was a way to draw public attention to the danger of nuclearisation in the Middle East. Organisations like the Bertrand Russell Peace Foundation, the Association for Peace in Italy, Mouvement la Paix in France, Abolition 2000, an umbrella organisation representing 700 nuclear disarmament groups world-wide, and the Geneva-based International Peace Bureau, another umbrella organisation comprising peace groups lobbied local politicians as well as the Israeli authorities and engaged in informational activities.

In early 1990 Amnesty International observers who had come to Israel for his trial called his conditions of imprisonment 'cruel, inhuman and degrading' – a category of ill-treatment one level below torture. They claimed that steps could he taken by the prison authorities to ensure Vanunu did not disclose more information as well as 'protecting' him from 'other prisoners' (another reason given for his isolation) without solitary confinement. There had been considerable discussion in Amnesty International, including pressure on the organisation's central committee from local Amnesty chapters, for Vanunu to be recognised as a prisoner of conscience. He fitted Amnesty's classification because he is non-violent, and his action was motivated by conscience, but since he had disclosed military secrets (which a country has a right to under international law) the organisation withheld the status. He joins an illustrious list which includes Daniel Elsberg, not accorded the status for disclosing the Pentagon Papers, and Nelson Mandela, who backed armed struggle.

Internationally acclaimed scientists who identify with the anti-nuclear lobby added their names to appeals to the Israeli authorities. When awarded the Nobel Peace Prize in 1995 Dr Joseph Rotblat of Pugwash, the anti-nuclear weapons organisation, singled Vanunu out in his acceptance speech for 'the exceptional price Vanunu was paying for "whistleblowing" '. Rotblat, who withdrew from the Manhattan Project in Los Alamos during the Second World War for reasons of conscience, becoming an activist in the non-proliferation movement, for which he was barred from entering the USA until 1964, argued that whistleblowing 'should become part of the scientist's ethos'. But Rotblat's sympathy for Vanunu was qualified by his belief that governments should punish those who reveal its secrets.

Vanunu has often been proposed by supporters for the Nobel Peace Prize. In 1987 he was given the Right Livelihood Award (worth $25,000), an alternative 'Nobel'-of-sorts dealing with issues like ecology and anti-nuclearism. Other prizes awarded to Vanunu included the 1988 Danish Peace Prize and the 1994 Sean McBride Prize of the International Peace Bureau.

The level of international support varied from country to country. Britain was the first country where an organised Vanunu campaign was launched. This is not suprising since the Vanunu affair began there. The Mossad abduction of Vanunu was enough to generate concern. Living in London, Meir Vanunu played an important role in the initial years of the campaign as a favoured speaker to groups. Meir tried to walk a thin line of aligning with the anti-nuclear movement while ensuring that prominence was given to his brother's plight. The UK campaign, coordinated by Ernest Rottker, a professional carpenter, and Rami Heilbronn, an Israeli-born psychiatrist, was characterised by seeking out 'elite' left-wing sympathy. By the early 1990s the UK Campaign to Free Mordechai Vanunu had assembled a respectable group of artists, writers, human rights activists and parliamentarians. These included playright Harold Pinter, actress Susannah York, Peter Benenson, Amnesty International's founder, and Bruce Kent, former chairman of the Campaign for Nuclear Disarmament.

The campaign had a useful channel for raising popular sympathy for Vanunu through publicity on the *Sunday Times* pages devoted to the campaign and more generally to Vanunu himself. Among its activities were a weekly vigil on Saturdays outside the Israeli embassy, lobbying of MPs and presenting early day motions in the House of Commons, and artistic benefit events for the Vanunu cause. (Its 'conscience-raising' ploys extended to propagating a 'Mr V hybrid clematis'; the flower, registered at the Royal Horticultural Society, has white petals, with a central light green vein of the Henryi variety, and the dark purple centre of the Nelly Moser variety.) Though considered one of the largest pro-Vanunu groups, it had only 2,500 on its mailing list. Yet its success in influencing policy was small. The UK campaign was held at arm's length by the Foreign and Commonwealth Office. While the Vanunu issue was occasionally raised in Parliament and while the subject of his imprisonment conditions was the subject of discussion with the Israeli authorities, successive British governments, including the Labour government, declined to press the Israelis for Vanunu's release, saying it was an internal Israeli matter. 'Anybody revealing sensitive military secrets in any country risks harsh punishment,' one British minister said.

Yet the Vanunu issue had disturbing echoes for Israel's image inside Britain. A petition with 17,000 signatures calling for Vanunu's release was presented to the Israeli embassy. Parliamentary delegations visited Israel, including one of Parliament's Human Rights group, which pressed the issue with Israeli officials. British lawyers attempted to sue the Israeli government in the British courts for Vanunu's abduction.

The North American campaign on Vanunu's behalf began in 1992. In contrast to the UK campaign, the American campaign engaged in more 'passive grassroots resistance', including deploying such tactics as activists forcing their way into Israeli consulates and the Israeli embassy in Washington – which often resulted in arrests. In 1997 demonstrators wearing Vanunu T-shirts blocked the entrance to the Nevada nuclear test site. It made only limited inroads with the American public. Though one of the largest campaigns in the world, with chapters in various major cities including Washington DC, San Francisco, New York and Chicago, its mailing list was limited to some 2,000 people.

Until his death in 2001, the campaign in the United States was led by Sam Day of Wisconsin. A former editor of the respected *Bulletin of Atomic Scientists*, Day had a long track record of anti-nuclear pacifism. Born into a privileged background, with parents who served as US diplomats in South Africa, he soon shed this status. He served six months in prison in 1989 for entering a missile launch site in Missouri; four months in 1991 for entering the Fort McCoy base, Wisconsin, to protest the Gulf War; and 16 months for unauthorisedly distributing peace literature at a base in Omaha where long-range nuclear weapons are stored. 'Vanunu did what we have been doing for years in the US. For Israel to keep its nuclear programme secret is dangerous in itself, as well as a bad example to other countries,' he said. 'Vanunu was a model for nuclear weapons workers elsewhere,' he added. In 1994 he was arrested seven times while demonstrating for Vanunu. In contrast to the UK campaign, Day believed that freedom for Vanunu the individual was part of the wider international struggle for human rights, peace and nuclear disarmament.

Day's most celebrated act of anti-nuclearism had occurred years prior to the Vanunu exposé when, while he was its managing editor, *The Progressive* magazine challenged a US law prohibiting the publication of information about manufacturing nuclear weapons. One of the magazine's reporters, Howard Morland, wrote an article entitled 'The H-Bomb Secret' on how to make a hydrogen bomb which drew wholly on interviews with scientists and information found in books. But, at the behest of President Carter, the US department of energy, which has responsibility for designing and manufacturing the US nuclear arms programme, got a federal judge to block *The Progressive* from publishing the article, claiming that it could help a foreign government or terrorist organisation to build an atomic bomb. After a six-month legal battle – and following the article's publication elsewhere – the US government climbed down.

Perhaps the most novel form of Vanunu campaigning was the decision in 1997 of a middle-aged couple from Minnesota, Nick and Mary Eoloff, to adopt Mordechai. Lifelong pacifists, the Catholic couple, who have six children, were impressed by what Mary Eoloff described as 'Vanunu's courageous war against nuclear weapons and by the manner he withstood the treatment to which he was subjected as a result of his adherence to his principles.' But for Vanunu himself the 'adoption' served as little more than a tactic in his struggle to leave Israel for the US.[6]

The Eoloffs were initially under the impression that adoption would win Vanunu American citizenship – which could subsequently help to get him admitted to the US – but this is limited to adopting children less than 16 years old.

By the late 1990s the US campaign to free Mordechai Vanunu had redefined its lobbying tactics and focused upon lobbying in Washington. Yet with Congress's sympathy for Israel, oiled by a powerful Jewish lobby, campaigning for Vanunu was an uphill battle at best.

In 1999 two Democratic (and Jewish) senators, Russell Finegold (Wisconsin) and Paul Wellstone (Minnesota), took up the matter with secretary of state Madeleine Albright. She told them, 'We do not wish to support and endorse his activities. The charges for which Vanunu was convicted are very serious. But Vanunu's moral deterioration [in solitary confinement] is one that ought to be reviewed on humanitarian grounds.'[7] The same year, US activists lobbied a dozen House Representatives in the US, led by Donald Dellum, a Californian Democrat, to write to President Clinton seeking his intervention in Vanunu's plight.

Later, in 1999, a year after Vanunu's release from solitary confinement, the US campaign, with the help of a part-time lobbyist on Capitol Hill, persuaded 36 Democrats – comprising 17 per cent of House Democrats – to write to Clinton to intercede and seek Vanunu's release from prison. Clinton replied,

> We are closely following the matter of Vanunu's incarceration. We are particularly concerned by reports [of the conditions] in which he is being held. I share your concerns on the matter of Israel's nuclear program. We will continue to raise these subjects with Israel.[8]

Although Vanunu campaigners were realistic enough to believe that the chances of Vanunu's release were not high – and were lessened yet further after the Republican victory in 2001 – in pushing the Vanunu case on Capitol Hill it had located a sensitive spot in Israeli officialdom.

In parallel with their efforts on Capitol Hill, members of the US campaign worked within America's anti-nuclear and peace lobby, recruiting the support of Professor Hans Bethe, a former director of the Los Alamos laboratory, and the Federation of American Scientists (FAS). Further afield, it got support from another whistleblower, Daniel Ellsberg, who leaked the Pentagon Papers, and from Americans who had been held hostage in Lebanon. It also won the ear of ex-president Jimmy Carter. The US campaign folded in 2005, a year after Vanunu's release from prison.

Three other countries which were directly involved in the Vanunu affair were Norway, Italy and Australia. Sympathy for Vanunu in Norway – which had supplied Israel with heavy water for its reactor – grew from the mid-1990s on, and centred around the efforts of lawyer Frederik Heffermehl, the president of the Norwegian Peace Alliance, an umbrella organisation for the country's peace movement. He was instrumental in Vanunu's nomination for the Nobel Prize. In 2001 he was awarded an honorary doctorate by Tromsø University, Norway's most northerly university, which had a long tradition of making such awards in human rights cases involving political oppression.

The Norwegian government took an active stance on Vanunu's plight from the mid-1990s on as a result of growing sympathy and mass petitions calling for Vanunu's release. Norway's key role in Israeli–Palestinian diplomacy, which resulted in the Oslo accords, gave the government the entrée to Jerusalem – far more influence than the small Scandinavian country could normally have expected. In 1995 its deputy foreign minister said, 'Notwithstanding that the Israeli authorities regard Vanunu as having harmed national security, we hope that the peace process will result in positive consequences for Vanunu.' Its foreign minister told the then Israeli minister Yossi Beilin, 'as Norway's involvement in the Israeli–Palestinian process grows, so do pressures inside the country in the matter of Vanunu.'

In Italy, a pro-Vanunu committee was formed in 1990 in the aftermath of disclosures of how Vanunu had been kidnapped from there, but it folded after a short while. The Comitato Libertà per Vanunu – whose founders included Supreme Court judge Amedeo Postiglione, a specialist in environmental law, and senator Giovanni Russo – revived in 1997 with the goal of reopening the official inquiry into the circumstances of Vanunu's disappearance. This followed the disclosure by an Israeli newspaper of how an Israeli naval craft had been involved in the abduction. But the Rome government declined to reopen the enquiry on grounds of insufficient evidence.

In Australia, pro-Vanunu activity centred around St John's Church, Sydney, where Vanunu had lived and was baptised before leaving to meet with the *Sunday Times* team in London. But after Reverend John McKnight left the church, activity declined. In 1996, after a church service marking ten years since the abduction (today the church has a replica of his prison cell next to the baptismal font in the corner of the sanctuary), the church's assistant pastor, Reverend Simon Henderson-Brooks, relaunched the campaign.

Elsewhere, pro-Vanunu committees existed in Belgium, Canada, Finland, France, Germany, New Zealand, Portugal and Sweden. For many the anniversary of the kidnapping, 30 September, was a key calendar date for such consciousness-raising activity as demonstrations outside Israeli diplomatic posts.

Church groups active in promoting peace and anti-nuclearism have also taken up the Vanunu issue, among them the Quaker movement, the Anglican Church, the Catholic Workers' Group, and the United Reformed Church or United Church. Most active was the Episcopalian Church; Vanunu was the recipient of the church's international award for 'courageous, and conscientious witness for peace and justice'. In 2000 Vanunu was elected Humanist of the Year by the Church of Humanism in New York. Yet it would be wrong to exaggerate the amount of support which Vanunu generated for himself. With the exception of the Episcopalian Church in the United States, none of the mainstream churches came out in active support – despite Vanunu's conversion to their faith. 'Vanunu had no influence in the mainstream Christian bodies because since the end of the Cold War, nuclear weapons have been of minimal influence really. Ninety per cent of the church leadership wouldn't even know who Vanunu was,' remarked Reverend Bruce Kent.[9] With the collapse of the Cold War, church attention turned from the Bomb to social concerns such as crime, housing and education. While the Church said that nuclear weapons were bad, nuclear deterrence, as the Pope said in the 1980s, was regarded as an acceptable solution in the short term if sugared by governmental promises of step-by-step disarmament. Other church leaders, including the Archbishop of Canterbury, have been hesitant in identifying with the campaign's goals, partly in order not to enter into potential conflict with Israel or the Jewish community. For this reason, Vanunu campaigners have attached importance to winning over Jews, and particularly rabbis, to their ranks. The US-based Jewish Peace Fellowship, which opposes nuclear weaponry, came out in support. A number of rabbis in the Reform Jewish movement have also done so. But both Vanunu's own rejection of his Jewish roots and the general reticence of Diaspora Jewry in publicly criticising Israel have made it an uphill battle.

There was a lack of coordination between the various Vanunu support groups. This was partly due to the difference in tactics, such as between the US grassroots anti-nuclear campaign and the more elite-orientated British campaign which was geared more towards the Vanunu cause alone. The Israeli support group, while important for providing those abroad with ongoing information about Vanunu's plight, was itself too strapped for supporters and finance to have fulfilled its potential uniting role among groups worldwide.

The Vanunu campaign took a revolutionary turn with the evolution of the Internet, which had the potential to bring the Vanunu cause to a potentially far wider audience. All the Vanunu support groups carried websites, with many having more than one site. One search elicited over 1,000 Vanunu-related sites.[10] On many of the sites the information covered background to the case and developments since Vanunu's imprisonment including his court appeals. Transcripts, for example of a Knesset debate on nuclear weaponry, appear on some. Sites also act as noticeboards for local activities of Vanunu support groups.

It would be wrong to exaggerate the level of international acclaim which Vanunu generated for himself. The Vanunu campaign never mushroomed into a truly international movement. In no foreign country did the Vanunu issue generate a widespread base of popular support like that enjoyed by Nelson Mandela in South Africa and Natan Sharansky in the Soviet Union during their struggles for freedom. One exception was a huge petition of 1 million Norwegian signatures demanding Vanunu's release from members of some 65 organisations in the country. The Vanunu issue was debated in parliaments, mostly as a result of initiatives by liberal and socalist politicians. The Green party initiated a debate in the Bundestag in 1987, and Italian politicians called on their government to investigate his abduction. In 1998 an Australian senate resolution called for Vanunu's release, as did one by 50 members of the Swedish parliament. Four such resolutions have been passed in the European parliament, in 1989, 1990, 1991, and 1997. In 1990 the European parliament called on the Israeli president to pardon Vanunu; failing this, aid and scientific cooperation between the European Union and Israel could be 'delayed'. But the realignment of the Middle East in the 1991 Gulf War, with Israel being identified with the US-led coalition, resulted in these cooperation agreements being implemented after all.

The subject of Vanunu's release did not move from the parliamentary arena to the diplomatic arena. With the exception of the Norwegian government, no foreign Western government called upon Israel to release Vanunu. Three Israeli premiers, Itzhak Rabin, Benjamin Netanyahu and Ehud Barak, were approached by their Norwegian opposite number to make such a gesture. Prior to Vanunu's release from solitary confinement other governments, like those of the United States, Britain and Germany, raised the issue of his imprisonment conditions but carefully stopped short of seeking his release, acknowledging that it was an internal matter for the Israeli government. And despite the direct interest of Italy and Britain in Vanunu's disappearance, neither turned the subject into a diplomatic *casus belli* with Jerusalem.

The absence both of a resonant movement of sympathisers abroad, in particular in the US, and of a wide support base in Israel, doomed the campaign. Ironically, the countries with the largest Vanunu campaigns, the US and Britain – both nuclear powers – were the least likely to pressure Israel concerning Vanunu's release. In those countries whose governments were more inclined to do so and which were anti-nuclear – Norway, the Netherlands, Germany and Ireland – Vanunu failed to generate interest and support among the public. Most surprising was the fact that Vanunu failed to generate support in Africa and Latin America, partly because the very absence of the Bomb in those regions meant there were no widespread anti-nuclear campaigns there. As superpower rivalry ended, concern for the danger of nuclear proliferation was replaced by concern for issues such as economic recession, unemployment and the environment. And even though the 1991 Iraq War reminded people of the danger of non-conventional weaponry in the region, there was no fallout for Vanunu's personal fate. The Vanunu campaign was little more than a public-relations annoyance, but it did ensure that the Israeli authorities were aware that there were groups monitoring his condition. It led Sam Day to conclude that 'I have little doubt that Vanunu won't be released before he serves his full 18 years. Our activity is above all educational. Opening people's eyes to the meaning of nuclear weapons is the best education.'[11] It remains to be asked whether pressure-group activity was the right approach in the case of a country where nuclear policy is central to its existence. 'Israel doesn't give in easily to pressure. We ought to have worked more through secret diplomacy to get his release,' said Frederik Heffermehl.[12]

Inside Israel, Vanunu was regarded as a traitor. The small minority abroad (not directly affected by Israeli nuclear policy) who supported Vanunu contrasted with the very, very small minority inside Israel (directly affected by the policy and by the region's military balance).

After the Vanunu exposé in 1986 a debate raged across the Israeli left over the rights and wrongs of Vanunu's action. In an article in the left-wing *Al Hamishmar*, Gideon Spiro, who later became one of the leaders of the pro-Vanunu campaign in Israel, caused some controversy when he compared Vanunu to a parent who punished a child for wanting to stick a metal wire into an electric socket:

> If a parent who prevented their child from being electrocuted were brought to trial on charges of child abuse, they would think that the system had gone mad. Vanunu feared that if the government succeeded in sticking a metal wire (a nuclear one) into a socket it would electrocute us all in a nuclear death.[13]

The newspaper's literary editor, Yael Lotan, who joined Spiro in the campaign, was more circumspect and compared the Vanunu case to the Israeli public's reaction to the 1982 Lebanon War. Most people supported the Lebanon War. Today this has been reversed. The majority now know that it wasn't a war, Lotan argued, but simply bloodshed caused by a few leaders who wanted to 'impose order' in a neighbouring country by force.

However, others like Yoram Nimrod, a Haifa University historian who had campaigned since the 1960s in favour of open debate on nuclear policy, said that Vanunu's disclosure was damaging, and that people would identify the cause of a non-nuclear Israel and nuclear disarmament with 'the treason of Vanunu'. And Levi Morav, a left-wing journalist, argued that a public debate did not require the colourful pictures of the reactor which Vanunu had taken to the *Sunday Times*. Even the centre-leaning socialist *Davar*, the organ of the trade union movement, editorialised that the way to advance his struggle should have been via the Knesset and the government.

Three months after the *Sunday Times*'s exposé the Committee for a Public Trial for Mordechai Vanunu was formed (later the Committee for Mordechai Vanunu). It had three objectives. First, that Vanunu should receive a public trial instead of the closed-doors trial he was given. Second, that the campaign's focus should be less on Vanunu's personality and more on the nuclear issue. Third, to encourage public debate on the nuclear question as a means of getting the country to sign the Nuclear Proliferation Treaty. This committee succeeded the Israel Committee for the Middle East Free From Nuclear, Biological and Chemical Weaponry, which had been established in the aftermath of the Chernobyl disaster. In 1996 it organised the International Conference on Democracy, Human Rights and Mordechai Vanunu, attracting internationally known names including Joseph Rotblat and Daniel Ellsberg.[14] But the pro-Vanunu campaign made little headway, and remained on Israel's political fringe. Popular Israeli support in favour of the possession of the Bomb hindered the committee from becoming a centre-stage political movement like the left-wing Peace Now movement which favoured territorial compromise for peace. At the beginning of the 1990s the Committee for Mordechai Vanunu numbered 50 members. Ten years later the number had risen to only 500.

Mordechai Vanunu was scathing in his criticism of the Israeli media:

> As a rule the Israeli media took a one-sided view of the affair. Why is it impossible to think about a second side? There is no democracy here nor any campaigning media. Show me one word which was written in my affair which did not come from the establishment.[15]

Yet a subtle change could be discerned among educated liberal Israeli opinion during the 1990s, not only favouring Vanunu's release from solitary confinement but even his early release. In addition to Hadash, the Communist party, and some also in the left-wing Meretz, among them Knesset member Zahava Galon, backed early release. Shulamit Aloni of Meretz, who had been communications minister, said in 1996 that no penal code allows one to 'send somebody mad'. Vanunu posed no danger. In the last ten years science and technology had changed. There was an element of revenge. The government should release him. Liberal writers and journalists such as Aryeh Shalev and Yaron London penned their support for his early release. Yehonathan Geffen, a *Maariv* columnist, argued in that newspaper that:

> If we free Vanunu now and realise that what he tried to do was be a total revolutionary, out of real fear for the atom bomb, it will not only be an act of kindness to Vanunu, it will also show the whole world that the fear of the atom bomb and the nuclear race scares all of us and sometimes makes people do desperate things just as dropping the atom bomb is a desperate act.

Part of the credit for the change in Israeli public perceptions goes to some artistic portrayals of the Vanunu message. These took the Vanunu question out of its political-defence paradigm, cracking open the stereotype which the defence establishment tried to foster of Vanunu as traitor. They range from Hanan Cohen's exhibit 'Who Will Press the Button?' (1993), to Micky Tropher's life-size figure of Vanunu (2000) which was constructed entirely of barbed wire, to Benny Efrati's exhibition entitled 'A Handful of Sweets, Summer 2048' which included an imaginary Israeli postage stamp with a portrait of Vanunu. In his documentary film, entitled *I am Your Spy*, Nissim Mossek (1997) filmed a car journey taken by Meir Vanunu to Ashkelon to visit his brother in prison. The constancy of film movement – interspersed with interviews with Hiroshima victims – was designed to transform the viewer from perceiving Vanunu as a traitor to a newer reality where the Israeli Bomb would be a subject of discussion by the Israeli public, and would eventually be dismantled. In 2001, Israel Television's Channel 2 broadcast Einat Fishbein's documentary on Vanunu and his campaign. Though sympathetic, the programme was disappointing because it failed to throw new light on the affair.

Most successful was Yigal Azarti's play *Mister V – Searching for Mordechai Vanunu*. Its performances in Israel won favourable reviews. Later, it toured North America and Britain. Performed in a space the exact size of the three-by-two-metre cell in which Mordechai Vanunu was held in solitary for twelve years, Jonathan Cherchi's one-man performance brought home the man's torture as memories, philosophical thoughts and hallucinations poured forth from his mind. As he paced out the dimensions of his constantly lit cell, Cherchi and Azarti attempted to exploit the idea of control: control of the individual by a state steeped in fear and self-censorship of the 'forbidden subject'. A clue to the play's success in breaking down the traitor stereotype was a poll conducted by a researcher from Tel Aviv University's Theatre Studies department. It found that 27 per cent of people who saw the play changed their opinion about Vanunu afterwards, and 89 per cent said the performance added new information about Vanunu's case.

But change was confined to segments of the liberal intelligentsia. It reflected the centrality of the Bomb as deterrent in Israel, including Israel One party or Labour party thinking. Nor did any government minister while in office favour an early release. Amnon Dankner of *Maariv* noted that Vanunu had damaged the most secret part of Israel's security and that whoever does so should know that if they extend a hand to the fire, they will get burned. In an editorial entitled 'A Third Off? For Vanunu', *Haaretz* opined, 'When the judges gave Vanunu 18 years the assumption was that he would serve 18 years and not be released for good behaviour. As a country based on law, we cannot afford to act lightly towards those entrusted with the most secret of information who break this trust. Vanunu could have chosen democratic ways to advance his views against Israeli nuclear policy.'[16]

After more than eleven years in solitary confinement Vanunu was released from it in March 1998, and allowed to mix with the rest of the prison population. Yehiel Horev, the chief security officer of the Israeli ministry of defence, was the official responsible for prison conditions and for Vanunu's release.

The process which finally resulted in Vanunu's release from solitary went back four years to December 1993. Using his status as chairman of the Knesset's statute committee, Knesset member Dedi Zucker of Meretz met with Vanunu, who told Zucker that the solitary confinement was unbearable. 'I had the impression that he had a very strong sense of mission and self-control. I did have the impression that he was sane,' Zucker said.[17]

Three years passed with no improvement in Vanunu's imprisonment conditions. International pleas to alleviate them went unheeded. Then in 1997 another member of the Knesset, Yossi Katz of the Labour party, took up the case after reading about them. It was while chairing the Knesset state comptroller's committee that his attention was drawn to the question of the imprisonment conditions of security prisoners. A lawyer from Haifa specialising in labour law, Katz had a track record on human rights. In sympathising with Vanunu's imprisonment Katz placed himself on the left of the centrist-inclined Israel One or the Labour party. But he distinguished between the imprisonment and Vanunu's crime of disclosing nuclear secrets.

Katz told Vanunu that if he would undertake not to discuss his work at the reactor, it might be possible to get him out of solitary. But Vanunu refused, saying that it would impinge on his freedom of speech. However, he was prepared to undertake not to discuss the names of other workers at Dimona because he 'respected their right of privacy'. Katz informed the Shin Bet head Ami Ayalon of Vanunu's willingness not to disclose workers' names, and Ayalon replied he had no objection to Vanunu being taken out of solitary. The matter, Ayalon added, was up to Yehiel Horev. The latter told Katz that Vanunu was no longer a security risk. So did justice ministry official Deborah Hen, who was responsible for the Vanunu file, and who was known for being unbending on security cases. The new police minister, Avigdor Kahalani, gave the order to release him from solitary.

At noon on 12 March 1998, Ashkelon prison governor Itzhak Gabbai entered Vanunu's cell and with an air of unusual formality, read out an official announcement. From now on the door to his cell would be locked only at night. Vanunu could come and go as he pleased.

With a feeling of apprehension, Vanunu emerged into the raucous prison yard where the inmates were mingling. He was nervous about how they would treat him. After all, he was a convicted spy. They were curious and there was no antagonism. He strolled round the yard, chatting with other inmates and staring at the factories beyond the prison walls – his first glimpse of the outside world in more than a decade. Vanunu had to reacquaint himself with such long-forgotten pleasures as chatting with passers-by, looking at the open sky, seeing plants and flowers.

The authorities had climbed down, it appeared; 1-0 to Vanunu. Disclosing or not disclosing the names of fellow workers at Dimona was never a factor in holding Vanunu in solitary. The issue was Vanunu's continuing refusal to undertake not to disclose the secrets of Dimona. With a pending appeal to the Supreme Court by Vanunu's lawyer, and against the background of growing international pressure, the Israeli government preferred to climb down before a court ordered it to do so. Yet in practice, the effect of solitary confinement for more than a decade had dulled Vanunu's memories of the classified secrets of Dimona, and he was no longer a 'danger to national security'. Vanunu's twelve years in isolation served the interests of the defence establishment in dulling Vanunu's memory and causing him to forget highly classified technical information from his work inside the reactor. With that achieved – and with Vanunu still remaining behind bars for another six years – there was little reason even for the hawkish security officials within the defence establishment to continue to insist on his being held in solitary confinement.

A month after he was taken out of solitary the Vanunu file came up before the prison parole board. To be sure, decisions by prison parole boards or by the state president are determined less by the prisoner's expressions of regret for the deed and more by the likelihood or unlikelihood of the prisoner committing the crime again. 'Yet', as Feldman said, 'if he did regret his action – and he was not going to – it might have helped.' In a letter to the Israeli authorities, Dr Ray Kidder, an American nuclear scientist who worked at the Lawrence Livermore Natural Laboratory,

> challenged any official asssertion that Vanunu possesses any technical nuclear information not already made public. Vanunu had little information because of his limited expertise in nuclear science and because of tight security restrictions at Dimona. Vanunu's information on plutonium separation techniques [is] readily available in other sources.'[18]

Vanunu said that he would not disclose any further classified information but would act within the law.

Yet the peculiarities of Israeli nuclear secrecy mean that anything short of complete silence would leave the defence establishment dissatisfied. The parole board failed to distinguish between the political interest of maintaining nuclear ambiguity and the question of whether Vanunu had more, still unrevealed classified information. An ex-civil servant, in referring to information he had previously disclosed without authorisation, in effect confirms its veracity. Presiding judge Ephraim Laron of the Beersheba District Court rejected Vanunu's parole request, arguing:

> Early parole is conditional on the level of danger which a prisoner poses. True, Vanunu is unable to describe technical components, but he can pass information ... which others could learn from ... , not necessarily about the nuclear weapon itself but about the ambiguity surrounding it. We cannot take a risk.[19]

Yet another possibility leading to freedom was a spy swap. Supporters of Vanunu raised the idea of an exchange with Jonathan Pollard, the ex-US naval intelligence analyst serving a life sentence in the US for spying for Israel. It would have been more palatable to mainstream public opinion on the centre and further right of the Israeli political spectrum than any decision to grant clemency or parole. But Katz failed to generate enthusiasm when he raised the idea with US embassy officials in Tel Aviv in 2000 – despite the Clinton administration's earlier concern about Vanunu's imprisonment conditions. Vanunu himself rejected any step towards freedom which was tainted with his being a spy: he had acted to help world humanity.

Even more bizarre was the arrest of a Ramallah Arab who planned to kidnap the mayor of Ashkelon to force the release of Mordechai Vanunu from Ashkelon prison. Learning in 1992 that an Israeli friend was about to meet mayor Benny Waknin, Iyad Damisi, a recruit to the Palestinian Fatah organisation, allegedly plotted to join his friend at the meeting and then take the mayor hostage and demand Vanunu's release from prison. But the plot failed to materialise after the meeting with the mayor was cancelled at the last moment.

11
The Reluctant Lobbyist

The *Sunday Times*'s relationship with Vanunu graphically illustrates the responsibilities and tensions of the news reporter–informant relationship. It raises questions regarding the obligations of the news organisation to protect the informant when his or her life may be endangered through revealing the information, its obligations when things go badly wrong, and the obligations of the informant to cooperate with the organisation. By contrast with the eagerness but ineptness of the pro-Vanunu groups, one potential source of support which could have been far from inept but which was less than eager was the *Sunday Times*.

How did the paper's management and 'Insight' team react after Vanunu had been abducted? There was a week's delayed reaction. On Tuesday, 7 October, two days after publication, members of the 'Insight' team debated whether to inform the police that Vanunu was missing. Some reporters said they should not bother since he had gone off on his own. But Peter Hounam said the police should be informed, and when Hounam said that if the team did not agree, he would inform the police of his own accord, they agreed. A formal complaint was lodged with the police, who carried out checks at the Mountbatten hotel but found nothing suspicious. Coffins which had been flown from Heathrow airport to Israel were investigated, and they discovered that a coffin had been despatched on the day Vanunu disappeared. They tracked down the family concerned and found that the matter was quite innocuous. Inquiries were made with the Home Office, which controls immigration, but the police file was closed after a couple of weeks. The inquiries to the Home Office did not, according to one 'Insight' reporter, 'go beyond the official level'.[1] Wendy Robbins, the trainee researcher on the 'Insight' team, was asked whether Vanunu had been in touch with her. But she notes that she was not asked about anything suspicious which might have given Vanunu away and offer a clue as to where he was. The then foreign secretary, Sir Geoffrey Howe, was asked to make an official request to the Israeli government for information. But a spokesman replied that 'we have no grounds for intervening with the Israelis'. When it was revealed that Vanunu had been abducted to Israel from Rome, the paper's management was not reported as having approached either the Italian government or the

British Foreign Office to take up the matter with Italy. Instead, the paper's 'Insight' team provided, in good faith, information it had discovered regarding Vanunu's abduction to the judicial inquiry under Judge Domenico Sica, set up to investigate Vanunu's claim that he had been abducted from Italy. Peter Hounam went to see Sica five times, providing the documentary evidence which the paper had gathered about Cindy and about Vanunu's abduction and which it used in preparing the articles on these subjects. Hounam made a statement to Sica regarding Vanunu's motives for speaking about his work. The paper also took Meir Vanunu to Rome to give his own statement to Sica.

There were precedents for *Sunday Times* journalists and informants disappearing or even being murdered. As mentioned earlier, in summer 1976 John Swain had been sent by the paper to report on the progress of the peasant army mobilised by the Ethiopian government against guerrillas in the northern province of Eritrea. Swain disappeared after leaving the town of Axum to the north of Addis Ababa, en route to the Tigrean province. He was the eighth Briton to disappear – kidnapped by Tigrean rebels. The British ambassador in Addis Ababa, Derek Day, turned to the Ethiopian government for assistance. A British consul then began the trip to Makale, the capital of Tigre province which borders Eritrea, but was not allowed to continue because of the security situation. Nor did the authorities allow a *Sunday Times* journalist who went to Addis Ababa to search further north. Notwithstanding a dispute between the Sudanese and British governments, the newspaper obtained from President Nimeiry, who in the past had intervened on behalf of Westerners missing in Ethiopia, a pledge of personal help to extricate Swain. He was finally released because an interview on the BBC World Service with Harold Evans, then editor of the *Sunday Times*, eased the rebels' suspicions that Swain was a foreign intelligence officer posing as a journalist. Anxious for favourable publicity, the rebels saw a certain value in releasing him.

When the body of the paper's chief foreign correspondent, David Holden, was discovered on the outskirts of Cairo in December 1977, two senior *Sunday Times* journalists flew to Egypt, and two others to Amman, where Holden had been prior to travelling to Egypt. By contrast, after Vanunu disappeared and was assumed to have been abducted to Israel the paper sent only a junior member of the 'Insight' team, Rowena Webster, to Israel. She did hire a leading civil rights lawyer, Dr Amnon Zichroni, who by coincidence was the lawyer Vanunu selected from a shortlist given to him by the prison authorities.

Vanunu was not a staff journalist with the paper. Just as Vanunu's own degree of obligation to the newspaper was small, so the newspaper's obligation towards him was smaller than if he had been a staff journalist. He came to the newspaper of his own volition, and was not in the same category as a staffer who disappears. 'Informants frequently disappear. He was not part of the *Sunday Times*'s staff in which case there is a moral obligation to find out where he is. Rather there is an obligation [on] the family to find out,' a former

Sunday Times staffer said.[2] 'If he had been a Frenchman, or a German who had got kidnapped, we might have had a different view but because he was a Moroccan Sephardi there was not so much interest in his welfare. There were those in the office who were a bit contemptuous of Vanunu,' an 'Insight' reporter said.[3]

Vanunu was not the first informant whose fate was to become a matter of concern to the *Sunday Times*. Anthony Mascarenhas, an Indian journalist living in East Pakistan, witnessed the rebellion and fighting which resulted in the independent state of Bangladesh, including the atrocities committed by West Pakistan in an attempt to quell the rebellion. He approached the *Sunday Times* to tell his story and, like Vanunu, requested that his name not be attached. But Harold Evans, the editor, said his name had to be attached because it was an eyewitness account. It was clear that he would be unable to go back to West Pakistan. Evans paid him some £15,000 for the story, which ran for two weeks, but recognised Mascarenhas' account as a continuing commitment, sending him back to bring his family out and absorbing him onto the paper's staff. Mascarenhas was spellbound both by the paper's integrity and by its journalistic instincts in recognising the story's significance.

To its credit, after Vanunu arrived in London from Australia, the newspaper discussed with him where he might settle after the publication of his story given that clearly he would be unable to return home. A number of possible countries were mentioned where he might make his new life. In addition to Britain, these included Canada and the United States (both his then girlfriend, Judy Zimmet, and his brother, Meir, lived in Boston). Australia was also mentioned, but Vanunu had not been enamoured of the country during his four-month stay there. Another possibility was New Zealand: Stephen Milligan, the paper's foreign editor, knew David Lange, the prime minister and an ardent anti-nuclear campaigner, and believed he could arrange for Vanunu to get citizenship. 'In practice', said Bruce Page, a former 'Insight' editor, 'you have to find a very specific environment. The newspaper has to be very intimately involved with the government in question. That means he would need to settle in Britain.'[4] Editor Andrew Neil said that the paper had told Vanunu that it would try to help him get citizenship when everything was over. But as mentioned in an earlier chapter, the paper made no known approaches beforehand, presumably because it thought Vanunu's case for application would be stronger once he had become an international political personality. If Vanunu had foreign citizenship and had given up Israeli citizenship – an idea that he himself was toying with – it could have discouraged the Israelis (assuming they were aware of the change) from planning to abduct him in the knowledge of the diplomatic repercussions which would follow.

Questions of judgement also arise because when Mordechai Vanunu first contacted the *Sunday Times* he said that he did not want his name connected with the exposé. Peter Hounam insisted that if the information was going to be published it had to be with Vanunu's name on it because its value was that for the first time somebody who possessed inside knowledge of the Dimona reactor was revealing its innermost secrets. It took Hounam some time to persuade Vanunu that his best security against being the target of a Mossad operation was to attach his name to the paper's exposé. There would have been a story even had Vanunu's wish for anonymity been respected because the 57 photographs which he had taken inside the Dimona complex were themselves of international significance. Of course the story had added value with Vanunu's name. But this should have been weighed against the real danger to Vanunu.

Vanunu was no ordinary informant. He was one of the most important informants the paper had dealt with during Neil's editorship. If there was limited rapport between the paper's staff and the oriental Israeli, the pride of the *Sunday Times* had still been wounded: a foreign government had abducted a very important informant. The limited reaction of executives on the paper is therefore most surprising. 'Most of those on the executive level had not come across a case like this before. Many of them did not believe that the Israelis could abduct one of their contacts from London,' an 'Insight' reporter remarked.[5] A big surprise was the absence of any newspaper editorial after the Israeli government formally issued its announcement that Vanunu was in detention in Israel.

According to Ivan Fallon, the deputy editor, Rupert Murdoch, the *Sunday Times* proprietor, was not asked to take up the matter. This is surprising given the good ties Murdoch had both with prime minister Margaret Thatcher and with Israeli political leaders. Since the days when Benjamin Netanyahu (Israeli prime minister 1996–99) had been his country's ambassador to the United Nations, ties had developed between the two men; more than once Netanyahu and his wife, Sara, had been given hospitality at Murdoch's London residence. 'Harry Evans would have been straight on to the proprietor. Thomson would have asked questions in Parliament,' Phillip Knightley said.[6] 'The day we begin asking our proprietor to bring pressure is the day we allow him to put editorial pressure on us. That is something we would not even consider,' Fallon said.[7] The ideal proprietor–editor relationship, however, is less one of excessively demarcated lines of responsibility and more one based on total non-interference by the proprietor in the running of the newspaper but ready availability if use of his contacts becomes genuinely necessary. By contrast, in the case of the *Observer* journalist, Farzad Bazoft, who was sentenced to death by the Iraqi regime, the chairman of the newspaper, 'Tiny' Rowland, turned to president Kenneth Kaunda of Zambia, whom he had known for many years. As a result, Kaunda, who had good ties with Saddam Hussein, sent a top-secret appeal to the Iraqi leader four days before Bazoft was hanged. (That was unsuccessful because Hussein had been inaccurately informed that Rowland's company, Lonhro, had supplied arms to Iran.) But a later appeal by Kaunda for the release of British nurse, Daphne Parish, who was with Bazoft at the time, was successful.

Where the *Sunday Times* could draw on negotiating muscle with the Israeli authorities was in relation to the additional classified information concerning production processes inside the reactor – highly sensitive from Israel's viewpoint – which it had not published. The 6,000-word published exposé was but a tenth the size of a far more detailed 60,000-word dossier of taped testimony which Vanunu had given the paper's reporters and Dr Frank Barnaby, who had acted as scientific advisor to 'Insight' on the Vanunu project. The paper was planning to publish more articles on Vanunu the following week, and about other aspects of Israel's nuclear programme including highly sensitive information concerning the question of Israeli–South African nuclear cooperation. There were also the 57 photographs which Vanunu had shot inside the nuclear reactor and elsewhere at the centre. Only a handful have ever seen the light of day. News International, parent company of the *Sunday Times*, ought to have opened discreet negotiations with the Israeli authorities with a view to returning the remaining unpublished information in return for a much reduced prison sentence for Vanunu.

Even Neil's statement when Vanunu was sentenced was devoid of direct criticism of the Israeli authorities for abducting the paper's informant. In his statement Neil said that the paper understood that a democratic government must protect secrets in the national interest and that most Israeli citizens regarded Vanunu as a traitor. Less than two months after Vanunu disappeared, in an interview with *Haaretz*, jollity even crept in. Asked by *Haaretz* London correspondent Shaul Zedka whether with Vanunu's disappearance the paper had cancelled plans to bring out a book, Neil replied, 'Now the book is much better.' Asked how Vanunu would be able to benefit from the book's profits, Neil replied, 'I really have to give it thought because it is possible that the Israeli government would impound the money.' When the correspondent remarked that the money might then go to finance Mossad activities, Neil's reply was that he was 'prepared to pass the money to the Mossad if they will tell me how they took Vanunu from here'.[8] To be sure, had Vanunu found sympathy among a significant section of the Israeli population, Neil's attitude to his abduction might have been different. In June 1990, after the Israeli Supreme Court rejected Vanunu's appeal against his 18-year prison sentence, Neil, in an open letter to then Israeli president, Chaim Herzog, published in the paper, lashed out at the court's decision. He wrote that if clemency was not given to the abducted informant Israel would be behaving on a par with prerevolutionary totalitarian regimes in Eastern Europe. 'By pardoning Vanunu you would demonstrate that Israel is capable of reconciliation, humanity and mercy,' Neil wrote.[9] A reply to the *Sunday Times* from one of Herzog's aides, rejecting the paper's appeal, was published by the paper; any appeal for clemency would have to come from Vanunu himself, wrote the aide.

According to Mordechai Vanunu, 'the *Sunday Times* have supported me, but they could have done much more to appeal for my prison release in the first years [of my imprisonment]. They could have provided more details of my case.'[10] Meir, Mordechai's brother, said: 'I have a very strong complaint about the way the *Sunday Times* behaved. They have failed to make a strong declaration regarding Mordechai's action. Did they think it was a moral one? They have ignored the whole issue.'[11] Fallon said,

> We weren't very morally indignant that Israel had the bomb. Nor were we very morally indignant that Israel had chosen not to tell its own population or the rest of the world about the bomb. We didn't feel very easy that Israel, under its own law, had prosecuted Vanunu, or even the fact that they kidnapped him. To us it was a matter of enormous international public interest that Israel did have the bomb and we thought the world should know and that the people of Israel should know – but that's up to the people of Israel.[12]

The paper was against Israel's nuclear capability being kept secret. In its editorial after Vanunu's release from solitary, the paper opined, 'unlike some of Vanunu's other supporters, the paper did not campaign against nuclear weapons. We are only asking the Israeli Government to exercise mercy, to commute Vanunu's sentence and release him from custody.'[13] Only a connoisseur of the fine art of 'news consuming' could appreciate that the sole raison d'etre of a news organisation is exposure, irrespective of political connotations which could be misconstrued by others. But the British and Italian governments could hardly be expected to take up Vanunu's disappearance in a serious manner if the *Sunday Times* itself appeared half-hearted. At best, Neil sketched a muddled defence of the free media. At worst, he attempted to rationalise publication of a good scoop. 'The security considerations were never part of our decisionmaking in the Vanunu investigation', an editorial executive said:

> It is not part of our job to consider Israeli security. If we had to balance the argument it would have been that nuclear secrecy is a bad thing and if we are in a position to throw some light on it we have a duty to.[14]

Yet the *Sunday Times* deliberately opened its pages to cover the various aspects and stages of the Vanunu affair. In the nearly 18 years from October 1986 to April 2004, the paper published 134 items relating to Vanunu. Given that these are necessarily tied to the news of the day, there was no even distribution over the period; nearly three quarters of the 134 items were published in 1986–87 (in the aftermath of Vanunu's abduction and the years of his trial), in 1998 (when Vanunu was released from solitary confinement), and 2004 when he was released from prison. Some of the reports were very lengthy. These included journalistic investigations into Vanunu's disappearance ('The Mossad's Tender Trap', 'How Israeli Agents Snatched Vanunu'), disclosures about the whereabouts of Cindy in Israel and in Florida respectively

('Revealed: The Woman from Mossad'), Vanunu's sea journey from Italy ('Riddle of Vanunu Ship'), Peter Hounam's own courtroom testimony, and a 'reconstructed' interview with Vanunu after his release from solitary confinement.

The paper published three editorials, calling for Vanunu's release from solitary and for his release from prison, in 1992, 1996 and 1998. Yet it had taken some six years until the paper published its first editorial, although it did report a statement by the editor after Vanunu was abducted in 1986, as well as the 1990 open letter from the editor to the Israeli president. The newspaper's letters section published eleven letters concerning Vanunu in the 1986–2004 period. The issue following Vanunu's prison release in April 2004 had a festive touch: a third of that issue's front page was taken up with a full-colour photo of Vanunu relaxing in East Jerusalem. There was a three-page feature about the release, and an editorial entitled 'Vanunu's Good Deed'. Weeks later it carried a further editorial decrying limits on Vanunu's freedom of movement and speech which the Israeli authorities had imposed upon him after his prison release. But over the 18 years there were few follow-up stories relating to the Israeli nuclear programme itself. Apart from the original Vanunu exposé and the follow-up pieces reporting reaction to the exposé immediately afterwards, the paper published three reports: on Israeli–South African nuclear contacts; on Israeli–Indian nuclear cooperation; and on Syrian willingness to dismantle its biological weapons capability if Israel dismantled its nuclear programme. The paper's daily sister, *The Times*, also covered Vanunu-related developments in its news pages and opened up its acclaimed letters page to the subject.

Important resources which 'Insight' could draw on were potentially embarrassing to Israel. 'We spent tens of thousands of pounds tracking down Cindy not just because it was a good story but because if we could resolve it, it would be one of the best ways of advancing his cause,' an 'Insight' reporter said. 'The reportage might embarrass Israel to the point where they would have to let him off the charges and let him go,' Robin Morgan, the 'Insight' editor said.[15] Yet to believe that Israel would release somebody charged with disclosing one of the nation's most important secrets because of some embarrassing information in a foreign newspaper displays a poor appreciation of the media's influence in international politics.

Morgan also said that 'Insight' hoped to provide the evidence for the British government to act. 'The reaction at the highest level in the British government was "You bring us evidence to show a couple of Mossad agents hitting him with a sack of sand in the street and we'll act," ' an editorial executive said.[16] Ironically, while the paper reported on the roles of the Israeli and Australian intelligence services it failed to investigate any MI5 or MI6 involvement, such as trailing Vanunu's movements in London, beyond claiming that two Special Branch men observed Vanunu's arrival at London airport accompanied by Hounam. 'Insight' concluded that MI5 had turned a blind eye to his disappearance but that they would not have tolerated any action on British soil. Yet 'Insight' failed to examine whether MI5 had actually been approached, and thus forewarned about Israeli intentions, or whether MI5 had actually told the Israelis that they would turn a blind eye.

Some believed that too much time was being spent on the story, that the story was over, and that it was time to move on to other things. It was, therefore, not surprising that the long article which Hounam wrote at the end of 1987, after he had given evidence in the closed-doors trial, describing the atmosphere and what he had said in the courtroom, was reduced to a quarter of its original length. The reporting was not always accurate: the paper's report on the eve of Vanunu's trial in September 1987 carried the headline 'Sympathy [in Israel] Grows as Vanunu Trial Opens'. Not only was this untrue, but the paper provided no evidence to support the claim. In reporting the information Meir Vanunu had given them about how his brother had been abducted and taken to Rome, 'Insight' claimed that Cindy wooed him with the promise of sex – but it was to happen only in her apartment, where she felt comfortable. How logical is it for a man on the run to fly to another country for sex just as he is about to have such a story published? Meir Vanunu denies ever having told the paper about the sex angle. 'They embellished [the] truth with the part about the sex. I never told them that,' he said.[17] According to him, the American woman offered to help Mordechai to contact the Italian press.[18] 'The newspaper was trying to sensationalise,' remarked Meir. 'Mordechai was a very philosophical man and they went and put a headline that the man went after sex,' he added.[19] The brother's protestations notwithstanding, Vanunu did flirt with the female reporters and researchers during the time that 'Insight' was checking his story.[20]

In Autumn 1992 an important change occurred when the newspaper launched a national appeal for alleviation of the solitary confinement in which he was being held and for his release from prison. In an end-of-year editorial comment entitled 'A Time for Justice' the paper opined, 'If Israel is to be seen as the civilised state on which it prides itself, it must relent in the case of Mordechai Vanunu – soon.'[21] The paper also launched an appeal among its readers to obtain cards it had produced showing two hands releasing a dove, one to be sent to Israel's president appealing for Vanunu's clemency, the other to be sent to Vanunu in jail to boost his morale. According to Meir Vanunu, the cards made his brother feel stronger and more determined to keep fighting.

Neil sought to justify the relative silence which characterised the paper's record in defending Vanunu up to 1992. In his autobiography he wrote, 'I did not want to join the international brouhaha because I feared boxing Israel into a corner would make her even more intransigent.'[22] Neil misjudged in thinking that treating Israel with kid gloves would make its government more flexible. Rather than the paper leading its readers, readers led the paper. In launching its clemency appeal the paper remained circumspect about Vanunu's action in leaking the information. Neil was quoted on the news pages as saying that the appeal was non-political and took no stance on whether or not Vanunu was guilty of some crime. To back up the appeal, the paper solicited and printed expressions of sympathy from mainstream public figures. A similar differentiation between Vanunu's original action and his imprisonment conditions was also drawn in an editorial in *The Times* entitled 'Time for Mercy: 2,200 days in solitary confinement are enough even for treason'. Circumspection notwithstanding, Neil's decision to launch a public campaign was a major step. The decision may be explained as having been taken for a variety of reasons. Vanunu had completed six years of imprisonment, a third of his sentence. A more moderate government in Israel had just been elected, raising any chances Vanunu had. The paper's appeal coincided with a low-key approach by the British Foreign Office to the Israeli authorities to ease Vanunu's imprisonment conditions. Sympathy for Vanunu had grown on the left within Britain. Moreover, there was criticism by some of Vanunu's supporters of a perceived lack of effort by the paper on behalf of its news source.

The same year saw the departure from the paper of Peter Hounam, who became an independent film maker. While he continued freelancing for the paper, mostly in covering Vanunu-related developments, the lack of daily attendance within the paper's portals by 'Vanunu's ambassador' meant that Hounam's influence in focusing the paper's continued attention on the case necessarily waned. Yet in 1998 Hounam managed to lobby the paper's editorial advisory board to beef up the paper's coverage of Vanunu's plight. After Andrew Neil left the editor's chair to take up freelance journalism he did not cut himself off from the Vanunu issue either. Indeed, in one sense he was now more free to speak. In 1997 Neil wrote a letter to *The Times* on the occasion of the state visit to Britain of Israeli president Ezer Weizmann, calling on him to intercede in Vanunu's plight.

In 1999, during a brief visit to Israel, Neil sought permission from the prison authorities to visit Vanunu – 'I wanted to tell Vanunu that I think about him, and that I would have handled matters differently' – but the authorities did not even reply to Neil.[23] His replacement, John Witherow, was a former managing editor (news), and the paper's reporter in the 1982 Falklands War. Witherow took the unusual step for the editor of a quality newspaper of publishing in the paper coupons for readers to send to the Israeli government on Vanunu's behalf. Some 4,000 coupons were sent to the government – a not insignificant figure. Two of the newspaper editorials published concerning Vanunu's imprisonment appeared during Witherow's editorship. In one of these, entitled 'Punishment Enough', published in 1996 on the tenth anniversary of the original Vanunu exposé, the paper editorialised that 'there could be no more fitting moment for Israel to show mercy'.[24] Witherow met with members of the UK Vanunu campaign. The idea of coupons was resuscitated again in 2004 after the limitations upon Vanunu's freedom of movement and freedom of speech were introduced by the Israeli authorities after his prison release.

Responsibility for coverage of the twists and turns of Vanunu's imprisonment lay with the foreign editor Sean Ryan, appointed to the post in 1998 from deputy news editor. Earlier Ryan had been the science editor. Notable during the Witherow-Ryan period were a second investigation into Cindy's whereabouts – this time she was located in Florida – and the interview of sorts which Asher Vanunu carried out with his brother after his release from solitary, and which the paper published in the form of a direct interview with Mordechai Vanunu. With Hounam's and Neil's departures, the only staffers still left on the paper who had been involved in the original exposé were Robin Morgan, who edited the paper's glossy weekend magazine, and the paper's legal advisor, Alastair Brett.

In the initial period following Vanunu's abduction, the newspaper played a significant part in Vanunu's defence, recognising that it had an obligation to assist with his legal expenses, thus resolving the internal debate over the level of its commitment to Vanunu. Key proponents of legal assistance included Brett and Hounam. According to Brett,

The affair has international ramifications, and has a major effect on the freedom of speech. If people cannot come to Britain and talk to a newspaper about what is happening in other countries because they are afraid they will be kidnapped, then it is a very sad day for the freedom of speech in Britain as well as internationally. Israel has behaved absolutely poorly: they have broken international law.[25]

As soon as Vanunu disappeared in October 1986, and before the Israeli government had even confirmed he was back in Israel, Rowena Webster had approached lawyer Amnon Zichroni to turn to the Israeli Supreme Court with an application for a writ of *habeas corpus*; this, together with a number of other factors, led the Israeli government finally to confirm that Vanunu was in detention in Israel. In addition to Brett maintaining contact with Vanunu's defence lawyer, the paper consulted international law experts in Britain regarding the best approach to take in the trial. Anthony Lester QC was consulted regarding the laws of conspiracy and kidnapping in order to ascertain whether British law had been broken. 'We looked at the international ramifications of somebody finding themselves charged in Israel when the charging state has committed an offence in bringing the person to trial in its jurisdiction,' a legal executive on the paper said.[26] The paper also reportedly contributed to some of the costs of the international conference on nuclear weaponry held in Tel Aviv, aimed at raising consciousness concerning Vanunu's plight, which drew participants from various countries.

According to a member of the Vanunu family, interviewed in January 1988, the paper had contributed US$28,000 towards the legal expenses of the defence which at the time were expected to total over $50,000. A source at the *Sunday Times* insisted that, with the exception of a small payment made by the family to Zichroni after they dismissed him as defence lawyer, the paper had covered all of the estimated US$50,000. However, after the trial ended in 1988, some bills sent to the paper by defence lawyer Avigdor Feldman were returned with a note that the paper had no obligation – which Feldman acknowledges. In one such letter, the paper wrote,

> There was never any commitment to continue paying Mordechai's legal expenses ... The *Sunday Times* accepts you have spent a considerable amount of time working on behalf of Mordechai, but you did so of your own volition and there can be no question of the *Sunday Times* reimbursing you either in full or in part for such work.[27]

Reading this, Peter Hounam – who was the only one among the reporters and executives involved in the original story who showed any interest in helping Vanunu by offering practical assistance or even moral support – felt 'ashamed that I was ever involved in the story and I'm sorry, Morde, I ever led you into trusting us with your welfare'.[28] While Neil would later write in his autobiography that the newspaper had paid many of Vanunu's legal bills, from the earliest days the paper has been publicly reticent about its legal involvement. Asked by an Israeli journalist in November 1986 whether the paper was paying for Vanunu's defence, Neil replied, 'No, we aren't involved in it. Vanunu is paying his lawyer.'[29] Another baffling aspect of the paper's limited involvement was that, despite early expectations, no senior executive from the paper, or from its parent company News International, testified on Vanunu's behalf at the trial: only Hounam did so. The lack of complete involvement was tempered, according to Brett,

> by the fact that Vanunu very largely caused his own problems by ignoring the advice given to him by the *Sunday Times*. But we can't say we don't have any responsibility at all because he is facing the treason charges as a result of having given the material to us.[30]

In part the paper's general reticence in campaigning for Vanunu could be explained by its wanting to distance itself from any linkage between Vanunu's fate and anti-nuclear groups. Yet it is questionable whether the paper would have been more active even if the Vanunu cause had not been linked by his supporters to the anti-nuclear campaign, because in the early days of 1986–87, prior to the launching of the UK Free Vanunu campaign, the paper was not noticeably active on Vanunu's case. The paper's reticence could also be explained both by its desire not to clash with the Jewish community, some of whose members were numbered among its circulation, and by Neil's interest in not embroiling and embarrassing the paper's pro-Israeli proprietor. Unless a newspaper editor is prepared to see the consequences of a disclosure through to their conclusion, whatever the reactions of others, it is obvious that the editor should not have gone ahead with the original investigation. The assistance which the *Sunday Times* gave at the legal level, and its series of disclosures on how Vanunu had been abducted to Israel, might be seen, by people wanting to make public important information which could result in their prosecution or worse, as proof that in such an event they could expect the paper's support. Yet a closer look has shown this to be only partially correct.

12
21 April 2004

Shortly after 11 am on 21 April 2004, Vanunu, dressed in a checked shirt and navy tie stepped into the yard at the entrance of Shikma prison, Ashkelon. On the other side of the prison gate hundreds of supporters had gathered, including over 100 activists who had flown in from abroad. These included the heads of Vanunu campaigns from amongst other places the US and Britain, supporters like Nobel Peace Prize winner Mairead Corrigan Maguire from Ireland, Bishop Ed Browning from the Episcopalian Church in the USA, the pastor David Smith from Australia, British parliamentarians Colin Breed and Jeremy Corbyn, and Shinji Noma, a Japanese peace activist from Hiroshima. Vanunu climbed onto the prison gates, and flashed the 'V' sign of victory to his supporters.

The longest day in Vanunu's life began the previous evening. Restive, unable to sleep, Vanunu wrote notes until 4 o'clock that morning, rising two hours later for the 5.45 am daily roster. At 8 am he began the final bureaucratic arrangements for his release. His brother Meir told him that hundreds of reporters and supporters were awaiting him outside the prison. Days earlier Vanunu had been briefed by Shin Bet officers, presenting with a list of dos and don'ts designed by officialdom to limit his freedom of movement and speech. Thousands of letters exchanged between him and his supporters, which over the years had helped him to survive the psychological strain of his solitary confinement, were taken away, together with notebooks, for a final inspection by the authorities to ensure that Vanunu would not be leaving prison with any classified information.

With a hostile group of demonstrators also outside the prison gates, including ordinary Ashkelon residents who came to vent their spleen on one whom they regarded as one of Israel's most notorious traitors, the prison authorities took the unprecedented step of letting press representatives into the prison forecourt rather than keeping them outside, so that the event turned into an impromptu press conference. Rejecting pleas from his brother Meir not to do anything provocative which could delay his release, Vanunu launched into a diatribe against the Israeli security authorities – a moment for which he had spent months if not years composing himself.

'Israel doesn't need nuclear arms,' he began, 'especially now that the Middle East is free from nuclear weapons [a reference to the overthrow of the Saddam regime]. My message today, to all the world, is to open the Dimona reactor to inspections. This bullshit, blah blah blah about nuclear secrets is dead. Since the *Sunday Times* article was published, there are no more secrets.

'I've suffered cruel and barbaric treatment from the Shin Bet but I say to the Shin Bet and Mossad: you didn't succeed in breaking me. You didn't succeed in making me crazy. I'm a symbol of the will to freedom. You can't break the human spirit. To all those who are calling me a traitor, I am saying I am proud and happy that I did what I did. I will continue to speak against nuclear weaponry.'[1]

The day came to a finale when Vanunu, with his brothers, Asher and Meir, a swarm of reporters and photographers, and supporters drove to St George's Cathedral in East Jerusalem. There, Vanunu participated in Communion and a thanksgiving on his release from prison. In a highly emotional encounter, some 150 supporters came to meet with somebody whom until then they had known only as the addressee of their correspondence over the years. The cathedral would become Vanunu's home while he was denied exit from Israel. As he was an Anglican convert it was incumbent upon the Church to give shelter to one of their members in distress, explained Bishop Riqah Abu-el-Assal, head of the Anglican Church in the Holy Land. The bishop had himself visited Vanunu years earlier in prison. Yet not a few members of the Anglican community in Israel, which numbered only 2,500 souls, were upset that the bishop had undertaken such a controversial action, placing the Church in the public limelight in Israel. Yet for Vanunu, staying on Church property gave him a semi-diplomatic immunity from any Shin Bet action to arrest him.

Vanunu and his release had all the ingredients of a media carnival – secrecy, the nuclear issue, the Cindy kidnapping, the lone individual fighting a bureaucratic security apparatus who acts according to his or her own rules, but most importantly somebody who had been silenced for 18 years and was now being released. For days and weeks beforehand the media covered the forthcoming release, giving it front-page treatment – both addressing such policy questions as the limits on Vanunu's freedom of movement and speech and revisiting past episodes of the affair. Vanunu's adoptive parents, the Eoloffs, were interviewed. Israel's TV channels carried live broadcasts of his release. On the day after his release, *Yediot Aharonot*'s front page had a page-length photographic front cover showing Vanunu sitting in the pews of St George's Cathedral with a pastor on either side as they all celebrated Communion, under the prize-winning headline 'Mordechai the Christian' – a contrast with the ancient Jewish Purim *megillah* saga of 'Mordechai the Jew', uncle of Queen Esther. For days afterwards, *Yediot Aharonot* and the rest of the Israeli media positioned reporters and photographers at the church's two entrances round the clock in a vain attempt to catch a glimpse of and talk to the ex-prisoner. On the day of his release *Yediot* had even despatched a photographer to the River Jordan in case Vanunu decided to travel there to be immersed in the holy waters.

Every foreign television station, and major foreign newspapers, radio stations and news agencies represented in Israel were outside the prison to record the release. In some European countries, such as Britain, Italy and Germany, there was a certain media hype in the days preceding the release. The London *Guardian*, for example, published extracts form the long correspondence over the years between British actress Susannah York and Vanunu. But most of the foreign media, including the American media, were satisfied with covering the release in the following day's news reports. Typically, the *International Herald Tribune* had a single 1,000-word report under the headline 'Israeli Scientist Asserts He's Proud of Act', with an accompanying photo of Vanunu's 'V' sign on leaving the prison.

Yet it was an opportunity for commentators in the serious international press to address the wider questions concerning Israeli nuclear secrecy. In a column syndicated in a number of US papers, Daniel Ellsberg, who leaked the Pentagon Papers to the *New York Times*, wrote that 'Vanunu is the pre-eminent hero of the nuclear era. More Vanunus are urgently needed. Can anyone fail to recognise the value to world security of a heroic Pakistani, Indian, Iraqi, Iranian or North Korean Vanunu making comparable revelations? This is what I should have done in the early Sixties based on what I knew about the secret nuclear planning and practices of the US. But I didn't have Vanunu's example to guide me.'[2] Britain's *Independent* editorialised, 'If Israel is the democracy it claims to be, Vanunu should be allowed the freedom to speak openly.'[3] The *Guardian* said, 'Vanunu may have been a traitor to the Israeli state but in exposing a secret which needed to be told he had shown a higher duty to wider humanity.'[4]

Envisaging the general media onslaught on Vanunu's release, the Israeli defence ministry, foreign ministry, interior ministry and prison authorities established a 'coordination committee' in order to formulate a common information policy. For example, it rejected one proposal to release Vanunu hours earlier – in the middle of the night in order to avoid the media barrage – arguing that a prisoner having finished his sentence should be released in the full light of day. Yet coordination, which as *Haaretz* reporter Yossi Melman remarked 'was supposed to be the committee's raison d'etre', did not work easily. For example, instead of releasing to all media outlets the video of an interview given by Vanunu while still in prison, defence minister Shaul Mofaz acceded to requests from Dan Margalit (Arutz 10) and Nissim Mishal (Arutz 2), giving the tape exclusively to them. Other Israeli news organisations were aghast at this step. Tempers only increased after Arutz 10 offered the tape exclusively both to *Yediot Aharonot* and to *Maariv* as a curtain raiser for that night's Dan Margalit programme.[5] The state was helped by Vanunu desisting from speaking to the Israeli media. He attacked the Israeli media for not covering 'one word' of his case, and for being fed by the government's propaganda machine. Notwithstanding that Vanunu had disclosed the nuclear secrets ostensibly in order that Israelis should know the truth about the nuclear project, he declined to speak to the Israeli media for the weeks and months after his release 'in protest at the limits imposed upon his contacts with foreigners'.

In the months preceding Vanunu's release the security agencies had concluded that Vanunu remained a security risk. This was the sum view of discussions between defence ministry chief security officer Yehiel Horev, Shin Bet director Avi Dicter, the Mossad and the Atomic Energy Commission. Their discussions centred around two questions: whether Vanunu still had in his possession classified security information about the reactor which had not been published in the original *Sunday Times* article in 1986, and if so, whether or not he intended to disclose it.

A search of his prison cell on the eve of the release found notebooks of detailed information about the nuclear programme which he had written in 1991. The *Sunday Times* itself had published only a fraction of the information which Vanunu had given the paper in 1986. In addition, Vanunu still had in his possession, as inconceivable as it may sound, two tapes of his two-day-long debriefing by the paper's reporters which had apparently not been discovered while he was in prison. Some of the information from the debriefing was not regarded by the *Sunday Times* as newsworthy – even if it had intelligence value for those working in the nuclear industry. Still other sections were intended to form the basis of more articles, but Vanunu's disappearance had meant the paper was unable to do additional checking of the information with its contact. Of some 57 photographs which Vanunu had taken inside the reactor complex and given to the paper, only a couple were ever published by the paper. Some of them were apparently passed by the paper to a number of anti-nuclear websites.

Over the years the authorities had been concerned about sentiments expressed by Vanunu to the effect that he would continue to disclose classified information once he was released from prison. He said he would be available to foreign intelligence services, including the CIA and the KGB. For example, in a letter written in November 1998 he said, 'The moment I am released I will publish all the secrets I have about Israel's nuclear weapons. This time I will go to Congress, the Senate, the White House, England, Europe. I will submit my testimony under oath.' In a letter to a supporter in 2000 he wrote, 'The only way is for American activists to inspect the Israeli reactor, to cut the fence around it; that will lead to the arrest and trial of people. This act needs to be repeated by many, many volunteers from many states, so that the issue will be raised in their countries, parliaments and governments.'[6] Yet as the release date got closer – and against the background of the authorities' deliberations over whether they should limit Vanunu's freedom after his release – Vanunu appeared to change tack. He said he would continue his campaign against nuclear disarmament but do so only within the legal framework. But officialdom remained unconvinced. In a letter to his supporters in the Autumn of 1999 he wrote, 'Let me know how the work is going in Washington, that maybe I myself will come to help when I am free … That will be my great moment – to survive all they are doing to me and still be able to continue my mission that they tried to prevent thirteen years ago by kidnapping and prison. So I will need your help and I [will] come to the US.'[7] The question facing the authorities was whether this letter implied simply grassroots agitprop action and not a disclosure of classified information.

The security authorities considered placing him in administrative detention, which would imply no telephone and no face-to-face connection with the outside world. However, they were overruled by the Government's legal advisor, Menny Mazuz, and state prosecutor Edna Arbel. Mazuz argued that that once a prisoner completes his prison sentence he or she returns to the citizenry. He questioned whether placing Vanunu in administrative detention would withstand a certain appeal by Vanunu to the Supreme Court as such a measure would amount to imprisonment at home. Accepting the Mazuz argument, the government, drawing on emergency regulations still in existence which dated from the British Mandatory period in Palestine, decided that Vanunu would nevertheless be required to inform the police of the area of the country in which he resided, would not be given a passport, would have limitations placed on his face-to-face contact with foreigners and on contact with them by mail, fax or e-mail. The prohibitions were exaggerated since the existence in Israel of the office of the military censor was designed to ensure the non-publication of classified information whether in the Israeli media or the foreign media. Both schools of thought – whether that of Mazuz as legal advisor or that of Horev as defence security officer – failed to distinguish between, on the one hand, the wider questions of nuclear policy which everybody including ex-officials has a right to debate (even though ex-officials might draw upon their previous experience and classified information to reach their informed views), and on the other hand, the disclosure of classified defence information.

The question of limiting Vanunu's freedom was the subject of a discussion in the Knesset's constitution, law and justice committee. Horev, in a rare appearance in front of a Knesset committee, was taken to task by some committee members for exceeding his powers and threatening the rights of the individual which ought to characterise a democracy. 'What type of secrets [does] Vanunu still possess?', charged Meretz member Zahava Galon, who had initiated the discussion. 'Treating Vanunu this way is a threat to individual rights and harming those rights also endangers the state,' the Labour party's 'Yuli' Tamir argued.

The question of limiting Vanunu's freedom produced a lively debate in the Israeli media in the weeks and days prior to 21 April 2004. Eytan Haber, a

Yediot Aharonot columnist and formerly the paper's defence reporter, said there was 'a need to follow him closely at all hours of the day and stop him from travelling abroad. So the world will scream? So humanitarian organisations will be on their feet? There is no choice. Israel's democracy has to protect itself.'[8] But Nahum Barnea, that paper's senior political writer, argued that 'Israel is unable to pursue a person after he has completed his prison sentence.'[9] But *Haaretz*, in an editorial headed 'Vanunu Is Being Freed', said, 'The ambiguity about Israel's nuclear capabilities, and Vanunu's behaviour on his release from prison, justify keeping track of his activities while respecting his personal liberties. It is up to the authorities to prevent him from once again seriously harming state secrets.'[10] The paper, which regards itself as liberal, failed to reconcile a prohibition on Vanunu going abroad with the need to 'to protect his personal liberties'. Worryingly, a *Haaretz* public opinion poll on the day of Vanunu's release found that overwhelmingly the Israeli public were close to the Horev line. Some 23 per cent of those questioned said that Vanunu should not be released at all. A further 24 per cent said that he should not be released as long as the security authorities regarded him as a danger. Some 27 per cent favoured his released under limitations (the Mazuz line). Only 17 per cent said he should be released without any limits and be allowed to travel abroad.[11]

The efficacy of the limits was tested by a number of interviews which Vanunu gave to the media, including to the BBC, the *Sunday Times, Washington Times, al-Hayat, al-Wassat* and Israeli Television's First Channel. Although in a couple of cases Vanunu gave the interview to an Israeli citizen, not to a foreigner, he nevertheless breached the prohibition on any press interviews. Though the *Sunday Times* interview for Peter Hounam was carried out by an Israeli citizen, Yael Lotan, it did not stop the authorities from arresting Hounam, throwing him out, and barring him from ever returning to Israel. Journalistic greed cost Hounam the direct personal contract he had wanted. The authorities held off from also arresting Vanunu. In one fell swoop the Israelis managed to cut Vanunu's lifeline to the *Sunday Times*. Though he was a household name, he still needed the *Sunday Times* to provide stage-by-stage coverage of the developments in his case.

Vanunu also gave addresses over the telephone to international peace gatherings. Though he was forbidden to do such things – which in Vanunu's own words were 'very risky' – there was little or nothing new in what he said, so that he thereby adhered to the key prohibition on disclosing new information. Yet by some of his actions Vanunu appeared to intend a certain 'spin', ensuring that he was a thorough nuisance to the authorities who denied him his rights. In the *al-Hayat* interview, Vanunu warned that a strong earthquake could crack the reactor, causing a radioactive leak throughout the region, and called on the Jordanians – whose border was only 40 kilometres from the reactor – to test for radiation exposure. A Jordanian government spokesman issued a statement to refute Vanunu's allegations and calm the population, but it did not stop worried members of the Jordanian parliament inviting inspectors from the International Atomic Energy Agency (IAEA) to come to inspect for themselves. A rare visit to Israel by the director-general of the IAEA, Dr Mohammed el Baredei, prompted Vanunu to request a meeting with him, without success, and to call upon him to visit the reactor 'to see if what I said is true'. In November and December 2004 Vanunu was placed under house arrest for periods of up to a week at a time for breaching the limitations imposed upon him speaking to the foreign media.

Vanunu proved to be a disappointment to his supporters. High hopes before his release that the man due to leave Ashkelon would become the figurehead of 'Vanunism' were dashed. Hopes that after 18 years in prison, where he had spent as much time steeped in history as in monitoring the international anti-nuclear struggle, he would come out with his own particular approach to nuclear pacifism, proved wrong. The interviews with the media shed little light on the issue. Indeed, his claim in one that Kennedy had been assassinated by the Israelis for, according to Vanunu, bringing pressure on the Ben-Gurion government regarding the Dimona project, was ludicrous and baseless. True, he was no political scientist or strategist, but many had hoped that as a student of philosophy he would leave prison equipped with a philosophical treatise on the moral questions of nuclear weaponry.

Vanunu's deeds, particularly the interviews he gave, hardly enhanced his appeal, presented by the Association of Civil Rights before the Supreme Court in June 2004, for the restrictions on travel and speech to be lifted. 'I said again and again that I don't have any more secrets. All the secrets I had were published in the *Sunday Times*. What is left is to let me speak and live my life as a free human being. After 18 years I have the right to live as a human being and not to be punished without [having committed any new] crime.'[12] But the Supreme Court panel, headed by court president, Judge Aharon Barak, accepted the prosecution's claim that notes and detailed diagrams as found inside his cell – in particular the 1991 notebook describing in great detail the work of the reactor, some of which had not been published in the original 1986 exposé – showed his true intentions. Vanunu lamely sought to explain that he had prepared the notes in order to exercise his mind and his memory, but the court said that 'this strange explanation does not hold water. It is enough to see the meticulous, painstaking labour that was invested in the scores of diagrams and pages of text. Moreover, whatever he had written in Hebrew he later took the trouble to translate into English. It is plain evidence of his intent that the material be published after his prison release.'[13]

On the face of it, the court's decision was surprising because Vanunu had not disclosed anything new in his media and public appearances. And the letters in which he had written that he planned to disclose more secrets were composed while he was suffering from being held in solitary confinement in prison and did not reflect his true feelings now that he had been freed. Yet from the original trial in 1987–88, through to the Supreme Court appeal, and Vanunu's other court appeals, the courts showed an unmistakeable inclination towards accepting the view of the security establishment. The ball game, in Mazuz's words, lay with Vanunu. If he played the game and remained silent the Supreme Court could overrule the regulations – which were renewable for twelve-monthly periods. It was surprising that Vanunu did not delay exercising his right to speak out until he was out of the country. Instead, his public actions in contravention of the regulations played into the hands of those in the justice ministry and defence community who sought any excuse to hold on to him. In March 2005 Vanunu was indicted for infringing the regulations imposed upon him – mostly for the many interviews he had given the media, as well as for attempting on Christmas Day 2004 to visit Bethlehem, which lies outside recognised national boundaries.

Foreign governments were not enthusiastic about intervening on Vanunu's behalf. He applied for permission to obtain political asylum in Denmark, France, Ireland, New Zealand, Norway and Sweden. But foreign governments in the main were not anxious to enter into what they regarded as unnecessary disagreement with the Israeli authorities. On the eve of his prison release, US under-secretary of state for arms control and international security John Bolton held talks with Gideon Frank, the Israeli Atomic Energy Commission's director-general, on the implications of the release. The two governments reached an apparent understanding that any request from Vanunu to enter the United States – Vanunu's favoured country – would be turned down. This was in line with the Nixon–Meir understanding under which the United States does not pressure Israel on the nuclear issue as long as Jerusalem does not initiate any public steps on the nuclear questions – of which Vanunu's plan to testify before Congress about Dimona was just one. The Bolton step hardly reflected a country which prides itself on being a democracy because all Vanunu sought to do was take the 'borderline' step of testifying before Congress that he had worked at Dimona, and that he could not reveal anything new but that this was his testimony as per the *Sunday Times* article – which was in line with US law forbidding a US government to grant foreign aid to a country with an unsupervised nuclear programme.

Vanunu learnt a bitter lesson about the realpolitik of international relations. He may have become the guru of the international peace movement but, as earlier when he was still in prison, it was quite another step for foreign sovereign governments to take up the issue. That could occur if Vanunu was awarded the Nobel Peace Prize, which his supporters in Norway had proposed over the years. If awarded it he would be following in the footsteps of the Burmese civil rights leader, Aung San Suu Kyi, who was awarded the prize in 1991, and of Dr Andrei Sakharov, who had worked on the Soviet atomic and hydrogen bomb projects and subsequently became disaffected with nuclear proliferation and more generally a campaigner for civil rights under the Soviet regime, which imprisoned him. He was awarded the prize in 1975. The house arrest of these two by the Burmese and Soviet governments respectively only enhanced their chances of winning the Nobel. Vanunu had a good chance of being awarded the prize, not only because of his imprisonment but even more so because of his strong anti-nuclear message. The founder of the prize, Dr Alfred Nobel, invented dynamite, and was concerned lest it be used for non-peaceful purposes. It was therefore not surprising that the Nobel Peace Prize committee awarded the prize in 1985 to Physicians against Nuclear Weapons, and in 1995 to Dr Joseph Rotblat, the British-Jewish nuclear scientist who opposed nuclear weaponry and nuclear testing from the 1940s and 1950s on.

As special as Israel's case for the role of nuclear deterrence in Arab–Israeli relations may appear to most Israelis and their supporters, and as mind-boggling as Israel's reasons for ambiguity and secrecy may appear, Vanunu had a highly moral message which, even with all the qualifications concerning his deed, should not be ignored by Israelis. Vanunu lived before his time, but precisely from this comes the recognition due to him. Were he to be selected for the Nobel Prize, Israelis would cry wolf, even anti-semitism, but in the longer term Vanunu's deed, and the Nobel Prize, would project a powerful message onto the broader canvas of Middle Eastern history. Israel should look to the day when the Jewish State, in showing moral leadership, will give up that part of its deterrent resources which draws upon morally reprehensible mass-destruction weaponry, as less moral states have already done, if only for lack of resources; and maintain its strategic 'qualitative edge' through alternative means, of which the joint US–Israeli Arrow anti-missile project is but one. If Israel is not prepared to take such a step today, it should certainly do so if and when the albeit slim chances of regional Middle Eastern peace develop. The great support which public polls inside Israel show in favour of a willingness to give up non-conventional weaponry in such a context bodes well for this.

When that idyllic era is reached – or if a Chernobyl-like accident occurs – how will Israeli and Jewish history look back upon one who was painted as the country's most notorious traitor? If Dimona is transformed into a museum, will Vanunu be memorialised by later generations of Israelis? How will the Mordechai Vanunu saga be rewritten by later historians? Will the web of contradictions behind Vanunu's half-baked deed be forgotten?

In 2004 it was difficult for the ordinary Israeli to understand Mordechai Vanunu. The mission which Vanunu had carved out for himself was incomplete. Dimona was no nearer being dismantled in 2004 than it was in 1986. The way to its dismantling was not via international public opinion, for which Israel did not care a fig, but through peace education and activism at home. No name conveyed the anti-nuclear message inside Israel better than that of Vanunu. Yet the student of philosophy broke every PR rule possible; instead of reingratiating himself with the target audience at home he searched for any means to alienate that audience. Not only had he converted to Christianity, and lived in Arab East Jerusalem, but he delegitimised the very existence of a Jewish State. In an interview carried out prior to his prison release, he said would happily go back to the country of his birth, Morocco. His refusal to speak to Israelis and do so in their language was mistaken. When Israeli media interest in his case was at its height in the weeks and months after his prison release, Vanunu lost much 'spin' on his anti-nuclear message. Sympathy for his case exists among elements in the Sephardi (Oriental) Jewish community, segments of Israeli youth, individuals in the country's growing environment lobby, sections of the left and the peace camp, and among Israeli Arabs. To many Israelis he appeared instead like a criminal running away from the scene of the crime. His own human rights were more important to him than his mission.

Israelis still following the Jewish faith after Vanunu, exploring the richness and diversity of the 'mother religion' of the three monotheistic faiths, and those left participating in the experiment of the first Jewish sovereign state for 2,000 years – which despite myriad shortcomings, of which nuclear secrecy was just one, could nevertheless look with a certain pride upon many social, economic and scientific achievements in the state's short 50-year history – were left by Vanunu's deed with such obvious and unanswered security questions as how Israel should defend itself when other Arab states such as Iran develop non-conventional weaponry, if only for intra-Arab regional reasons.

He disclosed his country's nuclear secrets because he felt he had a moral obligation – to 'come back to the battle', as he wrote at the time to his brother – to inform his countrymen about the nuclear programme. Vanunu's proclaimed goal was not just to inform but to see Dimona dismantled. And he went much further: for him, there was no need even for the State of Israel. Yet the existence of that state is axiomatic for any democratic call for free nuclear information. Only Vanunu knows the way out of this web of contradictions, if even he himself does.

13
The Bomb that – Still – Doesn't Exist

What was the international significance of Vanunu's disclosure? Did it affect the Israeli posture of nuclear ambiguity? What impact did the exposé have on Arab states with regard both to deterrence and to the Arab–Israeli peace process? Did the disclosure affect international efforts towards arms control?

The sensational information about Israel's nuclear programme given by Mordechai Vanunu to the *Sunday Times* confirmed Israel's nuclear dominance of the region. Data provided by Vanunu about the plutonium-production process enabled the newspaper and its scientific advisors to draw up their estimate that Israel possessed 100–200 warheads. According to Frank Barnaby, who debriefed Vanunu for the newspaper, the significance of his allegations was threefold. 'First, the actual size of the Dimona reactor is much larger, five or six times larger, than had been believed – thirty-two kilograms a year which is enough for about eight nuclear weapons.' Accordingly, Israel may have 150 nuclear bombs, or enough plutonium for them, each equivalent to the one dropped on Nagasaki, Barnaby said.[1]

Second, 'The most interesting thing that Vanunu told us is that Israel is producing lithium deuteride and tritium, the material needed for thermonuclear weapons,' Barnaby went on. According to 'Giora', an engineer at the Dimona reactor, the Vanunu exposé included revelations 'which had never before been published in international journals'.[2] Tritium's value in nuclear weapons is based on its high rate of fusion with deuterium and the large numbers of high-energy neutrons released in this reaction. The fusion of deuterium and tritium produces ten times as many neutrons as fission for the same energy release. These can produce an explosion equal to hundreds of thousands of tons of TNT, capable of destroying an entire city. According to Vanunu, about 170 kilograms of lithium-6 were produced in the three-year period 1984–87; while Vanunu was unable to provide evidence that Israel had produced thermonuclear weapons, this amount would be sufficient for it to do so.

'The third interesting thing is that his story and photographs prove that the French provided the Israelis with not only the Dimona reactor but also the plutonium processing plant.'[3] Even more information would have come out, further denting the image of ambiguity, had Vanunu not been abducted back to

Israel. The *Sunday Times* had planned to follow up the initial exposé, but was unable to check the reports with their informant.

The strategic significance of Vanunu's exposé is added to when it is placed against the background of the availability of delivery systems. Israel is believed to have delivery systems, manned aircraft and ballistic missiles for her nuclear stockpile of as many as 100 nuclear-capable Jericho missiles.[4] In 1989 Israel was said to have launched a Jericho missile which travelled 1,300 km, and a joint Israeli–South African missile reportedly reached over 1,500 km, bringing any Arab country as well as Russia within range. The Shavit missile being developed is intended to have a 7,000 km range, according to the London-based International Institute for Strategic Studies.

Up to the time of the Vanunu exposé, most estimates gave Israel a far lower nuclear arsenal – 20–30, for example. Yet the Vanunu exposé was not the first time that a higher estimate had been made. One estimate in 1981 said that Israel possessed 100 nuclear devices and in 1985 *Aerospace Daily* quoted unnamed sources to the effect that Israel might possess 200 nuclear weapons. But those estimates were not based on solid evidence. Vanunu was the first witness to give an inside picture of production at Dimona. Or as engineer 'Giora' observed, 'What was published up to now was speculation and assumptions of one kind or another. With the Vanunu exposé there are photographs and details. The man who worked at Dimona was able to speak from his own experience.'[5] The higher estimates of Israel's nuclear capability raised its deterrent potential. Asked to confirm a remark he had made at a journalists' briefing that the Vanunu exposé had strengthened Israel's deterrent capability, Shimon Peres, successively prime minister and foreign minister during the period of the Vanunu exposé, said somewhat lamely, 'I do not know – or at least not in an open setting … .'[6] Given the considerable strategic benefit to Israel's military posture gained from the estimate that it possesses 100–200 nuclear warheads, the *Sunday Times* and Barnaby suspected that Vanunu had been given just enough rope to take the photographs inside the reactor and make his disclosure to the newspaper. After all, the Mossad, according to one report, knew about Vanunu while he was still in Australia before coming to London for a month to be debriefed by the newspaper.[7] On the day after the *Sunday Times* published its exposé Yaakov Kirschen, cartoonist of the *Jerusalem Post*'s 'Dry Bones', drew a cartoon showing President Assad scowling at a newspaper and saying,

> Israel has the N-bomb? I don't believe it! Obviously, a lie planted by Zionist agents to scare us! On the other hand maybe they leaked the truth so that we would think that it was a trick and not believe it!'[8]

To what extent have Vanunu's allegations been accepted by nuclear scientists and, more importantly, by Arab states and other foreign governments? Not everybody accepted the *Sunday Times*'s estimate, although most increased their earlier estimates of the Israeli capability. In its own estimate made in 1987 that Israel possessed up to 100 nuclear weapons, the International Institute for Strategic Studies had agreed to a considerable extent with the estimate (which has not altered since then). US officials, however, while accepting the authenticity of Vanunu's technical data, challenged the estimate because it was inconsistent with other relevant information in their possession which suggested that Israel had no more than 50–60 plutonium-using devices. (Five years later, US intelligence estimates were that Israel possessed 60–80 nuclear devices.)

What baffled foreign officials and outside experts most was the question of the megawattage of the reactor. Megawattage determines the amount of plutonium which can be produced. Vanunu's claim that 40 kilograms of plutonium were produced annually would require a 150 megawattage. This led the *Sunday Times* to conclude that the reactor had been enlarged six times: Vanunu claimed that the 26 megawattage was increased to a 70 megawattage prior to when he started working there in 1976. US officials questioned the *Sunday Times*'s claim that the reactor's megawattage had increased six times from 24 to 150 megawatts. The French–Israeli agreement allowed for only a 24-megawatt reactor. It was again increased to a 150 megawattage while Vanunu was there. In its 'Public Eye Project', the Federation of American Scientists (FAS) compared declassified satellite photographs of the Dimona reactor taken by the Corona reconnaissance satellite in 1971 with satellite photos obtained in 2000 from the Ikonos satellite, and concluded that no new cooling towers had been constructed in the intervening 30-year period. It led FAS to question the Vanunu/*Sunday Times* estimate of 40 kilograms of annual plutonium production. Like US officials, FAS was more cautious and estimated that Israel might have enough for 100 weapons, but probably not 200.[9] True, a new cooling system was added when Vanunu was working there. But US officials remained sceptical because that would require a very large number of additional cooling units. US officials believed that the original 24 megawattage had not been changed substantially, but the reactor may have operated at about 40 megawatts because of cooling efficiencies permitted by the desert climate. Accordingly, they claimed that Israel had 50–60 warheads rather than the 100–200 estimated by the *Sunday Times*. The US estimate is based on the nine-year term when Vanunu worked at Dimona – the only solid information available. The dangers of generalising evidence from the 'particular' were emphasised by reports in 1992 that the three-shift day at the reactor had been suspended.[10]

Barnaby argues that reprocessing did not just begin on the day Vanunu walked through the doors at Dimona; his estimate includes some 60 warheads for the earlier period. Had Barnaby based this solely on the nine years Vanunu was there, he would agree with the US figure: 90 warheads, or a conservative estimate of 60, which assumes that the optimum quantity of plutonium is not reached due to factors such as wastage.

Throughout the 1990s, a number of US reports confirmed the *Sunday Times*'s estimate. A 1995 study by the Rand Corporation, commissioned by the Pentagon, estimated that Israel possessed 350 kilograms of plutonium in militarily usable condition, enough for 70 warheads. In 1993 the *New York Times* estimated that Israel possessed 50–200 warheads. A 1999 classified study by the US Department of Energy said that Israel had enough plutonium (300–500 kilograms) to manufacture at least 250 nuclear weapons. This meant that Israel was in sixth place in the atomic big league (after Russia, the US, Britain, France and China).[11]

Unnamed experts, quoted by *The Economist Foreign Report*, expressed surprise that Israel's plutonium-processing plant was underground since the operation is highly toxic – and radioactive; a minor accident could endanger the whole operation.[12] However, Dr Francis Perrin, former head of the French nuclear programme, told the *Sunday Times* that France had built the underground facility. There was also surprise when the components for bombs were said to be assembled beneath the reprocessing plant in Machon 2's underground facility, which would involve unnecessary risk.[13]

Vanunu's allegations aroused much interest in the Arab world, but attention was focused less upon the precise details of his claims than on the general issue and history of Israel's nuclear capability. According to Ariel Levite and Emily Landau, authors of *In Arab Eyes: Israel's Nuclear Image*, Arab reaction to the Vanunu exposé was twofold. First, that the details were entirely accurate, and second, that it was not the result of a security failure but an international Israeli effort to frighten the Arabs and to strengthen Israel's nuclear posture.[14] According to Dr Khadir Hamza, a senior scientist on Iraq's nuclear programme prior to his defection to the West in 1994,

> We did not believe that Vanunu would be able to enter the reactor and photograph whatever he wanted to. The Iraqis saw the Vanunu affair as a trick and he sits in prison in order that people will believe in a genuine leak. Imagine if he were freed – it would be clear that it was one big exercise.[15]

Some Arabs did not regard the information as anything new but rather as confirming what was already known. 'Vanunu is no Columbus,' the Abu Dhabi daily *Al-Atihad* wrote.[16] After the *Sunday Times* exposé Arab leaders did not rush to release statements condemning Israel, wishing neither to show they were 'being deterred' nor to arouse internal public calls for an Islamic Bomb. According to William Eagleton, former US ambassador to Damascus, Syrian president Hafez el-Assad appeared to accept Israel's nuclear potential as a matter of fact, but he would not refer to it in conversation with Western diplomats.[17]

Post-Vanunu reaction also took on a prescriptive tone, namely the question of how the Arab world should counter the perceived nuclear threat from Israel. According to Shimon Peres, and Abba Eban, who was chairman of the

Knesset's defence and foreign affairs committee at the time of the Vanunu exposé, the disclosure intensified the Arab arms race. Said Eban, 'One of the results of the affair was to turn on a red warning light in aggressive states. There is no doubt that the exposé added to enemy attempts towards a more equitable military balance.'[18] Peres added: 'The exposé sent individual states in the direction of an arms race.'[19] A Radio Damascus commentator said, 'The nuclear weapon does not need to exist in one place, or be the monopoly of one particular people.' Seeing the Vanunu disclosures 'as proof that conflict with Israel is unavoidable', the Egyptian opposition paper *Al-Shaab* said that Israel's nuclear potential 'obligates Egypt to adopt a nuclear option'.[20] In republishing the report from the *Sunday Times, Al-Shaab* wrote,

> our intention is not to arouse fears because of Israel but to arouse Egyptian public opinion and to declare to our government the iniquities successive Egyptian administrations since Sadat have committed against the country's national security in giving a one-sided advantage to Israel.[21]

According to the head of Israeli military intelligence, General Amnon Shahak, 'the Vanunu affair and publications about Israel's ballistic capability accelerated Syria's construction of a non-conventional capability in the sphere of chemical weaponry.' Yet this needs to be questioned. Also, when in 1960 the American U-2 spyplane photographed the construction of the nuclear reactor at Dimona, there was no major arms race. Given economic and technological limitations to achieving nuclear potential, it has not become a major issue on many Arab domestic agendas.

Arab will was mainly translated into diplomatic action. In one of a stream of Arab-initiated UN resolutions over the years which dealt with the Israeli nuclear progamme, Arab states' call for the United Nations to investigate Israel's nuclear programme was passed in the UN General Assembly by a majority of 92 to 2 (the two being the US and Israel), with 42 abstentions. A UN report published in October 1987 said that while it had no proof there is 'a strong impression that Israel possesses the potential to make nuclear arms'.[22] It offered as evidence Israel's reluctance to confirm or deny a nuclear arms capability, its contradictory statements regarding nuclear arms, and its refusal to sign the Nuclear Proliferation Treaty (NPT). A confidential report of the International Atomic Energy Agency (IAEA) on Vanunu's disclosure sounded an urgent alarm, and warned that Israel's nuclear programme 'had torn apart the fabric of the international atomic control system'.[23]

Vanunu's disclosure contributed to deterring Iraq from deploying non-conventional warheads in the 39 Scud missiles it launched against Israel during the first Gulf War. In the escalation in Autumn and Winter 1990 Israeli officials felt freer to allude to the nuclear programme than they had before Vanunu; there was little worth to a nuclear capability which could not be seen or at least hinted at. Rather than quoting the stock Israeli position that it would not be the first to introduce nuclear weapons into the region, Israeli officials responded to Iraqi threats made throughout 1990 to attack the Jewish state with its chemical weapons by promising to hit Iraq '100 times over', an allusion to an attack of mass destruction. Prime minister Itzhak Shamir, speaking to CNN in October 1990, said, 'Somebody threatening you with the most terrible weapons in the world has to think about certain responses to the use of such weapons.'

The story had little impact on official US policy. Repeating the standard position taken by successive US administrations, Charles Redman, the State Department spokesman, said at a briefing on the day after the *Sunday Times* article that the US is 'concerned by the existence of unsafeguarded nuclear facilities and have made our concern known to Israel. We have urged Israel to accept comprehensive safeguards.' The Secretary of Defense, briefed by his aides, was advised to tell any journalists asking about heavy water supplied by the US to Israel that as far as was known it was used for peaceful purposes.[24] The low-profile posture reflected the 1969 US–Israeli understanding in which the US has not pressured Israel on the Bomb as long as Israel did not go public on it. It has understood Israel's reluctance to sign the NPT. As long as Israel has enemies, is making territorial sacrifices towards peace, and as long as she behaves responsibly with her nuclear option, the US 'understands' Israel's nuclear needs. Washington, engaged in intensive efforts towards arms control, can still treat Israel as a 'special case' so long as the official cloak of secrecy remains.

But behind the scenes in American officialdom the revelations had considerable significance. President Reagan convened the Jason Committee – the administration's highest scientific advisory group – which meets behind closed doors to analyse major scientific national security developments in order to assess their impact on US strategy. The shedding of the ambiguity about Israel's nuclear programme extended in the US case far beyond the 6,000-word article printed in the *Sunday Times* because a copy of the original tapes of Vanunu's debriefing by the paper, comprising his detailed technical testimony – ten times the length of the article – reached US intelligence. Arms analysts at the Los Alamos and Livermore nuclear laboratories examined Vanunu's testimony, including the 57 photographs he had taken inside the Dimona centre. Seeing reconstructed replicas from the photographs showing warheads,[25] US officials were surprised at the scope of the Israeli programme. While they accepted the newspaper's claim that Israel was producing the neutron bomb, they disagreed with the estimate of the number of Israel's warheads, arguing that the statistics reflected the peak rate of production.

One area in the Jewish state's relationship with the United States which might have been affected by the *Sunday Times*'s allegations was congressional approval of the US administration's foreign-aid package to Israel. Observers pointed to the 1975 case when Congress held up the planned sale to Israel of Pershing surface-to-surface missiles which reportedly could be fitted with nuclear warheads. While the Vanunu disclosures were examined in the joint congressional committee on nuclear policy, there was no major initiative to cut off foreign aid. In fact, the quantity of US financial aid, and type of military hardware, did not change in the two years following the report. It also had less impact on the American peace movement than on the European peace movement where Vanunu became one point of focus in the anti-nuclear campaign.

Israel would later face another potential challenge from the US after the NBC television network claimed in October 1989 that Israeli–South African nuclear cooperation included the joint testing of an intercontinental missile over a 1,500 km range. Questions were asked in the media whether Israel had given South Africa access to US missile technology. Vanunu told the *Sunday Times* that he had seen South Africans at Dimona.[26]

Later, during the administration of George Bush senior, a change occurred. with concern about nuclear and chemical arms proliferation now high among US international priorities. US satellite intelligence attempted to follow Israeli activity at Dimona. Eban said that the Vanunu exposé created difficulties in obtaining supplies of certain raw materials for the nuclear programme.[27] These included, according to Peres and other officials, difficulties in obtaining such equipment as a supercomputer, which had been purchaseable prior to Vanunu.[28] The US now refused to allow the sale of supercomputers to Israel; they can be used in the development of nuclear weapons including simulating their launching. Instead Israel bought a less-developed model from Britain, and began development of its own at the Technion University in Haifa. Stiffer procedures for visits by Israeli scientists to American nuclear laboratories were also reportedly introduced.

The impact of the Vanunu exposé on US policy was felt in the first Gulf War. Publicly, US Defense Secretary Dick Cheney reacted to Iraqi missile attacks on Israel by remarking that the latter possessed the nuclear option.

The only diplomatic relationship significantly affected was Israeli–Norwegan relations. After the Vanunu exposé 'there were discussions with the Norwegians', said reactor engineer 'Giora'.[29] Or, as Yehiel Horev, head of the defence ministry's security department, said, 'Norway, according to reports, feels she was a partner in producing Israeli nuclear arms potential; [Norway] had originally thought that the heavy water it supplied to Israel was for peaceful purposes only.'[30] In 1959 Israel purchased 22 tons of heavy water from a Norwegian company. Heavy water allows nuclear reactors to run on natural uranium, which is widely available, rather than on enriched uranium which is scarce and tightly controlled – but which is vital for producing a chain reaction. Norway had imposed what were at the time unusually strict controls over the material, getting Israel's pledge to use it exclusively for peaceful purposes and obtaining the right to inspect operations to verify that Israel was adhering to its pledge. But Norway conducted only one inspection, in 1961, prior to completion of the Dimona reactor.[31]

The heavy water was supplied in 1958 under a pall of silence. The head of the Norwegian Labour party, Holin Lie – brother of former UN secretary-general Trygve Lie, and a leader of the underground Norwegian resistance to the Nazi occupation of the country in the Second World War – played an important part. When an Israeli socialist, Reuven Barekett, approached him with the request for the heavy water, it was approved – but it is unclear whether approval was given by the entire Norwegian cabinet or a small clique within it. When prime minister David Ben-Gurion visited Norway he was heard to to remark to his hosts, 'We give you sun, and you give us water.'

The close ties between Norway's leaders and the young Jewish state found expression in different crises. In 1969 a Norwegian company helped to bring five missile boats from the French port of Cherbourg – which Israel had ordered but which the French government had embargoed in the aftermath of the 1967 Arab–Israeli war. In 1973 the Mossad, engaged in an underground war against Palestinian terrorists, shot dead the wrong man, Ahmed Bouchiki, in the Norwegian town of Lillehammer. Norwegian police and defence officials did not expose the full involvement in the affair of Mossad agents, who were later given relatively light prison sentences.

After the Vanunu exposé Norwegian politicians and other public figures demanded to know the fate of the heavy water, pressing the government to take up Norway's right of inspection. In part the furore increased because five days after the *Sunday Times* article, another report, entitled *Israel's Nuclear Shadow*, was published by the Wisconsin Project on Nuclear Arms Control, which asserted that the heavy-water exports had been directly used in the manufacture of nuclear arms. Initially, the Norwegian foreign ministry rejected the Wisconsin Project's claims, saying that as far as it knew, Israel was using the heavy water for peaceful purposes. In February 1987 state radio carried a long programme on the country's heavy-water exports. After the Norwegian media took up the matter, the government said it would informally ask Israel to allow an inspection by the IAEA of the use of heavy water at Dimona. Initially, Israel rejected Norwegian requests that the heavy water be inspected by the IAEA on the grounds that the Norwegian supply had become mixed with other supplies, and that the IAEA was biased. But as parliamentary and public pressure increased, the Norwegian government told Jerusalem that unless it could inspect the heavy water, Oslo would insist on its being returned. In October 1987 Norway sent a technical team to Israel to carry out an inspection at Dimona, but it was not allowed into the reactor. In April 1988 the two governments initialled an agreement under which Norwegian inspectors would be allowed to see the heavy water in the first year, and in subsequent years the IAEA would be allowed to do so. (IAEA inspections are considered more rigorous than Norway's.) It was also a compromise for Norway: under the terms of the agreement they would be unable to determine whether in the long intervening years Israel had used the heavy water to manufacture nuclear weapons or whether the heavy water was Norwegian. Nor would the inspection take place at Dimona. Dr Gary Milhollin of the Wisconsin Project described it as a 'heavy-water whitewash'. The Norwegian parliament's foreign affairs committee rejected the compromise formula, insisting on knowing what had happened to the heavy water. This could only be discovered, the Norwegians said, if they had access to Israel's nuclear research facilities. After renewed negotiations Israel agreed in April 1990 to return to Norway the remainder of the heavy water which she had, 10.5 tons, which were used later by the Norwegians to produce isotopes in medical work. Israeli claims that the rest of the heavy water had been lost as a result of spillage and evaporation were regarded as 'exaggerated' by Oslo.

Norwegian TV carried a 50-minute documentary entitled 'Norwegian Heavy Water for Nuclear Weapons', which claimed that most of the country's heavy-water exports were being used to make nuclear weapons, rather than for peaceful purposes, as the Norwegian public had thought. In October 1988 Norway, the world's chief supplier (which by 1987 had produced 250 tons of heavy water), announced a ban on exports of heavy water apart from tiny amounts required for scientific research. The decision was a culmination both of the Norwegian–Israeli crisis concerning the diversion to India of 15 tons of heavy water supplied to a West German company, and to Israel of 12.5 tons supplied to Romania in 1986.

There was also no reaction to the *Sunday Times* exposé from the Soviet Union. Apart from raising their intelligence estimate of Israel's nuclear capability, the Soviets continued their practice of discouraging Arab states from requesting help with nuclear hardware. The most Moscow had done was to supply Arab states with advanced conventional weaponry, such as Scud missiles, and vague promises of protection in the event of nuclear attack.

Western European governments, anxious not to encourage Arab nuclear arms proliferation, also played down the Vanunu revelations. The French foreign ministry spokesman had 'no comment, none' regarding the previously mentioned claim by Dr Francis Perrin that France had helped construct a plutonium-processing plant at Dimona. Jean-Bernard Raymond, the French foreign minister, said 'Vanunu's exposé repeats what has been well-known for many years. The cooperation ended in 1959. Thirty years is certainly enough time for Israeli scientists to gather enough nuclear information without any connection to the French–Israeli cooperation of the 1950s.'[32]

Within the international scientific community, the revelations raised the level of discourse about Israeli nuclear capability. Israel's programme, according to one nuclear proliferation expert, was 'always hush-hush. Everyone was uncomfortable about mentioning it – everybody agrees there is no benefit in publishing it.' But 'it was out of the closet now', he added. Government officials opened up. 'Before Vanunu, the Israeli programme was treated with enormous secrecy by US officials, off-limits in even off-the-record conversations,' another expert remarked. 'Afterwards, though they wouldn't go into classified information, there was still enough in the public domain to start an educated discussion on the direction of the programme and the implications of the veracity of Vanunu's allegations.'[33]

Normally, a disclosure of significance by a newspaper, particularly one of international repute, would be picked up by other international news media. Yet the Vanunu exposé produced only minor waves. An examination of Nexus, the US-based electronic database monitoring over 2,500 publications, searching for stories containing the names 'Vanunu' and 'Sunday Times' for the period 1–20 October 1986 yielded only 24 articles. These included citations in the New York Times, Washington Post, Los Angeles Times, Chicago Tribune, Christian Science Monitor, the BBC and the news agencies of Reuters, Associated Press, and United Press International. Reuters gave the exposé most 'play', authoring ten of the 24 reports. Most reports were short, lacking in detail, and not placed prominently by the respective editors.[34]

The years following the Sunday Times exposé were followed by other disclosures in the media which further dented the ambiguity. IDR, the Swiss defence review, reported in 1987 the firing by Israel of a nuclear-capable Jericho missile with a range of 1,300 kms into the Mediterranean Sea. Israeli–South African nuclear ties were the subject of a disclosure by Time in 1989. That year saw the publication of Dr Frank Barnaby's book The Invisible Bomb,[35] which drew on part of Vanunu's testimony not included in the Sunday Times article. In Critical Mass: The Dangerous Race for Superweapons in a Fragmenting World,[36] two Americans, William Burrows and Robert Windrem, showed that Israel had progressed far beyond a primitive Bomb. It had developed a command, control, communication and technical intelligence apparatus to execute its nuclear doctrine. They claimed that at Be'er Yaacov, near Tel Aviv, the Jericho nuclear-capable missiles were stored. Nuclear research and even nuclear explosions were carried out at the Nahal Soreq reactor, which is under international supervision. A factory belonging to the Raphael arms industry in Yodfat in the Galilee region of northern Israel was a nuclear weapons design and missile development laboratory. Nuclear missiles were kept at the Tel Nof airbase and bunkers at the nearby village of Zecharya in the Judaean Hills. Jane's Sentinel reported in 1996 that Israel's nuclear capability would double with the arrival from the US of more F-15 fighter planes. In the northern Galilee region nuclear weapons were assembled and dismantled at Yodfat, and tactical nuclear weapons stored at Eilabun. The command base was divided between a huge underground strategic air command at the Nevatim Airbase in the Negev in the south and the 'Bor' (or pit) at army headquarters in Hakirya in Tel Aviv. With the appointment of Uzi Mahnaimi as its well-connected Tel Aviv-based Middle East correspondent, the Sunday Times ran a number of scoops including one in 1998 saying that Israel was planning a biological bomb which could ethnically distinguish between Arab and Jewish genes; and one in 2000 reporting the deployment of nuclear bombs on the Golan Heights, captured in 1967 from Syria. The same year saw a *Der Spiegel* report that missiles carried by Israeli submarines were nuclear-capable.

In 2002, some 15 of the 57 photographs that Vanunu had taken inside the reactor were screened on the website of the US Campaign to Free Mordechai Vanunu. (The 1986 exposé by the *Sunday Times* had included only a couple of the photographs.) These additional photos showed reactor and production panels, laboratory prototypes of nuclear weapon cores, glove boxes for handling radioactive plutonium and uranium, and machine tools.

In 1993 *Aviation Week*, drawing on satellite photos obtained from Russia, appeared to confirm earlier claims about locations in Israel where it said nuclear warheads were stored: the Tel Nof airbase; Be'er Yaacov, near Tel Aviv; and the village of Zecharya in the Judaean Hills, south-west of Jerusalem.

The following year, 1994, the London-based *Jane's Intelligence Review*, in an article in entitled 'Israel's Nuclear Infrastructure', drawing on satellite photos obtained from Russia and from the French commercial satellite Spot, printed eight pictures showing that infrastructure, which confirmed and added to information found by Vanunu. The author, Harold Hough, an Arizona-based analyst of satellite photography, claimed that three features in the photograph of the Dimona reactor gave away the location of the nuclear facilities. First, the reactor was surrounded by an extremely heavy perimeter fence with many patrols and roads. Second, the reactor was surrounded by heavy vegetation, despite being located in the arid desert, in order to screen the site from those on passing roads. Third, there was also an unusual amount of space inside the perimeter, to give defence in depth. Through examination of these and other features both at Dimona and at other sites in Israel, Hough was able to follow the development of the Israeli Bomb through its stages of production and deployment. In addition to Be'er Yaacov and Yodfat, Hough claimed that nuclear weapons were tested at Nahal Soreq, situated to the south of Tel Aviv, and that Jericho II tactical nuclear weapons were stored at Eilabun, which is not far from Yodfat. Hough described Zecharya, situated in the centre of the country, as the missile base and home of the strategic nuclear deterrent. Hough said that the area of the Judean site was naturally suited to the construction of underground bunkers, because it is composed of limestone and riddled with caves. 'By placing their nuclear deterrent in the centre of the country, the Israelis have placed it in a defendable area that would be one of the last parts of Israel to fall to an enemy,' Hough argues. But revisions by Hough to his various articles, scepticism about his theories concerning the precise functions of different installations, as well as errors in certain basic factual historical information on the area, have led some to question Hough's conclusions.[37]

Satellite photography also has its built-in limitations. Unless the satellite has the ability to send pictures back to earth, its information is neither continuous nor necessarily up-to-date; the satellite returns to earth once in six weeks, upon which the film is developed. The Dimona reactor itself – which appears in press photos as a sizeable domed structure – cannot be discerned even by a professional photo interpreter using the computer tapes from which the image was prepared. Only after careful study of general ground-level photos are specialists able to identify the precise location of the facility. Nor can satellite photos provide data on the capacities of particular installations or on the specific materials they may be using to produce weapons-grade uranium, how long the nuclear facility has been functioning, or tactical plans. Satellite-obtained information revealed only the roofs of hangars or 'the heads of people'. To make sense of the information provided requires collateral information, such as that provided by Mordechai Vanunu. Vanunu still remains today the only source who had direct access to information about Dimona – what is 'inside the hangars' – thereby acting as a channel of confirmation of the satellite information.

The exposé had little impact on Israeli nuclear policy itself. 'Israeli policy has not changed,' prime minister Peres told the Israeli cabinet meeting on the morrow of the *Sunday Times* report:

> We will not be the first to introduce nuclear weapons into the region. The government is used to sensational press reports on the subject of the nuclear research centre at Dimona, and we are not accustomed to accord them any recognition.[38]

Moreover, addressing fellow Labour party Knesset members, Peres said that the story 'did not weaken us'. There was increased reference in official Israeli declaratory policy to non-conventional deterrence. General Shahak said in December 1986, 'It was obvious to the Arabs that because of Israeli military strength and the backing it enjoys from the United States they will not be able to annihilate Israel in a military strike. The Arabs believe Israel also has a non-conventional power.' But there were those in the country's defence community who suspected that the 'security leak' was part of a PR exercise and could not believe that security at Dimona or the Shin Bet had been unable to stop the disclosure in time.

As before the Vanunu exposé, Israeli officials have since adhered strictly to the ambiguity posture. 'Israel's nuclear policy as perceived by the Arabs has not changed, will not change and cannot change because this is a basic foundation of our existence – which will influence future generations;' thus prime minister Ehud Barak in 1995. His predecessor, Benjamin Netanyahu – never at a loss in nuancing his policies – asked in 1998 by ABC 'This Week's Sam Donaldson, 'Does Israel have any thought of testing nuclear weapons?', replied:

> *Netanyahu:* 'The whole issue should be treated very, very carefully. We've emerged from a bipolar world in which the former Soviet Union exercised enormous responsibility in this area to an increasingly international disorder. We need to exercise responsibility in considering such questions.

Donaldson: You could have said 'No, we have no thought of testing nuclear weapons.' You have not. So, are we wrong to consider that you're considering it?

Netanyahu: You're asking me about something that would follow a decision of changing our policy, and we haven't changed our policy.

Donaldson: Just for the record, does Israel possess nuclear weapons?

Netanyahu: Well, Israel will not introduce nuclear weapons, and you can make of that what you want.[39]

Yet behind the declaratory statements differences in emphasis could be traced among key Israeli politicians. Netanyahu describes himself as 'a territorial hawk' but 'a nuclear dove'. In his book, *A Place under the Sun*, Netanyahu asks cryptically,

What shall we explode with a nuclear bomb? Nablus? East Jerusalem? Apart from the terrible human cost directly, there will also be radioactive fallout with many Arabs and Jews killed ... The Arabs believe that Israel refrains from using nuclear weaponry for international reasons, which reject such usage.[40]

The most divergent has been the architect of the nuclear ambiguity policy himself, Shimon Peres. Asked while addressing a meeting of Israeli newspaper editors and broadcasting heads in 1996, 'Anything new in the nuclear field?', he replied, 'Yes. Give me peace and we'll give up the atom. That's the whole story. If there's regional peace I think we can rid the Middle East of the nuclear threat.' Peres' comments were not a sudden knee-jerk response but well-calculated, a recognition that the role of the nuclear programme had altered as a result of changes in the international and regional Middle East environments. These included the collapse of the Soviet Union and with it the end of the Cold War, peace with Egypt (1976), with Jordan (1996) and the Israel–Palestinian accords in Oslo in 1993. 'Let's be fair and honest,' Peres said, speaking in 2000, 'Israel was left without a choice. We never built something to create Hiroshima. We built something to create an Oslo.' With a crippling defence budget there was good reason for defence goals to be aligned with new realities. The negotiations in the 1990s for indefinitely extending the NPT had refocused attention on Israel's refusal to sign the treaty because it required ratifying states to open their nuclear installations to international inspection. Abba Eban said, 'There was increased criticism in international public opinion of Israel's failure to sign the treaty.'[41]

It is a truism that once the nuclear arsenal is disbanded so will be the secrecy surrounding it. By Peres' raising of the subject of nuclear arms in diplomatic fora, the total secrecy in which it has been shrouded was lessened and policymakers were freer in their public utterances about it. For example, in a passing comment in a 1994 interview, Peres remarked, 'I am not invited to events. I make them. France, Dimona, Sinai. Nobody can take these from me.'[42]

A decade after his exposé Vanunu appeared to be making initial headway on the long road to regional disarmament. While Israel's declaratory stands in diplomatic fora focused attention on her non-conventional capability and, as a result, reduced the ambiguity, the stream of Israeli diplomatic statements did not veer too far from the standard one, first expounded by Ben-Gurion, that Israel would not be the first to introduce nuclear weaponry into the region, concluded Emily Landau of the Jaffee Centre.[43]

The Peres approach sparked a debate in the defence and diplomatic establishments over whether or not the country's nuclear capability should be affected by the peace process. Even though Peres saw the goal of Middle East peace as not just with Israel's immediate neighbours (Egypt, Jordan, Syria and Lebanon) but also with other states including those subsequently regarded as threatening, including Iraq and Iran, Peres' linkage of the subject to peace aroused the ire of many defence officials including those of the Israeli Atomic Energy Commission (IAEC). The latter view the nuclear ambiguity policy as something not to be altered in the foreseeable long-term future. The Bomb has served to deter the Arabs and, so goes their reasoning, there is no need to chance it even if a comprehensive Middle East peace comes about. The 'defence school' fears that removing the ambiguity would start a series of irreversible steps which would lead to nuclear disarmament – and, they believe, to the eventual breakup of any Middle East peace. The first Gulf War, and Iran's nuclear programme, justified Israel's 'non-policy', this school argued. The collapse of the Israeli–Palestinian peace process in 2001 underlined their concerns.

Peres first unveiled his new approach at the International Conference for the Removal of Chemical Warfare in January 1993, where he discussed the need for a nuclear-free zone in the Middle East similar to those zones existing in Africa and Latin America. In part the approach was raised to assuage Egyptian pressure on Israel to sign the NPT. At a series of meetings in Cairo between Peres, then foreign minister, and Egyptian foreign minister Abu Moussa, Peres projected that two years after an eventual comprehensive Middle East peace settlement Israel would begin negoitiations for a nuclear-free zone. But officials at Israel's defence ministry were furious and at prime minister Rabin's instigation the idea was dropped. At one of their meetings, Peres replied to Moussa's request to visit Dimona that such a visit would rob Israel of its nuclear option. 'Imagine to yourself', Peres told Moussa, 'that you visit inside Dimona, and you see there is nothing there, we will lose all our nuclear deterrence.'[44]

In 1993 Israel signed the Chemical Weapons Convention (CWC) under which ratifying countries undertook to report and destroy chemical weapons stockpiles. Even though Israel did not ratify its signature, its decision to sign aroused debate inside the defence community. Critics said it would weaken Israel's deterrence, and create a situation in which Israel would be the only state without a chemical capability. Arab states, including Egypt, Syria, Iraq and Libya, seeing their chemical capabilities as the poor man's Bomb to counter Israel's nuclear Bomb, did not sign. But supporters of the decision to sign, including Peres, argued that Israel's nuclear bomb capability had been strengthened, with Arab states concluding that Israel would use it even to counter a lesser, chemical or biological, attack. The US and India, in signing the CWC, said they reserved the right to use nuclear weapons if attacked.

Similar questions came up in 1998 with the Comprehensive Test Ban Treaty (CTBT), banning future production of enriched uranium. While Israel agreed, together with the other 60 members of the UN Disarmament Commission, to discuss the subject she said that she would not sign the treaty itself. With the treaty concerning only future nuclear stocks, the 'Peres school' saw Israel's agreeing to discussions as a confidence-building step in the new Middle East. 'It is necessary to find means not to be at odds with the whole world seeking nuclear controls and our maintaining our nuclear ambiguity,' Peres said. But others, including many in the defence establishment, said that even an agreement to dialogue was taking Israel down the slippery path to ridding itself of the nuclear potential which had served it so well. 'If Iraq and Iran obtain the nuclear bomb, we will not have a nuclear deterrent. Then we will need to call on our conventional arms deterrent,' said the then deputy defence minister Ephraim Sneh. 'In the meantime this is what we have and we cannot give it up.' The other member states of the UN Disarmament Commission were not faced with the non-conventional threats which Israel was faced with. In 2004 Israel also declined to sign the Fissile Material Cutoff Treaty (FMCT), which proposes to halt the production of nuclear materials capable of undergoing fission.

Other Israeli ministers disagreed with Peres' approach. 'Arms-control talks can go on for years because nothing is going to come of them,' Itzhak Rabin remarked in an Israeli Television interview. The Israeli public backs Rabin's scepticism. A 1995 poll found that 71 per cent of Israelis did not think there was a need to sign the NPT in contrast to 23 per cent who did.[45] Netanyahu declined even to discuss the CTBT with the Clinton administration. 'Don't delude yourself,' Netanyahu told the US president. 'The treaty pertains to matters which are of fundamental existential importance to us; we won't commit suicide.'[46] Ehud Barak, addressing the Knesset in 1999, said that Israel would continue to maintain a strategic deterrent capability even in peace time over whatever geographical or time range was required. Ariel Sharon had earlier opposed the government's decision to sign the CWC.

Peres' revised approach on non-conventional arms goes back already to the early 1980s. In 1982 the foreign ministry established a small department entitled the arms control and disarmament unit (ACD). It was the brainchild of Hanon Bar-On, the ministry's number two official. He argued that the ambiguity stance notwithstanding, it was better that Israel should be speaking in international fora because not being heard would cause even more damage. Up to then, the IAEC, a bedrock of those favouring total secrecy, was the sole body responsible for the 'public dimensions' of nuclear policy. Bar-On seconded Ephraim Teri, a veteran IAEC official, to head the fledgling unit – sparking not a little opposition from foreign ministry staffers jealous of appointments from outside the ministry.

In the unit's early days its task was mostly to gather information about arms developments in the Arab world as well as about the diplomatic positions adopted by Arab states on arms control. But gradually its functions widened to include preparing position papers on international arms questions and despatching delegates to international fora like the Vienna-based IAEA. During Shimon Peres' period as foreign minister in the late 1980s the unit was upgraded to a division and its head to assistant director-general. If nothing else, this was a signal to the international community of the seriousness with which Israel regarded the question. Peres' stance of carrying on a dialogue won diplomatic kudos for Israel. Whether even the 'Peres school' simply represents a tactical posture in an era of the Middle East edging forward to peace, only history will tell. The question itself is one more element in the uncertainty surrounding the chosen policy of ambiguity. But in practice, the division's raison d'etre was weakened by Israel's failure to take a clear initiative regarding its nuclear capability. The sole PR anthem was that Israel would like to take a major step towards disarmament, but that given the serious military threats from within the region it would be unable to.

In addition to international and Middle East regional efforts towards arms control, Israel's ambiguity stance has also to be examined in the context of changes in the Arab–Israeli balance of power resulting from advances in Arab military hardware. But experts have speculated that in the event of Israel's enemies obtaining the Bomb there will develop an urgent need to create a rational balance of nuclear weaponry between Israel and these states. In creating such a new rational framework Israel is likely to remove, at least in part, the ambiguity over its nuclear programme. A confirmed capability would produce a rational deterrent posture, more stable and less aggressive.

The possibilities of Iran's nuclearisation were regarded by Western intelligence as low even up to the mid-1990s. The nuclear programme that the Shah had initiated with the low-megawattage reactor at Isfahan had been put on hold after the Islamic Revolution in 1979. But a welter of reports since then has produced irrefutable evidence of Iran's efforts to become a nuclear power. According to *Jane's*, Iran has 17 nuclear research facilities. They include an underground enrichment plant near Ntanaz, 200 miles south of Teheran, and a plant at Arak for the production of heavy water. Faced with economic shortages, Russia and former Soviet republics have become ready sources of fissile materials and technology. In 1995, Russia contracted to supply Iran with two reactors at its top-secret Nekaa nuclear complex. Israeli diplomatic efforts to stem the flow of Russian nuclear technology have failed.

There were reports in the early 1990s that Iran had attempted to buy highly enriched fissile material from Kazakhstan. Nuclear materials have reached Iran from China. Pakistan was an important source for nuclear weapons technology and for weapons-testing data. Iran has also invested in delivery systems. In 1994, in return for oil supplies, Iran negotiated with North Korea to develop the No Dong 1 missile, which has a range of over 620 miles. In 2000, Iran successfully tested the Shihab missile, which has a range of 800 miles. More advanced missile-delivery systems currently under development in Iran have a range of 1,250 miles. All of these place Israel within range of the missiles.

Iranian nuclear goals are a subject that is hotly debated within Israel's defence community. Some in military intelligence regard Iran as an enemy. Another school of thought suggests that Iran is just a potential threat, not an enemy, and that the Iranian programme is aimed at dominating the Arab world.

In the event of Israel going public with its nuclear programme, remaining questions concern the US–Israeli (Nixon–Meir) understanding dating from 1969, and the congressional 'Symington clause' which prohibits a US administration from providing foreign aid to countries with unsupervised nuclear arms programmes. One proposal, outlined in a 1994 study by the US Council on Foreign Relations, recommends that Israel, together with India and Pakistan, be formally recognised as nuclear nations, thereby contributing to the nuclear deterrent being more stable and perceived as less aggressive.

14
Secrecy Ltd

Nine months before the Vanunu exposé, a poll by Tel Aviv University's Jaffee Centre for Strategic Studies found that 92 per cent of Israelis questioned believed that Israel possessed nuclear weapons; 54 per cent of those asked were sure that Israel had nuclear weapons and 38 per cent thought that Israel had them but were not sure. Only 7 per cent did not think Israel had them but were not sure.[1] To be sure, the first-ever disclosure by somebody directly connected with the Dimona project left few lingering doubts that Israel was a nuclear power.

Vanunu said that he wanted to bring the subject to the public, to open up debate not only abroad but inside Israel too. Given the general belief even before Vanunu made his disclosure that the country possessed the Bomb – which Vanunu appeared to be unaware of – and the support for the policy of secrecy, as well as the fact that Vanunu did not disclose any immediate danger from the reactor, it was difficult to justify Vanunu's deed. Yet Vanunu became the supreme symbol of the excessive secrecy surrounding the subject. His act went beyond consensus or no consensus inside Israel. It was a strident act of disobedience against the system.

Vanunu did not want merely to inform Israelis about Dimona; he wanted to arouse internal concern. Although Vanunu claimed in a letter to an Israeli newspaper, 'I broke the taboo. Now others will come. Nobody can stop it,'[2] few came. Vanunu had much less impact in 1986 than he had hoped, for without much official effort the breach in the taboo healed itself. Meir Vanunu said, 'Nobody can expect that after 25 years of taboo suddenly because of something even as dramatic as this, things will be turned upside down and be totally open and in public.'[3] Yet Mordechai Vanunu's act reflected a sheer lack of political wisdom and not a little naivety about international realpolitik. By disclosing Israel's nuclear secrets, he said in 2004 after his prison release, one was preventing Israel from using her weaponry, because all the world would now know and no one would let her use it. His point, he said, was that war is not the way to solve conflict. This has to come through peace.

Until the 1991 Gulf War, the Israeli public's orientation to the topic of non-conventional weapons, and especially nuclear ones, was remarkably dormant, making it a non-issue. When the public was asked over the years the open-ended question as to what major issue should be addressed by the government, the issue of nuclear weapons never came up – compared to a 10 per cent rate in American surveys. The debate in Israel on nuclear policy continued to be confined to informed and organised opinion, and academic symposia were held to consider Israel's nuclear options. The 1997 volume of *The Middle East Balance*, published by the Jaffee Centre for Strategic Studies, included a section on non-conventional weaponry in the Middle East. Confessing to some disappointment nine months after the *Sunday Times* article, Mordechai Vanunu bemoaned the fact that nobody wants to challenge the establishment, which is succeeding in removing the issue from the public agenda.

But the 1990s saw an incremental opening-up of the subject. The period was characterised by even more nuclear-related information entering the public arena in Israel after the Vanunu exposé. This was in no way due to Israeli policymakers being less secretive or their ceding to pressure for more information. Rather, once out the Vanunu exposé created a wider circle of data and a momentum for even more information. It occurred as a result of five related matters. In addition to the satellite photography discussed earlier, there were the first Gulf War; two environment-related developments: a leak from the Dimona reactor and a series of legal suits by ex-workers who had suffered radioactivity; and publication of a book chronicling the early history of the Israeli nuclear project.

Four years after Vanunu, secrecy lessened remarkably during and after the first Gulf War. There was probably greater informed discussion in Israel then about non-conventional strategy than at any other time in the country's history. Popular concern in Israel in 1990 and 1991 about the Iraqi threat stimulated public and media discussion about the threat and the options for an Israeli non-conventional military response. At no time was Israeli military censorship as liberal on this point as during this period. Unprepared to go public with its capability, Israeli officialdom encouraged journalists to write about the deterrent, thereby giving veiled warnings to Baghdad. Blunt allusions in the media to an Israeli nuclear capability, which in the past would have been blue-pencilled, were not prevented by the military censor. Dan Margalit, then a *Haaretz* columnist, remarked that while the government had to remain quiet, the media would do the government's job. Yet when the war ended so did the censor's short-lived approach. While the Vanunu exposé contributed to making this discussion more intelligent, it would be wrong to exaggerate his impact in stimulating the discussion. It was the war, the missile attacks on Israel, and the proposal of George Bush senior for regional arms control which provoked the debate.

In the aftermath of the first Gulf War there was an increase in public support in Israel for nuclear development. The public regarded nuclear weapons as the main threat. A Jaffee Centre poll conducted after the war found that 91 per cent of Israelis favoured development of nuclear weapons; in 1987, 78 per cent had said so. Even more noteworthy was an astounding increase in the Israeli public's willingness to deploy nuclear weapons: 88 per cent of those asked said after the war that they would tolerate use of nuclear weapons. Only 53 per cent had said so in 1987, and a mere 36 per cent in 1986. Most Israelis justified the use of nuclear weapons following a non-conventional attack by another country. A lower proportion, about half, supported the use of nuclear weapons in a desperate military situation; far fewer Israelis supported such use in more conventional military situations.

Despite the militaristic impression, there was also a contrasting public trend favouring arms control – suggesting a convergence between Vanunu's goals and those of the Israeli public. In the longer term Israelis favour the idea of arms control regarding non-conventional weaponry. In 1998, 82 per cent supported the notion of prohibiting armies in the region, including Israel's, from having nuclear, chemical, or biological weapons (by contrast only 56 per cent agreed to the idea of reducing the size of conventional forces).[4]

As a result both of the greater discussion during the first Gulf War and of the data about the Dimona programme provided by Vanunu, the 1990s were characterised by a further opening-up of public discussion about the nuclear subject in the media and academia. The censor's rule of thumb that what has been published outside the territorial jurisdiction of the state – and which is therefore no longer 'secret' – may be published inside the country meant that the Vanunu disclosure enabled an intelligent discussion of sorts on nuclear issues to take place. 'What I can publish today about nuclear arms policy today, I could never have imagined twelve years ago. Since the Gulf War I get almost everything past the censor. He still plays with the text, adding "according to foreign sources", but the ideas, including a first nuclear strike by Israel, are left in,' said a military correspondent.[5] An examination of Israel's three main Hebrew dailies and two TV channels found that during 1999, 165 nuclear-related items were published or broadcast – making nuclear-related items the most covered theme after Lebanon and the Palestinians. Broken down, the biggest nuclear-related sub-category concerned Israeli nuclear policy (49 items), with the second biggest nuclear theme being arms control and international treaties (24). Another big category concerned Vanunu. By contrast, nuclear radioactive waste and safety at the nuclear reactor resulted in only four and seven items.[6]

There were almost no major known instances in the 1990s of the censor blue-pencilling nuclear-related articles, but this may be due in part to journalists failing to gather any new information about the programme.

In 2000 Israeli Television broadcast pictures of the reactor for the first time (shot in 1968 and 1971).[7] Since the pictures had been taken from what had already been published – on the website of the Federation of American Scientists – it fulfilled the military censor's criterion. Yet Alex Fishman, the military commentator of *Yediot Aharonot*, said that 'while the 1990s saw a big improvement quantitatively, it [information] has not improved qualitatively.'[8] The censor still views the Israeli media as an integral element of the country's deterrent posture. Israeli officials believe that publication in Israel, even by journalists or independent researchers, could be interpreted as confirmation that the country possesses the Bomb. 'There is a basic difference between the nuclear subject and other defence subjects,' said Hanoch Marmori, then editor of *Haaretz*. 'In other subjects there is a black and white, but on the nuclear theme we need to play at politicians and use the government's style in nuancing articles against our will – requiring us to quote foreign sources, to which the censor often adds "if we are to believe the source". If we do not use the code "nuclear option", "nuclear policy" – but never "Israeli nuclear bomb" – the sentence is blue-pencilled,' Marmori said.[9] Brigadier-General Itzhak Shani, the then military censor, asked by a reporter in a *Haaretz* interview, 'Isn't it somewhat outdated after Mordechai Vanunu and others to attach the line "according to foreign publications" to every news item about the nuclear programme or to insist on the phrasing "strategic weaponry"?', replied curtly, 'I disallow the question. Phrase it differently and I'll answer you.' The reporter came back, 'Isn't it necessary to change the censorship policy regarding the nuclear issue?' Shani replied:

An excellent question. In my view, the censorship policy that has been used up to now, and will continue to be used, is very wise. If you take all the stories about the atomic bomb that have appeared in the Israeli press – from its sources and with the approval of the censor – you'll see that the contention that no discourse on the subject exists in Israel, is simply incorrect. Anyone who wants to delve into the issue can do so, as long as he goes about it in the appropriate manner.[10]

In asking the Editors' Committee (a framework within which newspaper editors and broadcasting chiefs are briefed on sensitive defence-related matters by senior policymakers) prior to the *Sunday Times* article not to go beyond 'quoting foreign sources' nor to report local or Arab reactions to the forthcoming disclosure, prime minister Shimon Peres illustrated how muddied are the lines between Israeli officialdom and journalists on the nuclear arms issue. The Israel Journalists' Association (the professional guild of journalists), which has long criticised the institution of the Editors' Committee as a means for officialdom to gag the press, later met to condemn both Peres and editors. Although in the end none of the assembled editors had objected to Peres' request, a formal vote was not taken, and Gershon Schocken, the publisher of *Haaretz*, went away from the Editors' Committee meeting believing that Peres' request had not been accepted. An editorial which *Haaretz* planned to publish alongside a reprint of the three-page *Sunday Times* disclosure was impounded by the censor. In protest the paper left its editorial column blank. About 70 per cent of a planned editorial in the left-wing *Al Hamishmar* was also censored. The misunderstanding between Peres and *Haaretz* originated in the absence of any objections to the former's request. At a subsequent meeting of the Editors' Committee, editors decided that in future a formal vote should be taken when a government minister or official requested non-publication of a specific piece of information. However, this would still leave the minister in the vulnerable position of having to volunteer information before obtaining the editors' agreement not to publish it. It was finally agreed that at the beginning of each meeting the chairman would clarify the rules of the game, and that the information would be non-publishable only if everybody agreed to it by vote then and there.

'Some journalists and editors identify with the ambiguity policy but nobody asks him or her whether they do,' Marmori said. Professor Gabriel Ben-Dor, a Haifa University political scientist, attacked the Israeli media for 'largely cooperating' with the Israeli establishment: 'No news organisation or journalist has said we will not comply with the ambiguity,' said Ben-Dor. But Marmori said, 'If Vanunu had come to us with his story I would not have published it, not because of the policy of ambiguity but for reasons of censorship.'[11] A public debate within the confines of the policy of ambiguity could be held without going into technical details of the programme. Initiatives by Egypt to raise Israel's non-signature of the Nuclear Proliferation Treaty (NPT) generated discussion of the nuclear policy inside Israel, as had the Gulf War beforehand. But Alex Fishman, a hardened reporter, says that 'without giving us the facts, the establishment has succeeded in stifling debate.' In practice, as one reporter put it, the Israeli Atomic Energy Commission (IAEC) 'has very few people who are prepared to speak to you'. And though the commission has an official spokesman, the occasions when he has spoken are few. During the 1990s these could be counted on one hand: after a radioactive leak from the Dimona reactor to a nearby crater in 1993; and an official announcement that the reactor would be shut down over the last weekend of the millennium in order to avoid any possibility of a nuclear accident – an announcement designed to calm public unease. When the author organised an academic conference on 'Nuclear Weaponry, the Public and the Media' at Haifa University in 1995, he had no difficulty in obtaining the participation of Israeli academics and journalists but the IAEC declined to send a speaker. The ultimate in official cynicism was shown when, while discussing the public and nuclear policy, Shalheveth Freier, the IAEC's ex-director-general, wrote in 1992 that he did not 'know of an instance of an official attempt to stifle public discussion of the nuclear issue'.[12] He placed the blame on academics who, in addition to not including an account of official attitudes to the Bomb in their publications, do not share the products of their research with governmental sources.

In covering the Israeli army, reporters are also faced with secrecy, such as that concerning the location of forces, level of preparedness of forces, and operational planning. Yet a steady stream of army communiqués and on-the-record and off-the-record briefings by the army spokesman and other military top brass, as well as the participation of military correspondents in military exercises, ensures a lively debate in the media, the Knesset, and among the broader public. 'There remains a threshold that without any information flow, no debate can be conducted,' said Fishman.[13]

The military intelligence surprises in the Yom Kippur War produced greater critical scrutiny of the armed forces after 1973. The next governmental agency to lose its public image of infallibility was the Shin Bet, the domestic intelligence agency, after the so-called 'Shin Bet affair' in the 1980s. In the 1990s, the Mossad became the butt of greater scrutiny over several bungled intelligence operations abroad. The popular image of glamour and stealth which characterised the Mossad has as a result been trimmed in recent years. One of the last sections of the defence community to enjoy a virtual absence of public and media scrutiny were the IAEC and the Dimona reactor. And, in an attempt to shore up the secrecy surrounding the reactor, in 2000 prime minister Ehud Barak brought back Abraham Shalom, the Shin Bet head disgraced in the Shin Bet affair, to strengthen security and secrecy at the reactor.[14]

If, like Vanunu, many Israeli journalists today call for freer information, in doing so most of them have different long-term objectives to Vanunu's. While Vanunu wants information and discussion in order to bring public pressure for dismantling the Bomb, the journalists see information as being vital for public discussion of the country's nuclear options. They want official information on aspects of the programme publication of which would not damage ambiguity, such as information about the reactor's safety, safety procedures within it, and arrangements for the disposal of radioactive materials.

In contrast to journalists, at the turn of the millennium most of the public still favoured nuclear secrecy. There is a continuous trend for an overwhelming majority in Israeli society to support secrecy, thus exercising the public's democratic right to limit freedom. According to the Jaffee Centre, 72 per cent of those asked in 1999 backed keeping Israel's nuclear plans concealed, compared to two-thirds in 1998, to 71 per cent in 1993, and 78 per cent in 1987.[15]

The same was true of the Knesset. Bipartisan support for the policy of ambiguity ensured that it was infrequently raised in parliamentary questions. Between 1995 and 1999 there were 13 nuclear-related parliamentary questions; these concerned the Iraqi nuclear capability, the NPT, and safety inside the reactor. If raised, the nuclear subject was invariably shunted off to the secure setting of the Knesset's defence and foreign affairs committee, sitting behind closed doors.

On 2 February 2000 the Knesset plenum was the setting for a rarified debate on nuclear policy. It followed an initiative by Communist Knesset member Issam Makhloul. The Knesset speaker, Avrum Burg, attempted to pass the matter to the committee, relenting only when Makhloul threatened to appeal to the Supreme Court that the full plenum debate the matter. Foreign diplomats and journalists filled the gallery. Not surprisingly, an attempt by the Free Mordechai Vanunu Campaign to get the prison authorities to allow Vanunu to attend the debate was rejected. The debate itself – which lasted only 52 minutes – was shallow and disappointing. 'The whole world knows that Israel is a large warehouse of nuclear, chemical, and biological weapons. Only Israeli citizens are kept in the dark about Israel's nuclear arsenal, and conditions at the reactor,' Makhloul said.[16] He declared that Iran and Iraq were 'threatened by Dimona', and not the other way round. Many Knesset members booed the debate, particularly when Makhloul slipped in a number of disclosures. He claimed that since the *Sunday Times* exposé the number of nuclear warheads had increased from 100 to between 200 to 300. He quoted reports that the navy's recently acquired Dolphin submarines were equipped to carry nuclear warheads, giving Israel a second-strike capability to respond a ground attack. He also quoted reports that radioactive waste from Israel is buried in Mauritania. Replying for the government, minister Haim Ramon repeated the well-practised cliché line that Israel would not be the first to introduce nuclear weaponry into the region. And turning to Makhloul, he asked, 'Do you want us to go and announce to Iran and Iraq exactly what we have?' That the debate was initiated by an Arab Knesset member hardly persuaded Middle Street, Israel of the virtues of debating the subject.

Haaretz came to Makhloul's assistance. In an editorial, entitled 'With All Due Caution', the paper opined:

> Israeli society is mature enough to open its nuclear 'black box' with all due caution and look inside. We can and must conduct a public debate on nuclear policy and deal with questions such as the future of the policy of ambiguity in a Middle East in which there will be a number of nuclear powers, and what kind of deterrence Israel needs in time of peace ... The maturing of Israeli society raises questions concerning matters such as the treatment of nuclear waste and the safety of the reactors, which until now have been swaddled in a thick blanket of secrecy. A discussion of this kind should be held without endangering confidential material of an operational nature and without exposing Israel to international pressure to divest itself of its protective armour.[17]

Legislative control of nuclear policy was still inadequate in the 1990s. 'I can't ever remember that we held a discussion on the Atomic Energy Commission,' remarked Ran Cohen, a member of the Knesset's state comptroller's committee. And Yossi Katz could not remember a discussion on nuclear policy during the year he chaired the defence and foreign affairs committee. Even ministerial oversight of the IAEC appeared wanting. Prime minister Ehud Barak left Danny Yatom, head of his policy staff, to deal with Gideon Frank, IAEC director-general. Barak later proposed appointing a minister to supervise the commission, as well as the intelligence community, but elections put paid to the idea.

As memories of the 1991 Gulf War started to dull, public apathy on the non-conventional weapons question had begun to return by the end of the millennium. An analysis of the content of the Israeli media on nuclear subjects in 1999 found that of some 165 nuclear-related items, the two popular mass-circulation papers, *Maariv* and *Yediot Aharonot*, accounted for only 35 per cent of them. Moreover, the news programmes of Israel's two television channels accounted for only 3 per cent. By way of illustration, when a programme in 2000 in the popular series 'Po-Politika', hosted by Dan Margalit, moved to the subject of nuclear weaponry, two-thirds of its viewers switched to the second television channel. However, there were signs of elite Israeli opinion becoming less inhibited in discussing the subject: some 42 per cent of the items appeared in the quality daily *Haaretz*.[18]

A separate challenge in the 1990s to Israel's ambiguity came from a novel direction. An Israeli-born researcher living in the United States, Dr Avner Cohen, used foreign archival sources to trace the history of the Israeli nuclear programme. The author came up with highly sensitive information. In particular, by using the US Freedom of Information Act he obtained archival material documenting US contacts with Jerusalem about Dimona, including the negotiations in the 1960s between prime minister Golda Meir and president Richard Nixon, leading up to the US–Israeli understanding of 1969. The Israeli authorities brought an assortment of pressures on Cohen while he was preparing the book. These included telephone calls from the security wing of the defence ministry, with veiled threats. On a visit to Israel in 1994 he was taken aside at immigration control at Ben-Gurion airport and informed by a police officer that his work was likely to infringe censorship regulations. Cohen did not submit his book for censorship clearance, partly because in 1994, when he submitted a single chapter to the censor, the latter, to Cohen's surprise, sent back the manuscript telling him, 'We are returning it without censorship, and we leave it to you to decide how to act.' When Cohen insisted that as an Israeli citizen he was obliged to get the permission of the censor, the latter replied, 'If so, the whole chapter is banned.' Cohen then appealed to the courts against this ban but according to him the courts, sitting behind closed doors, said that if he failed to reach a compromise with the censor it would take a long time for them to adjudicate in the matter.[19] At that point Cohen decided to publish the book, *Israel and The Bomb*, abroad. (The book itself, with the exception of a passing reference in the epilogue, all but ignores the details of the Vanunu exposé.)

The dilemma for the Israeli authorities is that it is not illegal to publish information learnt from foreign sources. To suggest that Cohen should not publish information gathered from the archives of the US government – and available to anyone else – is to introduce a double standard. Foreign corres-pondents of the Israeli media, who are Israeli citizens, freely gather information abroad from all sources and do not submit it to the censor for prior clearance. But, in addition to accessing US archives and interviewing US officials, Cohen also interviewed a long list of Israelis who had direct knowledge of the project. They included Professor Israel Dostrovsky, former IAEC director-general Shalheveth Freier, Shimon Peres, Zvi Dinstein, a former deputy defence minister, and General Yehoshafat Hakarbi, a former head of military intelligence. Cohen used these interviews to supplement information he gathered from the archives. He was able to recruit a number of former personalities like Professor Yuval Neeman who claimed there was nothing in the book which could harm Israeli national security.

Among other steps taken towards tightening up on secrecy about the nuclear programme were that personal papers belonging to Levi Eshkol, who was prime minister in the 1960s, and which included details of the nuclear programme which Cohen had used in his research, were removed from Eshkol's office on the orders of chief of defence security Yehiel Horev and deposited in the state archives. The Israeli authorities even managed to persuade the US National Archive to censor documents from the administration of Lyndon B. Johnson dating from 1968, which contained CIA assessments of the Israeli nuclear programme.

Greater public concern about the nuclear programme was generated after a number of environment-related crises at the reactor. They concerned safety aspects of the reactor, notably those of radioactive materials, whether affecting workers at the site due to poor safety standards or leaking to the environment around the site.

Following disclosure of a radioactive leak which had occurred in August 1992 to the Little Crater, a tourist attraction to the south of the Dimona reactor, the IAEC announced some eight months later, for the first time in the state's history, that radioactive waste was stored at Dimona. Up to then, nobody had disclosed whether radioactive waste was stored in Israel, let alone where. Weeks after the announcement came the media disclosure of the spillage of radioactive sewage from the oxidation ponds at the reactor into the crater. It was difficult not to conclude that the announcement had been intended to prepare the way for news of the spillage.

Vanunu himself had told Frank Barnaby about the burial of waste in barrels, but this point was not included in the *Sunday Times* article. It was later published in Barnaby's little-known book, *The Invisible Bomb*.[20] He said that radioactive waste from the reprocessing plant and elsewhere was mixed with tar, sealed in barrels, and buried. The official announcement helped to build up the scanty picture of what waste was stored at Dimona. Two types were stored there. The first was low-level radioactive waste from some 320 hospitals, research institutes and factories. The second was the highly enriched uranium rods used as nuclear fuel inside the reactor. These are highly dangerous. When the rods are replaced every few months with new rods they give out massive amounts of radioactivity, dangerous to humans, wildlife and vegetation. Dubbed 'the problem which refuses to disappear', this is an issue to which the nuclear industry has yet to find a long-term solution. Generally, the used rods are left in oxidation ponds for months, if not years, after which they are taken out and their parts separated. Some of these get reused. The remainder are buried underground in barrels for hundreds of years. In time a radioactive leak from the barrels could contaminate the Negev Desert's water table.

In an attempt to reassure the public following the announcement of the radioactive leak, Yossi Sarid, the high-profile environment minister, took a well-publicised tour of the nuclear research centre. It was the first time that any minister apart from the prime minister or defence minister had entered the portals of Dimona. Afterwards he said he had full confidence in the manner in which radioactive waste was stored. Environment ministry officials were subsequently given access to the nuclear research centre. Yet as many questions as answers were left. The IAEC's acknowledgement notwithstanding, no details were provided about specific safety measures taken for storage of different types of radioactive waste, particularly the uranium rods. Dr Danny Rabinovitch, a Hebrew University anthropologist specialising in environmental matters, remains sceptical as to whether the environment ministry has the know-how or the clout to provide the necessary supervision of the nuclear research centre.

Doctoral theses prepared by a botanist and a zoologist found radioactive effects on the vegetation and wildlife respectively in the Dimona area. Both theses were banned from publication.

In a further step to calm a distraught public, in 1993 the IAEC installed a monitoring station to follow radiation levels at Dimona. Situated in the local police station, its findings are open to the public. The reports are fed to a central monitoring station at Tel Aviv University.

A related question concerns the long-term safety of the reactor which, having been in operation for some 40 years, is old. While there are older ones, such as one in Canada which is 60 years old, and one in the US which is 48 years old, and while the Dimona reactor was built to Western standards and many of its parts had been changed, questions still arose. A fire broke out there in 1991, according to US officials. Paul Leventhal of the US Nuclear Regulatory Commission claims that the reactor suffers from safety problems. And according to Professor Uzi Even of Tel Aviv University, who worked at the reactor in the 1960s, it is old and dangerous and should be closed. Professor Even – who was almost put on trial on charges of disclosing nuclear secrets – said that 'the nuclear radiation discharged during the reactor's functioning causes a weakening of the building from which the reactor is made, the concrete and steel.'[21]

Inadequate safety standards further ensured that environment-related questions stayed on the public agenda. A stream of legal suits was brought against the IAEC in the 1990s by ex-workers at the reactor or their dependants who claimed that the ex-workers had got cancer as a result of their exposure to radioactive materials. Over 100 law suits, each demanding 1 million or more shekels in compensation, have been brought. These do not include other cases of cancer where the IAEC authorities agreed to give compensation (of no more than $100,000), or many cases, particularly of workers lower down the hierarchy, who for reasons of 'loyalty' or lack of means to pursue action have not taken up the matter.

These cases have resulted in much information about Dimona's safety standards coming into the public arena. For officials there was a danger that highly sensitive information about work methods inside the reactor would be exposed in the court appeals. But there was also bureaucratic manipulation of the so-called 'need for secrecy' in order to interfere in the due processing of the legal claims.

The two reactors – at Dimona and at the Nahal Soreq research centre – had autonomous arrangements for maintaining their own safety standards. An 1981 law had given the Israeli ministry of employment responsibility at workplaces for the health of workers who come into contact with radioactive materials. This included medical checks on employees. The environment ministry had responsibility for storage of radioactive materials at workplaces. However, in the cases of Dimona and Nahal Soreq, the law allowed for the IAEC to continue administering safety. This administration comprised three levels: Dimona's and Nahal Soreq's own safety department; the IAEC's licensing and safety division; and the Nuclear Safety Commission, whose members are appointed for a two-year period by the prime minister. However, after the death from radiation of a worker at Nahal Soreq, a 1992 Knesset inquiry under Knesset member Yair Tzaban favoured a new umbrella organisation, which would not be part of the IAEC, to supervise radioactive waste disposal. This was justified, the Tzaban inquiry concluded, because of the radioactive waste brought along civilian roads from hospitals, research institutes and factories for storage at Dimona; and because of an expansion of Nahal Soreq's growing involvement in selling its services to the civilian market.

But the IAEC said that the need for security and secrecy required them to carry out their own safety procedures. The workers' union countered with a proposal that the appointment of external inspectors should require the prior approval of the prime minister. In early 1992 the workers' union appealed to the Supreme Court to gain external ministerial supervision of safety standards. It was an extreme stand to take – the first such stand in Dimona's history – and reflected a breakdown in worker–employer relations. Their complaints acted as a form of confirmation of the fears for nuclear safety among the general public outside. The legal action by the workers' union never reached the courts as the prime minister's office drew up new safety regulations. These included a new laboratory and institute for measuring radioactive levels; more precise registration of radioactive materials; and more health inspections for workers. Jerusalem lawyer Richard Laster, a specialist in environment law, handled 70 of the legal claims.

IAEC strategy was to deny any causal connection between the 1992 death and the workplace. Given that it takes a minimum of seven years from exposure to radiation to getting cancer, it is difficult always to prove a causal connection. Defendants have been denied access to their own medical records; lawyers have had to subpoena the court to order the IAEC to release this information. There have even been allegations that medical records have been tampered with.

In the mid-1990s the IAEC referred to an internal survey of Dimona workers which found that the rate of cancer among them was no higher than the national average, and at times lower. But the Israeli authorities have 'for security reasons' steadfastly refused requests to disclose details of the sample. Suspicions were raised that the survey had been deliberately skewed. It was flawed partly because while the national population sample includes young children, youth, the infirm and aged persons, staff at the reactor are in the prime 22–60 age group, many with high physical fitness profiles. A 1995 survey conducted by the workers themselves in certain departments inside Dimona (among them 50 workers who had been suffering from cancer) found that cancer levels were twice the national average.

The IAEC suffered a major setback in 1997 when the case of Hayyim Itach, who had died of cancer aged 43, reached the Tel Aviv District Court. Itach had died of leukaemia, which his widow claimed had been caused after he came into contact with radioactive materials. While he had been instructed to don special protective clothing when handling such materials, his widow claimed that he had been exposed to radioactivity even when not directly touching them. Mrs Itach's attempts to get permission for an independent expert to enter Dimona to examine whether there was a causal connection between her husband's illness and his work, and to get access to his full medical records, failed. In her ruling Judge Hila Gentel accused the IAEC of showing 'contempt for human life' in its lack of safety precautions: 'The nuclear reactor is operating with its eyes closed, not taking necessary safety precautions against radioactive materials. The reactor's approach causes worry and outrage.' The court awarded the family damages of 800,000 dollars. Judge Gentel described the testimony of one of the prosecution's main witnesses, the head of Dimona's radioactivity protection unit, as 'unreliable'.[22] In a rare step the judge allowed testimony from Professor Baruch Modan, an internationally acclaimed expert in radioactivity and cancer, who linked Itach's cancer to his place of work. Modan testified in spite of the prosecution's protests. The prosecution even used Modan's former position as director-general of the Israeli health ministry to claim that the former civil servant could not give testimony against the government. The government appealed the court award and in an out-of-court settlement a much lower amount was agreed.

The Dimona workers have also turned to the parliamentary route. In 1997 the reactor's workers' committee took the unusual step of writing to the Knesset's defence and foreign affairs committee. Earlier, in 1994, it had turned to Likud opposition Knesset member Limor Livnat, who tabled a legislative proposal by which a worker at the reactor who got cancer as a result of radioactive exposure would be given state compensation. Livnat's proposed law would have linked cancer to the reactor worker's job. 'That way you safeguard the workers' rights and state security, as there is no need to reveal any information on exposure to dangerous substances,' Livnat said. Livnat based her proposal on an existing law which gives compensation to commissioned soldiers who die during military service. Later, Livnat's file, containing details of the workers and their illnesses, mysteriously disappeared from her Knesset office. The law passed its initial reading and was referred to the defence and foreign affairs committee. There it was put on ice. Under a compromise the committee proposed that Israel's National Insurance Institute, which is responsible for providing social security to the country's work population, would set up a special committee to determine whether there was a connection between illness and work at Dimona. However, the special committee failed to make a single financial award.

In an agreement reached in 1997 between the IAEC and lawyers representing the workers, it was established that the workers' claims could be settled by arbitration. It would ensure that sensitive details of work at the reactor would not be disclosed. An arbitration panel comprising three experts in radioactivity, one appointed by the IAEC, one by the victims' lawyers, and the third a mutually agreed appointment, would determine claims. However, due to bureaucratic foot dragging, ostensibly over working procedures, the panel did not meet. An attempt by the victims' lawyers to coopt a number of academic experts failed after the IAEC declined to give them access to victims' medical records because they did not possess security clearance. With patients dying in the meantime while waiting for their cases to reach the courts, time was playing in the IAEC's favour. In 2000, lawyers representing the families appealed to the courts to cancel the arbitration methods and return the matter to the courtroom. In 2001 victims and their dependants took to the streets and demonstrated outside the reactor. In 2003 a committee of experts appointed by the courts concluded that 33 out of 39 cases involving workers from Dimona and the Nahal Soreq reactor who had developed cancer could not be linked to the workplace. Although the legal claims remained unresolved, they did contribute to a major improvement in safety standards at the reactor.

Despite public concerns, the various environment-related crises failed to bring about the IAEC's 'Yom Kippur'. Both the limited 'fallout' – environmental damage to the Little Crater, and the general population not being affected by safety standards as opposed to workers inside – as well as a Machiavellian handling of official information about the spillages, enabled the commission to continue virtually unscathed.

The Vanunu exposé reported nothing concerning health and safety standards at Dimona. Vanunu himself provided useful information about Machon 4, where radioactive waste was dealt with. After debriefing Vanunu for the *Sunday Times*, Dr Frank Barnaby concluded that Dimona's health and safety standards were reasonable. Vanunu ought to have been aware of the poor work-safety standards which existed at the time he was there. Nevertheless, by drawing attention to the excessive secrecy in nuclear policy in general Vanunu played a useful role. As a result of Vanunu breaking the taboo of silence, workers became less inhibited from going public.

With the entry of non-conventional weaponry and warfare into the Middle East the need for public understanding has grown. The level of public knowledge among Israelis about new forms of warfare during the 1991 Gulf War was not high. Most Israelis failed to realise that chemical warheads are not dangerous because they dissipate into the air and cause little damage unless a warhead penetrates a residential area. Public knowledge regarding the biological threat is even less.

The demands on the Israeli psyche in a non-conventional war would be great. Research concerning civilian populations under stress shows that in wartime, once citizens have information about what is happening, and what they are able and unable to do about the situation, they have a feeling of control over it. In the 1998 war alert following a crisis with UN inspectors in Iraq, the long queues for gas masks in Israel reflected the failure in the years following the first Gulf War to sensitise Israelis to the phenomenon of citizens being the frontline troops. Israel's stance of ambiguity regarding its own reported nuclear, chemical, and biological capabilities makes it difficult for the government to go on the information offensive and build support at home. All that spokespersons are left with is to react passively, and advise civilians how best to protect themselves. In its entry on the army's home corps, which bore the brunt in the first Gulf War, the 2000 state comptroller's report called for removing some of the mystery surrounding the biological threat and for reducing public fear through information campaigns, not only in wartime but also in peacetime.

For Arab regimes in possession of non-conventional weaponry the panic in the 1991 war is a lesson in the deterrent power they possess over an enemy democracy. For Israeli leaders it is a portent of the likely political pressures that will result if and when Israel goes public with its capability. If an Arab country produces and declares possession of the Bomb, experts believe Israel will have to shed some of its ambiguity, with public pressure to learn more about Israel's capability being much greater. There will be a need for the public to understand the dynamics of strategic deterrence. Even seasoned military correspondents acquainted with conventional forms of warfare will have to re-educate themselves. A supply of data will clarify decades of speculation about what is and what is not true. The makeup of the nuclear programme will be much clearer, as will be the price Vanunu paid for providing his 1986 preview.

In such a scenario, Vanunu would be able to discuss openly some of the information he disclosed, without having to be unduly concerned about its effects on US foreign aid. While an Iranian bomb will widen still further the pro-Bomb lobby in Israel, an anti-Bomb lobby may also grow and become more vocal, one in which Vanunu is likely to play an important role.

15
Interview with Mordechai Vanunu

The author interviewed Mordechai Vanunu in Jerusalem on 29 July 2004.

Cohen: Mr Vanunu, you spoke to the *Sunday Times* because you felt that you had a moral obligation to inform Israelis about the nuclear project. Yet polls inside Israel have shown that there is wide support in Israel in favour of Israel possessing the Bomb. Polls also show that even before your disclosure most Israelis already believed their country possessed the Bomb. There was also wide public support in favour of the government's policy of secrecy. So, did you have a moral obligation to inform Israelis?

Vanunu: When I spoke, most Israelis may have believed that Israel possessed the Bomb but they did not know for certain. I disclosed that Israel had a larger amount of warheads than earlier estimates – today Israel must have 200 warheads. I revealed exactly what the government was doing. I also disclosed new information about the hydrogen and neutron bombs. Maybe the Israeli public support possession of the simple nuclear bomb, but do not support possessing the hydrogen bomb. In any case, I still have the right to inform them, and they can decide what they wish to do with the information.

Cohen: What about the majority of Israelis who support the ambiguity and silence around nuclear arms policy? In a democratic society, cannot the majority limit their own freedom whether in terms of artistic freedom or in defence-related information?

Vanunu: Regarding security secrecy, I don't accept that citizens can censor themselves. In a democracy people demand to know exactly what is going on.

Cohen: You wanted to change public attitudes, and dismantle Dimona. Do you think that retrospectively you might have played it differently: instead of leaking nuclear secrets to the media to have worked through peace education, to educate about the dangers of Hiroshima and Nagasaki?

Vanunu: After the Israeli public know precisely what is going on inside Dimona, only then can teachers teach against nuclear weapons. Teachers who talk about the Nazi Holocaust need to be aware of the existence of weapons which may cause a nuclear holocaust.

Cohen: Israelis now know the information you gave, and yet they still support possession of the Bomb. Do you think that you should become active not only abroad – where you want to go to campaign against the Bomb – but also at home, perhaps even running for the Knesset?

Vanunu: My mission was accomplished.

Cohen: Don't you think that you still have a mission inside Israel, to speak to those interested in your message?

Vanunu: I'd be happy to speak to Israelis once I can do so in a free way.

Cohen: When you spoke to the *Sunday Times* in 1986 were you already then against the Bomb in principle? Dr Frank Barnaby [the British nuclear physicist who debriefed Vanunu on behalf of the *Sunday Times*] told me that his impression was that you were not against the Bomb in principle, that you were not against Israel possessing a couple of warheads. Rather, you thought that the programme had got out of control.

Vanunu: I was against the Bomb before 1986. I saw the cases of Hiroshima and Nagasaki and was totally against it. I was always against the Bomb. In prison, this view became much more powerful and deeper. The world needs to get down to zero nuclear weapons – and Russia and the US have a big role to play in this process.

Cohen: Why were safety weaknesses inside the reactor not mentioned in the original *Sunday Times* exposé? Dr Frank Barnaby, in his own book published in 1989, wrote that safety standards were reasonable.

Vanunu: I told the *Sunday Times* everything. They have safety rules just like any reactor. There were accidents which I told them about. I told them about the [disposal of] nuclear waste.

Cohen: It is suggested that the Israeli Bomb has contributed to deterring Arab states like Egypt into making peace with the Jewish State.

Vanunu: Had Israel and her Arab neighbours achieved peace such as at the 1950 Rhodes Conference between Israel and the Arab States, including on the refugee problem, there would not have been any later need for the deterrent role.

Cohen: Where does one go from here? You made your disclosure. Most Israelis – even more today – support possessing the Bomb. The US government has a secret understanding with Jerusalem to look the other way and not bring pressure upon Israel on the question of the Bomb. How do you think those who oppose the Bomb should proceed? What lessons for protest action should be learnt from this case?

Vanunu: If Israel can be persuaded to make a real peace, then opponents of the Bomb will come forward and raise their voice and demand to get rid of all nuclear weapons. If there is no peace, nobody will listen to anti-Bomb campaigners. So my view is that the Bomb does not deter. They are keeping them in order not to make peace.

Cohen: Shimon Peres wants a regional peace which will be followed by disarmament. Dimona was built, Peres once said, to get to Oslo [where the 1993 Israeli–Palestinian accords were signed], not to Hiroshima.

Vanunu: Peres does not want a real peace with the Arabs. If Israel wanted one they could have got it. Israel is not ready to make peace, to have a Palestinian state. If so, the rest would have been easier.

Cohen: How do you rate the coverage your case received in the Israeli media?

Vanunu: As a rule, the Israeli media took a one-sided view of the affair. Why is it impossible to think about a second side? The function of a newspaper is to be objective. This press serves the establishment. This is not a respectable press which characterises a democratic country.

Cohen: How do you expect your views to get expressed in the Israeli media if you refuse to be interviewed by them?

Vanunu: You are assuming that this a democracy where everything is reported. Allow me to tell you, that there is no democracy here nor any campaigning media. Show me one word which was written in my affair which did not come from the establishment.

Cohen: Are you happy with the support which the *Sunday Times* has given you over the years?

Vanunu: I am critical of them. They have supported me, but they could have done much more to appeal for my prison release in the first years [of my imprisonment]. They could also have provided more details of my case.

Cohen: The *Sunday Times* still has a set of tapes of your two-day-long debriefing in London with the paper's reporters where you spoke in detail about your work.

Vanunu: Yes.

Cohen: Your story also appeared in the *Sunday Mirror*, which sought to discredit your account. Your contact man in Australia, Oscar Guerrero, offered them the story while you were in touch with the *Sunday Times*. Did you know that the Colombian intermediary was offering your story to the *Sunday Mirror*?

Vanunu: No I didn't know he offered them the story. Guerrero was concerned that he might not be paid by the *Sunday Times*. After Peter Hounam found that he could no longer trust Guerrero [after Guerrero had described Vanunu to Hounam as 'one of Israel's leading scientists'] Hounam tried to get close to me, being the source of the story, and felt that he did not need Guerrero any more.

Cohen: What hope do you have for Israel's younger generation and the chances of disarmament?

Vanunu: When I was released from prison after 18 years inside I found that the younger generation is more nationalist and more religious. So I hope that they will wake up and look to peace. But the situation is bad, and they are delaying the peace process by years.

Notes

CHRONOLOGY

i   Leonard Spector, *The Undeclared Bomb* (Cambridge, MA: Ballinger, 1988), pp. 386–7.

1 THE COST OF CONSENSUS

1   *Alternativa*, March 1987, June 1987 (Hebrew).
2   Avner Cohen, *Israel and The Bomb* (New York: Columbia University Press, 1998), p. 386.
3   *Maariv*, 10.5.1976.
4   Zeev Schiff, ' "The Delicate Subject" for which silence is not beautiful', *Politika*, March 1987 (Hebrew).
5   Interview with Charles Richards.
6   Interview with David Rubinger.
7   Interview with Gideon Berli.
8   Shlomo Aronson, *The Politics of Nuclear Weapons in the Middle East* (Albany, NY: State University of New York Press, 1992), p. 310.
9   *Sunday Times*, 30.5.2004.
10 Address, 'Nuclear Weaponry, the Public and the Media' conference, Haifa University, 1995.
11 *Haaretz*, 25.3.1976.
12 Asher Arian, Ilan Talmud and Tamar Hermann, *National Security and Public Opinion in Israel*, Jaffee Centre for Strategic Studies, Study no. 9, 1987–88 Series.
13 Ibid.
14 Interview with Menachem Shalev.
15 *Guardian*, 17.11.1986.
16 Australian TV, 'Four Corners', 31.8.1987; Israel Television, 'Mabat Sheni', March 1988.
17 Interview with David Kimche.

2 THE BOMB THAT DOESN'T EXIST

1   *Time*, 12.4.1976.
2   Ibid.
3   Ibid.
4   Andrew Cockburn and Leslie Cockburn, *Dangerous Liaison* (New York: HarperCollins, 1991).
5   *Haaretz*, 5.10.1986.
6   Fuad Jabber, *Israel and Nuclear Weapons* (London: Chatto & Windus, 1971), p. 114.
7   Leonard Spector, *The Undeclared Bomb* (Cambridge, MA: Ballinger, 1988), pp. 386–7.
8   www.fas.org/nuke/guide/israel/nuke3/index.html/estimate
9   www.fas.org/nuke/guide/israel/facility/dimona.htm
10 Louis Beres (ed.), *Security or Armageddon: Israel's Nuclear Strategy* (Lexington, MA: Lexington Books, 1986).

11 *Davar*, 29.12.1986.
12 Jabber, *Israel and Nuclear Weapons*, p. 114.
13 Frank Barnaby, *The Invisible Bomb: The Nuclear Arms Race in the Middle East* (London: Tauris, 1989), pp. 22, 25.
14 *Davar*, 29.12.1986.
15 Anna Gillespie, 'Current Nuclear Programmes in Third World Countries', in Frank Barnaby (ed.), *Plutonium and Security* (London: Macmillan, 1992).
16 *Yediot Aharonot*, 28.4.1994.
17 *Davar*, 29.12.1986; *Maariv*, 12.11.1986.
18 *Davar*, 29.12.1986.
19 *Maariv*, 12.11.1986.
20 *Haaretz*, 29.7.1997.
21 *Wehrtechnik*, June 1976.
22 *el-Hiyat*, 26.2.1967.
23 *Newsweek*, 11.7.1988.
24 *Observer*, 23.8.1987.
25 Frank Barnaby, 'Capping Israel's Nuclear Volcano', *Israel Affairs*, 2 (1), Autumn 1995.
26 Edwin Cochran, 'Deliberate Ambiguity: An Analysis of Israel's Nuclear Strategy', *Journal of Strategic Studies*, 1996. Cochran was a US army officer.

3 MORDECHAI VANUNU'S GAUNTLET

1   *Sunday Times*, 6.6.2004.
2   Interview with Meir Vanunu.
3   Interview with Rabbi Joshua Chalkowski.
4   Interview with Meir Vanunu.
5   Protocols of the Vanunu trial, no. 260497–8.
6   Ibid.
7   *Hadashot*, 7.11.1986.
8   *Davar*, 7.11.2004.
9   *Al Hamishmar*, 7.11.1986.
10 *Maariv*, 21.11.1986.
11 *Haolam Hazeh*, 11.2.1987.
12 Ibid.
13 *Sunday Times*, 5.10.1986.
14 *Haaretz*, 8.5.1989.
15 *Haaretz*, 5.10.1986.
16 *Hadashot*, 20.11.1987.
17 Interview with Reverend John McKnight.
18 Ibid.
19 Interview with Reverend David Smith.
20 *Sunday Times*, 6.6.2004.
21 For a discussion of Jewish thought on nuclear weaponry, see Reuven Kimelman, 'Judaism, War, and Weapons of Mass Destruction', *Conservative Judaism*, 56 (1), Fall 2003.
22 Letter to *New from Within*, 10.9.1987.
23 Protocols, no. 260312.
24 Yair Evron, 'The Nuclear Option: Needs an Airing', *Israeli Democracy*, Summer/Fall 1988.
25 Conversation between Mordechai Vanunu and the author.
26 *Hadashot*, 20.1.1987.
27 Ibid.

28 *Hadashot*, 20.11.1987.
29 *Haolam Hazeh*, 21.10.1987.
30 *Independent on Sunday*, 25.4.2004.
31 Interview with Dr Frank Barnaby.

4 DEVIL'S ADVOCATE

1 Interview with Robin Morgan.
2 *Sun-Herald*, 26.10.1986; *Jerusalem Post*, 7.11.1986.
3 Harold Hobson, Phillip Knightley and Leonard Russell, *The Pearl of Days* (London: Hamish Hamilton, 1972).
4 Interview with *Sunday Times* reporter.
5 Interview with Phillip Knightley.
6 Australian Television, 'Four Corners', 31.8.1988.
7 Interview with Peter Hounam.
8 Australian Television, 'Four Corners', 31.8.1988.
9 *Haaretz*, 5.10.1986.
10 Ibid.
11 *Sunday Times*, 30.5.2004
12 Interview with Peter Hounam.
13 Ibid.
14 Interview with Robin Morgan.
15 Interview with Dr Frank Barnaby.
16 Australian Radio, 'Forum', 22.7.1987.
17 *Sydney Morning Herald*, 29.10.1986.
18 *Sydney Morning Herald*, 29.10.1986; *Australian Jewish Times*, 27.10.1986.
19 Protocols of the Vanunu trial, no. 260017.
20 Ibid., nos 260017–9.
21 Interview with *Sunday Times* reporter.
22 Interview with Peter Hounam.
23 Interview with Eviator Manor.
24 Ibid.
25 *Time*, 12.4.1976.
26 Interview with Jane Biran.
27 Protocols, nos 260102–3.
28 Denis Herbstein, 'Changing Times', *Index on Censorship*, May 1986.
29 Interview, *Yerushalayim*, 23.4.1999.
30 Interview with *Sunday Times* reporter.
31 Ibid.
32 'The Man from Dimona', CBS News, 27.2.1988.
33 Leonard Spector, *The Undeclared Bomb* (Cambridge, MA: Ballinger, 1988), p. 138.
34 'The Man from Dimona'.
35 Frank Barnaby, *The Invisible Bomb: The Nuclear Arms Race in the Middle East* (London: Tauris, 1989), p. xi.
36 Interview with Hannah Zemer.
37 Interview with Ari Rath.
38 Interview with Robin Morgan.
39 Interview with Dr Frank Barnaby.
40 Ibid.
41 Interview with Robin Morgan.

5 THE SPOILER

1 Interview by author with Peter Hounam.
2 *Maariv*, 21.11.1986.
3 Israeli Supreme Court ruling, issued 29.9.1990.
4 Conversation between Mordechai Vanunu and the author.
5 Interview with Joe Grizzard.
6 Interview with Mark Souster.
7 Interview with Tony Frost.
8 Interview with Mike Molloy.
9 Interview with *Sunday Mirror* reporter.
10 Interview with Tony Frost.
11 Interview with *Sunday Mirror* reporter.
12 Ibid.
13 Interview with Tony Frost.
14 *Sunday Times*, 5.10.1986.
15 Interview with Tony Frost.
16 Seymour Hersh, *The Sampson Option: Israel's Nuclear Arsenal and American Foreign Policy* (New York: Random House, 1991).
17 *The Jewish Chronicle*, 19.9.1986.
18 Victor Ostrovsky, *By Way of Deception* (New York: St Martin's Press, 1990), p. 209.

6 A MOSSAD KIDNAPPING IN NEW PRINTING HOUSE SQUARE

1 Interview with Isser Harel.
2 *Maariv*, 14.11.1986.
3 Ibid.
4 Abraham Rotem, *The Invisible Syndrome* [in Hebrew] (Ramat ha-Sharon: Bar-Keren, 1999), p. 60.
5 Protocols of the Vanunu trial, no. 260035.
6 Peter Hounam, *The Woman from Mossad* (London: Vision, 1999), p. 28.
7 Louis Toscano, *Triple Cross* (New York: Birch Lane Press, 1990), p. 77.
8 *Hadashot*, 16.11.1986.
9 Australian Television, 'Four Corners', 31.8.1987.
10 Toscano, *Triple Cross*, p. 132.
11 *Financial Times*, 8.11.1986; *Observer*, 8.11.1986; *Daily Telegraph*, 10.11.1986; *The Times*, 12.11.1986; *Sunday Telegraph*, 16.11.1986.
12 Australian Television, 'Four Corners'.
13 Interview with Robin Morgan.
14 Interview with Bruce Page.
15 BBC, 'Breakfast Time', 28.11.1986.
16 Protocols, no. 260811.
17 Protocols, nos 260109–13.
18 Ibid.
19 *Hadashot*, 28.4.1987; *Maariv*, 29.4.1987.
20 *Hadashot*, 16.11.1986.
21 Ibid.
22 Ibid.

23 Interview with Wendy Robbins; see also Wendy Robbins, 'Betrayal', *New Moon*, December 1991.
24 *Yediot Aharonot*, 15.1.1988.
25 Interview with Wendy Robbins.
26 *Yediot Aharonot*, 15.1.1988.
27 Hounam, *The Woman from Mossad*, p. 88.
28 Andrew Neil, *Full Disclosure* (London: Pan, 1996), p. 427.
29 *Yerushalayim*, 23.4.1999.
30 *Haaretz*, 21.2.1988.
31 Ibid.
32 Hounam, *The Woman from Mossad*, p. 150.
33 *Haaretz*, 27.3.1998.
34 *Hadashot*, 21.3.1988; *Haaretz*, 21.2.1988.
35 *Hadashot*, 16.11.1986.
36 Ibid.
37 Australian Television, 'Four Corners'.
38 Interview with Meir Vanunu.
39 Australian Television, 'Four Corners'.
40 Ibid.
41 Ibid.
42 Ibid.
43 *Hadashot*, 16.11.1986.
44 *Financial Times*, 6.12.1986.
45 *Sunday Times*, 27.7.1997.
46 *ADI*, no. 271, 11.9.1995.
47 *Kolbo*, 24.3.1995.
48 Protocols, nos 260568, 260614.
49 Protocols, no. 260829.
50 Protocols, no. 260835.
51 *Enoshim*, 15.4.1994.
52 Protocols, no. 260627.
53 Ibid.
54 Ibid.
55 *Jerusalem Post*, 19.6.1987.
56 Protocols, no. 260712.
57 Ibid.
58 *Haolam Hazeh*, 30.3.1988.
59 Interview with Ivan Fallon.
60 BBC, 'Breakfast Time', 28.11.1986.
61 *Haaretz*, 19.11.1986.
62 Interview with Peter Hounam, *Haaretz*, 25.7.1996.
63 Interview with Robin Morgan.
64 *Jewish Chronicle*, 13.12.1991.
65 Interview with Wendy Robbins.
66 Interview with *Sunday Times* researcher.
67 Interview with Reverend John McKnight.
68 Interview with Wendy Robbins.
69 Interview with *Sunday Times* reporter.
70 Interview with Godfrey Hodgson.
71 *Yediot Aharonot*, 26.2.1988; interview with Mark Souster.
72 Protocols, no. 260633.

73   *Jerusalem Post*, 11.11.1986.
74   Interview with Menachem Shalev.
75   *Al Hamishmar*, 14.11.1986.
76   *New York Times*, 29.10.1986.
77   *Yediot Aharonot*, 10.11.1986.
78   Questions in the House of Commons, 7.11.1986.
79   Israel Radio, 4.11.1986.
80   Ibid.
81   *Jerusalem Post*, 24.6.1988.
82   Ibid.
83   *Hadashot*, 23.3.1990.
84   *International Herald Tribune*, 18–19.6.1988.
85   *Sunday Telegraph*, 18.12.1988.
86   *Yediot Aharonot*, 19.6.1988.
87   *Hadashot*, 20.6.1988.
88   Ibid.
89   *Al Hamishmar*, 29.12.1986.
90   Ibid.
91   *Maariv*, 25.12.1986.
92   *Weekend Australian*, 25.12.1986.
93   *L'Espresso*, 11.1.1987.
94   Ibid.
95   *La Republica*, 27.12.1986.
96   *Jerusalem Post*, 12.1.1987.
97   *Haaretz*, 16.8.1987.
98   Ibid.
99   Ibid.
100 *Panorama*, 26.9.1988.
101 Ibid.
102 *Jerusalem Post*, 25.10.1988.
103 *Kolbo*, 24.3.1995.
104 *Tikshoret*, December 1994.
105 *Haaretz*, 22.2.1988.
106 David Tinnin, *Hit Team* (London: Futura, 1976), pp. 56–9.
107 *Haaretz*, 21.2.1988.
108 Ibid.; *Hadashot*, 21.2.1988.
109 *Jerusalem Post*, 23.2.1988.
110 *Yediot Aharonot*, 7.4.1997.
111 *The Times*, 25.7.1988.
112 Interview with Isser Harel.
113 *Jerusalem Post*, 11.11.1986.
114 Interview with security source.
115 *Maariv*, 7.11.1986.
116 Letter from Dianne Stafford.
117 Letter from P.J. Monk.
118 Interview with *Sunday Times* reporter.
119 Interview with David Kimche.
120 *Independent*, 8.11.1986.
121 *Haaretz*, 27.10.1986.
122 *Al Hamishmar*, 28.10.1986.
123 *Jerusalem Post*, 4.11.1986.

124 *Financial Times*, 16.3.1987.
125 *Maariv*, 14.11.1986; *Sunday Telegraph*, 17.11.1986.
126 *Maariv*, 14.11.1986.

7   THE SECURITY FIASCO

1   Yoel Cohen, *The Whistleblower of Dimona: Israel, Vanunu & The Bomb* (New York: Holmes & Meier, 2003), p. 150.
2   *Haaretz*, 5.10.1986.
3   *Yediot Aharonot*, 7.11.1986.
4   *Hadashot*, 20.1.1987; *Yediot Aharonot*, 5.11.1986.
5   Protocols of the Vanunu trial, no. 260506.
6   Peter Hounam, *The Woman from Mossad* (London: Vision, 1999), p. 52.
7   Ibid., p. 56.
8   *Haaretz*, 14.11.1986.
9   Yossi Melman and Dan Raviv, *The Imperfect Spies* (London: Sidgwick & Jackson, 1989), p. 102.
10 Protocols, nos. 260804, 260812–14.
11 Protocols, no. 260810.
12 Protocols, no. 260806.
13 Protocols, no. 260633.
14 Protocols, no 260705.
15 Protocols, no 260743.
16 Frank Barnaby, *The Invisible Bomb: The Nuclear Arms Race in the Middle East* (London: Tauris, 1989).
17 Protocols, no. 260749.
18 Protocols, no. 260777.
19 Protocols, no.260775.
20 *Hadashot*, 15.10.1986.
21 *Israel Shelanu*, 7.11.1986; *Maariv*, 7.11.1986.
22 *Haaretz*, 10.3.2000.
23 Ibid.
24 Abraham Rotem, *The Invisible Syndrome* [in Hebrew] (Ramat ha-Sharon: Bar-Keren, 1999), p. 61.
25 *Economist Foreign Report*, 14.10.1999.
26 *Jerusalem Post*, 12.1 1.1986.
27 *Haaretz*, 4.11.1986.

8   THE STATE OF ISRAEL v. M. VANUNU

1   Unless otherwise stated, this chapter and Chapter 9 draw on the protocols of the Vanunu trial, which are in Hebrew.
2   *Jerusalem Post*, 19.6.1987.
3   *Jerusalem Post*, 4.9.1987.
4   *Haaretz*, 21.11.1986.
5   *Jerusalem Post*, 23.11.1986.
6   *Jerusalem Post*, 14.8.1987.
7   *Davar*, 28.8.1987.
8   *Jerusalem Post*, 14.8.1987.
9   *Jerusalem Post*, 28.8.1987; *Kol Hair*, 21.8.1987.

10 *Hadashot*, 23.11.1987.
11 Yoel Cohen, *The Whistleblower of Dimona: Israel, Vanunu and The Bomb* (New York: Holmes & Meier, 2003), p. 167.
12 *Jerusalem Post*. 28.9.1987
13 *Hadashot*, 31.8.1987, 1.9.1987.
14 *Hadashot*, 31.8.1987.
15 *Davar*, 3.9.1987.
16 Interview with Avigdor Feldman.
17 *Hadashot*, 24.3.1988.
18 Ibid.
19 Interview with Dr Frank Barnaby.
20 Cohen, *The Whistleblower of Dimona*, p. 171.
21 Ibid., p. 172.
22 Protocols of the Vanunu trial, no. 260600.
23 Protocols, no. 260525.
24 Protocols, nos 260539–40.
25 Protocols, no. 260568.
26 Protocols, no. 260753.
27 Protocols, no. 260572.
28 Protocols, nos 260600–01.
29 Protocols, no. 260631.
30 Protocols, no. 260692.
31 Protocols, no. 260677.
32 Protocols, nos 260677–8.
33 Protocols, nos 260680–1.
34 Ibid.
35 Protocols, no. 260681.
36 Protocols, no. 260709.
37 Protocols, nos 260710–11.
38 Protocols, no. 260711.
39 Protocols, no. 260713.
40 Protocols, nos 260713–14.
41 Cohen, *The Whistleblower of Dimona*, p. 184.
42 Protocols, no. 260742.
43 Protocols, no. 260750.
44 Protocols, no. 260745.
45 Protocols, no. 260756.
46 The defence's cross-examination of 'Giora' was banned from publication.
47 The prosecution's examination of 'the witness' was banned from publication.
48 Protocols, no. 260762.
49 Protocols, nos 260761–2.
50 Protocols, nos 260764–5.
51 Ibid.
52 Ibid.
53 Protocols, nos 260778–9.
54 Protocols, no. 260776.
55 Ibid.
56 Ibid.
57 Cohen, *The Whistleblower of Dimona*, p. 190.
58 Ibid.
59 Protocols, no. 260805.

60 Ibid.
61 Ibid.
62 Protocols, no. 260808.
63 Cohen, *The Whistleblower of Dimona*, p. 192.

9 PRESS DISCLOSURE = ESPIONAGE + TREASON

1   *Davar*, 2.12.1987.
2   *Maariv*, 2.12.1987.
3   Protocols of the Vanunu trial, nos 260827–8.
4   Protocols, nos 260513–14.
5   Protocols, no. 260148.
6   Protocols, no. 260184.
7   Protocols, no. 260187.
8   Protocols, no. 260187–8.
9   *Yediot Aharonot*, 3.9.1987.
10 Protocols, no. 260187.
11 *Haaretz*, 29.7.1987.
12 *Haaretz*, 29.7.1987; Protocols, no. 260142.
13 *Guardian*, 7.12.1987.
14 The testimony of Dr Frank Barnaby was banned from publication.
15 Protocols, no. 260067.
16 Ibid.
17 Protocols, nos 260017–18.
18 Protocols, no. 260022.
19 Ibid.
20 Ibid.
21 Protocols, nos 2600235–6.
22 Protocols, no. 260028.
23 Ibid.
24 Protocols, no. 260085.
25 Ibid.
26 Protocols, no. 260086.
27 Protocols, no. 260076.
28 Protocols, no. 260077.
29 Ibid.
30 Protocols, nos 260077–8.
31 Protocols, no. 260078.
32 Protocols, no. 260093.
33 Ibid.
34 Ibid.
35 Ibid.
36 Protocols, no. 260090.
37 Protocols, no. 260091.
38 Ibid.
39 Protocols, no. 260086.
40 Protocols, no. 260097.
41 Protocols, no. 260047.
42 Protocols, no. 260098.
43 Protocols, no. 260086.

44   Protocols, no. 260087.
45   Ibid.
46   Ibid.
47   Ibid.
48   Protocols, nos 260086–7.
49   Protocols, no. 260088.
50   Ibid.
51   Ibid.
52   Ibid.
53   Protocols, no. 260073.
54   Ibid.
55   Peter Hounam, *The Woman from Mossad* (London: Vision, 1999), p. 191.
56   Protocols, no. 260107.
57   Ibid.
58   *Jerusalem Post*, 28.8.1987.
59   *Yediot Aharonot*, 27.8.1987; *Independent*, 26.8.1987.
60   Protocols, no. 260149.
61   Protocols, no. 260312.
62   Abba Eban mentioned this volume in his testimony, but it is unclear exactly what it was.
63   Ibid.
64   Protocols, no. 260330.
65   Protocols, no. 260150.
66   Protocols, no. 260312.
67   Protocols, no. 260314.
68   Protocols, no. 260320.
69   Ibid.
70   Protocols, no. 260329.
71   Ibid.
72   Protocols, no. 260334.
73   Protocols, no. 260315.
74   Ibid.
75   Ibid.
76   Protocols, no. 260325.
77   Ibid.
78   Ibid.
79   Ibid.
80   Protocols, no. 260329.
81   Ibid.
82   *Hadashot*, 10.12.1987.
83   *Jerusalem Post*, 28.8.1987.
84   *Maariv*, 5.1.1988.
85   Yoel Cohen, *The Whistleblower of Dimona: Israel, Vanunu and The Bomb* (New York: Holmes & Meier, 2003), pp. 209–10.
86   Ibid.
87   Protocols, no. 260891.
88   Protocols, nos 260901–2.
89   Ibid.
90   Ibid.
91   Ibid.
92   Protocols, nos 260903–4.
93   Protocols, nos 260905–6.

94   Protocols, no. 260909.
95   Protocols, no. 260893–4.
96   Protocols, no. 260896.
97   Ibid.
98   Ibid.
99   Ibid.
100 Protocols, no. 260898.
101 Protocols, no. 260899.
102 Protocols, no. 260908.
103 Ibid.
104 Ibid.
105 Ibid.
106 *Haaretz*, 1.9.1987.
107 Protocols, no. 260914.
108 Ibid.
109 Ibid.
110 Ibid.
111 Protocols, no. 260915.
112 Ibid.
113 Protocols, no. 260916.
114 Protocols, no. 260915.
115 Protocols, no. 260916.
116 Protocols, no. 260917.
117 Ibid.
118 Ibid.
119 Ibid.
120 Ibid.
121 Ibid.
122 Protocols, nos 260853–4.
123 Protocols, no. 260916.
124 Protocols, no. 260919.
125 Ibid.
126 Protocols, no. 260920.
127 Ibid.
128 Ibid.
129 Protocols, no. 260924.
130 Ibid.
131 Ibid.
132 Protocols, no. 260925.
133 Protocols, no. 260925.
134 Ibid.
135 Protocols, nos 260929–30.
136 Protocols, no. 260281.
137 Protocols, nos 260281, 260291.
138 Protocols, no. 260284.
139 Protocols, no. 260286.
140 Ibid.
141 Ibid.
142 Ibid.
143 Ibid.
144 Ibid.

145 Ibid.
146 Protocols, no. 260287.
147 Ibid.
148 Ibid.
149 Ibid, no. 260288.
150 Ibid.
151 Protocols, no. 260289.
152 Protocols, no. 260288.
153 Protocols, no. 260289.
154 Protocols, no. 260290.
155 *Davar*, 4.11.1986; *Haaretz*, 4.11.1986.
156 Protocols, no. 260291.
157 Protocols, no. 260295.
158 Protocols, no. 260139.
159 Protocols, nos 260138–9.
160 Protocols, no. 260295.
161 Protocols, no. 260300.
162 Protocols, no. 260301.
163 *Hadashot*, 18.1.1988.
164 *Davar*, 24.1.1988.
165 Protocols, nos 260115–16.
166 Protocols, no. 260117.
167 Israeli Supreme Court ruling, p. 52.
168 Protocols, no. 260124.
169 Protocols, no. 260116.
170 Protocols, no. 260131.
171 Protocols, no. 260143.
172 Protocols, nos 260140–2.
173 Protocols, no. 260148.
174 Protocols, no. 260158.
175 Protocols, no. 260159.
176 Ibid.
177 Ibid.
178 Protocols, nos 260163–4.
179 Protocols, no. 260166.
180 Protocols, no. 260173.
181 Ibid.
182 Protocols, no. 260174.
183 Protocols, no. 260175.
184 Protocols, no. 260176.
185 Ibid.
186 Protocols, no. 260179.
187 Protocols, nos 260185–6.
188 Protocols, nos 260187–8.
189 Protocols, no. 260189.
190 Protocols, no. 260202.
191 Protocols, nos 260357–9.
192 Protocols, nos 260362–3.
193 Protocols, nos 260357–9.
194 Protocols, nos 260375–6.
195 Protocols, no. 260378–9.

196   Protocols, no. 260379.
197   Protocols, no. 260380.
198   Ibid.
199   Protocols, no. 260381.
200   Protocols, no. 260382.
201   Protocols, no. 260384.
202   Protocols, no. 260388.
203   Ibid.
204   Ibid.
205   Protocols, no. 260401.
206   Protocols, no. 260406.
207   *Hadashot*, 25.3.1988.
208   *Hadashot*, 24.3.1988.
209   Israeli Supreme Court ruling, p. 9.
210   *Hadashot*, 25.3.1988.
211   *Kol Hair*, 16.8.1991.
212   Israeli Supreme Court ruling, p. 52.
213   *Kol Hair*, 25.6.1993.
214   Conversation with the author.
215   *National Journal*, 30.9.1989.
216   *Haaretz*, 25.5.2001.
217   Protocols, no. 260568.
218   Protocols, no. 260567.
219   *Haaretz*, 30.4.2001.
220   Protocols, no. 260776.
221   *Haaretz*, 12.6.2000.
222   Protocols, nos 260184–92.

10   FRIENDS FROM AFAR

1   Samuel H. Day Jr (ed.), *Faith Under Siege: Letters from a Christian Prisoner of Conscience* (Madison, WI: US Campaign to Free Mordechai Vanunu, 1998).
2   Ibid.
3   Ibid.
4   Ibid.
5   *Maariv*, 12.12.1997.
6   *Haaretz* Magazine, 15.5.1998.
7   Newsletter of the US Campaign to Free Mordechai Vanunu, 1999.
8   Ibid.
9   Interview with Bruce Kent.
10   Search carried out in 2001 by Dror Moshe, student, Netanya Academic College, Israel.
11   Interview with Sam Day.
12   Interview with Frederik Heffermehl.
13   *Al Hamishmar*, 14.8.1987.
14   The conference papers were published in *Vanunu and The Bomb* [in Hebrew] (Jerusalem: Israel Committee to Free Mordechai Vanunu, 1999).
15   Conversation between the author and Mordechai Vanunu.
16   *Haaretz*, 20.4.1998.
17   *Haaretz*, 1.2.1998.

18   Newsletter of the US Campaign, 1998.
19   *Yediot Aharonot*, 25.11.2001.

11   THE RELUCTANT LOBBYIST

1   Interview with *Sunday Times* reporter.
2   Interview with former *Sunday Times* journalist.
3   Interview with *Sunday Times* reporter.
4   Interview with Bruce Page.
5   Interview with *Sunday Times* reporter.
6   Interview with Phillip Knightley.
7   Interview with Ivan Fallon.
8   *Haaretz*, 19.11.1986.
9   *Sunday Times*, 3.3.1990.
10   Conversation between the author and Mordechai Vanunu.
11   Interview with Meir Vanunu.
12   Interview with Ivan Fallon.
13   *Sunday Times*, 15.3.1998.
14   Interview with *Sunday Times* executive.
15   Interview with Robin Morgan.
16   Interview with *Sunday Times* executive.
17   Interview with Meir Vanunu.
18   *Palestine Focus*, January–February 1988.
19   Interview with Meir Vanunu.
20   Wendy Robbins, 'Betrayal', *New Moon*, December 1991; *Davar*, 14.11.1986.
21   *Sunday Times*, 12.12.1992.
22   Andrew Neil, *Full Disclosure* (London: Pan, 1997), p. 429.
23   *Yerushalayim*, 23.4.1999.
24   *Sunday Times*, 29.9.1996.
25   Interview with Alastair Brett.
26   Interview with *Sunday Times* legal executive.
27   Peter Hounam, *The Woman from Mossad* (London: Vision, 1999), p. 201.
28   Ibid.
29   *Haaretz*, 19.11.1986.
30   Interview with Alastair Brett.

12   21 APRIL 2004

1   *Haaretz*, 22.4.2004.
2   *Los Angeles Times*, 21.4.2004.
3   *Independent*, 22.4.2004.
4   *Guardian*, 20.4.2004.
5   Interview with Yossi Melman.
6   Newsletter of the US campaign to Free Mordechai Vanunu, Summer 2000.
7   Newsletter, Fall 1999.
8   *Yediot Aharonot*, 1.2.2004.
9   *Yediot Aharonot*, 20.4.2004.
10   *Haaretz*, 26.2.2004.
11   *Haaretz*, 21.4.2004.
12   *Jerusalem Post*, 12.7.2004.
13   Israeli Supreme Court ruling, 26.7.2004.

13 THE BOMB THAT – STILL – DOESN'T EXIST

1 ABC-TV, 'Four Corners', 31.8.1987; Australia Radio 2 FC, 'Science Show', 8.11.1986; BBC World Service, 'Outlook', 25.3.1988.
2 Protocols of the Vanunu trial, no. 260140.
3 Sources as note 1.
4 Frank Barnaby, *The Invisible Bomb, The Nuclear Arms Race in the Middle East* (London: Tauris, 1989), pp. 22, 25.
5 Protocols, no. 260140.
6 Protocols, no. 260291.
7 ABC-TV, ' Four Corners', 31.8.1987.
8 *Jerusalem Post*, 6.10.1986.
9 www.fas.org/nuke/guide/israel/facility/dimona-pir.html
10 *Haaretz*, 29.12.1993.
11 *Bulletin of Atomic Scientists*, September–October 1999.
12 *The Economist Foreign Report*, 13.11.1986.
13 The *Sunday Times*, 12.10.1986, 19.10.1986.
14 Ariel Levite and Emily Landau, *In Arab Eyes: Arab Perceptions of Israel's Nuclear Posture* (Jaffee Centre for Strategic Studies, Tel Aviv University; Tel Aviv: Papyrus, 1994), p. 52.
15 The *Sunday Times*, 2.4.1995.
16 *Maariv*, 23.11.1986.
17 David Twersky, 'Is Silence Golden? Vanunu and Nuclear Israel', *Tikkun*, vol. 3, no. 1, 1988.
18 Protocols, no. 260297.
19 Protocols, no. 260293.
20 *Maariv*, 23.11.1986.
21 *Al Shaab*, 14.10.1986.
22 *Haaretz*, 25.10.1987.
23 Ibid.
24 *Haaretz* magazine, 27.3.1998.
25 Seymour Hersh, *The Samson Option: Israel's Nuclear Arsenal and American Foreign Policy* (New York: Random House, 1991), p. 198.
26 *Time*, April 1994.
27 Protocols, no. 260329.
28 Protocols, nos 260145–6.
29 Protocols, no. 260145.
30 Protocols, no. 260765.
31 Gary Milhollin, 'Heavy Water', *Foreign Policy*, Winter 1987–88.
32 Reuters, 13.10.1986; *Sydney Morning Herald*, 13.10.1986.
33 Statements quoted in this paragraph are from proliferation experts interviewed by the author in the US, on a non-attribution basis.
34 Database search carried out by Jonathan Cutler, student, The Hebrew University's Overseas Students programme, Jerusalem.
35 Barnaby, *The Invisible Bomb*, pp. 22, 25.
36 William Burrows and Robert Windrem, *Critical Mass: The Dangerous Race for Superweapons in a Fragmenting World* (New York: Simon & Schuster, 1994).
37 *Haaretz*, 4.8.1997.
38 *Haaretz*, 7.10.1986.
39 ABC-TV, 12.5.1998.
40 *Jerusalem Post*, 24.12.1995.
41 Protocols, no 260318.
42 *Yediot Aharonot*, 13.4.1994.

43 Emily Landau, 'Has a Change Occurred in Israeli Nuclear Policy?', *Strategic Update*, The Jaffee Centre for Strategic Studies, Tel Aviv University, April 1998.
44 *Maariv*, 24.12.1995; *Jerusalem Post*, 5.5.2000.
45 *Yediot Aharonot*, 24.2.1995.
46 *Haaretz*, 18.2.2001.

14 SECRECY LTD

1   Survey by The Jaffee Centre for Strategic Studies, Tel Aviv University, 1987.
2   Letter to *Maariv*, September 1987.
3   Interview with Meir Vanunu.
4   *Strategic Update*, Jaffee Centre for Strategic Studies, Tel Aviv University, November 1988.
5   Interview by the author with an Israeli military correspondent.
6   *Haaretz*, 29.3.2000.
7   Israeli Television, Channel One, 15.8.2000.
8   Alex Fishman, address, 'Nuclear Weaponry, the Public & the Media' conference, Haifa University, 1995.
9   Hanoch Marmori, address, 'Nuclear Weaponry, the Public & the Media' conference, Haifa University, 1995.
10 *Haaretz* magazine 25.5.2000
11 Gabriel Ben-Dor, address, 'Nuclear Weaponry, the Public and the Media' conference, Haifa University, 1995; Marmori, address.
12 Shalheveth Freier, 'Who Stops Anybody from a Serious Public Discussion?' [in Hebrew], *Politika*, no. 44, 1992, pp. 22–3.
13 Fishman, address.
14 *Haaretz*, 20.7.2000.
15 Survey, Jaffee Centre for Strategic Studies, Tel Aviv University, 1999.
16 Debate in the Knesset, 2.2.2000.
17 *Haaretz*, 4.2.2000.
18 *Haaretz*, 29.3.2000.
19 *Yediot Aharonot*, 12.6.2000; www.seas.gwu.edu/nsarchive/israel/history/htm
20 Frank Barnaby, *The Invisible Bomb: The Nuclear Arms Race in the Middle East* (London: Tauris, 1989).
21 Sources as note 19.
22 *Sydney Morning Herald*, 14.10.1997.

Index